Higher than Hope

# HIGHER THAN HOPE

---

## A BIOGRAPHY OF NELSON MANDELA

Fatima Meer

HAMISH HAMILTON   LONDON

**HAMISH HAMILTON LTD**

Published by the Penguin Group
27 Wrights Lane, London W8 5TZ, England
Viking Penguin Inc., 40 West 23rd Street, New York, New York 10010, USA
Penguin Books Australia Ltd, Ringwood, Victoria, Australia
Penguin Books Canada Ltd, 2801 John Street, Markham, Ontario, Canada L3R 1B4
Penguin Books (NZ) Ltd, 182–190 Wairau Road, Auckland 10, New Zealand

Penguin Books Ltd, Registered Offices: Harmondsworth, Middlesex, England

First published in South Africa by Skotaville Publishers, Johannesburg 1988
First published in Great Britain by Hamish Hamilton Ltd 1990

Made and printed in Great Britain by
Richard Clay Ltd, Bungay, Suffolk
Filmset in Monophoto Times

A CIP catalogue record for this book is available from the British Library

ISBN 0–241–12787–4

*To Chief Albert Luthuli,*
*Dr Monty Naicker and Bram Fischer*

# I NEED

I need today oh so very badly
Nelson Mandela
out of the prison gates
to walk broad-shouldered
among counsel
down Commissioner
up West Street
and lead us away from the shadow
of impotent word-weavers
his clenched fist hoisted higher
than hope
for all to see and follow

*Sipho Sepamla*


Only free men can negotiate. Prisoners cannot enter
into contracts . . .
I will return . . .

*Nelson Mandela*

# Contents

## CONTENTS

# Foreword

I cannot remember how many friends volunteered to write the real family biography. Up to this point in the sad history of our land there have been numerous writings, some from complete strangers who know very little about the family. Over the years I have communicated this information to Mandela as best I could, since my visits to him in prison could be terminated at the mere mention of a name that was not of a member of the family.

For several years Mandela toyed with the idea of getting a friend of the family to write his biography.

There was no better person for such a narrative than Fatima Meer who knew Mandela from the early 1950s with her husband, Ismail Meer. Not only did Mandela request Fatima to undertake this task, he wrote to her and asked me to pursue her to get down to it and I did.

Fatima Meer was able to travel to Mandela's birthplace. That is how she was able to conduct interviews with Mandela's family. Professor Meer has tried her best to fill in the sketchy details of Mandela's formative years.

Naturally such a biography cannot be complete as some significant aspects of Mandela's life cannot be fully told without subjecting a large number of our people to state harassment and persecution. These are accounts of Mandela's underground days which are packed with historical drama as the African National Congress launched its underground direction.

The picture Professor Meer presents is that of an ordinary human being with natural emotions and desires and not an ancient myth which often provokes the tiresome questions:

'Why do children who were not yet born when Mandela was jailed eulogize this man?' 'Do you think the youth of the land really want a man they do not know to lead them if he is released?'

Written by a sociologist, the biography analyses the factors that drive a man, a flourishing young attorney, to give up everything for the Cause. That analysis is true of every one of those men behind bars. It also helps us to understand why a young twenty-year-old Solomon Mahlangu proudly sings his way to the gallows for the Cause, and why Steve Biko died. It explains why the commitment of these men and women has stood the rocky test of time.

Fatima Meer is not only a witness to history but she has herself made personal contributions to this Cause. Her independence of thought has at times been misunderstood, quite deliberately, by those whose ideologies differ from ours. We remain united by our commitment to justice, personal liberty and fundamental human rights.

*Nomzamo Winnie Mandela*
*18th July, 1988.*

# Preface

In one of Nelson's letters to me in the early seventies, he expressed the opinion that an autobiography was an excuse for an ego trip. I wrote back disagreeing. Some autobiographies, I said, were a people's essential heritage. In any case, what were his feelings about biographies?

A few months later I was at a mass meeting at the Bolton Hall in Durban, convened I think by the Black Consciousness group, for I have a clear recollection of Steve Biko on the platform. A message was whispered to me – from Nelson Mandela, I was told – sent through a newly released prisoner. He would like me to write his biography.

The prospect overawed me, though Nelson's confidence was flattering. Where and how did one even start making a beginning when the subject remained inaccessible? A few months later I made my one and only visit to Robben Island. Nelson said I should speak to Chief Jongintaba's wife; she was as his mother. His own mother was deceased by then.

I didn't get the opportunity to visit the Transkei. Neither did I have the confidence to embark on so important an assignment.

In early 1976, I was re-banned and confined to my neighbourhood in Sydenham, Durban. That same year, Winnie and I were among ten women detained at the Fort in Johannesburg. Towards the end of our five months detention, we had some opportunity to meet. Winnie and I began working on Winnie's biography/autobiography; the work was suspended on our release. We returned to the conditions of our banning orders, in our different cities, one of which was that we could not communicate with each other.

In 1984, when my ban expired, I visited Evelyn and Maki Mandela in the Transkei and they took me to Mqekezweni where Nelson had spent his childhood. I wrote about the visit to Nelson. He replied:

My dear Fatimaben,
Your nine page letter came when I was busy working on our reply to the State President's offer of release, and as important and urgent as the matter was, I instinctively pushed aside the draft until the following evening. Frankly, I just could no longer concentrate. The mind immediately went back many many years ago to a period in my life, the mere thought of which literally reduces me into a bundle of sheer sentiment.

As you know there are two Transkeis. One is the political entity which emerged in the mid-50s and which sparked off ugly polemics turning, in the process, friends, relatives, idols and their admirers into irreconcilable opponents and even enemies. This is the Bantustan whose capital you recently visited and whose leader you met.

Relatives from the Transkei often visit me. Paramount Chief Bambilanga, Chief Vulindlela Mtirara and others always bring some good news from that end. This year alone I had no less than four special visits, unlimited as to duration, from Acting Paramount Chief Ngangomhlaba Matanzima of Western Tembuland; my sister, Mrs Notancu Mabel Tumakhwe; Chief Zwelidumile Joyi. But the discussions were dominated by the highly sensitive and complicated question of the return and installation of the exiled Paramount Chief Sabata Dalindyebo and I had very little time for anything else.

You will, therefore, readily understand when I tell you that I was dangerously delighted to get your letter packed with so much information about the family. Even as I write now the spell on me is as overwhelming as on the day I received it. I have never imagined even in my wildest dreams that you would one day visit Mqekezweni, actually speak to members of the family and see the hut where I used to sleep. That letter was the proverbial cherry on top of the cake. I sincerely hope that you will be able to return with a camera and also visit the family graves at Qunu. Although not a single building now remains on my late mother's kraal, my sister Notatsumbana [now deceased] from the Great House still lives there and I would be glad if you could also see her. But Maki and Leabie will have to be there to interpret for you.

As far as the sensitive issues mentioned in the letter. I must point out that this reply will go through several hands before it reaches you, and it will, therefore, be unwise to discuss them fully and frankly. It may well be that one day we will be able to chat face to face when I will be able to expand. All I am able to say here is that Evelyn is a pleasant and charming person and I respected her even as the marriage was crumbling. It would be quite unfair to blame her for the breakdown.

My youngest sister, Leabie Makhutshwana Poliso blames two persons for the collapse of the marriage. Again, I can only tell you here, that in my present position, it would be quite indiscreet to attempt a thesis on the exciting adventures of more than thirty years ago. But I would be lacking in chivalry if I were to dismiss the allegation altogether. I will leave it to you to elicit the details when I see you.

You talk of the tall man [Kaiser Matanzima] to whom you were introduced at the 'palace'. You probably will not believe it when I tell you that he was once my idol. I introduced him to his great wife, Nobandla Agrineth, the daughter of Chief Sangeni, and George Matanzima, Sonto Mgudlwa [descendant of Jumba] and I were the best men at his wedding. In our [Madiba] clan he was the first to receive university education. He looked very well after me at Fort Hare and sent an encouraging message on the eve of the judgement in the Rivonia Trial and took interest in the family over the last twenty-two years of my absence. Although I will never agree to be released to a Bantustan, I must concede that he has fought patiently for my release throughout these years. We are still very close to each other, but something snapped inside me when he went over to the Nats. Indeed, politics have split families, hero and worshipper.

25 February 1985

I never revisited the Transkei, though I had hoped to. I was asked by Skotaville Publishers last year to provide the words for a book of photographs on Mandela by Alf Khumalo which they had in mind. As I have a tendency to be over-wordy, the result was this manuscript.

I offer this book as an addition to Mary Benson's pioneering work on Nelson Mandela. At best it is my interpretation of him. There can be no definitive biography of Mandela without full personal interviews with him. I hope that a biography based on such exhaustive interviews will be written one day. Better still, that Nelson will give us an autobiography.

I have tried as far as possible to interpret Mandela through Mandela's eyes. In so doing, I may have presumed too much and erred at times. For this I apologize to Mandela and hope and pray that he will have the opportunity to set the record straight.

I have leaned on the record of Thomas Karis and Gwendolen Carter (Hoover Institute Press, 1972–7) whose volumes have become a fundamental source of ANC history, and Tom Lodge's excellent volume *Black Politics in South Africa since 1945* (Longman, 1983). South Africans are indebted to them for their scholarly works.

I am grateful to the Institute for Black Research for bearing the typing and administrative expenses involved in preparing the manuscript; to Ramesh Harcharan for typing, to Dr Diliza Mji, Strini Moodley and George Sithole for their interviews, and to Phyllis Jordan and Kathy (Ahmed Kathrada) for their critical reading of the manuscript and their contributions to the revised edition of the biography. My daughter, Shehnaz contributed a labour of love, researching newspaper files; I thank her for that love.

Most of all, I am indebted to the Mandela family for their cooperation; to Evelyn and Maki for introducing me to the Mandela country and speaking to me of their lives as Mandelas; to Makgatho, Leabie and Ntombizodwa for sharing their memories of their beloved kinsmen; and to Nomzamo Winnie, for her time and patience, the hours spent in prison, in Brandfort and Soweto, recalling wonderful lives, hers and Nelson's, filling in details and checking the manuscript. Posterity is indebted to Winnie, to Maki, Zeni and Zindzi for sharing their letters, for it is through the letters that we enter the heart and mind of this most famous South African at this point in time.

Finally, we are indebted to Nelson Mandela for allowing us to publish his letters. Far beyond that, I am deeply indebted to him for his meticulous reading and correcting of the first edition and for the interviews he granted me, which have significantly enriched the second edition.

# Postscript

Nelson Mandela was ill in hospital when the South African edition of *Higher than Hope* was published. In September 1988 I visited the Tygerburg Clinic in Cape Town, where he was recuperating and left a copy of the book with the matron. For good measure, I also left one at Pollsmoor Prison. Nelson did not see the book until December. He wrote to my husband Ismail, on 10 January 1989, with this reference to the biography: 'Writing a biography without access to the subject of study can be a very difficult matter. There are chapters in *Higher than Hope* which clearly reflect this absence of contact. But I think that you have done a marvellous job for which the family will remain very grateful.'

In May 1989 at Nelson's request, my husband, Ismail, and I were granted a visit to Victor Verster Prison. Ismail was seeing Nelson for the first time in twenty-eight years, I in seventeen.

Victor Verster is a vast low-lying prison compound set among vineyards in the beautiful Franshoek Valley, overlooked by the Groot and Klein Drakenstein and the Simonsberg mountains. We were met at the main prison gates by Warrant Officer Gregory, who has been with Nelson for the last twenty-two years, moving with him from Robben Island to Pollsmoor and then to Victor Verster. He was in plain clothes and, as we saw later, so were the other guards who attended to Nelson.

He drove us to Mandela's prison house: we went past some hundred or more staff cottages, past the modest reception building, turned into an avenue of tall conifers flanked by an orange grove, heavy with fruit, and stopped in front of a padlocked gate. White cows with black markings grazed in a near by field and ducks came waddling up. There was a sense of infinite peace that not even the armed guard on the watchpost nor the guards lounging outside the small single-storey office block could mar. The gate opened, we alighted from our car and were handed over to an officer. The gate was locked behind us. We were conducted a few yards towards a concrete wall, another gate was opened and we were taken over by yet another officer, who led us through the backyard of what appeared to be a comfortable cottage, past a line of washing, to the front of the house. We entered a room, overlooking a swimming-pool, that we took to be the living-room; we discovered later it was the television room.

A sprightly step, and we were suddenly embracing Nelson Mandela.

I am not quite sure how I had expected to find him. His letters had been reassuring, but seventeen years ago when I had been allowed to visit him on Robben Island, I had been shocked by the emaciated, sallow face presented by the prison authorities through a glass pane. Mandela is a youthful seventy-one today: tall, debonaire and without a trace of fat on his lean frame. His hair is flecked with grey; his face remains unwrinkled; he smiles readily and often, his eyes crinkling at the corners; his laughter is deep-throated and spontaneous. He is as handsome today as I had found him hours before his arrest in 1962; the difference was that he was burly then, dressed in khaki, every inch the soldier newly trained in North Africa. Now he was immaculate in a three-piece suit, every inch the statesman ready to lead his country.

He led us into the spacious living room, and, after we had talked a little, took us on a tour of his tastefully furnished 'prison' in which every appointment bore the mark of decorative comfort.

The question kept recurring in my mind: what was all this about? As we talked and saw the deference shown him by the guards, it dawned on me that it was not only South Africa's disenfranchised who saw their hopes reflected in him but that the government too was hoping to resolve its problems through him.

I had come to despair for South Africa, my view of the situation considerably aggravated by events in Natal where state violence had become gruesomely distorted into violence of black against black. Nelson's optimism charged me with new hope. He had a perspective, I felt, that we outside had missed. Radical change was possible, and without further violence. I was left with the impression that Nelson was very much in command: it was not so much a matter of when he would be released, but rather of when the Nationalists would be ready to negotiate, for the two are inter-linked.

We spent a pleasant day together, and arranged that I would return in a fortnight's time to discuss corrections and additions to the second edition of his biography.

My second visit took place three days after Nelson's celebrated talk with President Botha. Nelson had gone through the book meticulously and presented me with a neat 39-page folio of amendments and additions typed by the Prison Department.

We decided that I would attend to the corrections at home, and that we should spend the day discussing other aspects of his life and filling in details on ground already covered.

We worked continuously, except for a lunch-break. Two more visits followed, so that, in all, I interviewed him for about eighteen hours. We worked on the dining-room table and, when the weather was warm, on the verandah, he in his corrugated cardboard sun hat made by Jeff Masemola. On my third visit I was told by the authorities that I had to finish work that day and that they would not allow me a further visit.

This biography then, while approved by Nelson Mandela, is based on very restricted contact with him. I had to travel a thousand miles for the interviews, and I was allowed to see him from 9 a.m. to approximately 3.30 p.m. lock up time was 4 p.m. when the staff left.

Nelson was frank and open, his memory remarkable. He remembered dates of events that had happened almost thirty years ago and he had clear recollections of people. I wrote up the new material and faxed it to him, so that when I met him again, he would have had time to read it and to make further corrections and amendments. The faxes were not given to him immediately. He had received them only on the morning of my last visit when we went through the material together. It meant that we were unable to explore any further new ground.

I came closer to Nelson Mandela during those three days than I had at any other time during my association with him. I found him to be a very good, honourable and humble man, a man of great tolerance, with a remarkable capacity to see the other point of view and to come to terms with it without compromising his own ethical position. He is the best person South Africa has to help the country out of the present quagmire of human and material bankruptcy. One can only hope and pray that he will be given the opportunity to move our country to the unity we all deserve.

*October, 1989*

PART I

# ROOTS

# CHAPTER 1

# In Search of the Boy Mandela

### QUNU

The sky is large in Qunu and one often sees little boys driving their cattle against it, their fathers' cast-off coats hanging low over their shoulders and knees.

The sky was the same sixty years ago, and the boys were the same, and one of them was Rolihlahla Nelson Mandela, A-a-a Dalibhunga!

It would be best for Nelson to tell us about his life in Qunu, but he has been in prison these last twenty-six years, and so the responsibility must fall on those who knew him, or knew of him, to recollect and recount his childhood. His sister Nomabandla, affectionately called Leabie, is one of them. She says:

Our father was Hendry Mphakanyiswa Gadla. Our father's great-grandfather was King Ngubengcuka who died more than a hundred years ago. He ruled over all the Thembus at a time when the land belonged to them and they were free. I don't remember our father. What I know of him is what our mother told me about him.

Our father's grandmother was from the *ixhiba* [minor, Left-hand] House of King Ngubengcuka, so her children did not inherit wealth and important positions. These went to the children of the *indlunkulu* [first house]. Our father was a chief but was subsequently deposed for insubordination. He rode a horse and he had enough cattle to marry four wives. Our mother, Nosekeni Fanny, was of the Right-hand House and was his third wife.

We lived with our mother in her three rondavels. That was

3

myself, my two older sisters and Buti, as we called Nelson. Our
mother had built them herself, with the help of the men in our
family who put on the thatch. We used the one hut for cooking,
one for sleeping and one for storing our grains and other food.

There was no furniture in our 'house', that is, no European
furniture. We slept on mats, without pillows, resting our heads on
our elbows. Our mother's 'stove' was a hole in the ground over
which she put a grate. When the food was cooking, there was
usually a lot of smoke for there was no chimney in our 'kitchen'.
The smoke escaped through the window.

As a general rule, a married woman in our area had her own
kraal and field, and our mother had hers. She planted and she
harvested and she took the mealie off the cob. We girls helped her.
We ground the mealies between two stones; we ground them when
they were fresh and we steamed them into a bread, and we ground
them when they were dry and stored them in pots. There was a
time, our mother said, when we did not have to buy mealie meal,
but for as long as I can remember we always bought mealie meal
because we never raised enough mealies on our land. But we never
bought milk and we never bought sour milk; we had cows and
goats and these gave us a good supply.

Our father was not a Christian. Our mother, Nosekeni (known
as Fanny in our church), was a devout Christian. She was most
worried about Buti's future, because the chieftainship would pass
to his brother of the *indlunkulu*. Our father decided that it would
be best for Buti to have a good education; then he would have a
good job. But schooling in Qunu did not go beyond the first few
standards, so our father spoke to his nephew, Chief Jongintaba,
acting paramount chief of the Thembus, and Jongintaba undertook
responsibility for Buti's education as he was required to do according to tradition, as head of the Madiba clan. Our father died when
Buti was ten and I had only just begun talking. When father died,
Chief Jongintaba sent for Buti and Buti went to live with him at
Mqekezweni.

I was very young then. Most of the time that I was growing up,
Buti was not in Qunu. When there was no man in our house to
help with the goats and the cattle, our aunt, our mother's sister,
sent her son Sitsheketshe to live with us.

Our kraal at Qunu was very busy and I had plenty of older
sisters to advise me, and sisters my own age to play with. There
were four of us in my mother's family: three sisters and Buti, but

our father had twelve children altogether. None of our mother's children or grandchildren live in Qunu now, but the ancestral home is there, and the graves of our ancestors are there. Our sister, Notatsumbana from the *indlunkulu* looked after the house and the graves up to the time of her death.


## MQEKEZWENI

The road to Mqekezweni turns off the macadam between Umtata and Engcobo. In dry weather it is hardened earth and dust; on rainy days it is mud and bog. In both seasons it is better for animal traffic than it is for mechanized.

The undulating country is criss-crossed by ravines, gouged out by sun and rain, and scattered with thatched huts lime-washed white and green.

The road dips and rises from the valleys to the crests of the hills, clouds cascade and bounce off the land. Every now and then the empty landscape is surprised by a small wattle grove or a mealie patch, or a herd of motionless sheep, or a solitary rider on a horse, or an occasional cow that stops midway across the road despite the rude hooting of an equally occa-sional car.

The road forks and one turn leads through a rusted iron gate to the Great Place, that was once the seat of Dalindyebo. Before him Ngangelizwe ruled in that region, and before Ngangelizwe, Mtirara and before Mtirara, Ngubengcuka from whose Left-hand House Nelson Mandela is descended.

Above the road is the school where the young Mandela completed his primary education, a crudely built rectangu-lar block under corrugated iron repaired many times over. A little apart is the stucco church, similar in structure save somewhat larger, and distinguished by the small 'gothic' windows, where Nelson prayed and learnt to be a Christian.

On the road is the courthouse, equally plain, but of red brick. Across the road is the royal dining-hall, a collection of three inter-linked huts under thatch, where Jongintaba entertained visiting chiefs and headmen, while the growing

Rolihlahla responded to their needs and listened to their wise talk.

Our car attracts the attention of people who have come to see the chief, and of the children just out of school who pause under an ancient tree and stare.

Mqekezweni was once a 'bustling capital', the meeting place of Thembu chiefs and headmen from the surrounding districts; today it is a dead end, of interest only to its marooned locals who come there to pray at the old church on Sundays and, on weekdays, to attend school or to see the chief about land, taxes, and disputes over boundaries and livestock.

Chief Zonwabele interrupts his proceedings in the red-brick building: his men come and ask our business; he sends us an escort to conduct us to Ntombizodwa, the daughter of Rhanuga, a cousin of Dalindyebo. We drive to the main house, a few metres away, a humble cottage of three or four bedrooms. We enter through the back door to the sitting-room, which leads on to a small front verandah, overlooking the backyard where fowls scratch in the sand.

We sit in carved imbuia chairs, upholstered in tapestry; heavily framed portraits of Dalindyebo, the *indlunkulu* and Jongintaba look down on us from walls papered in autumnal leaves. A very young and somewhat shy Nelson Mandela peeps through a cheap frame. The only other photograph in the room is of a group of women in church uniform.

Ntombizodwa, heavy with seventy years of eating and little activity, welcomes us. She is all that survives at Mqekezweni from the time of Jongintaba. A young woman brings refreshments: biscuits neatly arranged in a tiered silver tray, two large bottles of Sprite and glasses. She places these on the Victorian dining-table surrounded by its matching chairs and set off by a handsome chiffonier while we exchange introductory salutations. Once refreshed, Ntombizodwa, known as MaDlomo to those younger than her, accedes to our request and tells us what comes readily to her mind of the time Nelson spent at Mqekezweni.

I remember clearly the day he came. He was in khaki shorts and khaki shirt. He was shy and, I think, lonely. So at first he didn't say much. He brought a tin trunk with him and we children were curious to know what was inside. Nkosikasi No-England, the wife of Jongintaba, took him under her protective wing. I think she loved him as much as she did her own boy, Justice, and Nelson returned that love and came to see her as if she was his own mother. He and his trunk went into the rondavel there [pointing to a lime-washed, thatched hut a few yards from the main cottage] and he shared that rondavel with Justice, and the two boys were as brothers. Later they were joined by Nxeko [Bambilanga], brother of Paramount Chief Sabata Dalindyebo. The rondavel was very simply furnished: just three beds, a table and an oil lamp.

Even now there is no electricity in Mqekezweni. At the time Nelson seemed very much younger and I very much older, yet he was only four years younger than me. He saw me as an older sister and treated me as such. He was, as I remember, very well behaved and respectful of all the elders. He was diligent and hard-working both with his studies and with the chores that were assigned him at the Great Place.

We went to school together. I never knew him to give trouble to the teachers or to any of the girls in class. He attended school and church regularly and was as enthusiastic about Sunday school as any of us. Our school was very good and our teachers excellent. We had three teachers: Zama Njozela, Arthur Gcikwe and Mabel Mtirara. Two classes were held in one room, so that though I was in a higher class than Nelson, we were in the same room. We learnt English, Xhosa, History and Geography. We started off with the Chambers English Reader and wrote on slates.

The boys went to school in khaki; when they returned from school they changed into older khaki and did what I thought was a lot of romping in the fields, but it was all part of cattle herding. They also went bird-hunting with slings. They would defeather and roast the little things and enjoy the feast. In the evenings they milked the cows and brought in the pails of milk to Makhulu.

I think what they loved best of all was to race on the horses, when Jongintaba allowed them, which was not very often, Jongintaba was stern with us children as he was expected to be. He kept us at a distance, except when he needed to instruct us or reprimand us. He was very fair and just.

Nelson himself recalled Mqekezweni in a letter to a friend in 1985:

I have the most pleasant recollections and dreams about the Transkei of my childhood, where I hunted, played sticks, stole mealies on the cob and where I learnt to court; it is a world which is gone. A well-known English poet had such a world in mind when he exclaimed: 'The things which I have seen I now can see no more.'

22 February 1985

From prison, decades later, he wrote to a kinswoman of his indebtedness to Jongintaba:

Our families are far larger than those of whites and it is always a pleasure to be fully accepted throughout a village, district, or even several districts, accompanied by your clan, and be a beloved household member, where you can call at any time, completely relaxed, sleep at ease and freely take part in the discussion of all problems, where you can even be given livestock and land to build, free of charge.

As you know I was barely ten when our father died, having lost all his wealth. Mother could neither read nor write and had no means to send me to school. Yet a member of our clan educated me from the elementary school right up to Fort Hare and never expected any refund. According to our custom, I was his child and his responsibility. I have a lot of praise for this institution, not only because it is part of me, but also due to its usefulness. It caters for all those who are descended from one ancestor and holds them together as one family. It is an institution that arose and developed in the countryside and functions only in that area. The flocking of people to the cities, mines and farms makes it difficult for the institution to function as in the old days.

April 1977

Ntombizodwa says that schooling in Mqekezweni stopped at Std V.

Jongintaba did not consider that sufficient and so he drove his charge to Qokolweni in his Ford V8 and enrolled him at the higher primary school. When he passed his Std 6, there was a celebration and they slaughtered a sheep in his honour. Jongintaba bought him his school uniform and shining leather shoes and Nelson packed

8

his trunk and they drove in the Ford V8 to Engcobo, where he was enrolled at Clarkebury. He matriculated at Healdtown in 1938 and there was an even bigger celebration, for he was now to go to university. Jongintaba took him to a tailor and had a three-piece suit made for him. We thought there could never be anyone smarter than him at Fort Hare.

Kaiser Matanzima has the same feelings. He says, 'The two of us were very handsome young men and all the women wanted us.'

Nelson's own clearest recollection of those dandy days is of Ntselamanzi, a dancehall where the upper-crust of African society went ballroom-dancing in black suit and tie.

We spent hours learning to dance graciously. Our model was Victor Sylvester, the world champion of ballroom-dancing, our tutor, one of us, Smallie Guwindla. But as Fort Harians, we had a problem; while we learnt to foxtrot and waltz, the places where we could show off our talents were out of bounds. Undaunted, we sneaked out of our dormitories and presented ourselves at Ntsela-manzi. There was always the chance we might bump into one of our masters. We took that chance. One evening I spied a very lovely young woman. I went up to her and asked her to dance with me. She was in my arms, foxtrotting exquisitely. I asked her her name. She told me she was Mrs Bokwe. Dr Bokwe's wife! Dr Bokwe was with Professor Matthews. I looked across the hall and I saw the two gentlemen, my elders. I froze. I apologized profusely and conducted her to the esteemed company. I retreated hastily before any pair of authoritarian eyes held mine in cold rebuke, Dr Bokwe's or Professor Matthew's, but even though I had breached two rules, Professor Matthews never raised the issue with me. He lived up to his reputation of being a very good sport.

But [Ntombizodwa goes on] there was trouble at Fort Hare. Nelson got involved in a strike. There is always trouble about food, and he was sent home. Jongintaba was upset with him. He said he should apologize and return. But he was very obstinate. He said he would never go back.

Ntombizodwa pauses and it seems she has come to the end of her account of Nelson. But Nelson's eldest daughter Makaziwe reminds her about the cow incident. Ntombizodwa looks at her reprimandingly, and does not oblige, so Makaziwe, who will not be repressed, tells the story as she has heard it. Justice and Nelson, the latter suspended from college, decided to run away to Johannesburg, but they had no money so they took one of Jongintaba's cows and sold it to the local trader, Vigie Bros, and with the cash set off for the Golden City. But Jongintaba missed the cow in the evening. Someone reported that he had seen his two favoured *inkosanas* driving it to the store. Jongintaba confronted the storekeeper and soon had runners charging after the culprits. They were brought back, roundly chastised, the money returned and the cow herded into the kraal where it belonged.

Nelson corrects the story from Pollsmoor prison:

Ntombizodwa's objection to relating the cow incident was perfectly understandable in terms of countryside convention. Who would willingly vilify a beloved uncle by calling him a thief? But Maki also downplayed the incident. Justice [Zwelivumile] and I in fact sold two oxen and not one cow as she says. We used the money to dash to Johannesburg and after clearing many hurdles, we eventually reached the Golden City. No runners were sent after us, and we were never brought back. All that happened is that Jongintaba telegraphed the Induna at Crown Mines and demanded that we be sent back. As a result of the telegram, we were expelled from the mine. I am giving you only the bare bones on all these matters; you need to have the meat.

22 February 1985

Ntombizodwa grew pensive after an hour or so of talking. Then she said:

I have told you about Nelson's education and his college. But there was another education that we received at Mqekezweni and I believe that that education was very important to him, as it was to all of us. That was the education we received by simply sitting silently when our elders talked. We never made the slightest noise and our elders took no notice of us and it was as if they did not know we were there.

The chiefs and headmen from all the districts came to Mqekezweni and, their business done, they would sit in the dining-hall and

10

talk. As children we listened and we heard a history that was not written in our school books. They spoke of Thembu kings who had glorified the nation and of Thembu kings who had compromised and sold out to the British, and reduced the people to beggars.

The oldest of the chiefs who came to Mqekezweni was Chief Zwelibhangile Joyi. He was shrivelled and bent and so black that he was blue. He used to cough a lot; it would come in a convulsion and then trail off like the whine of a train whistle. He knew the history of the Thembus best of all, because he had lived through a great deal of it. It was from him that we learned about King Ngangelizwe. The years dropped from his body and he danced like a young warrior when he told us about how he fought in the King's impi against the British. Ngangelizwe, he said, was true to his people and generous to foreigners. We were all thrilled by his tales, but especially Nelson. I could see it did something to him, so that I am sure that Tatu Joyi's tales lived with him always.

Tatu Joyi said that the white people divided brother from brother, and split the people of Ngangelizwe into pieces and destroyed them in pieces. They told the Thembus that they were British subjects and that their great chief was the great white queen in England, but Tatu Joyi said that was a lie. A chief puts land beneath the feet of his people. Queen Victoria took away the land of the Thembu and put them into locations and put strange tribes between them, so that they would kill each other and remain forever weak against the white people.

We listened to Tatu Joyi and it made us angry that the British had done these things to us and ashamed that our ancestors had allowed these things to happen to them. Even then I saw that Nelson's anger was the greatest of all.

That is why he has spent his life in prison. He told the court of these things when they sentenced him. I could not be there, but I read every word he said and it was true and I heard Tatu Joyi in those words.

Nelson told the court at his trial in 1962:

Many years ago, when I was a boy brought up in my village in the Transkei, I listened to the elders of the tribe telling stories about the good old days, before the arrival of the white man. Then, our people lived peacefully under the democratic rule of their kings and moved freely and confidently up and down the country without let or hindrance. Then the country was our own. We occupied the land, the forests, the rivers; we extracted the mineral wealth beneath the soil and all the riches of this beautiful land. We set up and operated our own government, we controlled our own armies and we organized our own trade and commerce. The elders would tell tales of the wars fought by our ancestors in defence of the fatherland, as well as the acts of valour by our generals and soldiers during these epic days.

The structure and organization of early African societies in this country fascinated me very much and greatly influenced the evolution of my political outlook. The land, then the main means of production, belonged to the whole tribe and there was no individual ownership whatsoever. There were no classes, no rich or poor and no exploitation of man by man. All men were free and equal and this was the foundation of government. Recognition of this general principle found expression in the constitution of the council, variously called *imbizo* or *pitso* or *kgotla*, which governs the affairs of the tribe. The council was so completely democratic that all members of the tribe could participate in its deliberations. Chief and subject, warrior and medicine man, all took part and endeavoured to influence its decisions. It was so weighty and influential a body that no step of any importance could ever be taken by the tribe without reference to it.

There was much in such a society that was primitive and insecure and it certainly could never measure up to the demands of the present epoch. But, in such a society are contained the seeds of evolutionary democracy in which none will be held in slavery or servitude, and in which poverty, want and insecurity shall be no more. This is the inspiration which, even today, inspires me and my colleagues in our political struggle.

7 November 1962

# CHAPTER 2

# The Past

The Thembu lineage is traced twenty generations back to the patriarch Zwide who ruled in the fifteenth century. Beyond that date, historical records fade into prehistory. One late-nineteenth-century government report claims that the Tambookies, as they were called, 'were found in 1688 by shipwrecked sailors, occupying the country between the Bashe and Umtata Rivers'.* They were described as having abominable heathen customs and as an idle race of people. Such violent impressions were conjured to justify the exploitation and destruction of a proud people.

Commenting on the physical beauty of the region of his birth, Nelson wrote to Winnie:

The story of our grandfather Langasiki fascinated me a great deal and I hope you are able to collect more of such historical snippets from C. K. before his death. Few places have moved me as the Mkhomasi valley. I first saw the river's mouth in September 1955 when I drove along the South Coast road from Durban to Port Shepstone, and the majestic beauty of the landscape caught me at once. I saw the valley twice in February 1956 on my way to and from Umtata and crossed it between Richmond and Ixopo.

I found that part even more awe-inspiring than its coastal region. If I were not driving the Oldsmobile I'd have found it quite difficult to hold my nerve as I had to keep my foot on the brake continuously, as the road turned and twisted down the steep slope to the river. On crossing the bridge, I couldn't resist the temptation of stopping, getting out and surveying the beauty that surrounded me. Can you guess when and with whom I next saw it? I hope you

* Department of Native Affairs Blue Book and Magisterial Reports, 1851–1902.

are not going to be jealous now. Come, guess, who was it? Yes, a woman! Yes, oh yes, you are quite right, in June 1958 [on their return journey after their wedding] with you! It flatters me much to discover that that wonderful garden was once the territory of a man from whose loins we come. It is one of the most beautiful regions in the country.

14 May 1976

It was to Tatu Joyi that Nelson turned to understand the past. That Thembu sage laid the foundations of his historical perceptions. At Fort Hare, and later in Johannesburg, Nelson researched government reports on the tribes of the Eastern Cape, recorded in the late nineteenth century, and these confirmed the broad outline of Tatu Joyi's detailed recall.

Tatu Joyi recounted that before the white people came each clan lived in peace with other clans. According to legend they – the Zulu, the Pondo, the Thembu, the Xhosa – were all children of one father, but as the clans multiplied so they fell under the protection of district chiefs, and each chief was the founding father of *isizwe* (nation) and *isizwe* came to be known after him. But when *isizwe* grew too large for a single chief to control, then it re-grouped under his sons. Very often the re-grouping occurred because of quarrelling between men of authority, and most often the quarrelling was between sons of common loins but different wombs. Tatu Joyi said a chief's strength lay in his many wives and the numerous children they bore him, but he said there was also weakness in that strength. Sons of different wombs quarrelled over power. According to Nguni law, the chieftain-ship could only pass to one son, and that son was the son of the Great House. The chief chose his successor, but, said Tatu Joyi, the successor was always a centre of envy and if he was not strong, or if he did not protect his people and settle disputes with justice, and so lost their respect and love, he opened the way for his brothers to dispute his authority and his people to leave him and follow someone who would protect them better.

That is how, according to Tatu Joyi, the Nguni, who lived between the mountains and the sea in the great land that stretched from the River Kei northwards on the east coast

14

and across the Zambezi and beyond, became divided into Zulu, Xhosa, Pondo, Thembu, and into the many clans with their many chiefs and their headmen. And that is also how the quarrelling began that made them weak in the face of *abelungu* (white people) who came across the sea with their rods of fire against which African spears were nothing.

They were few in numbers, but great in intrigue. They looked about for weaknesses in the tribes; they scratched in the history and looked to see who had quarrelled with whom in the past and who was quarrelling with whom in the present and there they poured poison and worked their witchcraft. They set brother against brother and while the brothers fought, they took the land. The children of the Zulu king, Senzangakhona, fought against each other and cleared the path for the Boers, and the children of Faku and Ngubeng-cuka divided the Pondos and Thembus into patriots and traitors.

Tatu Joyi said that *abantu* could match neither the white man's gun nor his cunning, nor could they cope with his God; above all, he said, they were defeated by the white people's papers, which took by law, *their* law, what they could not take by war. That was their witchcraft and magic.

He told them about a white man who came to Ngangelizwe one day and asked for land. He gave him land and that, Tatu Joyi said, was the greatest mistake King Ngangelizwe ever made: The *abantu* shared land as they shared water and air, but *abelungu* took the land as a man takes a wife. That white man brought a piece of paper and made Ngangelizwe put his mark on it. He then said that the paper gave him possession of the land and when Ngangelizwe disputed that, the white man took him to the white court and the court looked at the paper and said Ngangelizwe had given the white man 4,000 morgen of land. The court also said white people needed the land of the Thembus to protect themselves from the Thembus!

Nelson read in the Blue Book how the teachers drained his people of their wealth: 'The system practised by a large number of traders in the territories of giving almost unlimited

15

credit to the customers is rapidly impoverishing the Natives. Many who were wealthy a few years ago are reduced to poverty ... The credit system must in a very few years greatly impoverish the Natives.'*

In the time of King Ngubengcuka, the Thembus occupied all the land between the Indwe and the Kei Rivers. His son, Paramount Chief Mtirara, virtually sold his dominion to the British for a retainer of £400 a year. The British grip over Thembuland tightened when Mtirara's successor, Ngangelizwe, sought British protection against the Gcalekas. Tatu Joyi said that they quarrelled over a small matter. Ngangelizwe had married the daughter of the Gcaleka paramount chief, Sarhili.

Tatu Joyi explained that husbands will beat their wives when provoked, but when the wife is the daughter of a paramount chief the husband reaps the wrath of a paramount chief, and that is what happened to Ngangelizwe. Sarhili invaded Thembuland and defeated Ngangelizwe. That is when the Thembu king ran to the British and lost his kingdom without realizing it. They supported him against Sarhili, but in return they took control of his kingdom, for his protection, dividing it into four districts and appointing a magistrate over each. The king was king in name only.

Ngangelizwe awoke to the enormity of his action when the British helped themselves to Indwe. There was resistance against the British. The king's brothers, Siqungathi and Matanzima, and the chiefs of the Qwathi and Gcina tribes, Stokwe Ndhela and Gecelo, led the fray, but Thembu was divided against Thembu, and the British conquered the 'rebels' and deprived them of their land, ripe for harvesting and gave it to the 'friendly' Thembus. But, Tatu Joyi said, even the 'loyal' Thembu were not allowed to eat the harvest; that went to the magistrate. Their reward was bitter; they were put into locations, and moved from even these at the whim of the white people.

The Thembu, Tatu Joyi said, would have won, and kept

* Blue Book, 1895, p. 53.

16

their land, had they remained united, but there were those who wanted power over Ngangelizwe and the enemy promised them that power, so they went to the enemy.

The Xhosas, according to Tatu Joyi, were a great people when the white men crossed the Fish River. There were many chiefs, all children of Paramount Chief Phalo, whose great-grandsons were Gcaleka of the Great House and Rarabe of the Right-hand House. Then the white people came and there was war. For a hundred years the Xhosas fought the white people to save their land and their customs. Growing impatient, the white people decided to destroy the Xhosas by perpetrating an unimaginable evil. They simulated the *izinyanya* (the ancestral spirits) and tricked them into destroying themselves.

Sarhili's most renowned councillor was Mhlakaza, the wisest of all the seers of the Xhosa. Sarhili respected and believed him. So the white people set a trap for Mhlakaza. One day when his niece was fetching water from the stream she heard voices and saw strange men, and when she was about to run in fear they restrained her and asked her to send her uncle, Mhlakaza, to them. She did. He came and the trick was so clever that he believed they were the *izinyanya*. He saw among them his dead brother who had been an even greater seer than he, and his brother told him of the Russians, the powerful enemy of the English, who would come to liberate the Xhosas. He asked them to prepare for the coming by killing the cattle and leaving the fields fallow.

Tatu Joyi said that to this day they were unable to explain how so wise a man as Mhlakaza could have fallen for so terrible a trick. He must have been bewitched and in turn he bewitched Sarhili, the king, who ordered his people to do as the *izinyanya* had directed. So they killed their cattle and did not sow their seeds. They waited for the Russians to come from across the seas and liberate them, but they never came. Instead there was famine and death and that is how the Gcaleka were conquered.

The Pondos were the last of all the tribes to be conquered by the Europeans in Southern Africa. Pondoland was annexed by the British in 1894. Thembuland had been annexed nine years earlier.

Tatu Joyi said that Mqikela was the king of the Pondo and the son of the famous Faku. He was the brother of Ndamase, who became the senior chief in Eastern Pondoland. In the time of Faku all the land between the Umzimkhulu River and Umtata, and between the sea and the mountains, was Pondoland. Then Shaka began the *imfecane* because he wanted to control everyone. There was terror in the country, and the tribes fled, many never to return to their ancestral land. Faku, whose people were the largest and the wealthiest of all the tribes, retreated to Umgazi. The *ibongi* of Shaka's brother Dingane boasted:

> He destroyed the cattle of Sigenu
> He destroyed the cattle of Sangwena
> Who fled and sank into Umzimvubu
> Oh! take them by their heads and
> Submerge them in the waters
> Do they not see the destroying bird is wrath?
> He is raging
> He is the lightning of the earth
> The lion returns
> The king of Zulus returns victorious.

But, Tatu Joyi said, there was little truth in the boast. Faku had chosen discretion instead of valour and bided his time. He returned in 1842 when the Boers defeated Dingane mainly through the treachery of his brother Mpande, only to find himself blocked by the Boers. They were stronger because of their guns. Being wise he turned to the other white people with guns, the British, who were only too eager to help. But the Pondos returned to only a part of their original Pondoland. The man who helped them to do so was Theophilus Shepstone, missionary turned statesman, and the price he extracted was the paramount chieftaincy of the Pondos. It was all written on a piece of paper and Faku and all the important chiefs were made to sign that paper.

*

Nelson later, much later, when he was a lawyer, found a copy of that treaty recorded in a *Government Gazette*. It read:

We hereby for ourselves, our heirs and successors and for and on behalf of our respective tribes acknowledge and profess that from and after the execution hereof Theophilus Shepstone, Esquire, is and hereafter shall be, the Paramount and Exclusive Chief and Ruler of ourselves and the tribes belonging to us, as also of the country or territory now occupied or hereafter to be occupied by us or any of us or any part or portion thereof.

And we ... acknowledge Theophilus Shepstone, Esquire, as such Supreme Chief or Ruler, as effectively and to all intents and purpose, as firmly as if he ... had been or had become such Paramount Chief or Ruler by succession according to our laws or usage.

The treaty which was signed with a cross by Faku on 5 June 1854 at his Great Place, Ezizindeni, also gave 'Theophilus Shepstone, Esquire, the full and complete control of Port St John' [the trade line to the Cape]. Identical treaties were similarly signed by the heads of six other tribes: the Nikwe, Mbulu, Xesibe, Boto, the Twana and Ngutyana. The chief of the last was Madikizela who married Faku's eldest daughter, Mqwabe. Chief Madikizela was the great-grand-father of Winnie Madikizela, who married Nelson Mandela.

During the life of Faku the British wanted little beyond a *de jure* presence in the area, so that, in effect, Faku, up to his death at the reputed age of ninety, reigned supreme. But his sons Mqikela and Ndamase were beset with all the problems the treaty produced and suffered the humiliation of deposition.

Ndamase was Faku's eldest son, but he was already an old man at the time of his father's death, and that was probably why Faku named his younger son, Mqikela (no older than Ndamase's own son, Nqwiliso), his heir. Ndamase felt that he had been overlooked, and there were many who encouraged that feeling in him. But Ndamase was too frail in himself to enter into conflict with Mqikela. Besides, he had

19

crossed the Umzimvubu in 1845 and established his capital in Eastern Pondoland. Mqikela refused to be bullied by whites. For that reason he was disliked by both the English and the Boers. They used his nephew, Ndamase's son, Nqwiliso against him when it suited their purpose.

They did not like Mqikela because, Tatu Joyi said, he refused to be their 'dog'. He insisted on being a proper chief like his father; above all, he refused to give them Port St Johns which brought in a lot of money from shipping. In addition, Mqikela collected licence fees from the numerous white traders, who bought maize, tobacco and ivory from the Pondo. Tatu Joyi said that the one thing that gives white people indigestion is a rich black man. Mqikela was getting rich with the licence money and they did not want him to have that money. Nelson's own research revealed that when Mqikela insisted on his fees, saying that the traders had paid to Faku, so they should pay to him, the British resident, Mr Oxland, had replied haughtily:

You talk of Faku's time. Let me just point out that things are very different today to what they were when Faku was alive. The Government was then far from you. In those days there were many people and much land between the Government and the Pondos. Today, however, the Government is closer on your border. You are hemmed in on every side.

You are like a stone in the middle of a river. You will do well to reflect on this, and it will be pleasing for you to think that you have such a powerful friend and neighbour as the Government.

But, Tatu Joyi said, there was no pleasure for Mqikela as the British were busy taking his land and his people. The Xesibes had been taken and turned against him because the British said there was copper on their land and they wanted the copper. They sent a British force to protect them from Mqikela. And they simply took the fertile Rhode for the white farmers. They pretended that they bought the land because they paid Chief Mota £600. But the Rhode was not Mota's to sell. Mota was a *mthakathi* (witchdoctor) who had converted to Christianity and had become an *impimpi* (spy).

When Mqikela refused to sell Port St Johns to the British, they simply declared that that part of Pondoland was not his to sell anyway. It was his nephew Nqwiliso's, and General Thesiger (who later became Lord Chelmsford) sailed to the Port from the Cape, surveyed the 3,500 acres they required, paid Nqwiliso £1,000 and annexed it as British territory. Tatu Joyi said they could not tolerate Mqikela because he treated the British traders in his territory as his subjects. He tried the Englishman Bell for murdering a Pondo and made him pay fifty head of cattle, saying: 'We do not, as the English do, execute murderers. We make them pay reparation.' For this, and because he gave refuge to fugitives from British 'injustice', he was accused of breaking Faku's treaty. The British summoned him to depose him and put Nqwiliso in his place.

Tatu Joyi maintained that a man is a chief because the generations before him made him one, because in the years he was growing up he learnt to be chief, and because his people knew him to be chief. The land was his, the people were his, the cattle were his. He did not cease to be chief because white people wrote in their books that he was no longer chief. He was chief in the mind and hearts of the people. How could a paper change that?

Mqikela ignored the British summons, and his followers took up their sticks and assegais and threatened to go to war. They openly insulted the magistrates and the British residents and terrified the small white community. They stirred up such a fury that both chiefs, Mota and Nqwiliso, abandoned the British and came scurrying back to the Pondo fold.

The British residents warned them that the Government never took up the assegai until forced to do so, and then it never stopped until it broke up all the people and pulled down the houses of all the chiefs; that two years ago when the Gcalekas had attacked the Government, it had destroyed them so that they were now a scattered people and their chiefs were living like bucks in the bush. The same had happened to Cetewayo and it would happen to them.

And it did when the British annexed Pondoland.

So, said Tatu Joyi, *ubuntu* (humanity) of the African kings came to an end and the tyranny of the white people had been established.

The young Nelson, tutored at Tatu Joyi's feet, was fired to regain that *ubuntu* for all South Africans.

PART II

# THE STRUGGLE

CHAPTER 3

# Johannesburg

In 1941 Johannesburg was a sprawling, high-rise city that had reaped the benefits of a European war. Its industry in gold had been compounded by other industry, almost literally converting the rest of the country into its hinterland. Hundreds of thousands of male migrants poured in from the African reserves of the four provinces in search of the work the city offered.

As many came with proper authorization as did not, and as many found jobs in factories as found temporary accommodation in prisons. While there were jobs in the city, there was no housing, not even sufficient land for 'squatting'. But there were 'non-European' townships established just after the First World War, before the white government totally contained blacks with laws, mostly about where they could not live.

Sophiatown, Newclare, Martindale and Alexandra were stacked with rows and rows of single-roomed barracks, with forty or more people sharing a toilet and a tap. The only municipal housing provided close to the city was the Eastern and Western Native Townships, a fenced-in compound of 2,000 red-brick, two- and three-roomed houses, planned for no more than 13,000 people.

That was the Johannesburg into which Nelson stepped in 1941. Neither he nor Justice had the problem of authorization or accommodation, or of a job – at least not immediately. They had come to South Africa's industrial heart, to experience life there, so that they could begin to understand their own place and destiny in their motherland.

They had one solitary address to Crown Mines, where an

old *induna* of Jongintaba was an overseer. They made their way to that destination. The *induna* was honoured to extend his hospitality to the two members of the royal kraal.

But, within days of their arrival, Jongintaba's man tracked them down. Justice returned, for he had filial obligations he could not escape, but Nelson convinced his guardian that it was best for him to pursue his studies in Johannesburg and become a lawyer. Jongintaba realized that it would in fact be the culmination of his duty to Hendry Gadla. So Nelson stayed in Johannesburg with the reassurance of his guardian that he would continue to care for him, even in that great city, for as long as his assistance was required.

Nelson moved in with a family in Alexandra Township. He fondly recalled his days there in a letter to his youngest daughter, Zindzi:

Often as I walk up and down my cell or as I lie on my bed, the mind wanders far and wide, recalling this episode and that mistake. Among these is the thought whether in my best days outside prison I showed sufficient appreciation for the love and kindness of many of those who befriended and even helped me when I was poor and struggling.

The other day I was thinking of the home in 46, Seventh Avenue, Alexandra Township, where I lived on my arrival in Johannesburg. At that time I was earning the monthly wage of two pounds (R4,00) and out of this amount I had to pay the monthly rent of 13/4d plus bus fare of 8d a day to town and back. It was hard going and I often found it quite difficult to pay the rent and bus fare. But my landlord and his wife were kind, not only did they give me an extension when I could not raise the rent, but on Sundays they gave me a lovely lunch free of charge.

I also stayed with Rev Mabuto of the Anglican Church on 46, 8th Avenue, in the same township, and he and Gogo, as we fondly called his wife, were also very kind, even though she was rather strict, insisting that I should take out only Xhosa girls. Despite the fact that my political outlook was still formative, Healdtown and Fort Hare had brought me into contact with students from other sections of our people, and at least I had already developed beyond thinking along ethnic lines. I was determined not to follow her advice on this particular matter. But she and her husband played the role of parents to me rather admirably.

Mr Schreiner Baduza, originally from Sterkspruit, lived as tenant with his wife in 46, 7th Avenue. He and Mr J. P. Mngoma, although much older than myself, especially the latter, were among some of my best friends in those days. Mr Mngoma was a property owner and father to Aunt Virginia, one of Mum's friends. Later I was introduced to Mr P. Toyana, father-in-law to the brother of the late Chief Jongintaba Mdingi. He, Mr Toyana, was a clerk at the Rand Leases Mine. I used to travel there on Saturdays to collect his rations – samp, mealie meal, meat, peanuts and other items.

Much later my financial position slightly improved, but I hardly thought of those who had stood on my side during difficult times; nor did I ever visit them except once or twice only. Both the Mabutos and the Baduzas came to live in Soweto and I visited the Mabutos on a few occasions. I met both Messrs Toyana and Baduza on many occasions but not once did I think of returning their kindness. Both in the late forties and early fifties Mr Baduza became a very prominent figure in the civic affairs of Soweto and our association was limited to that level.

1 March 1981

In another letter he described an awkward moment as he familiarized himself with the city's consumerism:

Shortly after my arrival in Johannesburg in 1941, I bought some meat in a provision shop next to the Cathedral. When I reached my room in Alexandra I asked Notosini, then a young lady of about six, to tell her elder sister to cook it for me. She had a short, sharp mischievous laugh which she quickly suppressed. 'Ivuthiwe, Buti,' she said. It was smoked beef and, as a 'mampara' from the countryside, I thought it was raw meat.

2 October 1977

But there were also shocking experiences in those early Johannesburg days. He recalls one:

In 1941, I went to visit my teacher who had taught me in Standard Ten. He was a good qualified teacher and a graduate, married to an equally well-qualified nurse. They lived in Orlando East. I found the house shut and a terrible smell emanating from within, of herbs and medicines. It was clear that a professional herbalist was doing his job. His wife came out as I was about to knock on the door. She was pale with shock and said that her husband had become ill and was suffering from pain in the joints. She said that it had started when he had begun his studies in law, and accused me of bewitching him.

I was very troubled and went straight to Anto Lembede and told him of my experience. He only laughed.

In another letter he wrote:

Talking about Klerksdorp reminds me of some aspects of family history I never had the opportunity to relate to you, about some of the old families. On a Friday evening in the early 1940s, I entrained from Park Station to Klerksdorp. The train consisted of 3rd-class coaches only and was crowded and riotous. I reached the town at midnight. I took a taxi to my destination. I knocked on the door and the next moment I was part of the family. I was welcomed by a sporting, intellectual, tall, soft-spoken and steady person in many respects similar to Ngutyana. Early in the morning we went out sightseeing in a setting that differed from the open spaces in the south of Johannesburg only in that it was more wild with fairly thick bush and rookies. I immediately fell in love with the place because it reminded me of Mvezo on the banks of Umbhashe where I was born. We were together for several years until politics drastically cut down moments of pleasure. I am sure that when I return you will eagerly accompany me to that old spot in Klerksdorp and then to the south of the Golden City where history really begins.

15 May 1977

While Nelson recalls his early days in Johannesburg with such affection, the impressions of a young nurse trainee who lived a few doors away on Eighth Avenue, Alexandra, were very different. She saw Nelson as a nice young man, fresh from the rural area, lost in the squalid dynamics of the sprawling township. She felt sorry for him and decided to help. She spoke about him to her friend, Albertina Totiwe, a fellow nursing student at the Johannesburg General Hospital, who in turn mentioned Nelson to her fiance, the resourceful Walter Sisulu. If anybody could help the young man, she knew Walter could.

Walter had practically grown up in Johannesburg. His mother was a strong, caring woman, highly respected both in her home area and in Orlando. No one referred to him by name, but they all knew of the white foreman who had come as a road builder to Engcobo in the Transkei many years ago, fallen in love with the young Sisulu girl and then abandoned her and their two young children. MaSisulu never looked at another man. She devoted her life to her children. She took them to Johannesburg, found lodgings in Alexandra Township and worked as a washerwoman to put them through high school.

In 1941 she was one of the few fortunate people with a house in Orlando, and she shared it unstintingly with relatives, no matter how far removed.

Nelson and Walter met in the city and the two young men became friends almost instantly. Walter invited Nelson to stay with them at MaSisulu's house; Nelson accepted the invitation. Nelson recalls: 'Walter arranged for me to be articled with Attorney Lazer Sidelsky, an LLB graduate from Wits, a white man, who practically became an elder brother to me. Walter also bought me a suit for graduation when I passed my BA in 1942.'

Walter did not only draw Nelson into his home, he also drew him into his world of politics and human concern. In the course of time he drew him into marriage to his cousin, the petite, pretty Evelyn from Engcobo.

CHAPTER 4

# The Sweep of Politics

━━━━━

Nelson's political history began in Johannesburg and his political work was largely concentrated there. Many experience that metropolis as the palpitating heart of South Africa. Nelson, in those distant years, found Johannesburg to be the centre of his universe. The city engulfed and challenged him, but he soon learnt to manage her. He came to understand her awesome complexities and, above all, her politics. He responded to her from the standpoint of Orlando, and it was this response that eventually developed and sustained him as the people's leader.

Nelson was at the centre of an emergent African urban culture, pushing through the poverty and the post-war repression of the forties.

In the streets of Sophiatown, Newclare and Alexandria, it was an exuberant, unabashed response to those who thought themselves better. Both defiant and defensive, it had an element of the subterranean about it, for it was forever watchful of the police, at times on the run and almost always vulnerable to arrest. It was a culture that went with degrees of inebriation and crime. American movies, American gangsters and American jazz fuelled it. It had its own rhythm and the penny whistle piped it in happy notes that evoked a dizzy mood and shaped the dance in shebeens.

It spoke its own language, an impudent mix of African, Afrikaans and English, which came out in loud, tough, staccato talk. Non-book in origin, it became a distinct literary style in the African-focused media and it produced angry, frustrated, township writers, as it did musicians. It was the womb from which Bloke Modisane, Can Temba, Casey Motsisi, Miriam Makeba and Dolly Rathebe were drawn.

Complementing this township culture was that of the university-educated African, the doctors and lawyers, teachers and school principals – men and women of discipline and Christian commitment (sometimes Marxist commitment) who took western civilization and its liberal and socialist promises literally and were determined to realize them on the African continent. Nelson became inbued with that culture and, in turn, influenced it. He met ex-Fort Harians: Oliver Tambo, William Nkomo and Lionel Majambozi; he met A. P. Mda, Congress Mbata, Jordan Ngubane, David Bopape and Anton Lembede, and he renewed his association with Victor Mbobo, his former schoolmaster from Healdtown. They exchanged ideas and developed a consciousness that crystallized into the ideology of Africanism and African nationalism. They identified with the culture of the townships, the art and musical forms, bursting to be recognized; they intellectualized and organized those forms. They coordinated the political and cultural, so that there was a duplication of personalities in the emergent educational, literary, artistic and political bodies. The fact that among them were editors of the leading African newspapers of the time, Jordan Ngubane, M. T. Morane and H. I. E. Dhlomo, gave them a significant reach to the reading and thinking public.

They were a small group of men, a dozen or two, who took upon themselves the formidable task of awakening the slumbering African giant and rousing him into self-realization. Anton Lembede wrote in *Inkundla Ya Bantu* in May 1946: 'A new spirit of African Nationalism, or Africanism, is pervading through and stirring African society. A young virile nation is in the process of birth and emergence. The National Movement imbued with and animated by the national spirit is gaining strength and momentum.'

They were the heralds of that momentum which they pursued through the African National Congress Youth League, described in their manifesto as 'the Brains Trust and power station of the spirit of African Nationalism; the spirit of African self-determination'. They declared: 'At this power station the League will be a coordinating agency for all youthful forces employed in rousing popular political consciousness and fighting oppression and reaction.' *

While the Youth League manifesto of 1948 concentrated on the political, it made a special point of supporting 'the cultural struggle of the African people' and encouraged 'African artists of all categories and emphasized that African works of art could and should reflect not only the present phase of the national liberatory struggle, but also the world of beauty that lies beyond the conflict and turmoil of struggle.' †

They decided that the only way to wield power within the ANC, and to transform it into a militant African organization, was through establishing their own wing, the African Youth Congress.

The idea for the Youth League, according to Nelson, came from Dr Lionel Majambozi, who was a medical student at the time. He and his fellow student, Dr William Nkomo, both of whom Nelson knew from Fort Hare, were members of the Young Communist League; Dr Nkomo was also a member of the Communist Party. Nkomo became the President of the Provisional Executive of the Youth League in 1943 and Majambozi, the Secretary. Nelson says:

We were very critical of the ANC. We felt that it was out of touch with the masses. But we did not distance ourselves from it. On the contary, we wished to work with it and through it. We accepted it as the foundation of African Nationalism, but felt that its encumbents had little concept of that Nationalism.

We succeeded in persuading the ANC Conference in 1943 to establish a youth wing and then drew up a constitution and manifesto which we took to Dr Xuma, the President General, for his approval. There was a great deal to admire in Dr Xuma, despite his distance from the masses and his authoritarianism. He had lifted up the ANC from its moribund state in the 1930s. He had assumed the Presidency with only 17s. 6d. in the coffers but had soon raised this to £4,000. We were also aware of his international importance. He was widely travelled and respected by

* G. Carter and T. Karis *From Protest to Challenge*, Volume 2, Hoover Institute Press, Stanford University, 1977, p. 331.
† ibid., pp. 300, 336.

traditional and modern leaders, both in South Africa and the neighbouring states. King Sobuza, Tshekedi Khama and Hastings Banda stayed with him when they came to Johannesburg, and he was on first-name terms with the Secretary of Native Affairs and several Cabinet Ministers. He exuded a sense of power and security, real or otherwise. Our meeting with him was genial. He was in a way flattered by the attention we younger men were paying him. He accepted our consititution and manifesto.

And so in 1944 the young men met at the Bantu Men's Social Centre and formed the Youth League. Anton Lembede was elected the first President and Nelson, David Bopape, A. P. Mda, Walter Sisulu and Oliver Tambo were among those elected to the Executive Committee.

Enshrined in the policy statement of the Youth League was Lembede's philosophy:

The white man regards the universe as a gigantic machine hurtling through time and space to its final destruction: individuals in it are but tiny organisms with private lives that lead to private deaths: personal power, success and fame are the absolute measures of values, the things to live for. This outlook on life divides the universe into a host of individual little entities which cannot help being in constant conflict thereby hastening the approach of the hour of their final destruction.

The African, or his side, regards the universe as one composite whole; an organic entity, progressively driving towards greater harmony and unity, whose individual parts exist merely as inter-dependent aspects of one whole realizing their fullest life in the corporate life whose communal contentment is the absolute measure of values.*

The social dynamic was not based on conflict, but on the humanitarian impulse for harmony. It was an analysis that rang true for Nelson for it reflected his rural roots.

On the Witwatersrand campus Nelson discovered another world, open and multi-racial, which both sympathized with his Africanism and rejected it, not aggressively but somewhat patronizingly. His mind was tugged at by liberalism and

* Carter and Karis, op. cit., p. 301.

Marxism. He drew close to his fellow law students, Ismail Meer and J. N. Singh. He met Zainab Asvat and the Cachalia brothers in Fordsburg and Dr Dadoo in End Street, and through them he was introduced to the Indian passive resistance. They were engaged in resistance against the new Land Act that condemned them to segregation, by law, throughout the country. Nelson was impressed by their organization. They were not Africans, but they too were oppressed and they were fighting their oppression actively and militantly, though non-violently.

He enjoyed the open-house hospitality of the Pahads. Amina Pahad cooked mounds of rice and large bowls of curry, and when it was meal time all those present washed their hands and sat down to eat, without the formality of an invitation, in the same way as they had done at Mqekezweni. He noted how strongly and how proudly they maintained their culture, how they ate with their fingers without any embarrassment. At times he stayed over-night at Ismail Meer's flat, and they discussed matters of cultural pride and inferiority, segregation and racism, and wondered what they should do about them.

He met Violaine Junod, Ruth First and Joe Slovo, Harold Wolpe, Rusty Bernstein and Hilda Watts, Bram and Molly Fischer, Betty Du Toit, the Harmels, the Weinbergs and, through them, entered radical white society.

The Fischers, Bernsteins, Harmels, Weinbergs, Ruth First and Joe Slovo, were members of the Communist Party; Ismail Meer and J. N. Singh were, in addition, members of the Natal Indian Congress and Moses Kotane, J. B. Marks and Dan Tloome of the ANC.

Though drawn to them socially and stimulated by them intellectually, he remained politically aloof from them. He did not quite understand how they fitted into the African future. At Joyi's feet he had learnt of the weaknesses of their chiefs that had lead to the enslavement of their people. Fort Hare had lifted him out of tribe and into the concept of an African nation. How did whites, Indians and Coloureds fit into this nation? Did they fit in at all? The thought bothered him. He was, like Lembede, an Africanist and critical of Dr Xuma who flirted with Liberals and Indians and Communists, but his personal friendships were modifying this position; he was taking in the different worlds and learning to live in all of them, and they were challenging his African exclusivism and preparing him for that international humanism that upholds him today.

They boarded the bus, Nelson and his three Indian fellow students: Ismail Meer, J. N. Singh and Ahmed Bhoola. It had barely taken off when the conductor turned to them and said: 'Hey, you are not allowed to carry a kaffir.' They were taken aback and confused, not quite comprehending who the conductor was referring to. 'That kaffir there,' the conductor clarified, pointing to Nelson. A heated exchange followed. The four erudite young men confronted the middle-aged, semi-literate Afrikaner with his racism. Where, they asked him, had he got the word 'kaffir'? Did he understand its meaning? Nelson demanded where he had got the notion that he could not travel in the same bus as his friends. The conductor had no words to match theirs. He responded by stopping the bus at the next stop and calling a policeman. They talked in Afrikaans, which the four students did not understand. Then the policeman turned to Ismail Meer and said, 'You are under arrest for carrying a kaffir and disturbing this conductor in his duty.' The students began to protest. The policeman was having none of it. 'You,' he said turning to Nelson, 'you better come with us as well. We will need you.' The four young men were forced off the bus and they walked to the charge office. The police took Nelson aside and advised him to made a statement against the Indian who had 'carried' him in the bus illegally, and who had behaved cheekily to the conductor, but Nelson would have none of it; so they said they would have to charge him as well. He told them that they were welcome to do so.

Ismail was ordered to appear in court the next day, which he did, accompanied by his fellow students and his advocate, Bram Fischer. The magistrate was delighted to see Bram. He had just returned from the Orange Free State where he had had the honour of meeting Bram's father, the Judge President. 'He is in excellent health,' he told Bram.

None of this escaped the four students. With such geniality between attorney and magistrate preceding the case, they could not but have a smooth ride. The conductor cut a very poor figure in the box, and the magistrate was pleased to give the verdict in favour of the Judge President's son.

Bram Fischer, a man of brilliance, rare integrity and great humility, and he was a member of the Communist Party. Nelson came to admire and love him, but he could not accept his view of the South African conflict, that it was essentially a matter of class and not race.

He discussed these and other theories deep into the night with his close companions, men with whom he shared tribal roots, common jokes and common fears. The more they discussed, the more convinced they became that the ANC, with its prevailing structure and programme, lacked the capacity to confront and overcome the white rulers, that it was tending to play a secondary role even in the mobilization of the African people, that it was the Communist Party with its foreign ideology and white leadership which was tending to pre-empt it among African workers. The Communist Party organized trade unions, supported strike actions, and ran literacy classes. The ANC which should have been in the forefront was standing by and simply fitting into initiatives taken by the others. It neglected the African workers, whom the Communists adopted. The Youth League blamed Dr Xuma, President General of the ANC, in particular, for this state of affairs. They felt that he lacked a deep ethnic sympathy and had no sense of the masses, that it was Communists and Indians who organized mass action and the ANC followed. In the process, African interests were subordinated to others and the African people were enjoined to support essentially non-African programmes.

They argued that South Africa was an African country and that the leadership should be African. They were specially concerned about members of the CP who infiltrated the ANC. If the Africans had anything at all, they believed, it was their fraternity, their national identity, and that identity had to be protected from non-African intrusion.

They attacked the ANC for supporting, and participating in, the Native Representative Council and the Advisory Boards, and began calling for their boycotts.

It was above all in the Youth League that Nelson developed his political orientation and strategies. Lembede and Mda were intense, almost humourless, and intellectually intimidating. Nelson learnt from them but did not always agree with them. Intellectually he was closer to A. P. Mda than to Anton Lembede. He admired Mda's clarity of thought, his precision, the logical sequence of his oratory. He found Lembede somewhat in the air, tending to obtuseness and, when delivering a speech, becoming distracted by a side issue and losing the main course. He saw him more as a visionary, a dreamer, than a politican. He appreciated the two men's African exclusivism and identified with it theoretically, but he was simultaneously touched by the worlds of the Cachalias and the Harmels. He could not quite see their viewpoints as wholly alien from his own. Within the Youth League, he felt closest to Oliver Tambo and to Walter Sisulu.

He enjoyed M. B. Yengwa, modest and sharp, who reflected his strong nationalism in his grasp of Zulu history. They would spend hours listening to him as he regaled them with the bravery of Zulu warriors, giving details of the numerous battles fought with the English and the Boers, how each regiment got its name, who the leaders were and how the battles were planned. When he had done with the exploits of war, he recited extensively from the poems of H. I. E. Dhlomo, who was also the President of the Natal Youth League.

Later, when Nelson became General Secretary of the Youth League under A. P. Mda, he met Godfrey Pitje, H. Chitepe, C. N. C. Mokhele, Robert Mugabe, William Nkomo and S. M. Guma, who founded the Fort Hare Branch of the League. Later still, he met Gatsha Buthelezi and they formed a friendship that survives to this day. They were all Youth Leaguers together and they would, in different ways, lead

37

their people as heads of states, as revolutionaries, and in many other roles.

In Walter Sisulu's house they relaxed, laughed and teased each other about the women they loved and courted. Walter was about to be married. Nelson's attention was caught by his demure young cousin, Evelyn, from the Transkei.

# CHAPTER 5

# Evelyn

───────

Evelyn Mase came from Engcobo, not far from Nelson's home area. She arrived in Johannesburg at about the same time as he did to complete her schooling. Her father, a mine worker, had died when she was an infant, leaving her mother with six children to raise single-handedly. Mercifully, perhaps, three of them died, leaving Evelyn's mother grief-stricken but with a lightened burden. Quite illiterate, she struggled to put her surviving children through school. All three did well, especially Evelyn, but her mother did not live to see that. She died when Evelyn was twelve. Just a few months before her death, as if in anticipation of the event, she had entrusted Evelyn to her brother. He cared for her as if she were his own daughter. When she completed schooling in the Transkei he sent her to her elder brother in Johannesburg so that she could go to high school and eventually take up a profession. Her mother had wanted her to become a nurse and Evelyn was determined to fulfil her mother's desire.

Evelyn came to stay with the Sisulus where her brother was living in 1939. Walter's mother, MaSisulu, was the sister of their father's deceased first wife. This relationship, and because they came from the same area in Engcobo, gave them claim to a place in the Sisulu home.

Soon after Evelyn's arrival, her brother married and was allocated a house in Orlando East. She went to live with him but continued to be a regular visitor at the Sisulus' where she met Nelson. She recounts:

I think I loved him the first time I saw him. The Sisulus had many friends. They were such genial, generous people and Walter had

39

lots of friends who came to their home, but there was something very special about Nelson. Within days of our first meeting, we were going steady and within months he proposed. Nelson spoke to my brother and he was overjoyed, the Sisulus were overjoyed. Everyone we knew said that we made a very good couple. We were radiant on the day of our marriage which took place at the Native Commissioner's Court in Johannesburg, as it was then called, but we could not afford a wedding feast. That was in 1944.

We had problems, many problems, and most important was the house problem. There was literally not a house nor a room to be rented within reasonable distance of my work and Nelson's. My sister and her husband, the Mgudlwas, offered us accommodation. My brother-in-law worked at City Deep Mines as a clerk. My sister, Kate, stayed at home and looked after their two children. They had three rooms and they gave us one. There was no question of paying towards board and lodging. They were family. We shared what we could together but, with Nelson working part-time because he was studying and I earning only eighteen pounds a month, there was not all that much to share. Yet we were happy together.

Within a year I was expecting our first child. We were very excited, and Nelson's joy was there for all to see when Thembi was born. He had arranged for me to be confined at the Bertrams Nursing home, and he came there loaded with nighties for myself and baby clothes for our son. When I returned home, there was this beautiful cot he had bought.

We were allocated a two-roomed in Orlando East and early in 1947 we moved to a three-roomed match-box house, No. 8115, in Orlando West. The rent was 17s. 6d. per month. The house was not just for us. It meant that we could now have our family to live with us, just as we had lived with my sister. Nelson's sister Leabie was the first to join us and she was also the first member of his family I met. I had not even met my mother-in-law when she came. Nelson was too busy and had no time to take me to Qunu. He used to write to his mother and send her money orders. Nelson enrolled Leabie at Orlando High and assumed responsibility for her education as he was expected to do.

In 1948 we had our second child, a girl. We named her Makaziwe. Although Nelson was kept very busy, particularly on account of his political work which was taking more and more of his time, he

40

helped with the children and enjoyed doing so. Makaziwe was frail at birth and required a lot of nursing. Nelson was very tender with her. She became very ill at nine months and died within days. We were heart-broken.

In 1949 Nelson's eldest sister wrote to say that their mother was unwell. Nelson arranged for her to come to Johannesburg to see medical specialists. She stayed with us after that and filled our house, providing it with a gentle authority and giving it the dignity of the older generation which it had lacked. She was weak and distraught on arrival, but gained strength quite rapidly. My feeling is that her illness was due to the fact that she had missed her son. We got on very well together and Makhulu was a great help both with housework and the children.

Makhulu's presence gave me the opportunity to take a more active interest in the Nursing Union. I had been roped into the Union by Adelaide, who later married Oliver Tambo. Adelaide was vivacious and very persuasive. She and Gladys Khala had strong feelings about the rights of nurses, and particularly about the discriminatory wages of black nurses. I shared those feelings, and I threw in my weight with them. We held meetings at the General Hospital and at Darragh Hall. Nelson was pleased with my involvement and very supportive.

We settled into a happy, crowded family. Nelson was a highly organized person and very regular in his habits. He was up at the crack of dawn, jogged a few miles, had a light breakfast and was off for the day. He liked doing the family shopping and I was more than happy for him to do so. He enjoyed bathing the babies in the evenings and there were occasions when he took over the cooking from us women.

We had many visitors, especially from the Transkei. They came and put up with us for long periods. We made them feel that the house was their own and they had every right to it. We made the beds on the floor when there were too many of us. We never felt that there wasn't enough room. Somehow there was always room. Kaiser Matanzima was one of our regular visitors. He usually came with several men. He was close family and Nelson loved and admired him.

Nelson was at that time studying law at Witwatersrand University and Evelyn was the effective breadwinner in the family. For Nelson, politics and his studies combined and

41

interacted, and he was dedicated to both, but politics had the edge on his academic pursuits.

But it was never all politics and all studies. Nelson had a hearty zest for life. He took to amateur boxing; he enjoyed the cinema; he enjoyed the multi-cultural evenings at the International Club of which he became Secretary. Reverend Sigamoney was then Chairman. At the Club he met whites on a non-political basis and formed some firm friendships.

As the fifties approached so Nelson became intensely drawn into active politics and was often away, several days at a time, organizing in the Transvaal townships. The reception of the Youth Leaguers was always spontaneously friendly. Hospitality accepted, bedding provided, their host usually proceeded to introduce them to influential locals so that they could establish the basis for a Youth League branch.

Things were coming together in both Nelson's private and public life. His family was growing; they were taking care of Leabie; and the arrival of his mother gave them all a sense of stability and security. His studies, too, were drawing to a close.

The new decade would open for the Mandelas with the birth of their second son, Makgatho; for the ANC with a new programme of militant protest.

CHAPTER 6

# Defiance

In 1947 the Youth League was plunged into momentary gloom with the premature death of its brilliant President, Anton Lembede. Nelson had been with him in his office during the lunch-break. Later that afternoon he suffered an intestinal obstruction and was rushed to hospital. That evening Walter informed Nelson that Lembede was dead.

It seemed impossible to think of the Youth League, which had become such a great part of their lives, without the presiding influence of his impressive mind. A. P. Mda succeeded Lembede as President, with Nelson as General Secretary. The political demands on Nelson's time increased dramatically. He maintained a low political profile until the fifties and rarely participated in the heavy debates at conferences or spoke at the larger meetings. The minutes of the 1949 ANC Conference do not record any contribution from him. Neither is he reflected as a vocal participant in the minutes of the Unity talks between the ANC and the All African Convention (AAC) in 1948, to which Oliver Tambo made a special contribution. His election as Secretary of the ANC Youth League appears to have been the first step towards his popular recognition.

In 1948 A. P. Mda wrote to the Youth League branch leaders, introducing the Secretary: 'N. D. R. Mandela Esq., BA, a law student', and asked them to liaise with him. It was in that year that the Youth League launched a vigorous campaign to establish itself nationally. A great deal of the responsibility for this mammoth task fell on the Secretary. He came into contact with branches and branch officials, with ANC leaders in other provinces, and with officials of organizations with which the League had decided to cooperate, such as the Communist Party and the Non-European Unity Movement (NEUM). People were generally impressed with Mandela. I. B. Tabata, doyen of the Non-European Unity Movement and prominent on the All African Convention, was one of them, and he followed up the young man's visit to him with a long letter from Cape Town, dated 16 June 1948. In it he asked if Mandela could give him any good reason why he had joined the ANC, apart from the fact that his father had been a member. (Nelson had no knowledge of this and wondered if Tabata had information he did not possess.) Tabata continued: 'I am conscious of the fact that because of your youth, you did not have the opportunity of living through the events leading up to the 1936–1948 period' and he proceeded to analyse these for him, blaming the failure of Non-European unity on the ANC. Tabata saw the solution in the All African Convention. Unity, he concluded, 'evaded the Non-Europeans', because each organization wanted to subsume all others and because political differences denegrated into personal squabbles. He concluded:

Now, Mandela, it is time I gave you a rest and, incidentally, myself, too. If you curse me for having written so long a letter, remember that you have yourself to blame. I have added this last page because I think it is of paramount importance for a man, and especially a young man entering politics, to establish the habit of basing his action on principles. He must be ready, if necessary, to swim against the stream. Thus armed, he is protected against the temptations of seeking popularity and ephemeral success.

In the following December the ANC and AAC held a Unity Conference. The event was historic in that it brought together 165 delegates (115 from the ANC), but nothing came of the talks.

While the Unity talks with the AAC failed, the ANC moved closer to the Indian Congress. The catalyst was the terrible riots in Durban in January 1949 when, under white

44

instigation, Africans attacked Indians. The military and navy intervened, and within a week 130 people were dead.

The Indians were at the time the prime target of white rancour. They had just waged a very successful Passive Resistance campaign against apartheid, and had brought South Africa's racism into world focus at the United Nations. South Africa faced India at the debating table, much to the former's discredit. In this tense situation the boxing of an African's ear by an Indian employer provided the strategic opportunity for whites to deflect burgeoning African resentment over their poverty-stricken existence on to the Indians. Whites went about openly provoking Africans to act against the 'coolies', who, they said, were the cause of the trouble. The Natal Presidents of the ANC and NIC, A. W. G. Champion and Dr G. M. Naicker, issued a joint statement calling for restraint from the two peoples.

The ANC Working Committee, in a statement signed by the President General, appealed to the African people 'not to allow themselves to be used by other people who desired to further their own political ends at the expense of the African by fostering race hatred'. The statement went on to blame 'the Union policy of differential and discriminatory treatment of various racial groups as the fundamental contributing cause of racial friction and antagonisms. It has rendered the African the football and servant of all which he silently resents. It has given him an accumulation of grievances and a sense of frustration which find expression in unpredictable actions of violence or otherwise, to which no section is immune.' *

The national executives of the two congresses established a joint council to improve Afro-Indian relations. Nelson and his colleagues were sceptical of such moves, seeing them as empty gestures, a papering-over of the animosities of racism. The Youth League remained as unimpressed by this overture as it had by the Xuma–Dadoo – Naicker Pact of 1947, which had agreed on Afro-Indian cooperation on specific issues.

* Carter and Karis, op. cit., p. 286.

Unity, the Youth League argued, could only happen on the initiative of the ANC.

There were members who went further and said it could happen only after Indians already lived with Africans and dropped their own race prejudices against them. So Bloke Modisane wrote: 'Even intellectually I could not rationalize the discrimination of the Indians. But the African and the Indian politicians concluded the alliance, gambling to chance the issues of inter-group relations.'*

Yet the Youth League was undergoing significant change. Its 1948 manifesto rejected the extreme form of Nationalism which reserved 'Africa for Africans' and hurled the whites into the sea. It conceded that 'the different racial groups had come to stay', that 'the Indians were an oppressed group and they had not come to South Africa as conquerers and exploiters'. Some members of the executive were even having second thoughts about working alone and a few months before the Durban riots had met members of the Transvaal Indian Congress to thrash out differences. The fact that a number of the Youth Leaguers and Indian Congressites already had warm social relations had encouraged them to do so.

They had talked for a number of days in the office of J. B. Marks in Rosenberg Arcade, Market Street, Johannesburg. The Youth League had insisted on recording every word in long-hand. Thoughts had to be interpreted sentence by sentence, so that the words could be written accurately. 'It was eventually Walter who broke the ice,' recalls Ismail Meer. 'He said, "We have talked enough. These people are sincere. There is no reason to doubt them. Let us work together where we can."' But this was not to be for two more years.

The major issue of conflict between the ANC and the NEUM at the time was the former's participation in pseudo, racially structured governing bodies such as the Bunga, the Native Representative Council and the Local Advisory Boards. Nelson had an instinctive reaction against such in-

* Bloke Modisane, *Blame Me on History*, Ad. Donker, Johannesburg, 1986, pp. 141–6.

volvement shared by the Youth League in general, but he realized that until they took control of the ANC and radicalized it, there was little they could do. However, when they did take command, they were still unable to prevail on their senior members to resign from these institutions; worse, they found that some Youth League members began to rationalize that it was preferable for local councils to be under ANC control rather than in the hands of reactionaries. For Nelson there was only government control. He was critical of white liberals and, of white members of the Communist Party who stood for the 'Native' seats in parliament, though he did not openly condemn the elections as such because of the ANC's continued support for them.

It was a matter of deep embarrassment to front-rank Youth Leaguers that the ANC still continued to support the Native Representative Council and the advisory boards, whereas the Non-European Unity Movement with its large Coloured membership in the Cape had rejected all collaboration with the government, and the Indians too had not only rejected communal franchise but had waged passive resistance against it. Mandela, Tambo, Mda, Sisulu, Njongwe and Bopape burnt the midnight oil hammering out ways and means of solving this predicament. Even as they did so, in 1948 the new Nationalist Government eliminated the NRC and the Bunga, and relieved them of all further discussion on the issue.

Smuts or Malan, United Party or Nationalist, both were white Prime Ministers, both racist, both oppressive and tyrannical. What Nelson did not foresee was that the Nationalists would legislate for their political security with such vengeance that in a few years practically all organized resistance would stop. The simple wearing of ANC colours would become a criminal offence liable to five years' imprisonment; and the death penalty would be used with such impunity that it would make South Africa the foremost hanging country in the world.

The assumption of Nationalist power coincided with the radicalization of the ANC. Within months of the Nationalist victory, the Youth League took control of the ANC. Diliza Mji recalls the historic December 1949 ANC Conference in Bloemfontein where the coup occurred:

We congregated at the Botshabelo Location, putting up with residents who were prepared to accommodate us. There were no hotels for blacks in those days, and even had there been, we would not have had the money to pay. Both the ANC and the Youth League were holding conferences at the same time in the local community hall. The All-African Convention was also in conference not far from us.

We had prepared well. The President delivered his address. The clapping that followed was hollow and restricted to the older members who were in the minority. I moved the resolution of no confidence. Eddie Manyosi seconded me. A shock wave went through the hall. Never in the history of the ANC had the President been criticized. In retrospect I feel that I was too brash, but that was the prevailing mood of the youth.

Members of the old guard tried to defend Dr Nxuma but they were out-voted by us.

Having rid Congress of its President, we faced the dilemma of finding a suitable replacement. We couldn't put forward one of ourselves, we lacked the prestige.

It so happened that the President of the AAC also lost his position that year, so we went to Dr Moroka and offered him the presidency of the ANC. He accepted. He was barely suitable, but at that moment he was 'our' President.

We elected a first-rate Secretary in Walter Sisulu.

In those days A. P. Mda was the fire-brand among the youth leaders. He was an Africanist who never changed his position. We were all Africanist, but in different degrees. I was considered diluted. Nelson was to my right. He was closer to Mda. Tambo, I could never lay my finger on. He was the perfect diplomat. Both he and Nelson had a way of hiding their feelings. Mine always poured out for all to see. Walter was the most open of all of us when it came to working with other race and ideological groups.

The 1949 conference adopted the Youth League's programme of action and instructed the new executive to call for a national work stoppage on 26 June, in protest against the Nationalist Government. But at a meeting chaired (to the consternation of the Youth Leaguers) by their President General, Dr Moroka himself, the Indian Congress and the Communist Party called for a national stay-away on 1 May. The Youth Leaguers were incensed. The Indians and Communists were pre-empting their strategy and, worse, bamboozling the African mass into thinking that it was an ANC call by using Dr Moroka on their platform. There were angry murmurings about how the ANC President could have allowed himself to be exploited.

The Youth League opposed the May Day call, but despite the opposition, the 1 May stay-away was a success, though the day ended tragically when police opened fire, allegedly to protect workers returning from work. Nineteen people were killed, thirty injured.

A rank-and-file Youth Leaguer recalls that slaughter as follows:

I saw the police rehearsing their roles in the drama of murder unfolding before us; it was a cool, calculated, cold-blooded dress rehearsal.

We lined the street to watch, with silent awe, the spectral parade, we did not cheer or wave flags; we stood there spellbound, transfixed as by a stately, slow and solemn funeral train. There was a promise of death and we could sense the horror in that promise, and yet we could not turn our faces aside, turn our backs to it. Then suddenly, as if in fulfilment of that promise, an order was shouted through the loudspeaker. The people were given three minutes to disperse, but the people mumbled and shuffled their three minutes away.

The mounted police steered their horses into the crowds, galloping into men and women, charging into mothers with children strapped on their backs; screaming women and children were running from one horse and baton into another; men were collapsing under baton wallops, falling to the ground before the galloping horses. I saw a mounted policeman charging in the direction of a woman running for shelter, heard her terrified scream as she fell under the horse, the rider almost falling off his mount from the sheer force of the blow. He had meant to cudgel her but had missed.

Then it happened, I mean the action which has caused the death of many people in countless riots. Someone threw a stone and it bounced off the shoulder of a mounted policeman, then there was another, and another.

They started running, even though their bodies may not have moved more than three feet; it was the mind which was running. They were holding their rifles high in the air, scampering about in a confused retreat. They may not have been supermen, but they were not men either; and although their mind was running, the bodies would not follow until they had been ordered to. We were throwing stones at a machine fitted with discipline. It was a victory to us.

The order to open fire disciplined them into juggernauts of death; from that moment on there was no excitement, only death. The rifles and the sten guns were crackling death, spitting at anything which moved – anything black. The police selected their targets at random with persistent accuracy. The shooting, the screaming, the dying, continued for what seemed like the whole day, and the snap staccato of the guns echoed from all round Sophiatown; and the smell and the decay of death spread over the township, over the burning cinders and the smog.*

There were those who blamed the Communists and the Indians for the deaths, but by mid-year the Youth League saw the wisdom of working as a broad liberation front. A National Day of Protest was called for by the ANC, together with the South African Congress, the African People's organization, the Communist Party and the Transvaal Council of Non-European Trade Unions. The response of the people would be a test of their commitment to further, more daring action. The Indian Congress and the Communist Party pledged their support, and a coordinating council was set up under the joint secretaryship of the Indian and African congresses, represented by Yusuf Cachalia and Walter Sisulu respectively. Nelson was placed in overall command as national volunteer-in-chief.

Diliza Mji was sent to organize Natal. A medical student, he took time off from his studies. He recalls: 'I stayed with Dr Naicker in Durban and operated from the NIC (Natal

* Modisane, ibid., pp. 141–6.

Indian Congress) offices. It was the NIC that carried the day, J. N. Singh, Debby Singh, M. P. Naicker and Ismail Meer were conspicious among those who pulled their weight. We couldn't count on the Natal ANC dominated by A. W. G. Champion. Natal always goes its own way. It is always *yase* (of) Natal. It formed its own breakaway ICU (Industrial and Commercial Workers Union) in 1950. The Natal ANC continued a conservative stance and now, of course, we have Inkatha.'

The team was charged with an unusual energy and a remarkable dedication, the like of which had not been known before. There was a seriousness of purpose, a belief that they were set on a course that would win the people their rights. They aimed to coerce the Nationalists to share power with them.

Nelson was required to be almost everywhere at once. He travelled as rapidly as he could, mostly in buses and trains, coordinating branches and stimulating support to ensure success. But despite his heavy schedule, in which he gave little thought to himself, he remained constantly aware of Evelyn's pregnancy, and when the time came was at her side to welcome his second son Makgatho into the world.

The response to the 26 June national stoppage was overwhelming in Durban, Ladysmith and Port Elizabeth; but was relatively poor on the Rand. Over a thousand Indian workers suffered dismissal in Durban, and white bosses openly threatened to replace them with African workers, but timely action on the part of the Natal Indian Congress averted a crisis. The workers realized that this was the typical divide-and-rule tactic of the authorities; and the quick and effective material support organized mainly through the generosity of Indian shopkeepers restored failing spirits. At the same time, it brought Indian trade unionists to the realization that as long as Africans were kept outside the union fold, there would be no unity of workers: the government and its police, representing the bosses, would use workers to stab each other in the back, and it would be experienced as a racist stab.

The very positive Indian response in the first joint action

significantly modified the isolationist Africanism of the new ANC leadership and spurred it to plan the Defiance of Unjust Laws Campaign along the lines of the 1946 Indian passive resistance. Nelson was volunteer-in-chief; Moulvi Cachalia, the brother of Yusuf Cachalia, his deputy. Dr Moroka, Dr Dadoo, J. B. Marks, Walter Sisulu and Yusuf Cachalia made up the planning committee. It was a unity of Indian and African in ethnicity and, to some extent, Marxist and Nationalist in ideology, since Dadoo was a member of the CP. They worked together as a team with neither the ethnic nor ideological factors intruding into the day-to-day planning.

The campaign opened with a letter to the Prime Minister, demanding the repeal of all unjust laws. As expected, the Prime Minister ignored the letter, but banned seven members of the Communist Party from membership of practically all organizations and from attending all gatherings. In April mass protest rallies were held throughout the country. In May the executives of the ANC and SAIC (South African Indian Congress) met in Port Elizabeth and announced at a press conference that their volunteers would begin their defiance of unjust laws on 26 June.

Disciplined batches of Africans and Indians, accompanied by vast bodies of supporters, filed out to deliberately break specified racial laws.

In Boksburg African resisters led by Walter Sisulu and Indians led by Nana Sita defied the laws that required them to obtain special permits to enter a African township. They were all arrested and swiftly removed to prison. In central Johannesburg Nelson and Yusuf Cachalia instructed fifty African resisters as to their conduct on arrest and waited for the clock to strike 11 p.m., curfew time, while hundreds of supporters sang and danced in solidarity. As the chimes died away, they moved out into the street and were instantly arrested, bundled into the police vans and driven to prison. Nelson and Yusuf were released on bail by the movement because they were not in the batch of volunteers for that night but mainly because they were required to campaign in the Transvaal.

In Natal Chief Luthuli and Dr Naicker led the resisters; in the Eastern Cape, it was Dr James Njongwe, Robert Matji, Raymond Mhlaba and Mr Tshume. The campaign caught the popular imagination, ANC membership soared and resisters poured in. The authorities grew alarmed; in July they countered in their own macabre manner. Nelson was jerked out of bed in a pre-dawn police raid. His house was surrounded by the police. The net was cast wide. The homes of twenty other Transvaal activists were raided. They were all arrested. This was the first instance of a Nationalist technique which would become commonplace in the years to come. The activists were brought before the court and released on bail. In future there would be no trial, no bail, but in 1952 the Government was still learning its tyranny. All were found guilty as charged, but given suspended sentences.

The arrests exposed the weakness of Dr Moroka. He distanced himself from his colleagues and engaged his own independent lawyers. It so soured his reputation that he was displaced as President at the next election by Albert Luthuli.

Albert Luthuli gave the ANC enormous respectability. An ex-teacher (he had taught for seventeen years), a Methodist lay preacher, and Chief of the Makholweni tribe in Groutville, he was a marvellous orator, a powerful singer, and extraordinarily wise and erudite. He drew the admiration of both radical and liberal, and both Africanists and Democrats within the ANC claimed him as their man.

Nelson's regard for Luthuli grew all the more when, summoned by Pretoria and ordered to choose between the ANC and his chieftainship, he refused to give up either, leaving the Government to do its damnedest. They deprived him of his chieftainship, as he had expected, and he countered:

'I was democratically elected to this position in 1935 by the people of Groutville Mission Reserve ... I have been dismissed ... I presume by the Governor-General as Supreme Chief of the 'native' people of the Union of South Africa. In so far as gaining citizenship rights and opportunities for the unfettered development of the African people, who will deny that thirty years of my life have been spent knocking in vain, patiently, moderately and modestly at a closed and barred door?'

Luthuli and Mandela, as President General and General Secretary of the ANC, constituted the most formidable top executive the ANC had ever known. Their oratory was breathtaking. In 1951 Nelson was elected President of the Youth League and in 1952 he replaced the banned J. B. Marks as President of the Transvaal ANC. He was also elected as one of the four Deputy Presidents of the ANC. Nelson's power and popularity were spreading everywhere, yet he remained genial, accessible and modest, though he swore like a trooper when the occasion demanded.

In the hurly-burly of the organizational activity that sapped his strength, yet bouyed his spirit, there was hardly any time for pause or thought. As the volunteer-in-chief, Nelson had a mammoth task travelling throughout the country, coordinating branches, canvassing recruits and raising funds. He gave his time voluntarily, abandoning his practice and his family, and expecting nothing in return apart from the liberation of his people. The membership of the ANC grew from a few thousand to an estimated 100,000. The ANC depended on membership fees for its running expenses, and these were very modest: 2s. 6d. per annum. There is evidence that these fees were not always collected. The result was very little money in the coffers. Fortunately halls, chairs and public-address systems could be obtained from supporters as 'donations', and printers were prepared to give long-term credit. There were enormous travelling expenses, but these were borne by the activists themselves. Those with cars shared with those who hadn't. Rarely, if ever, organizers travelled by plane though they covered long distances; bus and train were the most usual modes of public transport. The telephone, especially long-distance, was used sparingly. Money was required, above all, for full-time organizers.

They estimated that with a paid-up membership of 30,000 and an income of £2,000 per annum, the organization could function efficiently, but even a regular income on that basis was difficult to come by. So the organization subsisted on whatever it could, and it was a wonder that it continued at all. It survived in the final analysis on the enthusiasm and commitment of leaders and followers. The Eastern Cape was by far the best organized area.

The ANC had very little access to the media and was virtually ignored by the white media. It had started its own paper *Abantu-Batho* between 1912 and 1913, but circulation was small and the paper finally died in its second year. During the fifties, the ANC relied on the left-wing press, most prominently the *Guardian* and then, after its banning, on *New Age*. Nelson contributed to the radical monthlies, *Liberation* and *Fighting Talk*. The white media virtually ignored the ANC.

As the success of the Defiance Campaign ensured the ascendancy of the ANC, the nagging fears about non-African interference began to wane. Nelson realized that the struggle would remain essentially African, since Africans were both the most oppressed and the most numerous group, but that non-Africans had a significant part, in that a non-racial democracy was possible only through a multi-racial liberation movement. His antagonism against 'foreigners': against Communists, whites, Indians and Coloureds subsided and in the course of time disappeared. In 1952 Mandela, the Africanist, emerged, with Sisulu and Tambo, as the arch non-racial democrat, ahead even of the Christian democrat, Luthuli.

Even as Walter and Oliver moved to an integrationist position and accepted all South African democrats as equals in the liberation struggle, so the Africanists, lead by Mda, crystallized into an internal opposition. They formed a watch-dog committee, and kept a close eye on non-African initiatives in the struggle. The fact that the leadership in the Defiance Campaign was shared almost equally by Indians and Africans, but that the vast body of resisters came from the African rank sowed tension, a tension aggravated by the imbalance of 71 per cent of the resisters coming from the Eastern Cape, which had no Indians at all.

A. P. Mda expressed fears that Indians and white Communists were taking over African Nationalists; Jordan Ngubane accused Dr Dadoo of appropriating the ANC; and Selope Thema accused Indians of exploiting Africans, and Marxists of leading them into internationalism before they had consolidated their nationalism. The authorities joined the fray by propping up the herbalist Bhengu in Natal who launched a racist anti-Indian attack through his newly founded Bantu National Congress.

Perhaps Nelson and his colleagues were ahead of their time, and maybe also ahead of their people; they had had the opportunity to develop a capacity to handle the intellectualism of white radicals and liberals, and also the cultural difference of the Indians – most Africans, impoverished and illiterate, had not. The top leadership, sharing common professional standards, could talk, work, eat and dance together, but inter-race commensalism stopped at that point. There was no fraternity of teachers irrespective of race, and teachers predominated in the rising African bourgeoisie, and there was no fraternity of workers across the race barrier, and workers constituted the masses.

But whatever the problems, the Defiance Campaign withstood them, and the 'passive resistance' of the ANC won admiration and friends from white members of the newly founded Congress of Democrats and the Liberal Party. Prominent among the latter was Patrick Duncan, the son of a past Governor General, who joined the ranks of resisters. Internationally, South Africa's treatment of its black population became a major issue at UNO.

As the Defiance Campaign progressed, so Evelyn, Nosekeni (Nelson's mother) and Leabie settled down in a household run by women. Nelson spent heady, brief periods at home and a great deal of his time was devoted to playing with the boys. He and Thembi were the best of friends; they jogged and boxed together, played on the floor and on the bed – Nelson roughing him up until he screamed with laughter, with Makhulu scolding Nelson that he would give the boy a stomach-ache from all the excitement.

In 1952 Nelson was away from home more than ever. Thembi had started school and Makgatho was a toddler. Evelyn had always wanted to do midwifery, but marriage, pregnancy and, most of all, financial stringency had prevented her from studying further. The Mandelas decided that it was as good a time as any for her to fulfil her ambition. Nelson had started earning and the family was no longer dependent on Evelyn's wages, but the most important fact was that Makhulu was there, strong and caring, to look after the children. So Evelyn set off for Durban and enrolled for midwifery at King Edward VII hospital. She recounts:

I lived in the nurses' quarters. Nelson visited me whenever his political work brought him to Durban. He would come to fetch me at the nurses' quarters, usually with Ismail Meer, who was then married to Fatima. They lived in a two-roomed house in Umgeni Road. It was little different from our Orlando house. We would spend the night there; the Meers would move out of their only bedroom, so we could have some comfort and some privacy.

The Defiance Campaign continued vigorously. Nelson was everywhere, travelling to Cape Town, Port Elizabeth, Johannesburg, the Transkei. The hard work paid dividends; volunteers swelled the rank of resistance. The bannings of leaders and activists had not stemmed the rising power of the African people. The Government grew desperate. Realizing that the strength of the Campaign and its international support lay in its non-violence, it acted to slander it with violence.

The Eastern Cape, with its long history of African and Boer confrontation, was targeted as the point where the Africans could be most easily provoked to violence. There is no evidence of deliberate government machinations in this respect, but the facts appear implicit. The authorities, who had banned all open-air meetings in the area, now gave the ANC special permission to hold a mass prayer-meeting in East London in October. As the meeting proceeded, the military moved in and within moments converted a peaceful gathering into a bloodbath. Eight Africans were killed, and dozens lay injured. Passions were roused and an infuriated mob went on the rampage, attacking all symbols of white power that they encountered. Two whites were killed, one of them a nun whose body was found mutilated. The violence spread to Port Elizabeth and Kimberley. The ANC was shocked and confused. It did not know how to handle violence as it was committed to non-violence. The Government used the tragedy to justify the passing of a spate of new repressive laws that made passive resistance itself illegal. Practically every organizer of the Campaign was banned in 1957, including Nelson. Deprived of its marshalls, the ANC called off the Campaign.

It was Nelson's first banning order; he was banned from all gatherings and confined to Johannesburg. The order deprived the Transvaal ANC of the physical presence of its President at its regional conference that year. It did not, however, preclude his address from being delivered *in absentia.* He worked on it, using it as an opportunity to analyse their position and to consider a new strategy. He focused on the Campaign and on the increasing armoury of repressive laws the state was using against them.

Starting off in Port Elizabeth in the early hours of 26 June and with only thirty-three defiers in action, and then in Johannesburg in the afternoon of the same day with 106 defiers, it spread throughout the country like wild-fire. Factory and office workers, doctors, lawyers, teachers, students and clergy; Africans, Coloureds, Indians and Europeans, old and young, all rallied to the national call and defied the pass laws and the curfew and the railway apartheid regulations. At the end of the year, more than eight thousand people of all races had defied.

Between July last year and August this year, forty-seven leading members from both congresses in Johannesburg, Port Elizabeth and Kimberley were arrested, tried and convicted for launching the Defiance Campaign and given suspended sentences ranging from two months to three years, on condition that they did not again participate in the defiance of unjust laws. In November of the previous year, a proclamation had been passed which prohibited meetings of more than ten Africans, Contravention of this proclamation carried a penalty of three years or a fine of three hundred pounds. In March of the following year, the Government passed the so-called Public Safety Act which empowered it to declare a state of emergency and to create conditions which would permit it the most ruthless and pitiless methods of suppressing our movement. Almost simultaneously the Criminal Laws Amendment Act was passed which provided heavy penalties for those convicted of defiance offences. This Act also made provision for the whipping of defiers, including women. It was under this Act that Mr Arthur Matlala, who was the local leader of the Central Branch during the Defiance Campaign, was convicted and sentenced to twelve months with hard labour plus eight strokes by the magistrate of Villa Nova.

He told the Conference that 122 activists, including many trade union officers, had been served with notices and black-listed under the Suppression of Communism and the Riotous Assemblies Acts. He explained that such repressive measures made the continuation of the Defiance Campaign futile.

The masses had to be prepared and made ready for new forms of political struggle. We had to recuperate our strength and muster our forces for another and more powerful offensive against the enemy. To have gone ahead blindly as if nothing had happened would have been suicidal and stupid. The old methods of bringing about mass action through public mass meetings, press statements and leaflets, calling upon people to go to action, have become extremely dangerous and difficult to use effectively. The authorities will not easily permit a meeting called under the auspices of the ANC, few newspapers will publish statements openly criticizing the policies of the Government and there is hardly a single printing press which will agree to print leaflets calling upon workers to embark on industrial action for fear of prosecution under the Suppression of Communism Act and similar measures. These developments require the evolution of new forms of political struggle which will make it possible for us to strive for action on a higher level than the Defiance Campaign.

From now on, the activity of congressites must not be confined to speeches and resolutions. Their activities must find expression in wide-scale work among the masses, work which will enable them to make the greatest possible contact with the working people. You must protect and defend your trade unions. If you are not allowed to have your meetings public, then you must hold your meetings in the factories, on the trains and buses as you travel home. You must make every home, every shack and every wood structure where our people live, a branch of the trade union movement and never surrender.*

It was clear to Nelson that the ANC could not survive in its existing form, that continuous police harassment would make it impossible for it to continue long as a legal entity, that the Government would ban it sooner or later, as it had the Communist Party. He knew that the Organization was riddled with spies, and knew that they were too gullible, too trusting, to protect themselves from those spies. He therefore proposed a new structure for the ANC, one that would intensify participation at the grassroots level and simultaneously transform it into an underground structure, if necessary.

He proposed small street-based cells. The proposal was accepted and identified as the M (for Mandela) Plan. The M Plan was discussed at local and national levels. It was first implemented in 1953, immediately after the banning of the ANC; in the 1980s the youth spontaneously used a very similar organizational network to counter the intensified repression of the Nationalist Government.

Even as the ANC prepared new offensives, the Nationalists extended the frontiers of oppression. In 1953 they enacted a series of new laws: the Bantu Education Act, designed to undermine the African's intellect and possess his psyche; the Bantu Authorities Act, devised to control every metre of his physical existence; and the extension of passes to women, to violate the African family. It seemed that the repression of the African had been completed, but this was only the beginning – the racists would come up with more horrific inventions.

Nelson's banning order removed him from the public platform. He could no longer engage in open political ac-

* 'No Easy Walk to Freedom', Presidential Address, ANC Conference, Transvaal, September 1953.

tivity, and there was a limit to what he could achieve clandestinely. This meant that he had more time for his family and for his studies. He passed his attorney's admission exam. Normally he would have celebrated the event, but his banning precluded such occasions. He could not be present at social gatherings, nor even at private family ones.

That year he opened his legal office at Chancellor House and, a few months later, formed a partnership with Oliver. It was with a sense of excitement and achievement that they put up their signboard, moved in their furniture, and opened their doors to their first client. They were assured of a very successful practice because of their enormous popularity and reputation as people who really cared for the poor.

The Transvaal Law Society, however, intervened and tried to stop Nelson from practising at all. It objected to his conviction for defying unjust laws. But if the Law Society opposed him, the Chairman of the Johannesburg Bar, Walter Pollak, defended him *pro amico*. He continued in his practice, but not for long, for when his banning order expired, he rejoined Oliver in active resistance. They treated their legal work as part time; resistance and revolution were their full-time vocation.

Yet Nelson savoured his experiences as a lawyer and, years later, he recalled them in a letter to his daughter Zindzi:

I've visited the Eastern Transvaal several times, especially Carolina where I defended Mr Harry Matyeka and other clients in that area. I well remember the year 1954 when I first went there. It was probably the first time for them to see an African attorney after the old generation of Dr P. I. Ka Sema. I was received warmly and courteously treated by everybody, including the magistrate and the prosecutor. They were curious and all sort of questions were asked. The court was packed out.

On one occasion I appeared for a medicine man who was charged with witchcraft. Again the case attracted many people from the surrounding villages, this time not so much because they wanted to see me, but in order to find out whether the country's system of justice could be applied to such a man. Once more I realized the tremendous influence still exercised by diviners amongst people, black and white, in small country towns. In the course of the proceedings my client sneezed violently and his whole body quivered terribly. There was almost a stampede and people who sat near him, including court officials, almost ran out. Fortunately for him, he was found not guilty, but I fear that some people were convinced that his discharge was not due to the insufficiency of evidence but to the power of his herbs.

8 November 1977

There were other interludes. He became specially friendly with Gordon Bruce, an insurance agent, who succeeded him as secretary of the International Club when he was forced to resign due to pressure of political work. The Mandelas and Bruces were Methodists and at times they attended church together. They thought nothing of asking each other for special favours. One day Bruce phoned Nelson and asked if he would fetch his wife, Ursula, from work. He had been held up in a meeting. Ursula was blind. It was five o'clock, the downtown traffic was heavy and Nelson was forced to park his car a block away: 'I collected Ursula; she rested her hand on my arm and I led her to the car. If looks could kill I would have been dead that day. I had the feeling that the scores of whites who passed us by were ready to spit on us. A kaffir boy escorting a white woman!'

It was a lasting friendship. During his underground episode, Nelson lived at one stage in the same neighbourhood as the Bruces and spent evenings with them. They named their son, David, after his underground name. David became a conscientious objector and was sentenced to two years' imprisonment in 1988 for refusing to join the army, co-incidentally on the anniversary of Nelson's arrest, 5 August 1961.

# CHAPTER 7

# Nationalist Repression

The mid-fifties saw the Nationalists at their strongest; their tyranny appeared invincible. They passed laws with impunity, monstrous laws that deprived African, Indian and Coloured people of their homes and land.

As if to revitalize them for the battle that would follow, Walter Sisulu and Duma Nokwe took advantage of being smuggled out of the country to raise the liberation issue abroad. It was the dream of every young black person to breach parochial bounds, to stretch out into the world, to experience that world at first hand. Few could realize that dream. The more prominent of the founding fathers of the ANC had had such opportunities. Excluded from South African institutions of higher learning, they had been hand-picked by their churches and helped to obtain academic training in the United States and Britain. Later, with the establishment of Fort Hare, university education in the humanities became available to Africans, Coloureds and Indians. Nelson's generation of the African élite was thus by and large home-cultivated. None of the Youth Leaguers had been overseas. In the mid fifties the Eastern bloc invited members of the ANC to attend their youth festivals, all expenses paid. Walter Sisulu, Duma Nokwe, Robert Resha, Lindi Ngakane and Alfred Hutchinson attended the youth and student festivals in Bucharest, Rumania, in 1953. They spent five momentous months abroad, impressed by the socialist orders. They also visited Britain, Israel and China. In his own country Walter had never been considered important enough to be heard on the radio, but Radio Peking relayed his message to the Chinese people.

In 1955 Moses Kotane and Moulvi Cachalia met Pandit Jawaharlal Nehru in Indonesia at the Bandung Conference. He arranged Indian travel documents for them and promised financial assistance for the struggle against racism. Kotane and Cachalia also met President Nasser of Egypt, and Chou En-lai of China at the Conference.

Nelson was not destined to go abroad, not then. Too many things stood in his way at the time. His opportunity would come, years later, and under very different circumstances. The contacts he would make then would change the whole course of South African history and earn him life imprisonment.

The ANC Conference, meeting at the end of 1954 in Queenstown, heard glowing reports of the progress in the Soviet Union and China, and in the newly liberated countries, and it received messages of solidarity and support from abroad. The ANC was not alone. A whole new world was with them.

Nelson was first banned in 1952 under the Riotous Assemblies Act for six months. Between June and September 1953 he had a brief respite and was again free to participate openly in the struggle against apartheid. It was not too soon either, for the Government began just then to implement its notorious Group Areas Act, which reserved practically all urban and developed South Africa for whites.

The western areas of Johannesburg: Sophiatown, Newclare and Martindale were the first targets of government attack. While predominantly African, they were extraordinarily mixed neighbourhoods by South African standards, with large Indian and Coloured populations. The new law demanded their summary removal.

The ANC and TIC launched a programme of massive protest meetings. Robert Resha was Chairman of the Sophiatown branch, the most powerful ANC branch in the Transvaal at the time. Nelson threw his weight behind the campaign. At one particular meeting, Nelson's presence of mind saved the police from being attacked by an infuriated audience. The Odin Cinema was full to capacity, and Nelson,

Yusuf Cachalia and Walter were among those on the platform. Yusuf was addressing the meeting when the police
surrounded the cinema, and a contingent entered the hall,
marched up to the platform and arrested him. There were
cries from the audience, tempers flared. Nelson grabbed the
mike and burst into a revolutionary song. The audience
joined in, the danger passed: the police retreated. Nelson
wondered how long his own patience would last. In September 1953 he was banned again under the Suppression of
Communism Act, which confined him to the Johannesburg
Magisterial district, ordered him to resign from the ANC
and a host of other organizations, and forbade him to attend
any gatherings.

Government action intensified; houses were bulldozed and
Africans began to be removed to an arid waste near Orlando,
incongruously baptized Meadowlands. Tiny sites were
cordoned off; the only amenities offered were sanitary
buckets in corrugated iron shelters. Families were ordered to
pick up their lives from the western areas and restart them
there. The people grew frantic.

In the face of police presence and the fear that they might
lose even those sites, the resistance petered out despite the
ANC's attempt to provide temporary shelters. How long
would they have the ANC shelters? they asked. The ANC
had no land to provide them with permanent homes. Bad as
Meadowlands was it offered land and they could put up their
shacks.

The Africanists within the ANC, who later formed the
PAC, exploited the situation and, amazingly, accused the
leadership of protecting the interests of landlords and of
ignoring tenants! They said that the ANC had called for a
boycott of Meadowlands because they did not want the
landlords in the western areas to lose their tenants! The split
was intensifying and developing ugly manifestations. It
became increasingly apparent that the Africanists were preparing for a major confrontation. Their real grievance was not
the ANC's resistance to the removals but its partnership
with the Indian Congress. Nelson understood the sentiment

all too well, since only a few years ago it had been his own. But practical experience and good political sense had convinced him that racism could best be toppled by a democratic front of all anti-racists, that African exclusivism encouraged an African racism which could become as diabolical as Afrikaner racism. Nelson thought how macabre it was becoming: the Africanists and Afrikaners, pursuing diametrically opposing goals, were levelling common accusations against the ANC. At the same time Dr Xuma, whom they had criticized just a few years before for his indiscreet liaisons with Indians and Coloureds, was now turning the tables and accusing them of conceding to alien influences and losing their African identity. Nelson wondered if it was possible to heal the rift. Yet in the early 1950s the Africanists did not constitute a threat. Their attention was, moreover, diverted by the sudden extension of passes to women and the women's immediate resistance.

South Africa's racist–capitalist system is structured on a careful monitoring of the movement of black labour. Until 1952 the pernicious pass system that controlled the entry of black job-seekers was restricted to black men. But that year the Government, responding to the rising rate at which black women were entering domestic service and secondary industry, announced that their movement too would be controlled by passes. This was met by spontaneous uprisings of women in urban and rural areas. Groups of angry women, already organized for other purposes but most extensively as members of local church groupings, *manyanos*, and the ANC Women's League, protested at police stations and pass offices. In Natal a young doctor, Margaret Mgadi, led the onslaught. Indian, African and Coloured women united in the Durban and District Women's League and organized protest marches under the presidency of Bertha Mkhize. Lilian Ngoyi, Bertha Mashaba and Frances Baard gave the lead in the Transvaal and Florence Matomela in the Cape. In 1954 150 delegates from throughout the country met in Johannesburg and founded the Federation of South African Women. The Federation centralized protest in Johannesburg, climaxing in the march of 20,000 to the Union Buildings in 1956.

Nelson was kept close to the women's resistance, mainly through Lilian Ngoyi. He admired her magnetism and profound understanding of the people's passion. She often came to him for advice. He thought that there was some tension between the ANC and the women: the ANC felt at times that the women were slipping away from the main struggle; and the women felt that the ANC was not as sensitive to their issues as it should be.

The Nationalist assault on African education intensified in the mid 1950s. Against this, as against the removals in the western areas, the ANC found itself helpless. Nelson wondered which was the more pernicious, the bulldozing of the people's homes or of their minds through a sinister education programme.

Dr Verwoerd spelled out the rationale of Bantu Education:

I just want to remind honourable members that if the native in South Africa today in any kind of school in existence is being taught to expect that he will live his adult life under a policy of equal rights, he is making a big mistake.*

There is no place for him in the European community above the level of certain forms of labour ... for that reason it is of no avail for him to receive a training which has as its aim absorption in the European community ... Until now he has been subject to a school system which drew him away from his own country and misled him by showing him the green pastures of European society in which he is not allowed to graze.†

It was a chilling declaration, and one that attacked the African ethos to the marrow. Nelson reviewed the position of African education. Mainly in the hands of mission societies, it was already deplorable, but it was not isolated from the general stream. The new system would attempt to limit the perceptions of the African child and diminish his expecta-

* *Hansard*, 17 September 1953.
† Statement to Senate, June 1954.

tions. Nelson was determined to do everything in his power to save the African children from such a fate:

When this Bill becomes law, it will not be the parents but the Department of Native Affairs which will decide whether an African child should receive higher or other education. It might well be that the children of those who fight the Government and its policies will almost certainly be taught how to drill rocks in the mines and how to plough potatoes on the farms of Bethal.

The teachers were already alerting the people to the dangers of Bantu Education. They saw their own profession under attack. The Cape and Transvaal Teachers Associations were highly politicized; the Cape body had a long tradition of working in the rural communities. Their campaigns against the Act in fact led the way to a people's struggle.

Nelson's reaction was to boycott Bantu Education schools and to replace them with the ANC's own schools. It was a response he shared with his colleagues. He told the 1953 Transvaal Conference:

You must defend the right of African parents to decide the kind of education that shall be given to their children. Teach the children that Africans are not one iota inferior to Europeans. Establish your own community schools where the right kind of education will be given to our children. If it becomes dangerous or impossible to have alternative schools, then you must make every home, every shack, every rickety structure a centre of learning for our children. Never surrender to the inhuman and barbaric theories of Verwoerd.

The ANC announced an indefinite boycott of all schools from 1 April 1955 (the date set by the Government for the transfer) and called for a 1,000 volunteer teachers. The main problem was funding: teachers had to live and there was no money to pay them. White radicals and liberals and the church came to their assistance. Together, under the chairmanship of Father Trevor Huddleston, they established the African Education Movement (AEM).

Older members on the ANC Executive sounded a note of caution that the ANC did not have the capacity to confront the problem. The youth and women thought otherwise. Bantu Education had to be resisted at all cost. Nelson was agitated by the rift that loomed within the organization. Nelson, Oliver and Walter saw clearly that this was an issue on which the feelings of the people far outstripped the caution that was advised. Leadership implied leading the people's outrage, effectively and positively. He felt strongly about setting up alternative schools and suggested that if the only solution lay in all of them becoming teachers and running the schools themselves, they should do so. The ANC launched its boycott campaign. The Youth League went from house to house and canvassed late into the night. On 1 April they began pre-dawn marches in the townships, calling on the children to stay away from the schools. Women picketed the schools, pulled out the children who 'strayed' into them and directed them to the ANC schools.

Simultaneously the AEM set in motion its alternative school programme. Teachers came from all races and the movement gained ground: the number of AEM schools increased, the standard of education improved, Bantu Education appeared threatened. The Government countered by passing a law that made all schools, apart from those registered by the Department, illegal. The police raided the AEM schools and the authorities closed them down. They re-emerged as cultural clubs but it was a losing battle. Nelson realized that given the choice between abnormal education and no education at all, parents had no alternative but to opt for education, whatever its content.

Educationists have called Bantu Education education for barbarism, and warned that it, more than any other Nationalist act, contained the seeds that would destroy apartheid. Bantu Education produced the generation of Steve Biko and the ideology of Black Consciousness. It roused a black youth, compliant and apathetic in the 1950s into the fighting-force of the 1970s and 1980s. They not only made the townships ungovernable, but revitalized the organizations-in-exile with a massive transfusion of freedom-fighters.

But that was a time yet to come. In 1954 Nelson prepared

for the Congress of the People. He had suffered a second banning order, this time for five years, but his contribution to the planning and implementing of this congress, essentially the brain child of Professor Z. K. Matthews, was considerable.

CHAPTER 8

# The Congress of
# the People

At the 1953 Cape Provincial Conference of the ANC, Professor Matthews moved for a National Convention of all South Africans to draw up a Freedom Charter truly representative of all races. The proposal fired the imagination of the general body of the ANC. Two hundred organizations, including the National Party and its official opposition, the United Party, were invited to the first planning meeting at Tongaat, Natal, close to Groutville, where Chief Luthuli lived under strict banning orders. Few organizations responded to the invitation. Apart from the Liberal Party, the Labour Party and some trade union representation, the planning meeting was reduced to the Congress Alliance: the African and Indian congresses and the newly established Congress of Democrats (COD), the South African Council of Trade Unions (SACTU) and the South African Coloured Peoples Organization. Subsequently, even the Liberal and Labour Parties withdrew, feeling out of place in an organization they considered too far to the left.

The Congress of the People was destined to be the first, and last, expression of the Congress Alliance as a legal structure in the country. But the Alliance would enter South African history as the main target of the Government's numerous treason trials. These would begin with the prosecution of the COP itself.

The COP would also provoke a split within the ANC and give birth to the Pan-Africanist Congress. The Africanists objected strongly to the 'domination' of non-Africans and

71

non-ANC members on the organizing council of the COP. Only two of the eight-man council were ANC members. The COD, with no more than a hundred or so members, had equal representation with the ANC. Was this the shape of things to come? they asked. Was it the intention of the ANC to hand over the country to non-Africans? Were Africans being asked to relinquish their country to others? The Freedom Charter would lay strong emphasis on sharing the country with her own people.

There was no doubt at all that the COD had practically no constituency and that the ANC provided the mass. But what of it, Nelson reasoned. If one thought racially, then all the COD had to do was join the whites and it would have a large constituency. If the COD was small, it was precisely because it was bursting the walls of racialism and for that reason was welcome. Nelson, Walter and Oliver threw themselves into grassroots-level organization of the congress, attending area meetings, and explaining the purpose of the Congress of the People. The COD, having less field-work, precisely on account of its negligible constituency, concentrated on the writing of documents: COD members wrote the Call to the Congress of the People. Nelson found it beautiful; that its authorship was white did not bother him. But later he realized that in a society as racially entrenched as South Africa's, it bothered others. The fact that some of the clauses did not reflect the general ANC viewpoint exacerbated the accusations that the COP was Communist-dominated. The strongest protests came from the Western Cape where the Africanist tendency was strong and where ANC members were particularly resentful of the COD because of its participation in the Coloured elections.

Notwithstanding these problems, the preparations for the COP proceeded smoothly. Thousands of suggestions were collected at branch meetings, following enthusiastic small group discussions on the kind of society the people would like to see in South Africa. These proposals provided the basis for the first draft of the Freedom Charter. Nelson studied that draft and approved of it. The draft was accepted by the ANC working committee. Unfortunately no one took it to the banned President General, and few outside Johannesburg saw it. That aggravated the brewing controversy over the planned congress.

The congress assembled at Kliptown on the morning of 26 June 1955. Nelson watched the proceedings from a distance. He sat disguised, at the house of a friend overlooking the square, with other banned colleagues. The gathering was as impressive and as large as they could have wished for. The people were there, in gold, black and green, massively African, though the 2,884 delegates included 672 'non-Africans', almost half of whom were Indians.

Anthony Sampson, described the scene:

Large African grandmothers, wearing Congress skirts, Congress blouses or Congress cloths on their heads, traipsing around with baggy suitcases; young Indian housewives, with glistening saris and shawls embroidered with Congress colours; grey old African men, with walking sticks and Congress arm-bands; young city workers from Johannesburg, with broad hats, bright American ties and narrow trousers; smooth Indian lawyers and businessmen, moving confidently among the crowd in well-cut suits; and a backcloth of anonymous African faces, listening impassively to the hours of speeches that are the staple of any Congress meeting.*

As Nelson saw it, precisely the people who had been called to the Conference had come:

The people of South Africa, black and white, African and European, Indian and Coloured, the farmers of the reserves and Trust Lands, the miners of coal, gold and diamonds, the workers of farms and forests, of factories and shops, the teachers, students and preachers, the housewives and working and businessmen and professionals – and they had all gathered to talk of freedom.

But he saw too the immense turnout of police. Those in uniform were visible to all, the plain-clothed to only the seasoned few; these nudged the others and pointed them out. The people jeered and laughed at the police while they took photographs and notes.

* Anthony Sampson, *Treason Cage*, Heinemann, 1955, p. 106.

But the joke was on the congressites, for the police were preparing evidence for the massive treason trial they were about to institute, and though the trial would fail, it would keep their leaders trapped and well-nigh impotent for four long years.

The proceedings opened with the presentation of special awards. Father Trevor Huddleston was the first to be called to the rostrum. The square filled with laughter, and then with applause, as the popular priest, forced to stop in his acceptance speech by the terrible din that erupted from the Public Works Department which went into a sudden fit of activity, said: 'I have never known the South African Railways to be so efficient as they are this afternoon, and I am sure it is a demonstration to this congress by the Minister of Transport.'

Chief Luthuli and Dr Dadoo were banned and so could not be present to receive their awards. Nelson's eyes dimmed when Dr Dadoo's frail old mother went up to receive the award on behalf of her son.

The first day's proceedings went smoothly. Young Kathy (Ahmed Kathrada), though banned, was very much in the spirit of things and in touch with volunteers who reported on the proceedings. The food, he reported, was first-class and the service efficient. Nelson couldn't resist the temptation to be part of the crowd. He had a rough and ready 'disguise' and moved about unrecognized. It felt good to be one of the people. The Freedom Charter was being discussed. He stood alongside a bearded Transkeian who listened intently. He marvelled at the concentration of the people as each clause was read, translated and affirmed with a thunderous shout of *Afrika!*

He returned to his vantage point the next day. Yusuf Cachalia, referring to the police, said to Walter, 'The dogs just stand there and do nothing.' As if responding to his challenge, the police suddenly acted. They broke into the gathering. A battery of Special Branch men escorted by an armed battalion climbed on to the platform; one of them took the microphone and announced that they suspected treason and that no one was to leave until the names of all delegates were taken. It was 3.30 p.m. Soon it would be dusk. The police set up tables and brought in hurricane lamps. They worked late into the night while a cordon of armed police, mounted and on foot, sealed off the conference square. Somebody started singing softly, sadly; the strains were taken over by the whole congregation. Each delegate was interrogated and searched at the police table. All documents found were taken and sealed in envelopes. All literature left on the conference tables or set up for sale on other tables was confiscated, and so was the money left in tills and boxes. European delegates received special attention of being photographed.

Nelson's immediate reaction was to stay, in case his help was needed. But they decided to leave for Johannesburg and call up an emergency meeting to assess the situation. All in all, they concluded, the Congress of the People had been a great success, and that the police action, if anything, contributed to that success. It gave the lie to the Government's stance that it did not care about the Congress or fear its influence.

The National Action Council devoted itself to popularizing the Freedom Charter. Report-back meetings were held in all major areas. Attendances were encouraging. The Durban meeting at Curries Fountain, the vast football ground, was a sea of faces.

But with acclaim, there also came dissension. Most disturbing were the murmurs from senior leaders, especially from the President General, Chief Luthuli. He had not seen the draft, partly because he had been grievously ill at the time. Worse, Professor Matthews, who initiated the idea, also had not read the first draft of the Charter.

The National Executive met at Chief Luthuli's home on 30 July to try to settle differences in approach to the Charter. The meeting agreed that the National Conference had to endorse the Charter before the ANC could be said to be in support of it.

However, the meeting ratified the million-signature campaign in support of the Charter, suggested certain amendments, accepted that the provincial executives should recommend the Charter to their constituencies and finally approved that a permanent Consultative Committee replace the National Action Council.

The National Conference in Bloemfontein, attended by three hundred and seven delegates from eighty-one branches, however, did not adopt the Charter. Dr A. B. Xuma wrote a hostile letter to the conference on the Charter, and when Dr Letele, the Acting President, moved that only portions of the letter be read, the Africanists went into an uproar.

It was only in April 1956 that the ANC adopted the Charter at a special conference in Orlando, amidst heated controversy between the Africanists and 'Charterists', in the process of which Natal's proposed amendments barely came up for discussion. The last thing Natal wanted was to strengthen the hand of the Africanists.

The Africanists rejected the Charter because they claimed it was written by whites and because some of the clauses had non-Africanist overtones. They accused the COD of hijacking an indigenous nationalist movement to bolster the Soviet bloc. They alleged that the charter was a negation of the 1949 ANC programme of action and the ANC was handing over initiative to the other race groups. The murmurings were always there; the difference was that they grew louder in 1955. The tragedy was then that almost the entire ANC leadership was banned, leaving the organization to the second-tier leadership which, to a considerable extent, was Africanist in orientation. That leadership muscled in and provided a powerful challenge, especially in the Orlando Youth League. It was led by such accredited ANC men as Potlako Leballo, Zeph Mothopeng and Peter Raboroko. They were reinforced by Josiah Madzunya. Nelson, Oliver and Walter had to deal with their hostility, the more bitter because it was the hostility of friends turned foe. MacDonald Maseko, a member of the national executive of the ANC and chairman of the Orlando Branch, had already been expelled for his reckless militancy and racism: he had wanted to rid the executive of foreign influences and cut links with the Indians. The Africanists criticized those who had accepted invitations to the Soviet-inspired world youth festivals and condemned the ANC for participating in Advisory Board elections. Their criticisms were publicized in their newsletter, the *Africanist*.

Nelson realized that the attacks were coming at a time when the provincial leadership was weak. He despaired over the incompetence, bad bookkeeping and, most of all, the poor public relations of branch leaders. He feared that these would be exploited by their adversaries to gain an upper hand.

Matters came to a head on 31 July when the Africanists held a Lembede Memorial Service and inaugurated Heroes Day. In clear contradiction to ANC commemorations, which were non-racial in focus, Heroes Day was Africanist. Significantly they claimed Lembede, the original Africanist, betrayed by his colleagues, as their own.

The conflict was sharpening; within two years it would end in an irreconcilable division and the Pan-Africanist Congress would be born.

CHAPTER 9

# Parting with Evelyn

Dissension in the ANC was not the only conflict Nelson faced during this period. He also faced dissension in the family. The marriage that had appeared to have been solidly founded and sealed with four births began falling apart. It had withstood economic problems, but it was shaken by the pressures of separation. Evelyn herself felt that she had paid a heavy price for her midwifery, that her absence had led to the estrangement of her husband. Nelson was extremely attractive to women, and he was easily tempted by them. His family meant everything to him; he probably did not believe a passing liaison would place it in jeopardy. He probably also expected Evelyn to be more tolerant and less puritanical.

Evelyn says that though they had lived apart for periods in 1952–3, she had been happy in her love for Nelson, and had felt quite secure in his love for her.

In 1953 I was again pregnant. At the end of the year I passed my exam. I was overjoyed, more so because I would be reunited with the family. I returned home to a warm welcome and subdued celebration for Nelson was under a banning order. The banning gave him more time with us and secretly we welcomed it. Makaziwe was born the following year.

I could not place my finger on it at first. Nobody would tell me. Then the gossip reached me. Nelson, I was told, was having an affair with a woman member of the ANC. I knew this woman and admired and liked her. She visited us often and I got on well with her. I did not believe the rumour at first, but unable to bear it, I turned to Nelson. Who else could I have turned to? He was angry that I questioned his fidelity. The woman was an important ANC leader and that was all there was to it, he said. But the gossip continued, and there were those who tried to console me by claiming he was bewitched. There was also another woman and this one started coming home, walking into our bedroom, following him to the bathroom. What was all this about I demanded, and declared that I would not allow it, that if she had work to discuss with him, she should confine it to his office and not pursue my husband into my house in that unseemly manner. Nelson was enraged. He moved his bed into the sitting room. He grew increasingly cold and distant. I was desperate. I went to see Walter. I don't think Nelson ever forgave me for that. He accused me of broadcasting our problems. He stopped eating at home and took his washing to a cousin. Then he started sleeping out.

The rift between us was soon public knowledge. I was embarrassed and deeply pained. Leabie and Makhulu were feeling the strain. Makhulu returned to Qunu. I think she couldn't bear to see our family being torn apart. I went to see my brother, who was then living in Orlando East. He spoke to Nelson and then said to me, 'If the man has stopped loving you, if something or someone has killed that love, there is nothing you or anyone can do about it.' I realized for the first time that I was losing my man, if I hadn't lost him already.

Yet I made one last attempt. I went to see Kaiser Matanzima. Nelson admired him and was close to him. If Nelson would listen to anyone, I thought he'd listen to him. K. D. spoke to Nelson, but Nelson's reply was that he no longer loved me.

Leabie, recalling this period, says:

I can't tell you how we lived through that time – the two people we respected, suddenly turning on each other. We all depended on them and when they went on like that, it was as if the ground below us was breaking and we were falling. It was *ubuthi* [black magic], that is what it was.

Evelyn speaks of the day when the silence between them broke and matters came to a head.

Nelson used to keep 20 cent pieces for the children to take to school. Thembi was allowed to take one 20 cent piece each morning. I had always complained that the money was too much. On this morning Thembi helped himself to two 20 cent pieces instead of one. I scolded him. Perhaps I went too far. In my anger and frustration I must have burst out against Nelson for spoiling him. I may well have been too harsh on Thembi. Whatever it was I said in those moments, the months of unspoken breach exploded in a torrent of words.

It was after this incident that I left our home and went to live with my brother. Nelson came to see me at my brother's and told me to forget the incident and return home. I returned home. I was desperate to save the marriage, even if it meant clutching at a straw. But there was no thawing of the freeze. That chilling, unbearable distance continued. I realized that I had no marriage. I moved out and went to live in the nurses' quarters. Perhaps I imagined that if I reversed the situation and I walked out, instead of him, he would come to his senses and realize that he needed me to keep the family together. If that was my feeling, I was totally mistaken. Nelson never came to see me at the nurses' home nor did he send any messages to me. I had initiated the separation. A year later, I moved in with my brother. Perhaps if I had been patient, if I had tried to understand why he had turned away from me, perhaps things may have been different and I would still be his wife. He was the only man I ever loved. He was a wonderful husband and a wonderful father.

The children moved between us, from Orlando East to Orlando West. Maki was only two at the time and much too young to understand what was going on. Makgatho, at five, was young enough not to be bothered by it, but Thembi, who was eight, suffered intensely.

In a way I continued to delude myself that since there were children between us, there was a marriage between us. But this changed when a friend drew my attention to a notice in the paper, a whole year and more after I had moved out of my house. 'Your husband is divorcing you,' she said. I froze, unable to respond. I had heard vaguely that Nelson was going out with a social worker from Baragwanath Hospital. It was just one more woman, I had thought. He would discard her like he had the others. Nelson's devotion to the children would keep our marriage, if not in fact, in name at least.

I had got used to that position, now I faced a divorce. I went to see a lawyer. I did not oppose the divorce. It went through. We did not quarrel about the custody of the children. The court gave me custody. Since Nelson had not paid lobola, he did not have rights over the children according to African law. This distressed him very much and he arranged with my brother to pay the lobola and my brother said that since he had ill-treated me, he would accept it. So Nelson did one of these rare things, paid lobola after the marriage had ended. He, in fact, lobola'd the children.

Nelson's second son, Makgatho, remembers his father as both loving and disciplining.

We used to do lots of things together, Daddy, Thembi and I. We would wash in the bedroom. He would bring the water there, wash us first and then he would wash. In the evenings he would take us into town and buy us ice-cream. We used to love listening to his stories. He would tell us about olden times and explain to us how the trouble had started between black people and white people. Even though I couldn't understand all of it, Thembi could. He would try to make us understand why he was so often away from home, why he had to attend all these meetings, what the struggle was all about. He used to take us to the Masuphatsela meetings, that is, the ANC Young Pioneers in Orlando West.

He was very popular where we lived. When he would leave the house and get into our car, the children would come running and they would shout *'Afrika! Mayibuye!'* We would feel so proud. Daddy would explain the meaning of the words to us. He would tell us that they were not just words, that when the people called *Mayibuy'i Afrika* they meant that they wanted what was theirs returned to them.

Daddy was very athletic. He exercised a lot and he made us exercise with him. We used to jog together. We did shadow boxing against the wall. I used to think that if Daddy went in the ring he would beat anyone. He would take us to boxing tournaments at the Bantu Men's Social Centre. He used to play indoor games. He took us with him, as I remember, every evening, and we also played there with boys our own age.

On Saturdays Daddy took us to a cinema in Fordsburg. He would leave us there in his car and he would come to fetch us. The three of us, Thembi, Maki and I would go together.

Daddy never beat us, but if we did anything wrong we would get a lesson from him that was worse than a beating. I remember one time, I wanted to go to the swimming pool. It was Saturday afternoon. I asked him for money for the entrance fee. He asked how much? I thought a bit and I asked for double the amount I needed. Daddy knew. But Daddy didn't say anything, but he followed me, which I did not know. He saw that my friend was waiting outside. He called me in and he asked my why I had lied about the money. I felt so ashamed I could hardly speak. He kept asking me. Then I said that I wanted the money for my friend, my friend did not have money to go swimming. Daddy said it was good I thought about my friend, but it was terrible that I lied. Why did I lie? I said I was afraid and he said I should never be afraid of truth.

It was very bad for us when my mother left our house. It was like I stopped having a house. I didn't know where I should stay. I think it was worse for Thembi, but then he was at boarding school at Matatiele. We stayed with our uncle because our mother stayed with him. Then we stayed with Daddy. Granny was there. She was always happy to see us. But Daddy wasn't always there. So it seemed better to stay with our mother. But I stayed with Daddy on weekends.

Nelson was sensitive to the effect of his breach on his children, and he attributed the meaning of one dream, during his confinement, as reflecting this stress.

The night of 24 February, I dreamt arriving at 8115 finding the house full of youth dancing away a mixture of jive and *infiba*. I caught all of them by surprise as I walked in unexpectedly. Some greeted me warmly, whilst others simply melted away shyly. I found the bedroom equally full with members of the family and close friends. You were relaxing in bed, with Kgatho [Nelson's son Makgatho], looking young and sleeping against the opposite wall.

Perhaps in that dream I was recalling the two weeks in December 1956 when he was six and when I left Makhulu alone in the house. At that time he was living with his mother in O. E. but a few days before I came back he joined Makhulu and slept in my bed for a couple of days. He was missing me very much and using the bed must have relieved the feeling of longing a bit.

15 April 1976

# CHAPTER 10

# Treason Arrest

If Nelson's political life was hectic, his personal life was disconcerting. His mother was unhappy about his breach with Evelyn. She wanted them to resolve their differences and return the family to its former harmony. Nelson knew that he could not. The breach was hard on both of them, on Evelyn because of the loss of Nelson, on Nelson because of the disruption it created in the lives of the children. What hurt most was Thembi's distress. He was not only a son, but also a friend, and Nelson worried about how he could re-establish the trust that had been there and which had been shaken.

But he had little time to console Thembi, or the other children. A few weeks before Christmas there was a sudden pre-dawn swoop. He was surprised in his bed by the urgent banging. He knew it was the police. He opened the door. They told him he was under arrest, that he should pack a few things and accompany them, but not before they had searched the little house, turning it upside down. Makhulu watched, crying within herself. Nelson comforted her as best he could, with the tenderness in his eyes rather than in the words he spoke.

He discovered later that he was only one of the 156 people who had participated in the Congress of the People to be arrested.

The State called it 'Operation T'. The *Golden City Post* reported on 9 December 1956:

All the arrested were flown to Johannesburg in military aircraft; all appeared before a Johannesburg magistrate; all were remanded for hearing to 19 December, and all spent at least one night in the Johannesburg Fort.

Police tried to cloak the departure of the Dakotas carrying the arrested people from Cape Town, including Mr L. B. Lee-Warden MP, Native Representative; Mr Lionel Forman, an advocate, who had to be provided with special medicine because of a heart ailment; Mr Fred Carnenson, former MPC, and Mrs Sonia Bunting, wife of Mr Brian Bunting, a former member of parliament.

Police found Mr Ismail C. Meer, banned official of the Indian Congress, an attorney, in bed at the home of relatives. He was recuperating from a major operation. Because he could not be moved he was placed under house arrest and a policeman was posted in his bedroom. The guards were changed three times during the day . . . his two children, unaware of what was going on, played in the room. Three-year-old Shamin Meer devised a game of her own choosing, believing the policeman on guard to be a tram conductor and presenting him with tickets to be clipped.

Mrs G. M. Naicker reached the airport just as Dr Naicker was crossing the tarmac to the waiting plane. He turned and waved to her and she responded.

Seventeen people were arrested in Port Elizabeth and about fifty detectives visited their homes in Korsten and New Brighton. All were flown to Johannesburg. Police searched the offices of the ANC branch and several trade union offices.

The Fort Prison in Johannesburg suddenly became a concentration of the country's most dedicated democrats. The warders had their problems. One treason trialist recalls:

The great evening ritual was the counting of the prisoners. The warders never got it right. One evening, after endless counting and recounting, they literally claimed there was one African too many and one Indian short. Their eyes settled on Joe Matthews whose hair was somewhat longer than most Africans'. 'You'll do,' they said, 'you're Indian,' and so the problem was solved.

The preparatory trial opened in the Drill Hall in Johannesburg two weeks after the arrests. There was a huge demonstration outside and a thunderous welcome each time a police van stopped and disgorged a batch of accused. The police panicked and fired into the crowd, the people panicked and ran helter-skelter. The trialists froze in fear. Fortunately no one was killed, though twenty-two were injured.

The hearing began with the 156 accused locked in a cage. Someone attached a placard: DON'T FEED. The counsel for the defence expressed its rage and the accused were granted bail.

Nelson was happy to be back with his children. He opened his home, small and crowded as it was, to treason trialists from other areas. There were no hotels for 'non-Europeans' in Johannesburg in those days and, even if there had been, most trialists would not have been able to afford them. Besides, the obligations to friend and kin would not have allowed it.

The trial brought together local leaders from throughout the country. Many had known each other by name but had never met. Now it was as if the entire leadership was in constant conference. They talked and planned during lunch and in the evenings. They were invited by church groups and by liberals to meet dignitaries from all parts of the world. Such meetings were important public relations exercises. Bishop Reeves and Alan Paton formed a Defence Fund, and it became important for prospective donors to be reassured that they were not being asked to help irresponsible extremists, that these were people of integrity. All this was happening before the established social orders of the world would wince at the shock of 'terrorism'.

While practically the entire resistance movement became embroiled in the trial, another liberation organization was formed in Cape Town in 1957: the Ovamboland People's Congress, which would later become the South West African People's Organization (SWAPO). It sent its first recruits for military training to Egypt in 1962. In 1966 the ANC prisoners on Robben Island were joined by a large contingent of SWAPO guerrillas and party leaders, among them Toivo Ja Toivo. SWAPO was an ANC ally.

CHAPTER 11

# The Pan-Africanist Congress

Within a month of the opening of the preparatory examination there were massive bus boycotts throughout the country. They began in Alexandra Township, spread to the Reef, and extended to Pretoria, the Eastern Cape and the Orange Free State. Banned and chained to the Treason Trial, Nelson felt frustrated and helpless.

It was then that the full impact of the trial was brought home to him. He swore in anger. The Government had cut them off from the people and interrupted valuable community work; worse, the trial left the field wide open to the Africanists who were growing in strength. He saw them as small-minded and reactionary, and feared that the new and inexperienced ANC men left in the field would not be able to cope with them.

As the boycott intensified, so People's Transport Committees sprouted in the townships. It was a spontaneous resistance movement and the ANC was pleased that their man, Alfred Nzo, headed the seven-member coordinating committee of Nationalists, Africanists, Conservatives, Trotskyites and the tribalized Madzunyites. Six thousand walked daily to work, rather than pay the increased fares they said they could not afford; their voices raised in slogans that would stand the test of time: *Asikwela*, 'We won't ride', *Asinamali*, 'we have no money'.

But Nelson knew that there were limits to a people's endurance, that if the resistance was not properly guided, it would result in frustration and disaster. The bus boycott was hardly the end of the struggle. It was one episode in a conflict he saw stretching ahead for several years to come. As time would prove, his own calculations were too optimistic, and those of his adversaries reckless.

Nelson saw two problems: the people's own over-estimation of their capacity to endure and the exploitation of this faulty perception by opponents of the ANC, mostly by the Africanists and, to a lesser extent, by the breakaway NEUM faction calling itself the Movement for Democracy of Content (MDC). He feared also that the Government, unrelenting and angry, would use the slightest provocation to embroil the marchers in bloody violence.

It was commerce and industry, whose labour turnover was seriously affected, that made the first overture. They offered to subsidize their employees. Later, the subsidy was extended to all commuters. The Drill Hall group discussed the offer. Should the people accept the compromise or continue the boycott? There were those who argued that the total subsidy offered would not last more than twelve weeks. What after that? How could the people be expected to give up a four-month struggle for a twelve-week solution? The Africanists and the MDC agitated for a continuation of the struggle. ANC activists in the field agreed with that assessment. The Government, on its side, threatened to bring the boycotters to their knees. It saw any 'victory' on the part of the people as an ANC victory. To counter that it began a sinister propaganda campaign against the ANC, accusing it of master-minding the boycott through underground insurgents. This was followed up with mass arrests. In Alexandra Township alone, 14,000 people, including 500 taxi-owners, were arrested for the flimsiest of reasons.

Nelson and his compatriots discussed the situation with their men in the field. Members of the Liberal Party and Bishop Ambrose Reeves came to give their counsel. The Bishop was a pillar of strength against apartheid. Both Chief Luthuli and Professor Matthews admired and trusted him. Oliver, just prior to his arrest in 1956, had been accepted for ordination by him. Ultimately, the prime considerations were how much longer the resistance could survive, and how soon after the compromise offer was turned down would the Government move in?

The Africanists and the MDC were making impetuous calls to the people to stock up food and to prepare for a prolonged stay-away from work. The ANC by contrast was cautious as the leaders, trapped in the Trial and distanced from the field, did not have a direct understanding of the issues.

Nelson refused to see the issue as a contest between political forces or for the solution to depend on who could outdo whom in revolutionary zeal. He feared, above all, that the people's sacrifice would be squandered, and that they would have nothing in return. He didn't agree that they should back down and compromise but, unable to take the field himself, he could not very well come up with a more militant solution either. The ANC's decision was to call off the boycott and accept the subsidy.

The Africanists were waiting for just that decision. They now accused the ANC of selling the people's struggle for a mere £25,000. The ANC lost support in Alexandra and even more in Evaton. The boycott was in fact more successful in Evaton than in Alexandra, and continued for a longer period, primarily because of the stronger bargaining power of the Transport Committee. It was made up of young ANC men and two local members of the Transvaal Indian Congress, one being Solly Nathee, a fellow treason trialist. That committee was prepared to set up its own transport company. It gained important concessions from the bus company and would have fared well, but for the attack from the Basotho.

The Basotho, largely migrant males, were not represented on the committee and the boycotted bus company exploited this. In particular it manipulated the thuggish elements, the white-blanketed Basotho, who had achieved a notorious reputation as 'Russians'. There were the forerunners of the reactionary *witdoeke* (white head-bands) of the 1980s, mobilized by the system and its agents to counter the people's resistance. In 1956 the boycotted bus company hired them to attack the boycotters and picketers. Despite this the Evaton commuters made significant gains. Their support went to the Africanists because they were active in the field.

The trial that held the ANC leadership hostage, the poor ANC showing in the bus boycott, and poor organization at branch and regional levels seriously dented the popularity of the ANC at this time. Nelson worried about the sheer in-competence and high-handedness of some officials and des-paired over the bad book-keeping and poor accounting of others. It gave the Africanists ground to attack the presiding leadership from within, so forcing the organization to follow an Africanist stance. Leballo and Madzunya were making significant gains in the townships. The ANC had called for a national stay-away from work in protest against the 1958 white election. Leballo and Madzunya, though ANC mem-bers, openly campaigned against the call, holding the white election irrelevant.

Both men had an almost uncanny capacity to sway the crowds. Leballo had seen service in the Second World War as a Basotho national. A colleague described him as 'blunt, rash and a fierce public speaker with a haranguing style directed at the raw emotion of his audience'. He could whip up the youth into fanaticism. Madzunya, an earthy per-sonality, as rough as the soil he hugged, and messianic in rhetoric, had a strong appeal for the migrant tribesmen whose instincts were still rooted in rural politics and who found the urban scene strange and uncomfortable.

Matters heated up at the 1958 ANC Transvaal Confer-ence. Several branches had already petitioned the National Executive about the alleged corruption in the Transvaal Executive. At the conference Madzunya and Leballo led the opposition against the Executive. The conference erupted in accusations and counter-accusations.

Oliver, sitting on the platform, had a grandstand view of the mood of the floor, and counselled the chairman to concede to the petitions, but his counsel fell on deaf ears. The chairman preferred confrontation. Leballo called for the resignation of the Executive and received overwhelming support. The chairman, faced with defeat, closed the meeting and started singing the national anthem. Most of the hall remained seated, clearly demonstrating its rejection of the chairman. That evening angry Africanists raided the ANC offices and made off with the ANC car.

The National Executive, realizing how critical the situation was, took matters into its own hands; it persuaded the Transvaal Executive to stand down, promised the petitioners new elections, and convened the postponed conference. At the same time, as a show of strength, it expelled Madzunya and Leballo for their continued opposition to the official call for the stay-away. Leballo formed an anti-Charterist Council and put up Madzunya as its candidate for the provincial president.

Things appeared to be falling apart and the task of putting them together, of reorganizing and strengthening branches, fell above all on Nelson, Walter and Oliver. After a full day at the trial they had a few concentrated hours in the office that brought in essential private income; they became immersed, late into the night, meeting, discussing, advising, planning and hoping, almost against hope, that things would improve.

The 26 June 1958 stay-away was a disaster; and the postponed Provincial Congress produced a highly publicized opposition. Madzunya made an impressive entry with his blanketed followers; Leballo was vociferous; Tambo, in the chair, calm. Chief Luthuli opened the conference with his usual dignity. He made a pointed reference to the new and dangerous tendency within the ANC to revert to racism in the guise of nationalism.

There was some heckling and stamping of feet at the back of the Orlando hall, but the marshals had this quickly under control. Trouble broke out when the credentials committee questioned the *bona fides* of a number of 'delegates' brought by the Africanists. Argument and anger followed these delegates to their homes and neighbourhoods, and they returned to the conference the following day, heavily reinforced. Some tense moments followed when it seemed that they would lash out against each other. But suddenly the Africanists decided that there was nothing left in the ANC to fight about. They would leave it and go their own way. They withdrew and sent in their statement of resignation and their resolve to establish their own organization.

This is a political battle aimed against the oppressor. We are not a para-military clique engaged in the murder of fellow Africans . . . In 1955 the Kliptown Charter was adopted which, according to us, is in irreconcilable conflict with the 1949 Programme, seeing that it claims the land no longer belongs to the African people, but is auctioned for sale to all who live in this country . . . We have come to the parting of the ways and we are here and now giving notice that we are disassociating ourselves from the ANC as it is constituted at present in the Transvaal.

We are launching openly on our own as the custodian of the ANC policy as it was formulated in 1912 and pursued up to the time of the Congress Alliance.

Two months later the Africanists met in the same Orlando Hall and formed the Pan-Africanist Congress. They elected as their chairman a university lecturer, a man of intellectual brilliance, Robert Sobukwe. Nelson knew him well. He had been a strong Youth Leaguer and an important ANC man. He was sorry to see him as an opponent.

Sobukwe was among those who had founded the Fort Hare branch of the ANC Youth League. Nelson recalled his brilliant address at the prestigious 1949 graduation ceremony on behalf of the students. In the Defiance of Unjust Laws Campaign they had been brothers, courting imprisonment and sacrificing their livelihoods in the process. Now they stood in opposition, and would be caught up in the abuse each organization would hurl against the other. In the very next year they would commit themselves to action, separately and competitively, but they would reap together the harvest of blood, banning and exile that would ensue.

Nelson had defended Sobukwe in the Standerton court when, following his participation in the 1950 campaign for 26 June, he was threatened with expulsion from the Education

Department. He had also defended Zeph Mothopeng, the other PAC leader. They had trusted him and now 'Robbie', as he called Sobukwe, evaded him when he asked for his presidential speech and the PAC policy statement. 'Nel,' he said, 'I've got it at varsity,' or, 'Nel, as soon as I have a moment, I'll get it to you.' 'Robbie was always cautious,' Nelson recalled, 'playing his cards close to his chest, but very honest.' Nelson eventually got the documents from Leballo. 'Leballo,' says Nelson, 'was completely different from Sobukwe, very outgoing and almost incapable of secrecy. When I told him I was trying to lay my hands on their documents and not getting anywhere, he said, "We'll never give them to you. We know what you'll do with them" (whatever he meant by that), and then proceeded to invite me to his home where he gave them to me!'

The PAC had a following in only two centres, Johannesburg and the Western Cape, but they burst on to the political scene with new zeal and vigour. They set up a labour alliance with anti-SACTU trade unions and formed the Federation of Free African Trade Unions (FOFATUSA) under Jacob Nyaose and Lucy Mvubelo.

The ANC lost support in the Cape because it continued to support white candidates who contested parliamentary seats to represent blacks. NEUM, a major political tendency in the region, had popularized boycott and made 'collaboration' a virtual crime. The ANC supported the COD candidate standing for the native seat. Those in the ANC who supported boycott, moved out and joined the PAC.

The Coloured elections proved disastrous, with most Coloureds boycotting and those participating turning their backs on the COD candidates and supporting the United Party.

The year proved, all in all, to be one of white consolidation behind the Nationalists as they increased their majority, and one of black fragmentation. Not only did a split occur within the ANC ranks, but the All African Convention, meeting in conference that year, clashed with its youth affiliates on ideological grounds. Sons of Young Africa (SOYA) and the Cape New Era Fellowship. They were found to be too

Marxist in orientation, emphasizing class as the crucial basis of the South African conflict almost to the exclusion of race.

In the midst of all this political upheaval something wonderful happened in Nelson's personal life. He met Winnie Madikizela. Her brightness and beauty overpowered him. Adelaide Tsukudu, Oliver's fiancée, introduced them. Nelson wooed Winnie in his own way, within the confines of his banning order and in between his daily attendance at the Treason Trial, and at the numerous meetings outside of it. She visited the Drill Hall. He introduced her to his friends. He sent her to Durban to spend time with the Meers; he sent her to his aunt in Orlando. It was as if he wanted them all to see her through his eyes, to know her goodness and her beauty as he knew them. She visited him in his office; they went out for the occasional drive into the country. Soon his photographs (her favourite Nelson, the boxer) were always in her bag. She was clearly in love with him. When his divorce came through, he did not propose to her. He told her that they would be married and introduced her to his children.

Makgatho recalls the divorce of his parents and his meeting with Winnie.

I was eight years old at the time, schooling in Orlando West where our house was, but living with my mother in Orlando East. Thembi was at boarding school. I can't remember Maki. My mother read in the newspaper that my father was divorcing her. It didn't worry me too much. As far as I could see that had already happened a long time ago. My parents were living apart; we were going up and down between them, from Orlando East to Orlando West, then from the West to the East. In the dispute, I took my father's part. I can't say for sure whose part Thembi took but maybe he took my mother's part. I remember one time at home when there was big trouble between them. I don't know what it was about, but I sided with my father.

In 1958 Thembi was home from school. We used to go to Daddy's office and we would drive to Orlando with him. Then one day we stopped somewhere and we picked up Winnie. She was very friendly. I thought, What a pretty lady. She was talking and her eyes were shining. I liked her. We met her many times after that, usually at Daddy's office. I thought nothing about it. Then one day Daddy told us that Winnie was going to be our new mother. That seemed strange to me. I talked about it with Thembi later. I said to him: 'Daddy is going to stay with Winnie and Winnie is going to be our new mother.' It upset Thembi, but he said nothing.

Then when I went to visit Daddy in Orlando West at our house, I heard my aunts and my grandmother talk about Daddy's wedding. They were all very excited and they were making big plans.

I continued visiting Daddy after his marriage, and to spend weekends with him. Winnie was okay to me. I regarded her as my mother, like my father wanted me to, and this upset our mother. She didn't want me to go there at weekends, but I went.

Evelyn recounts:

I heard from Thembi that Nelson was marrying the social worker from Baragwanath: her name was Winnie Madikizela. I thought, how ironic, that it was not any of the women we had quarrelled over that had finally ended our marriage, but a newcomer. Oh! Winnie was not responsible for the break, but because he wanted to marry her there had to be the divorce.

My brother returned to Engcobo about this time and I took over his house in Orlando. The children continued their visits so long as father and grandmother were there, but when they disappeared, father, because he was imprisoned, and grandmother, because she returned to Qunu, they practically stopped going to their father's house, except when there was some specific need.

Nelson paid maintenance for the children as long as he was in a position to do so, but after his arrest and imprisonment, I became responsible for them. For a while school fees were paid. Winnie bought them clothes. But Winnie, too, had her children to look after.

Whatever the problems that broke the marriage, Nelson, thinking back and commenting on the episode through the conduit of censored letters, wrote: 'Evelyn is pleasant and charming and I respected her even as the marriage was crumbling. It would be quite unfair to blame her for the breakdown.'

25 February 1985

PART III

# WINNIE

# CHAPTER 12

# Bizana

There was no rejoicing on the day Nomathamsanqa went into labour for the fourth time and produced yet another daughter. She had prayed hard for a son as she had to contend with Makhulu (whose name was Seyina, but none had survived to call her that), who blamed her for the birth of daughters, and reminded her that their grand-patriarch Mazingi had considered girls a waste of time and had ordered them killed at birth.

Makhulu's ululations had sounded across the *inkundla* (yard) and floated into the valley when Nomathansanqa's first child and *indlalifa* (male heir) had been born, but on the two succeeding occasions she had turned away in disgust and remarked: 'You are wasting our time!' However, Makhulu had then proceeded to love and in turn to discipline her grand-daughters.

Three months after the birth, the family gathered in the little corrugated-iron church building in Dutyiwa, a rural location in the district of Bizana in the Transkei, and christened the child Nomzamo Zanyiwe Winifred Madikizela. Her parents simply called her Ntombi (girl) and, when she went to school, Winnie. Makhulu's wishes were later realized when Nomathamsanqa gave birth to two boys, Lungile and Msutu, although girls never stopped coming, and later there were Nobantu and Nonyaniso.

Winnie is an Ngutyana, one of the stronger clans of the Pondo. Her great-grandfather Madikizela was a marauding chieftain in the Umkomaas district of Natal in the second quarter of the nineteenth century. His ferocity was such that it won him the fighting men, land and cattle on which his reputation stood. But even he could not withstand the power of uShaka, the great Zulu King, and caught up in the great *imfecane* (the Zulu invasion) he moved with his followers and cattle south into Pondoland where he threatened Faku's domain. The wise Faku decided that it was better to have Madikizela with him than against him, and gave him a sister in marriage. The Madikizelas from then on were also known as the nephews of Faku.

When the British signed a treaty with the Pondos in 1848, Madikizela of the AmanGutyana was one of the four major chiefs, together with King Faku, with whom individual treaties were signed.

The AmanGutyana finally settled near Izingolweni between Port Edward and Bizana. Winnie's grandfather, Chief Mazingi, had twenty-nine wives, and they presided over his numerous residences between Mbongweni and Dutyiwa. He was both a prosperous farmer and a trader. His landholdings were vast and he reaped a good harvest of maize and grazed large herds of cattle and sheep. The missionaries intrigued him, as they did many other chiefs. He gave the Methodists permission to settle at his Great Place, Kamkhulu, and was so impressed with their superior skills that he abandoned his god for theirs. A teacher was engaged, a school started and the new generation of Madikizelas were directed from the fields to the classroom where, painfully taking pen in hand, they prepared to learn the skills that would make them as clever as the white people. Chief Mazingi was determined that his children would be lifted out of the unlettered past that had made his people vulnerable to conquest. His senior wife, Seyina, large-bodied, big-hearted and with a laugh that rang out across the fields, was his business manager and the mother of six sons, the eldest of whom, Kokani, was the father of Winnie.

Three of Seyina's sons, including Kokani, became teachers, one qualified as an agriculturalist and one joined her in the business. The youngest, Xolane, went to work on the mines, where he almost instantly contacted phthisis and died.

Seyina resisted Christianization for as long as she could.

When finally she succumbed, she laid aside her *isidwebe* (leather skirt) and stepped into a simple dress of German print. Yet inwardly she remained Nguni and although she attended church she continued the Nguni rituals to preserve the happiness of her home. These rituals touched her six sons and three daughters and became part of their inner peace.

Seyina lived a great deal in the past, which went against her daughter-in-law Nomathamsanqa's Christian conscience, since she saw it as a past steeped in the pagan values her family had abandoned two generations ago. There was a tension between the two women on account of their different world-views, and because they competed for the affection of the same man, Kokani. Winnie was always aware of this.

My mother was, by Makhulu's standards, a modern woman, a schoolteacher. She did not dress like the other women in the village. She and Aunt Jane were different. For one, they never wore doeks [headcloths]. They wore crocheted hats and they rarely wore German prints. Makhulu held my mother responsible for inhibiting her son, my father, from becoming a chief and a real man by taking more wives. When he announced his intention to marry her, Makhulu had told him that he was out of his mind, that he was marrying a 'European' not a Muntu, and a man not a woman. 'Marry a wife,' she had advised, 'not a fellow teacher.' But having made her point she held her peace with her son, and blamed the woman for the *takhati* [witchcraft] she had put on him.

Seyina saw her son suffering an affliction from which she could best save him by drawing him even closer to her. When he set up home with the teacher woman, her concern for him grew even greater.

When Winnie was barely five years old she accompanied her mother, Nomathamsanqa, to her secret praying place in the fields where she talked to God about her family and their welfare in this world and the next. Winnie gained the impression that there was something different about Makhulu's Christianity and that it would not take her to their mother's heaven. She also gathered that this did not trouble her mother very much, for she never included Makhulu in her earnest entreaties to make them into fuller Christians. It also seemed to her that Nomathamsanqa was afraid that she might not find Kokani in her heaven, for she never omitted to ask Him to make Kokani into a good Christian and to deliver him from the evil influence of Makhulu. Winnie thought that God was not paying her mother too much attention in this matter.

Makhulu, on the other hand, talked to grandfather's spirit in the cattle kraal and the children listened. She was forever asking him to strengthen her sons, and not to be too upset by their European ways; at times she would present him with complaints against the one son or the other, or ask his assistance in chastising a daughter-in-law.

Winnie noticed that her mother came in for more than her fair share of criticism. This disturbed and embarrassed her because of the cousins who were listening in, but the children never discussed what they heard during such eavesdropping. They knew that if the mother of one was criticized today, it would be the turn of the other tomorrow.

Though Christian and an active member of the church, Kokani dared not ignore the cult of his forefathers, his mother was there as a living insurance against that. There were special occasions when the ancestors would be called upon in the cattle kraal and offered the finest and best-loved beast in their herd. Winnie's eldest brother, Makhulwa, would lead the ceremony outside the kraal. Makhulu would take over from him, chanting: 'We are congregated here in your name. We hope that the blood we spill will honour you and drive away any anger we might have incurred. Be with us in all things. Protect us. Bring us prosperity and peace.' The beast would then be taken into the kraal and the young men would slaughter it, and then cook it, dividing the meat carefully according to seniority: first to the men, then to the women and finally to the children.

Winnie recalls: 'That was a good time for us, for everyone would be in a happy mood, we children sitting on our mats and sucking at our bones, the men near by, drinking their beer and relating their stories, we listening in – though I suppose we were not intended to, but nobody minded.'

Winnie grew up in two homes: her mother's and her grandmother's, as different as the women who presided over them. Nomathamsanqa's house was a collection of seven rondavels, while Seyina's comprised twenty. Nomatham-sanqa's family was limited to her husband and children, Seyina's overflowed with aunts and uncles and dozens of cousins. There was always a festive atmosphere about Seyina's house with lots of cooking, eating and drinking, Makhulu presiding over it all with an exuberance that clearly derived from the time she had managed her husband's vast *umuzi* (homestead).

Winnie remembers her grandmother's house as a kraal of many rondavels set in what appeared to her 'a huge garden of trees and pecking ground for the many fowls and their chicks'. The cattle kraal stood about half a kilometre from her father's plantation.

Nomathamsanqa rarely visited Makhulu, but Makhulu strode into her house at will. It was, after all, her son's house and she filled it like some supreme goddess, sending No-mathamsanqa into a corner. Winnie says:

When she came, our house rang with the authority of her boom which swelled from out of her great bosom. My father's veneration for my grandmother sent all of us into fits of awe, and when son and mother retired into the sitting room, we children were sent away and warned not to be a nuisance while the *indaba* [discussion] continued for an hour or more. It seemed that when Makhulu had matters of importance to discuss she preferred to use our mother's sitting room.

In Nomathamsanqa's house everything was neatly con-tained and nothing allowed to be out of place. She was forever checking things and arranging them in order, cleaning and polishing as if that was what life was all about. Winnie says:

We girls took turns to start the chores at dawn. We were scolded out of our sleep to pick up sticks and scraps of paper that littered the yard, to sprinkle the bare earth with water to keep down the dust from blowing into the house and settling on the high-gloss

Victorian furniture. Our mother was so strict that when she sent us to collect wood or water she would spit in front of the fire and warn us that we had to be back before the spit dried. We knew better than to tarry and made the two-kilometre run in record time as we knew that if we did not, we would go without supper or be slapped.

At Makhulu's house, work was a kind of play, which proceeded in a rhythm which was both languid and exciting. Makhulu taught us to weave grass mats and make clay pots. The hours passed in talking, teasing and story-telling. She taught us to brew beer, with constant tasting and consulting, and when she tired of us, she shooed us into the yard where we drew patterns in the sand amongst the scratching fowls and chickens and played a kind of hopscotch.

Makhulu taught me things that my mother had taken care to see I'd never learn. She took me into the ways of our ancestors, she put the skins and beads that had been hers when she was a young girl on me and taught me to sing and dance. I learnt to milk cows and to ride horses and to cook mealie porridge, mealies with meat, mealies with vegetables, and I learnt to make *umphokoqo* [Pondo porridge] the way Makhulu made it.

On the days that a beast was slaughtered and meat was cooked, Makhulu would recline in the doorway, great pot in lap, and carve out portions for each of us with her knife as we filed past her with our plates and spoons. It was always adults first, children last, because Makhulu said we had our whole lives ahead of us and we would go on eating, but the adults were dying.

It was Makhulu who first drew my attention to the fact that there were people who had a different colour, that there were white people. She called them *aba Nyephi* and said they were thieves. They gave nothing without money: 'See the white doctor,' she told us, 'if you go to him and you are sick, he does not care to make you well. He cares for the money you take him. But *inyanga ya komkhulu* [herbalist of the clan], he cares for you. He treats you. And he does not ask you for money. These *aba Nyephi* are no bigger than us, but their appetite for land and cattle, and for other things we cannot even imagine, is as large as of giants. They have swallowed our land and our cattle, and they just sit to take more. One day we will be paupers.' A bad person and a white person were the same things in her mind, and when a child stole sugar or bread she rebuked: 'You mustn't be like an *aba Nyephi*.'

Makhulu had no use for the things the *aba Nyephi* made and

sold in their stores. She said they were made to trap black people into buying them – that way they stole all their money. She warned that they would take all the black people's land in the same way. There was no furniture in her rondavel, only cowdung neatly levelled and shining clean [as a floor], and grass mats and little stools made of rough wattle. But she made two concessions to the white man's industry: a blanket she wore around her shoulders in the winter, and the German print she wound around her waist.

Our family was very regular at church, and Sunday was set apart for worshipping and visiting and helping neighbours in distress. We went as a family in our cleanest and neatest clothes. I tried to like church, as my sisters did, but found myself bored. It was the same each Sunday, standing and singing the same hymns, sitting and listening to the same sermon. And at the end of the quiet part the same noisy part would follow, as the priest railed against the sins that had been committed and called on the sinners to stand up and repent. There would then be such a chorus of weeping and wailing, of beating of breasts and screaming, it would scare the children, but mostly it bored me.

After church we children went to Sunday school conducted by Mtokelikozi who managed to produce prizes for the best pupils. Christmas was a special occasion; our father saw to that. Everyone got new clothes, the children got toys, presents were exchanged and an ox slaughtered.

Winnie's maternal grandmother was very different from her paternal one, Seyina. Winnie went to stay with her for a while. She was a staunch Christian, an activist in the Methodist church. She cooked European food and sewed European dresses, the prettiest that Winnie had ever seen, and she wore these in great style, following a toiletry that took hours each day. First would come the bath, and when Winnie stayed with her it was her special duty to fetch the water from the river. Next came vigorous washing of the body, followed by the rubbing in of mineral jelly that Granny had prepared herself by boiling together candle wax and paraffin. Then she would comb her hair, till it stood stiff and long about her head and Winnie would be invited to plait it in a dozen little plaits. Undressing each night was as ceremonial as dressing each morning. Granny would take off her clothes carefully and stretch them out under her mattress so that all creases would be pressed out and they would be perfect for the morning wear. Her maternal granny was also very particular about household cleanliness.

It was the two grandmothers who lived all over again in Winnie when she grew into womanhood. She derived from Makhulu her imperious authority and from Granny her love for smart clothes and an obsession with cleanliness.

Of all the women in the family, Winnie admired her mother's sister, Aunt Phyllis, most of all, for she was highly educated, having graduated from Fort Hare, and was, like her father, a teacher. She was also the first secretary of the YMCA. Winnie did not see much of Aunt Phyllis in her childhood for she lived in the Transvaal on the East Rand, but they met a great deal when Winnie went to study in Johannesburg.

Of her daughters, Nomathamsanqa found Winnie the most troublesome and the most wilful. Although she never suggested anything by word or deed, Winnie, even as a child, sensed that she was not what her mother had wanted, so she tried to be a boy which only aggravated the situation: 'Why can't you be a girl like other girls? Why all this running around with the boys? Why all this falling and scratching yourself? And why do you take Nonalithi with you?' Nomathamsanqa would demand. Then she would turn on Nonalithi and berate her for being led by the nose.

Winnie also had the impression of being the ugly duckling of the family. She recalls a particular Sunday when she accompanied her mother and sister to visit Reverend Gabela.

My mother and sister were very light complexioned. My mother's eyes were almost blue and her hair was longish. The Reverend's wife admired my sister: 'What a lovely child. She will grow to be a great beauty.' And then, turning to me, 'And what is the name of your little boy?' I hated the Reverend's wife from that day onwards.

If I looked like a boy I thought, I would behave like one. So I played with the boys, the sons of the farmhands, and they taught me to fight with sticks and lay snares for small animals. I crept into the cattle kraal with them and lit fires and roasted the birds they caught and ate them as men did.

She found no difficulty in being accepted into the boys' group. It was because she was tall and strong and able to outdo most of them in stick fights. The children would climb trees and lie waiting for each other. Then they would jump down on their 'enemy' and the fighting would be fierce.

Nomathamsanqa believed that to spare the rod was to spoil the child, and her stick fell most often on Winnie who had earned the reputation of being wilier than the other children. On one occasion, provoked by her elder sister Nonalithi, Winnie made a knuckle duster out of a baking powder tin by knocking a nail through it. The next round in the sisters dispute was fought with this weapon. The nail penetrated the inside of Nonalithi's mouth and she had to be taken to Dr Thompson in Bizana for the wound to be stitched. The beating that Nomathamsanqa gave Winnie was so ferocious that it affected her for the rest of her life.

With all this going on, Winnie, unsurprisingly, got the reputation of being the trouble-maker of the family. When the sisters quarrelled, which was all too often, it seemed easiest to stop the disagreement by giving Winnie a few resounding smacks; whenever a child went to Nomathamsanqa with a complaint, she knew who the culprit was and punished Winnie.

Winnie could not, dared not, accuse her mother of loving her less than she loved her sisters, but she felt an injustice. Often she cried out, not knowing that it was from the pain of that injustice. Her father would intervene, not to condone but to console, and she was grateful to him. Such acts of 'mercy' drew her father closer, despite a great aloofness from his children and demand that they respect him in a formal way. They were trained to stand up when he entered a room and to sit only after he had. He never touched them in affection or in anger. Those gestures were left to their mother.

Winnie loved her uncle Lamginya who treated her as a

favourite niece. He was a bus driver, and the best occasions were when he piled the children into his bus and took them for a drive. He was playful and affectionate and, unlike her parents, cuddled and kissed them.

When Winnie turned six her father enrolled her in the infant class at his school. She took her place with a hundred other children. She spent three years there, then, when the Department transferred her father to Mbongweni, she went with him. The family sold the farm, the house and a large number of chickens and established a new home at Mbongweni not far from the Madikizela *komkhulu*. Their standard of living deteriorated. Home was three rondavels, not six as before. The cattle kraal shrunk in size and the farmhands disappeared. Kokani ploughed the land himself and the children helped. Winnie recalls:

A large portion of the work fell on me because I was tall and strong and because I was in a lower class at school and did not have as much schoolwork as the others. I led the oxen and Father drove the plough. We both hoed together. Even though the work was hard I never complained as I was too overcome by the specialness of this new relationship with my father. We hardly spoke, but his gentle presence gave me support. It was as if God walked with me. We were up at dawn to disinfect the mealies; we interrupted our work to eat breakfast and then we set off for school together.

We had beehives in the forest – the forest did not belong to us, but everyone conceded that the beehives did. When the time was right my father would set fire under the hives to drive away the bees after which he would collect the honey comb and give it to Mother to boil to extract the honey and bottle it. We also raised chicks and sold eggs. Nonalithi and I were put in charge of the incubator. We took turns sitting in the incubation room watching the temperature. When it rose too high we would run to call our father, who would put matters right.

I was ten years old when my youngest brother was born. He was to be my mother's last child, and the death of her. It was as if she had been living just to give birth to this precious son. She became very ill. She lay on our father's iron bed and my aunt came to help with the nursing. We were unhappy with our aunt's nursing so

Nonalithi and I took turns to go to school so that one of us would always be with our mother.

It was then that Nomathamsanqa drew Winnie close to her. She would call her to sit beside her with the baby. Her eyes, hollowed into her face and grown dim with fever and vomiting, would look at her as if from a great distance, then rest on the baby in Winnie's arms. At times she would stretch out a limp hand to stroke the baby, but the effort was usually too much and her hand would fall beside her on the bed. When she talked to Winnie, it was always about goodness, and how she should make her life pure and good. Winnie listened earnestly, taking in every word as if it were a precious treasure. She did not always understand, but this did not matter. In those days mother and daughter and the baby, sometimes sleeping, often crying, were bonded tightly.

Nomathamsanqa's illness weighed heavily on Kokani who walked dejectedly about the house. He would sit for hours with Nomathamsanqa and then would lock himself up with a pile of exercise books and work late into the night. He said little to the children and avoided them, afraid that they would see the pain in his face and wonder at his weakness.

When her end drew near, the elders gathered around Nomathamsanqa's bed.

Nonalithi and I did not know what to do, so we retreated into one of the rondavels, and waited in fear. Then, towards dawn, a horrible shriek broke the silence and our older sister Nikiwe burst into the rondavel sobbing and beating her breasts and we knew the worst had happened. We flung our arms around each other and wept and it was as if our sorrow would never end.

Our house filled with relatives, and they remained for a whole month, leaving us no space for our private sorrow. Black cloth was brought out and black dresses made on our mother's old sewing machine. Our heads were shaved and we were put into the black dresses and the outer walls of our house were painted in black ochre and our mother's body was placed in a black box.

After the funeral, life was never the same. Nonalithi went to live with our aunt Mpiyonke at Mzize, Nikiwe and my elder brother returned to their boarding schools. I remained at home with the baby and my father. His sister came to live with us, but it was left to me to care for the baby. When my mother died he was still on her breast and so he cried all the time because he missed her. Often I had to sit up with him all night.

But in the tragedy, there was also happiness. I grew very close to my father in those days. I washed his clothes at the river and we went to school together. My father would bring me the *Farmer's Weekly* to read for I was helping with the farming. 'Read,' he would say, 'then you will understand better. See what they say about those worms in the mealies. I shall get the disinfection powder.' My father was at the time a member of the Bunga and I missed him terribly when he went to meetings at Umtata.

The *makotis* [married women] in the neighbourhood came in their long German print dresses and their black doeks pulled low over their brows to check on *Mamomncinci* [small mother] as they called me, and to offer their help which I always politely declined.

At this time there was a Miss Jane Zithutha who joined our school. She was especially good to me, called me into her office and gave me sweets. Makhulu questioned me closely about the sweets and gave knowing nods. Miss Zithutha lived about one kilometre from us, renting a room at my paternal uncle's place. At times she gave me a letter for my father and asked me just to leave it on his table in his bedroom. Then my father asked me to go and stay with her. He said she was alone and afraid and needed company. Makhulu gave more knowing looks, more nods.

Miss Zithutha later became possessive and jealous about her relationship with the widower, Kokani. She made the fatal mistake of complaining to Makhulu about her son. She listened coldly and then said: 'I hear. Now you tell me, what did you have for breakfast?' Confused, Miss Zithutha listed the food. 'And for lunch?' And for supper?' And each time Miss Zithutha bore testimony to the good food she had eaten. Makhulu then said, 'You are well fed, you are well clothed, you are well housed. What do you want from my son?'

Nature intervened where Makhulu left off.

One day the clouds darkened and a wind blew up and there was thunder and lightning. Makhulu asked me to fetch the cattle from the field. 'Quickly,' she warned, 'the storm is coming fast.' I was still herding the cattle when there was a terrifying noise and a horrible scream from Miss Zithutha's hut, and the sound of a crash that resounded for miles. There was a shaft of lightning; the tree in front of her hut crashed and fell; and tree, hut and Miss Zithutha were all enveloped in one great blaze. Father was running and shouting, I was crying. Miss Zithutha was dead.

Soon thereafter our aunt became ill. We nursed her as best we could, but within days she too was dead. Then Nikiwe fell ill. She was at boarding school at the time. I had finished primary school and was waiting to be sent to boarding school myself for there was no further schooling available in the area. Now Nikiwe was sent home and it seemed as if some strange spirits had taken possession of her. She wailed the whole night and kept us awake; she spoke in a strange language; her body went into spasms and there were times when she had to be tied to the bedstead to prevent her from harming herself.

My father brought home Flathela. He was *inyanga* [traditional herbalist] and known to be able to see witches, to talk to them and to coax them out of the strange places in people's bodies where they took possession of them and ruined their lives. Flathela saw the matter as concerning our whole family. He put *mthi* [medicine] all around our rondavel and burnt a large number of strange objects in Nikiwe's room. He then had our heads shaved, and made us sit in a semi-circle; and our cheeks were incised and black muti was rubbed into the incisions. Flathela then approached Nikiwe and, pressing her head with the palm of his hand, addressed the witches within her in a tongue we could not understand. He pleaded and scolded. He beat her and she cried out in strange sounds and they said it was the witches within her. Then she collapsed and lay still, and when she awoke, it was all over. Flathela had exorcized the witches, so we believed then.

My brother suddenly arrived home. He had completed his studies, having matriculated and gained his teacher's diploma, and was appointed to a school in the district. He brought this woman with him, or rather we assumed that what he brought with him, completely wrapped up in a blanket, so that we saw not even a part of her limbs, was a woman. It was in the morning and the time was about 7 a.m. He stood outside, with this figure draped in the striped *ibhayi*. He sent me to his bedroom and asked me to see that it was swept and clean and the bed made up. I asked no questions. I checked out everything as he instructed. Nobody had touched his room since he had left a week ago. We all knew better than that. It was clean and neat. He then asked me to stand before my father's door, and while I did so, he slipped this woman in the blanket into his room. He then asked me to prepare food and bring water for washing into the room. Then he locked the woman in the room and went away. Nobody spoke about the locked room or the woman within for the rest of the day. In the evening my brother returned with our uncle and they went into my father's room and they shut the door and talked for a long while.

The following day, while everyone pretended not to look, my brother took the woman in the blanket into a separate hut. I caught a glimpse of a pretty, fair hand. Then a lot of women came and joined her, but none of us saw her for she remained hidden behind a curtain that the women had thrown before her. She remained like that for a whole week, and in that week her relatives came and talked with our elders.

At the end of the week, our uncle returned with the menfolk from Chief Lumayi, for the woman in the blanket was his daughter, and she had already become registered in marriage to my brother.

We now slaughtered an ox and my aunt, Dadobawo, went behind the curtain, with the new, long, green print dress she had made and our brother's *makoti* emerged out of her seclusion for the first time, *ixakatho* [breast cloth] around her shoulder, her head elegantly wrapped in *ukuhlo* [headcloth]. She was very light complexioned and very beautiful.

I do not know to this day why it happened that way. Why there was no wedding in the way our mother would have wanted it, with veil, and marching to the pulpit, and singing and praying.

Perhaps it was the way she had been brought into the house, without consultation with my father. Perhaps it was my father's fastidiousness, but he never took to his daughter-in-law and she did not stay long with us. She and my brother left us to set up house on their own.

My father did not remarry until 1955. He married Hilda No-kikela, a school principal. As could be expected Makhulu did not approve. She did not go to meet the bride. Instead she remained seated in her place and ordered that the bride be brought to her. 'That old hag,' she said, who had come to take her son's money and eat her grandchildren's wealth. The bride came, covered in her veil, and a beast was brought to Makhulu to be slaughtered in honour of the presentation. But Makhulu stopped the ceremony.

110

'We're all full now. Nobody is hungry. Stay the blood-letting. We'll slaughter when we are hungry. This doesn't deserve any slaughter.'

By then my baby brother was already at boarding school. We got on very well with our stepmother. She was a considerate and wise woman.

I completed my standard six in 1946. It was the happiest day I had known yet. My father slaughtered a sheep and demonstrated his pride in me. I, who had been rejected by my mother, was honoured by my father in a way he had never honoured any of his other daughters before. I prepared to go to boarding school at Emfundisweni, in Flagstaff, a hundred miles from home. Two iron trunks were packed, one with clothes, the other with food. Makhulu said all that food was a waste of my father's money. My father bought me my first overcoat. Up to then I had wrapped myself in a blanket to keep the cold away. I left by bus with other children who were headed for the same school.

I spent three years at Emfundisweni and passed my junior certificate exam there. In my final year I took a 'boy' because everyone else had a 'boy'. It meant writing little notes and looking at each other in church – all at long distance. I did not realize then that after my marriage it would still be a long-distance affair.

After Emfundisweni it was Shawbury Hight, run by the Methodists. I prepared for my matric there. It was an eventful year. I became politicized there. Our teachers, Fort Hare graduates, were members of the Non-European Unity Movement and I was influenced by them. But I also read about the ANC in *Zonk* magazine.

We were on our way to Tsomo on a school excursion. Our bus stopped at Flagstaff for petrol and we alighted briefly to loosen our limbs. One of my companions drew my attention to a dwarf who was gazing at me. He came up to speak to me. 'Do you know what a pretty girl you are?' My companion whispered, 'Khotso!' Khotso was a legend in our district for his great wealth and his many wives. He squeezed a ten shilling note in my palm and said, 'This is the first instalment for your lobola. You will be my wife when you have grown fuller.' I was deeply embarrassed but my friends laughed and helped me to spend the money.

In my final year at Shawbury, my school work suffered. I had always done well, never falling below fifth position in my class, but that year my report placed me thirteenth and my father, for the first time, reprimanded me. 'What is the trouble?' he asked. 'What is it that is getting into your head now?' He had plans for me but if

111

I went on like this they might as well be abandoned, he said. I felt ashamed, but I could not tell him my problem. How could I discuss such a matter with him? The real trouble was that I had matured too quickly, I looked older than my years. Still a girl, my body had grown into womanhood, so much so that I was often mistaken for a teacher when we went out to play netball. Worst of all, the assistant principal was making passes at me. I was one of the prefects at the school and had to fetch the keys to the book-shelves from him, and when I did he would slip a tightly rolled note into my hand. The first one humiliated me so much that I cried, and when others followed I confided in Ezra Malizo Ndam-ase, my fellow head prefect who was also supposed to be my boyfriend. That was the sort of thing the girls at the school did, paired you off with somebody and that was as far as it went. Ezra Ndamase would have died rather than make a pass at me, but we worked on some of our subjects together and shared duties as prefects. I told Ezra mainly because he was around on one or two occasions when the note was so slyly pushed into my fingers and I thought he'd seen the note and he was probably thinking that I was a bad girl.

I cried and I said: 'How could Sir do a thing like that? How could he? How could I learn from him when he did a thing like that? How could I?' Ezra did not know what to say or how to comfort me. It was all too much for him. He felt too embarrassed and just kept quiet and that made me wish that I had never told him.

The assistant principal taught us three subjects, and after those notes I could not learn from him, and I could tell neither my father nor our housemistress Mrs Mtshali. She was such a stern woman, much like my grandmother. She regularly inspected us girls. I, as prefect, had to help her strip them, and if she found anything wrong with one she would make her lie naked on the floor and beat her with a whip. It was a shameful thing to happen to a girl. If I told Mrs Mtshali about the notes she would say I had provoked the sin in the assistant principal's heart and she would make an object lesson of me, beating me naked on the floor, and for that to happen to me, a prefect! What a disgrace that would be! So I kept silent and was sorry that in my initial distress I had talked to Ezra, who I now felt was the last person for such confidences.

# CHAPTER 13

# Johannesburg

Winnie passed her matric in 1952, and her father, ambitious for her, considered sending her to Fort Hare. But a nephew, returned from that institution, had warned against it: 'There are too few girls there and the boys are always after them. It is not a place for a girl from our home.' So Kokani settled for the Jan Hofmeyr School of Social Work for his daughter, slaughtered a special beast for her well-being, and entrusted her to his farm manager who was going on business to a place near Johannesburg.

They counselled her closely about the big city. She was warned to beware of strangers; Johannesburg was full of *tsotsis* [hoodlums] who abducted young girls. Her grandmother, Makhulu, had wailed, 'Why does the child go at all, so much education already. Why doesn't she remain at home?' But Winnie was never intended to spend her life in her grandmother's world.

The man and girl travelled from Bizana to Kokstad by bus, and then took a train to Pietermaritzburg to board another for Johannesburg. But that train was not due to leave until the next day, so they spent the night in an empty coach, vacating it at dawn before they were discovered. They spent another night on the train, on the hard third-class benches, and in the morning Winnie awoke as Johannesburg approached. The old man told her that he would get off three stations ahead of her destination and then she would be alone. He repeated the terrifying warnings of her parents and told her that she should wait for Mrs Hough, who would come to fetch her, and under no circumstances was she to ask directions of strangers.

Winnie alighted from the train at Park Station on a January morning in 1953, an iron trunk on her head and a food basket in hand. Mrs Hough identified the rural school-girl in her black lace-up shoes and blazer, and soon had both trunk and girl deposited in her car and on the way to the Helping Hand Hostel.

Winnie relates her experiences at the hostel and as a social work student.


The other girls were smart, they used creams and powders and sweet smelling soaps. They went to bed in nightdresses and in the morning in dressing-gowns. I slept in my petticoat and slipped into my dress the moment I got out of bed. They unashamedly dressed and undressed in front of each other, and felt nothing about standing naked beneath the showers where others saw them. I was ashamed of being naked. Nobody saw me bath, and I was so secretive about my person that stories went around that there was something wrong with me. Had my room mate, Sarah Ludwick, not taken a hand and sorted me out I might not have lasted at Jan Hofmeyr. She was older and, or course, totally at home in Johannesburg. She introduced me to the brassiere, to sanitary pads and cosmetics, to nighties and pyjamas, high-heeled shoes and smart dresses.

Money of course was the problem. Part of it my family solved. My father had inherited a wattle farm from my grandfather. White traders came to buy the bark, and my sister Nonalithi attended to the business and sent me five pounds a month. She also sent me my first pretty dresses. I wrote and told her how unsuitable my clothes were and sent her some pictures cut out of the newspaper advertisements showing the current fashions. She bought suitable material from the local store and my cousin, our maternal aunt's daughter, Nomazotsho Malimba, who was a dressmaker, made this up for me. I was very proud of the dresses they sent me, especially as my roommate approved of them. But the money was not sufficient. Fortunately I was awarded the Martha Washington bursary. I also earned money babysitting for the Philippses, doing the washing for some teachers and cleaning the school windows.

Within months I burst out of my shell, and looked no different from the other students. I distinguished myself in sport, especially netball, shotput, javelin, softball. I had many nicknames. They called me 'Steady but Sure', 'Commando Round' (because of my round face), 'Pied Piper' because of my long nose, 'The Amazon Queen' and 'Lady Tarzan' because I solved problems the simple way, using physical force, as I had done way back in my childhood days when I had defended myself against older boys who came marauding into our mealie fields at harvest time.

I joined the Gamma Sigma Club and there met students from the Witwatersrand, St Peter's Seminary and the Wilberforce Training College. There was an old piano in the hall and students who could thumped away at it. I learnt to dance and joined the choir, and I attended NEUM meetings in an obscure hall in Doornfontein. My best friend there was the beautiful Pumla Finca who later did her master's degree in Sociology and who now lives in the States.

I realized just how I had changed in Johannesburg when one day our principal at Jan Hofmeyr, Dr Philipps, invited me to meet some visiting American professors over dinner. They had wanted to see a typical rural tribal girl, and I certainly fitted the definition. But one look at me and they showed their disappointment. They wanted to see 'a real native', as they put it, to photograph.

The school gave us a lot of practical experience. My first stint was in the Salvation Army Delinquent Girl's Home, Mthutuzeni. There was no such thing as a delinquent girl back home. Some of us were more spirited than others, but none had problems with their parents or had dared to live on their own. The very idea of doing something our parents might disapprove of set our hair on end. At first, the girls in the Home struck me as no different from those back in Bizana, but the difference became all too apparent in a short while. They came from broken families; some did not know their parents at all. There were those with an identity crisis, those who were confused, depressed or uncontrollably quarrelsome. I eventually got through to some of them, not through social work theory, but through sports.

My second assignment was in the Transkei at the Ncora Rural Centre in the district of Tsolo. I enjoyed that very much. I felt at home in my rural environment. I was excited at the time with what the centre was achieving in farming and in organizing communal markets *indali*. People brought their produce and bartered with each other.

I met the Matanzimas there. George Matanzima was very friendly and very hospitable. He already had a flourishing legal practice then and was a member of the ANC. People with problems came to see him and he helped the tribesmen in whatever way he could, never charging for such services. He had a car, the only person I knew who did, and was generous in sharing it with others. He was equally generous with his money and could be counted on to give it to good causes. The other lawyer in practice in the Transkei at the time was Letlaka, also a prominent ANC member, who later joined the PAC and went into exile, and was then brought back into the Transkei by Kaiser Matanzima when the Transkei became independent.

I attended tribal meetings for the first time. Women were excluded from these, but I qualified as a social worker. K. D. Matanzima was the chief of the Emmigrant Thembu and the meetings were held at his Great Place, Qamata, in a large hall that could accommodate a thousand people at a time. The hall was always full. The chief, lean, upright and aloof (Nelson to this day refers to him as The Cigarette), addressed the tribesmen. I was impressed by his oratory, but noted his rigid, dictatorial manner. He did not consult his tribesmen; there was no discussion at these meetings.

But my stay at Ncora was cut short. I heard that Chief Qaqauli was planning to *thwala* [abduct] me for his son who was studying at Fort Hare. The boy had never seen me, nor I him, but I had caught the chief's fancy as a daughter-in-law. I knew the custom. His tribesmen, white-blanketed Thembu, would ride over on their horses and await their chance to pounce on me and carry me away. I would then be locked up while the chief's son would be brought from college and the marriage would be forced on us. My father would be presented with the *fait accompli* and he would be forced to accept lobola.

Winnie had seen that happen to women back home, seen the desperation in the eyes of those new brides when they crawled out of the thatched huts after their incarceration to be received by the waiting, chanting women who smeared them with the bile of goats, dressed them in ankle-length German print dresses and, tying black *doeks* low on their foreheads, presented them to the kraals as the new *makotis*. She remembered the sister-in-law whom her brother had abducted. Winnie returned to Johannesburg rather than risk Chief Qaqauli's men and an ignoble fate.

*

Barney Sampson was dashing and debonair, all attention and good humour. Barney was fun and he knew all the fun places. They were soon going out together, to dances and parties, the cinema, to other social events. Barney was a clerk and a part-time student. He rented a room in a white back yard and appeared to spend most of his money on clothes. Winnie shared his love for clothes and the two young people would step out fashionably dressed.

Winnie could not have asked for a more devoted, more elegant companion. She relaxed in his company; he joked and made her laugh, and she enjoyed herself with him. But he did not go down well with her family. They questioned his name 'Sampson' and wondered about his family – issues that meant nothing to her. Practically the whole of 1957 saw them together. Perhaps if Nelson had not entered her life just then, she might have married Barney. But there was just as great a probability that she might not have, Nelson or no Nelson, for Barney, a marvellous escort and great fun, was practically non-political and politics, even then, were important to Winnie. What put her off about Barney was his obsequious manner when it came to white officials. There was an incident at the station buying tickets. Suddenly there was a blast of verbal abuse: 'You bloody kaffir, cheeky boy, throwing money at me!' Barney was cringingly apologetic. Winnie squirmed. He should have stood up to the false accusations, she thought.

Winnie's family attended her graduation ceremony. The representative from the Education Department presented the awards. She smiled radiantly and stretched out her hand to receive hers. He ignored her hand. Her smile disappeared and she withdrew her hand awkwardly. She had never felt so embarrassed in her life. For a moment she was distracted by the flashing of a bulb. She saw the man behind the camera who later introduced himself as Peter Mugubane and promised to send her some pictures. But for her, the day was spoilt.

Baragwanath Hospital created a post for the first medical social worker. Winnie started her career enthusiastically, without the slightest premonition that it would be short-lived. All too soon, she was inundated with cases; relatives had to be traced, funerals arranged, accident claims sorted – usually for injuries sustained at work.

In her first year, K. D. Matanzima visited the hospital and they brought him to talk to her about her work. Winnie reminded him that they had met before at Ncora. He appeared to have no recollection of that meeting, but was clearly charmed with the present one. He said he would welcome an opportunity to discuss further plans for Ncora. Winnie was flattered and, as good as his word, he sent a tribesman to fetch her the next day, so they could talk. She met him at No. 8115, Orlando, a house that within a year would become her own.

The chief's attentions to her continued and he eventually asked her to become his second or third wife. She declined. By then she had met Nelson. Winnie saw him passing by in his car with Diliza Mji and his wife, both medical students at the time, as she waited for the bus. Her hostel mate, Adelaide Tsukudu, who was going out with the equally famous Oliver Tambo, talked about Nelson incessantly. One day she met the three of them together, returning from a meeting or party. Adelaide stopped and introduced her companions to Winnie, who was dazzled by the bronze giant with his mop of thick hair, parted on the side, and a smile that affected her as nothing else had in her life.

She was soon seeing a lot of him. He invited her to use his office if she needed a quiet place for studying and took her to visit his friends. If Winnie had any doubts about his feelings for her, these were dispelled one night at the Bantu Men's Social Centre. They were attending a fund-raising ANC dance; suddenly knives were flashed and shots fired. Winnie ducked under a table; Nelson was beside her, dragging her out, leading her to his car. She saw in his concern for her safety that he loved her.

# CHAPTER 14

# The Wedding

Nelson was convinced in heart and mind that Winnie was the woman he wanted to marry. It became important to introduce her to his friends who were at the Drill Hall, where the preparatory examination of the Treason Trial was in progress. He arranged for Winnie to join them there just before the lunch recess.

The defence lawyer, Vernon Berrange, was on the floor cross-examining a witness when she arrived. Nelson saw her instantly and when the court adjourned was immediately at her side. He led her to the open quadrangle to meet some of his colleagues locked in a circle of conversation: Chief Luthuli, Professor Z. K. Matthews, Moses Kotane, Dr Naicker, Walter Sisulu and Ismail Meer. They were all charmed by her but in an aside Kotane said to Nelson, 'Such intimidating and seductive beauty does not go with a revolutionary!' Nelson laughed and turned to ask if Winnie had heard. She was looking at him, smiling expectantly, but when he repeated what had been said she flared up in anger. 'You have no sense of humour,' he chastised, and continued laughing.

Over the weekend he fetched her to visit his friends, the Bernsteins, in the white suburbs. Winnie found it all very new and exciting. She sat in the living room, demure and happy. The people were so relaxed, sipping wine and nibbling snacks. There was no sense of colour in that company; they were all just people together. Later they went into the back garden to watch rabbits in a hutch.

Nelson's divorce came through in 1957, and in 1958 he announced their marriage. He did not propose but took it for granted that they would marry. That was what the long courtship had been all about. Winnie told Barney Sampson, who took it badly. She was in Nelson's office when the hospital rang. Barney had taken an overdose of pills. Nelson rushed her to hospital where she spent a great deal of time with Barney and helped him to recover. She arranged for him to recuperate in Durban at the FOSA (Friends of the Sick Association) settlement where her sister was a nurse. Barney got over his disappointment and is happily married today.

In early 1958 Nelson told Winnie that she should go to Bizana to inform her parents of their intention to marry. They could then prepare for the men of his kraal to visit with a formal proposal. Early on a Friday morning Winnie set off with her uncle, Alfred Mgulwa, for Bizana. Her father was surprised but happy to see her. By Saturday evening she had not yet plucked up courage to broach the subject and she had to leave the next day. Her mother was preparing the tea tray to take to her father in the sitting room. Winnie produced a photograph of Nelson in his boxing gear. 'Ma,' she said, 'this man wants to marry me. I've come to get your approval because I also want to marry him. His name is Nelson Mandela.' Hilda caught her breath. 'I hope it is not the Mandela of the ANC. I hope it is only the name?' Winnie confirmed that it was the very man. Her mother called a child to take in the tea and then told Winnie she was mad, the man had a charge of treason hanging over his head. He would be in prison sooner or later. What life did she expect to lead with a man who was married to his politics? Why did she think his first marriage had failed? But when she saw that Winnie's only response was to gaze at the photographs, she realized that her counsel was falling on deaf ears, so she went to talk to Kokani. She returned after a while to say that he wanted to see her. Her father said he admired Nelson and would be the last man to stand in his way, but the road he had chosen was difficult and she was much too young and far too inexperienced to accompany him on it. She saw the great sadness on his face when he eventually accepted the situation and said, 'God be with you.'

Nelson sent his childhood friend and nephew, Chief Justice Mtirara, and Dr Wonga Mbekeni to arrange the lobola. Kokani slaughtered two fine beasts and beer flowed and meat sizzled as Madiba and Ngutyana clans joked and sang and heard each other's praises.

In Orlando they celebrated the engagement at Aunt Phyllis and Uncle Mzaidume's house. Aunt Phyllis spared nothing and the champagne flowed. Winnie was radiant in the light green gown Nelson had bought her. The engagement ring was slipped on and there was the usual applause and banter from ANC comrades, boxers and family members. The evening made the social columns in the Johannesburg *World*.

At the time of her engagement Winnie was living with Aunt Phyllis. Nelson decided that she should move in with his aunt, Nonqonqoloza Mtirara, so that she could become accustomed to his family. He was probably thinking of his mother's continuing unease at the turn of events. She had not quite reconciled herself to his divorce. She worried about the children who lived with Evelyn. She knew how confused they were over their parents' separation and feared that the divorce and the impending marriage would aggravate matters. Out of deference, mostly to the children's sensitivities, she had not involved herself in Nelson's new arrangements. But, once married, Winnie would live with her and the children would, she hoped, return to live with them too. Nelson thought that the time spent with his aunt would serve as a convenient transition into the family. Winnie obliged, though not without resistance.

The marraige was set for 14 June 1958. This was the first wedding in Kokani's house. There had been marriages before but never a wedding, for Kokani's other children had preferred to make their own arrangements which he had been forced to accept. In the case of Winnie it was different. She had consulted him and he was determined to spare nothing. Moreover, he was no longer a poor teacher, but a prosperous businessman. He had several shops and a fleet of buses, and his customers and tribespeople expected some share of this new prosperity. His daughter's wedding provided the appropriate opportunity.

Nelson applied for a relaxation of his banning order. He was given six days' leave of absence from Johannesburg, but was to confine himself to Bizana and strictly to the affairs of his marriage. He drove the bridal car which included the bridesmaids, his sister Leabie, Georgina Lekgoate and Helen Ngobese (now a medical practitioner).

Kokani had invited Aunt Phyllis to help with the social graces – YWCA women were considered to be specially adept. Aunt Phyllis took Aunt Mary with her to supervise the cooking in three-legged iron pots. Duma Nokwe, Scrape Ntshona, Lilian Ngoyi and Ruth Matseoane made up the rest of the party. Among the V.I.P's who attended were Chief Madikizela, Dr James Njongwe and his wife Connie, Drs Wilson Conco, Margaret Mgadi and Victor Tyamzashe, Attorneys G. Vabaza, Templeton Ntwasa and Toni. The most treasured piece of luggage was the wedding gown, white satin, loving sewn by Ray Harmel, Michael's wife. The Harmels were very close friends and among the small group of white political activists totally committed to the struggle for human rights.

Nelson recalls: 'The wedding party left Johannesburg at midnight on 12 June and reached Bizana the next day in the afternoon. As we were expected to reach the bride's place, Mbongweni, at dusk we spent some time at Dr Gordon Mabuya's place, where he and his wife, Nontobeko, entertained us.' But the journey was catastrophic for Winnie. Her excitement and nervousness brought on a fit of diarrhoea. Nelson had to stop the car four times while she, in embarrassment and pain, took to the bushes, protected by Aunt Phyllis's concern and sense of decorum.

They finally reached Mbongweni at the propitious time to be met by a great chorus of ululations led by Winnie's step-mother, Hilda. The groom was quickly separated from the bride, and with his party escorted to Simon Madikizela's house, which had been prepared for the *abekhwenyana* (groom's party).

Winnie's sisters and aunts fussed around her and put her to bed. Her cousins teased and Makhulu scolded them and said that Winnie had most surely been bewitched. Nelson discreetly sent his friend Dr Mabuya to examine her. Winnie's malady continued for two full days, and was subdued only after the wise ministering of Makhulu. And for those two days, and up to the time that the bride was conducted to the altar, Nelson was placed out of bounds by the elder Madikizela women.

The wedding day alternated between the sombre proceedings of church and the riotous dancing of Makhulu. It began for Winnie, with the bridal ablutions in a large iron bath filled with warm water. Aunt Phyllis helped her with her toiletry, and at last she slipped into her wedding gown. Relatives waiting in *inkundla* leapt into a joyous dance as she stepped out into the morning sun. Makhulu's shrill ululations led the chorus.

The Madikizela kraal was black with the horses of the tribesmen. They tied these up and boarded the buses to travel out to the church, twenty kilometres away at Ludeke mission. The bridal car was bedecked with ANC colours. Kokani went ahead and waited for the bride at the church door in his new black suit, carnation in lapel. The father led the bride up the aisle and heads turned to look at them. The small page boy stumbled but quickly regained his step and his minute companion remained demure. The choir sang 'Lizalise Idinga Lakho', a hymn the Reverend Tiyo Sogo had composed on sighting Table Bay after years of study in Britain. The wedding ring was slipped on Winnie's finger, the Reverend Madikiza pronounced them man and wife, and the choir joyously sang a Xhosa hymn. The Reverend Gadama, in tribal skins, intoned the rites of the *imbongi* (praise-singer) and rang out the praises of both lineages.

The wedding party drove to the Madikizela ancestral home, occupied at the time by the eldest son, Mpumelelo, and proceeded to the burial ground near the cattle kraal. There they abandoned themselves to dancing, singing and merrymaking.

Nelson presented headcloths to the elder Madikizela women, and each danced up to him to receive the gift and ululated her appreciation. Then the bride's retinue walked round and round the Madikizela kraal in demonstration of the virginal purity of their daughter – the young women leading, the older ones following. Nelson and his retinue made a parallel chain. The hoary-headed Makhulu leapt in what seemed to be a final tribute to life and fertility, sweat trickling down her cheeks and nose. Winnie burst out laughing just when the mood changed and her kinsmen sang of the sadness of their parting with her: '*Baya Khala Abazali*' (your Relations are crying). It was the signal for the bride to wail and cry. Nikiwe nudged her. The bride was indecently happy, and here she was leaving her ancestral home. 'Pretend to cry,' Nikiwe exhorted. 'Wipe your eyes, look down!' But how *could* Winnie? The sight of Makhulu, her large breasts bouncing, her mouth raised skywards in ululation was too much for her. Nelson was laughing and Winnie was convulsed. Her sister-in-law quipped, 'How can she cry?' she has found a prince.' Nelson had caught up with Winnie and was claiming her to lead her to his people. Aunt Phyllis lifted the bride's veil; frank, laughing eyes met the grooms. 'Look down, look down!' Nikiwe urged again. 'A bride does not look at her in-laws like that!' But Winnie's joy was too full for any simulated embarrassment.

In all the excitement the groom's party was caught off guard by the Madikizela men and Duma Nokwe was ceremoniously kidnapped. They demanded their traditional ransom. Kokani paid a goat, but Duma owed them an ox that was never paid.

Bridal party and guests settled down to dinner, served from the large three-legged pots near the cattle kraal: *umnggusho* (samp with beans) and the many salads that the women had prepared under the supervision of Aunt Phyllis.

In the late afternoon the great company travelled to Bizana where the town hall had been hired for the first time to an African. Scrape Ntshona banged out the wedding march. Bride and groom obliged and walked to it. The speeches followed and Kokani's was everything the occasion demanded: admiration of Nelson for his commitment to the country, love for his daughter, deep foreboding for the future. 'This marriage will be no bed of roses; it is threatened from all sides and only the deepest love will preserve it' and advice to his daughter, 'Be like your husband, become like his people, and as one with them. If they be witches, become one with them.' Nurse Nozipho Mbekeni, sister to Wonga, responded on behalf of the groom in an equally impressive speech.

The cake was cut, thirteen tiers into as many pieces as there were guests; the fourteenth left intact, and wrapped up carefully, for the bride to take to the ancestral home of her groom in Thembuland. Nelson never managed to take Winnie there and so the fourteenth tier remains in its wrapping to this day, awaiting Nelson's release to complete the last wedding rite.

After five days of feasting, bride and groom took their leave so that Nelson could comply with his banning requirements and return to Johannesburg in time. Kokani led his daughter and son-in-law to the hut where he had stored their presents: grass mats, clay pots, small animals and poultry – all alive and kicking. Nelson declined the gifts for, after all, they had been given in recognition of the Madikizelas. But he did accept two fowls as a gesture. He wished later that he had not bothered for the fowls ran out into the veld when they stopped for a picnic lunch. Bride and groom found themselves chasing after them until they knocked into each other and fell laughing. They left the fowls to their dubious freedom and proceeded homeward.

The sun had not yet set when they reached Orlando and the time was therefore not propitious, according to tradition, for them to start their new married life. So they drove to Lillian Ngoyi's house and waited until dusk set in. They then drove to house No. 8115, where Nelson's mother and a large party of friends and relatives welcomed them and they settled down to yet another feast.

A few weeks later the Madiba tribesmen arrived and Winnie was officially and ceremoniously admitted into the tribe and given the name Nobandla.

# CHAPTER 15

# The Mandela Routine

The new bride settled into the Mandela home. There was much in it that displeased her, but she left untouched the small study Nelson had partitioned off from the front room. It was warm with his personality – a bookshelf, a display cabinet, three cane chairs, a couch against the wall and, dominating it all, a picture of the bearded Lenin, prophet-like, addressing a huge crowd.

The household rose early. Nelson was up at 4 a.m. and started his day with an early morning sprint. He liked the emptiness of the streets and the half-light just before doors burst open and people poured out to queue for buses that would take them to work. He breakfasted on orange juice and toast, at times a raw egg and a small portion of porridge.

Makhulu remained at home with her grandchildren, including those who had come from the Transkei. Nelson, Winnie and Leabie set off to take the bus; Winnie to the hospital, Leabie to the Orlando Children's Home and Nelson for the trial in Pretoria.

Nelson's day was taken up by the court, so he spent the evenings, and late nights, attending to his legal practice and ANC work. As a result he usually returned home when the clock had started counting in the new day; in addition, he rarely spent weekends with the family.

Nelson was a lavish spender. He had a permit to keep drinks in the house (all 'non-Europeans' had to have these permits in those days) and though he did not drink himself, he saw to it that his guests never went dry. His grocery purchases were exotic; he liked experimenting with food.

The year 1958 was one of the leanest that the Mandelas

faced. The trial dragged on. The routine never changed: waiting for the buses that took the women to work and Nelson to the trial in Pretoria; the long dreary hours of court submissions. It had gone on for three years. The office rent was too high and the practice was crumbling. There was hardly an income to talk about, the family was growing and needs escalating.

Evelyn was not happy about her sons' education; schooling was a problem in Johannesburg as the education was poor. She discussed the matter with K. D. Matanzima during one of his visits and he suggested that she send the boys to school in the Transkei and he would keep an eye on them. Evelyn asked K.D. to discuss the matter with Nelson, which he did. Nelson wholly approved. The rural environment and discipline at the mission boarding school would be good for the boys. He took his sons shopping, fitted them out smartly and gave them over to Matanzima. However, when he later heard that his youngest son, Makgatho was ill in the Transkei, he broke his ban and drove down there to fetch him. Nelson respected his ban up to a point but he was not prepared to police himself. Long trips, however, were tiring: he had to travel by night to return in time to appear in court and to sign the weekly register at the police station, as he was forced to do in terms of his banning order.

The marathon treason trial was in its fourth stage. In January 1958 the indictment against sixty-one of the accused was quashed. Thirty-one still remained charged, and Nelson, Walter, Lillian Ngoyi and Helen Joseph were among these. Nelson grew close to Helen during this period. He knew he could depend upon her; in his years of incarceration, he would find her a pillar of strength to his family.

In July 1958 Winnie found that she was pregnant. By October 1958 Johannesburg's women were in a ferment of protest against passes. They organized a deputation to the office of the Native Commissioner. Winnie, a member of the Orlando West branch of the ANC Women's League, was among those elected to the deputation. They began their march to the Commissioner's office. Within hours they were surrounded by the police, packed into police vans, whisked off to Marshall Square and locked up in police cells. Their spirits, if anything, were heightened by the arrests, their sense of fraternity strengthened. They sang and were glad to be with each other. Later in the day they were removed to the Fort, where they found hundreds more of their fellow resisters milling in the main hall and on the balcony of the second-floor cells. They greeted their arrival with ululations and shouts of *Amandla!* (power!). The warders lined them up, stripped them to their skins, ordered them to squat and to spread their thighs wide apart for vaginal examinations in search of contraband items. Then they were ordered to dress and sent into their cells.

Nelson came to see Winnie as soon as he heard of the arrests, and could obtain permission. There was little time for personal exchanges. He told her that they were arranging legal representation for the women and that he was proud of her.

In prison Winnie clung to Albertina Sisulu as she was afraid on account of her pregnancy. Albertina was older, more experienced and, above all, a nurse. Winnie spread out her mat next to Albertina's and was reassured by her knowledge, her competence and warmth. In the second week Winnie began bleeding but Albertina allayed her anxiety. The bleeding stopped.

As the numbers of arrested women swelled, so the conditions in the prison deteriorated. There was the terrible stink from the sanitary buckets. In the morning they were obliged to eat their breakfast in the foul air and the queue for the shower was endless. At the end of the third week there were 2,000 prisoners and not enough floor space to bed them at night.

A large contingent was then herded under heavy police guard, and after dark, through the back gate into a basement cell in the men's section. In the morning they were moved out before six and returned to the women's section.

The women were eventually brought to court, tried, found guilty and offered the option of imprisonment or a fine. The ANC paid their fines and the prisoners were released.

The hospital gave Winnie notice terminating her services. Earnings dwindled but friends helped and her father sent a welcome sum.

Just past midnight on 4 February 1959, Nelson arrived home after a meeting to find Winnie alone and in great pain. His mother had returned to the Transkei and Leabie was at the hospital as a trainee nurse. He fetched Aunt Phyllis and together they rushed the expectant mother to hospital in the early hours of the morning. They were told that it would be quite some time before the baby would be born and were advised to leave.

Nelson went on to Pretoria for the trial. He returned to the hospital towards evening with Duma Nokwe to welcome his new daughter. He held the yellow mite with a mop of black hair and announced that she was a true Mandela and a princess. Chief Mdingi named her *Zenani* (what have you brought) and the Madikizela's gave her *Nomadabi* (battles) and *Nosizwe* (of the nation).

Two days later Nelson brought a beautiful layette for Zenani and a week afterwards he arrived with a huge bag filled with the prettiest of nighties for Winnie.

Makhulu returned from the Transkei to help with the baby, and when Winnie arrived home she was welcomed by two matriarchs, Nelson's mother and Walter Sisulu's. They fussed over the *mdlezana* (feeding mother) and the baby. To Winnie's horror they called in *inyanga* to strengthen the baby with a herbal bath. Winnie wasn't having any of it. Such care had been taken of the baby all these days; she had been meticulously protected against infection. Now they wanted her dipped in germs. Her mother-in-law pointed out that all her grandchildren had had the traditional bath and that they were the picture of health. She pointed to Maki and Makgatho who hovered affectionately around the baby. But not only did the *mdlezana* remain unconvinced about the baby bath, she also blankly refused to drink the herbal tea they had prepared for her. Instead she proceeded to consume all the wrong foods, as they saw it – coffee and eggs – things they thought would dry up her milk.

Years later, the baby grown into a woman, and a mother herself, Zenani sent her father a photograph of her baby, Zaziwe, he responded:

Zazi's picture at once reminded me of you shortly after you and your mum returned from Bara Maternity wards in Feb '59. You'd be fast asleep even as she bathed, dried, smeared you with olive oil, turned your skin white with Johnson's baby powder and stuffed your little belly with shark oil. It's family photos, letters and visits that keep on reminding me of the happy days when we were together, that make life sweet, and that fill the heart with hope and expectation. Thanks a million, darling!

Nelson undertook to teach Winnie to drive, but soon realized his mistake. They had arguments all the time. Winnie kept making the same mistake, and as he saw it continued to ignore his directions. A man teaching a woman to drive on an Orlando road, especially a husband and wife, is a rare sight and bound to attract a crowd; when the husband is the famous Mandela, the interest is compounded. The lessons proceeded amid exuberant calls of *Amandla*, but when the car 'stalled' and exposed the famous couple in an obvious quarrel, the youth, out of respect, melted away. Nelson stormed out of the car, banging the door behind him. He went home, stripped to his shorts and punched out his anger on the boxing-bag. That is how Winnie found him when she returned an hour later. They ignored each other for a while. He showered and lay down on the bed. She came over to massage him and the quarrel was over. He fetched the car and they went to visit their friends, Ismail Matlhaku and his wife, Martha, who ran a high-class shebeen. They gave themselves up to sensuous enjoyment in the luxury of deep pile and velvet drapes and converted the afternoon's 'tragedy' into an evening's comedy as they laughed over the driving lesson.

Winnie had vowed never to lose her individuality when she married, but to remain her own person. But Madiba, as she called him, was overpowering.

In the little time I spent with him, I discovered only too soon how quickly I would lose my identity because of his overpowering personality – you just fizzled into being his appendage, with no name and no individuality except Mandela's: Mandela's wife, Mandela's child, Mandela's niece. Thriving in his glory was the simplest cocoon to shield in from the glaring public, or to boost your extinct ego. I vowed that none of this would apply to me.

Winnie needed to work. Nelson understood that and when the Johannesburg Child Welfare had a vacancy for a social worker, Winnie applied for the job and got it. Zenani was then five months old and Winnie left her in Makhulu's care. Winnie wanted above all to return to university but they could not afford the fees. She applied for a bursary and was interviewed by Fred van Wyk and Ellen Hellman of the Institute of Race Relations, but they turned her down. Ellen Hellman said that Winnie, who earned R44.00 per month, at the time, was earning more than graduates and did not really need a second cheque. Their attitude infuriated Winnie.

Within months of Zenani's birth, Winnie was pregnant again, but the pregnancy did not go well. Winnie began to bleed. Fortunately Nelson was home and he rushed her to his friend, Dr Mohamed Abdullah, who was living at the time in the Coloured township of Albertsville. Winnie miscarried virtually at his door. The Abdullahs were all concern and medical attention. They kept Winnie at their home and nursed her overnight, allowing her to leave only when she had recovered sufficiently to be hospitalized.

A few months later Winnie was pregnant again, but this time she was stronger and happier.

PART IV

# LIFE-SENTENCE

# CHAPTER 16

# Sharpeville

The year 1959 had opened ominously with a white parliament headed by the father of apartheid, Dr Verwoerd, who proceeded to convert the reserves into Bantustans and cut them off from the developed South African sector. It also saw a split in the official opposition and the emergence of the Progressive Party which stretched out a hand to the ANC, not in alliance but in negotiation and understanding. The Black Sash women's organization added a further component, small but effective, to the anti-apartheid white contingent of churchmen, liberals and socialists.

The emboldened government prepared for violence. Patrick Duncan, a Liberal Party member, reported in *Contact* that the Minister of Defence had told his army officers, 'You must not think we are arming against an external army. We are arming in order to shoot down the black masses' (26.12.59). That year Britain delivered eighty Saracens to the South African military.

In Windhoek police opened fire on a crowd resisting removals and killed fourteen people. It was the beginning of the massacre that would follow a few months later at Sharpeville and that would direct the ANC on a new course, and Nelson to his historic prison sentence.

While the state violated black life, the law courts continued the Treason Trial. The prosecution alleged and the judges questioned whether violence was not in fact the ANC's intent. Nelson listened to the evidence of Chief Albert Luthuli. The prosecutor was trying his level best to establish the ANC as a violent organization. He read out a statement allegedly made by Robert Resha: 'If you are a true volunteer and you are called upon to be violent, you must be absolutely violent. You must murder, murder. That is all.'

*Prosecutor:* I put it to you, Mr Luthuli, that Resha made this speech and he gave these instructions to the volunteers because that was exactly what volunteers were expected to do? And you know that?

*Luthuli:* I don't. Because Resha would be expected to lead the volunteers along the policy of Congress. Now if Resha as a general departs, he departs as Resha. It has nothing to do with the policy of the African National Congress, definitely.

*Prosecutor:* Mr Luthuli, negotiation was never contemplated, and you knew that?

*Luthuli:* It has been all along anticipated. My Lord, even at this moment, we would be very, very happy if the government would take up the attitude of saying, come let us discuss. We would be extremely happy in fact even to discuss, even if at the end of the discussions we didn't agree.

*Prosecutor:* It is sheer hypocrisy to make a statement like that and you know it. That was never your attitude.

The prosecutor's examination of Nelson was as follows:

*Prosecutor:* Now what I want to put to you is this: do you think that your people's democracy could be achieved by a process of gradual reforms? Suppose as a result of pressure, the ruling class were to agree next month to a qualified franchise for the Africans, an educational test perhaps . . ., and the next year, as a result of further pressure, a more important concession is made; a further concession is made in 1962 and so on, over a period of ten or twenty years; do you think that the people's democracy could be achieved in that fashion?

*Mandela:* We demand universal adult franchise and we are prepared to exert economic pressure to attain our demands, and we will launch defiance campaigns, stay at homes, either singly or together. If the Government should say, 'Gentlemen, we can't have this state of affairs, laws being defined, and this whole situation created by stay at homes. Let's talk.' In my own view I would say, 'Yes, let us talk,' and if the Government said, 'We think that the Europeans at present are not ready for a type of government where there might be domination by non-Europeans, we think we should give you sixty seats, the African population to elect sixty Africans to represent them in parliament; we will leave the matter over for five years and we will review it at the end of five years.' In my view, that would be a victory, my Lords; we would have taken a significant step towards the attainment of universal adult suffrage for Africans, and we would then for the five years say, suspend civil disobedience, we won't have any stay at homes, and we will then devote the intervening period for the purpose of educating the country, the Europeans, to see that these changes can be brought about and that it would bring about better racial understanding, better racial harmony in the country. I'd say we should accept it, but of course, I would not abandon the demands for the extension of the universal franchise to all Africans. That's how I see it, my Lords. Then at the end of the five-year period we will have discussions and if the government says, 'We will give you again forty more seats,' I might say that that is quite sufficient. Let's accept it and still demand that the franchise should be extended, but for the agreement period we should suspend civil disobedience; no stay at homes. In that way we would eventually be able to get everything that we want; we shall have our people's democracy, my Lords. That is the view I hold – whether that is Congress's view I don't know, but that is my view.

The judge then asked him what he would do if the Government did not 'soften in its views'.

*Mandela:* I don't think that the Congress has ever believed that its policy of pressure would ultimately fail ... the Congress expects that over a period, as a result of these pressures, together with world opinion, that the Government notwithstanding its attitude of ruling Africans with an iron hand, the methods which we are using will bring about a realization of our aspirations.

*Prosecutor:* ... is it not ... that the African National Congress held the view, and propagated the view, that in resisting pressure by the Congress, that the ruling class, the Government, would not hesitate to retaliate – would not hesitate to use violence and armed force against the Congress next?

*Mandela:* Yes, the Congress was of that view, my Lords. We did expect force to be used, as far as the Government is concerned, but as far as we are concerned we took the precautions to ensure that violence will not come from our side.

Nelson emphasized that in organizing 'stay-at-homes', pickets were never used, as in strikes, to avoid police provocation.

*Prosecutor:* As far as you know, has the liberation movement continued to manifest itself?

*Mandela:* Yes, it has. Congress has become much more powerful and much more strong today.

*Prosecutor:* And in your opinion is the possibility of this violence to which you refer therefore heightened – increased?

*Mandela:* Oh yes; we feel that the Government will not hesitate to massacre hundreds of Africans in order to intimidate them not to oppose its reactionary policy.

*Judge:* I want to know whether the Congress Alliance discussed or considered whether white supremacy in South Africa would, without a show of arms, surrender that which if surrendered would mean its end?

*Mandela:* The Congress considered . . . the whites being eager to retain political power exclusively for themselves . . .

*Judge:* Was that considered?

*Mandela:* That was considered. It was also considered that through this policy of exerting pressure we will force the whites by using our numbers, our numbered preponderance, in forcing them to grant us what we demand, even against their will. We considered that, and we felt that that was possible.

*Judge:* How would you use your numbers to force white supremacy to give what you want?

*Mandela:* For example by staying at home and not going to work, using our economic power for the purpose of attaining our demands against the wall of prejudice and hostility which we encountered, that they can never remain indifferent indefinitely to our demands because we are hitting them in the stomach with our policy of economic pressure. It is a method which is well organized.

138

While the charade of debate continued in the courthouse, the country outside headed for its worst crisis.

The year 1960 consolidated the parting of the ways between black and white in a way that no single year has done in the history of South Africa. Sharpeville brought to a head black agony and white tyranny. For Nelson it encapsulated his life. Sharpeville was the beginning of the end of his personal, physical freedom in the country. He was still making daily trips to Pretoria to sit before the judges. He had closed his office in Chancellor House, Fox Street – he couldn't meet the rent – and was operating some sort of practice from a fellow attorney's office. He had a large household of dependants and massive family responsibilities, but the massacre at Sharpeville subordinated everything else in his life.

The months preceding Sharpeville saw a deepening of apartheid and the prospects of defeating it becoming all that more difficult. The new law, ironically named the Extension of University Education Act (1959), excluded blacks from 'white' universities and proposed special tribal and racial colleges. It was an extension of Bantu Education into the universities. What additional detrimental effect would this have on future youth, Nelson wondered.

There was racial discrimination at Wits, his university. Black people could not swim in the beautiful pool opposite the library, they could not attend any socials, or take part in any sport, and there was very limited, segregated hostel accommodation for Africans; but in the lecture room and the library there was integration and Nelson considered this important.

In 1959 thoughts focused strongly on using black economic power to coerce change. Messages in this respect kept coming from the rank and file.

Nelson's observation that the people were growing impatient with ANC strategy strengthened. They were in the third year of the Treason Trial. For all that time, the Government had held key activists hostage in court, forcing them to listen to a selected record of their past activities while they remained shackled from direct action in the present. The people were resorting more and more to spontaneous and localized action: the women's protest against passes was the most explosive and extensive indication. It was as if they were putting the ANC to shame for its lack of militancy. The reports of infuriated women storming police stations and Native Commissioner's offices came flooding in. In Natal alone, 2,000 women had been arrested. They had caused astronomical damage to beer halls and in Cato Manor such fury had been aroused during a beer raid that nine policemen had been killed.

The Eastern Cape branch of the ANC initiated a boycott against Rembrandt Tobacco. Nelson felt that it was time to coordinate anti-apartheid activities. A National Anti-Pass Planning Council set up in 1958 had recommended the use of economic power: industrial action and strikes. It calculated that the African people had a purchasing power of £400m per annum and if this was withdrawn the whites would be hurt where it mattered most. The report was read at the Mass National Conference in Johannesburg on 30–31 May, and there followed a call for a boycott of potatoes in protest against the sub-human treatment of African farm labourers. The proposal received unanimous support. But Nelson continued to have the feeling that they were not going fast enough, that the people were wanting to go further, that either the 'leaders' had a higher level of tolerance for apartheid or that the 'leaders' were unfamiliar with the true depths of the people's suffering. He grew more and more convinced that the existing ANC structure did not allow for sufficient participation, that they were misguidedly concentrating on organizing people rather than on consulting them. Street-based cells, he believed, would intensify consultation and strengthen commitment. These would at the same time lay the basis for an underground network in the event that the ANC was banned. He had a premonition that this was about to happen.

Others felt that the organization was not sufficiently strong at the centre, that too much power was dissipated at provincial levels. Nelson saw a measure of truth in that criticism as well. Looked at any way the ANC was in need of overhauling.

The last legal ANC conference in the country opened with a massive attendance of 8,000 at the Curries Fountain sports ground in Durban. The conference declared 31 March 1960 as anti-pass day, and planned mass deputations to Bantu Commissioners' offices throughout the country. In 1952 they had announced defiance, now it was deputations! Nelson felt they were moving backwards. How could they move forward, what resources could they muster? What strategies, what energy remained untapped?

The PAC, in the first flush of its new dawn, entered the fray with messianic zeal. It announced: 'In 1960 we take our first step, in 1963 our last, towards freedom and independence.' Unrealistic or not, the PAC was casting a spell in some regions, even beyond the expectations of the zealots. Nelson thought that foolishly they were giving themselves just three years to end apartheid.

At its founding convention, the PAC set itself a target of 100,000 members within a year. At the first and only conference it held in South Africa, in April 1959, it claimed 24,664 members and 101 branches. Almost half the claimed support was in the Transvaal and half in the Cape. If the figures could be relied on, then it was a tremendous achievement.

Nelson shuddered at the crude racist statements made by some of the PAC members, but hardly believed that they suffered from real racism and that deep down their desire for African exclusivism was fuelled by the horrendous inferiority of Africans in the country; one could not throw the sentiments of an Africanist into the same basket as those of an Afrikaner nationalist. He sympathized with the aspirations of PAC intellectuals for an African destiny, for an African unity that embraced the entire continent from Cape to Cairo, Madagascar to Morocco. But how practical was Pan-Africanism, and to what extent was it an unattainable ideal: good to hold, but unwise to bank upon?

His deepest problem with the PAC was its denial of the

rights of minorities under the subterfuge of the 'one nation' ideal. The Manifesto of the Africanist Movement stated:

The African people will not tolerate the existence of other national groups within the confines of one nation. For the healthy growth and development of the African nation it is imperative that all individuals must owe their first, and only, loyalty to the African nation, and not to their ethnic or national groups ... Within the social limit of the African nation there will be room for all individuals who identify themselves nationally, intellectually and spiritually with the African nation. *

This struck him as empty rhetoric and an evasion of the abounding South African reality that they had all been raised in racism, and injected with a racist mentality, and this necessitated the guaranteeing of minority rights as a prelude, at least, to a non-racial democracy.

Besides, there were deep-rooted historical identities that could not be denied; after all, what was the first experience of human solidarity but in the family, in the clan, in the tribe? These constituted real identities, the nurseries for larger solidarities, for Pan-Africanism, and they were ethnic identities. It was co-existence on the basis of equality.

One could neither wish away race, nor wish in liberation. The PAC behaved as if that was all one had to do and it would happen. Nelson considered the PAC campaign ill-conceived and rather competitive. It sought to rush in where the ANC, with its generations-deep experience and wide-ranging support, feared to tread. Instead of working with the ANC against passes, the PAC sought to pre-empt the ANC call by ten days. It invited the ANC to join the PAC, an arrogant and irritating gesture. But it was not the arrogance that prompted the ANC to reject the invitation; they recoiled against the irresponsible and unreal mood of the PAC campaign.

Nelson had always admired Robert Sobukwe: his integrity, incisive intellect and eloquent oratory. But his new messianic stance, his apparent belief that all he had to say was 'follow',

* Carter and Karis, op. cit., p. 521.

and that the people would do so and passes disappear, was flabbergasting.

But Sobukwe was drawing support. In Cape Town 2,000 gathered at Langa to hear him detail PAC targets: initially, the abolition of passes and a minimum wage, not of £20 a month as the ANC Alliance had demanded a few years back, but £35. Sobukwe's instructions to his followers were read out at all meetings.

The African people have entrusted their whole future to us, and we have shown that we are leading them not to death, but to life abundant. The only people who will benefit from violence are the government and the police. Immediately violence breaks out we will be taken up with it and give vent to our pent-up emotions and feel that by throwing stones at a bar-room or burning a particular building we are small revolutionaries engaged in revolutionary warfare. But after a few days, when we have buried our dead and made moving graveside speeches and our emotions have settled again, the police will round up a few people and the rest will go back to the passes, having forgotten what our goal had been initially. Incidentally, in the process we shall have alienated the masses who will feel that we have made cannon fodder of them, for no significant purpose except for spectacular newspaper headlines ... We are taking our first step in the march to African independence and the United States of Africa. And we are not leading corpses to the new Africa. We are leading the vital breathing and dynamic youth of our land. We are leading that youth, not to death, but to life abundant. Let us get that clear.

Yet within weeks this man of peace would lead the youth to the very death he sought to avert, because violence, as Nelson so well knew, was the only response the government would make to Sobukwe's non-violence. In time to come to justify State violence the Government would hold in its courts of law that non-violence was in effect violence.

Nelson marvelled at Sobukwe's intense Gandhian tone in *Contact*, 16 April 1960:

We are not going to fight or attempt to fight, insult or attempt to insult, provoke or attempt to provoke the police in their lawful duties. We are not going to throw stones at the police or do anything that is going to obstruct the police . . . nobody is carrying money, knives or any dangerous weapons with himself tomorrow.

We have the continent on our side. We have history on our side. We will win.

To the people, Sobukwe announced:

I, myself, Mangaliso Sobukwe, or one of the PAC leaders, acting on my behalf will call off the struggle, after our demands have been fully met.

Fellow Africans, the hour for service, sacrifice and suffering has come. Let us march in unison to the United States of Africa.

Nelson was amazed at Sobukwe's expectation that all he had to do to avert violence was to be non-violent himself. He found it ironic that while purporting to be African, the campaign had all the aspects of an Indian passive resistance struggle, even to the extent of informing the authorities of intentions.

Sobukwe wrote to the Commissioner of Police notifying him that the campaign would begin on 21 March, that he had instructed the African people not to be provoked to violence, and requesting the Commissioner to instruct his men similarly. He then began a rather lonely four-mile march from his home in Mafolo to the Orlando police station. It appeared to be a case of a prophet having no honour on his home patch but on the way he was joined by 150 followers, including Leballo. They reached the police station and announced to the official in charge that they did not have their passes on their persons. They defied the police to arrest them, which they did.

There were no demonstrations in Natal or in the Eastern Cape, but the situations in Vereeniging, some forty miles from Johannesburg, and in Cape Town, were explosive.

Resistance had continued in the Vereeniging region since the bus boycott. The townships, neglected by the ANC and picked up by the NEUM and now PAC, had deteriorated into unspeakable poverty and disease through government policy. The people responded easily to the simple call to leave their passes at home and surrender to the police. What could they lose? And maybe, just maybe, some miracle could

144

happen. The PAC pickets efficiently directed those who came to the bus stops to the police stations. By 10 a.m. there were 4,000 demonstrators in Vanderbijlpark, 20,000 in Evaton, 5,000 in Sharpeville.

In Cape Town the Africans suffered more than any other African from influx control. Reputedly the most liberal city, it was the least tolerant of a permanent African population. The colonizers had bred their own Coloured labour force and did not require Africans. As a Coloured preferential labour area, Africans were, as far as possible, to be excluded from Cape Town. Thus, where other cities provided some housing for Africans and tolerated a measure of family life in segregated townships, Cape Town provided practically no family housing. Langa, established in 1927, was populated essentially by male migrant workers and Nyanga was an emergency squatter community started in 1956. But poverty in the rural areas compelled work-seekers to go to the mother city. The authorities expelled as many people as they could and then pretended that the thousands who escaped their net were, in fact, not there; they totally ignored their existence. By 1960 residents of both townships had almost reached the end of their tether and were ripe for mobilization. To aggravate matters, there was wholesale repatriation of Africans considered to be illegally in the townships and large-scale curbs on male immigrants seeking work.

The PAC, under the leadership of university students, Philip Kgosana and Nana Mahomo, had recruited 1,000 members by the end of 1958 and established a number of branches. It had also developed a good working relationship with the local Liberal Party, particularly with Patrick Duncan and his *Contact* journal group. The two groups shared a deep antipathy to Communism and by extension to the ANC because of its alliance with the COD.

On the morning of 21 March almost 2,000 people responded to the PAC call. They marched to Philippi police station and declared that they did not have passes. 'Arrest us!' they demanded. Their names were recorded and they were told to come to court.

In the Vereeniging complex the State showed signs of losing its nerve. Police reinforcements poured in, aircraft hovered above the protestors, and in Sharpeville the State unleashed one of its most brutal attacks in the history of the country. The police opened fire on the peaceful demonstrators and within minutes left sixty-nine dead, shot mostly from the back, and 180 wounded. In Cape Town people had continued to gather throughout the day. By evening there was a gathering of 10,000 at Langa. A heavy police contingent moved in and baton-charged the crowd. Two people were left dead. Incensed groups armed themselves with whatever they could find and attacked government property and any non-African on sight.

Nelson was devastated as the reports came pouring in. What could he do? What could they do? It was as if every one of the sixty-nine dead were his close friend or relative. They were his people, his flesh and blood, fellow South Africans murdered by a brutal Government. The Sharpeville massacre left him trembling and sick. He faced his comrades in grim silence. This wasn't a time to say 'I told you so' to the PAC. Something had to be done.

The world was horrified by the massacre. In South Africa the situation was getting out of control: there was panic as prices on the stock exchange began falling and fear about the country's cash flow. White civilians rushed around buying guns, and artillery training centres sprang up overnight. Commerce and industry, fearful for their survival, called for reforms, but the Verwoerdian Government was the toughest the Nationalists would produce. It was convinced it could ride the tiger.

Chief Luthuli announced that 28 March would be a day of mourning. The people would stay at home and burn their passes.

From his cell Sobukwe supported the call, albeit somewhat ambivalently: 'We are not opposed to Luthuli's strike call. We go further. We say the people must stay away forever!'

In Cape Town it seemed that this was already happening. African workers had begun a stay-away on 22 March, follow-

146

ing the Sharpeville shootings. By 28 March the country had responded as one to the Chief's call and there was a 100 per cent stay-away of workers; Langa and Nyanga were on their sixth day of strike action. The PAC had taken virtual control of the two townships, and was organizing massive relief. The people were inundated with material support, mainly of food, from a large range of organizations, regardless of political affiliation: Brian Bunting from *New Age* moved in supplies but Patrick Duncan's *Contact* group was the crucial life-line. With commerce and industry almost paralysed, the PAC had achieved a certain leverage, pass arrests were temporarily suspended, food supplies were allowed into the townships and the people were allowed to bury their dead without interference.

Nelson fetched Duma and the Chief on the evening of 28 March and in Orlando, watched by hundreds, the three burnt their passes. As they did so, thousands of bonfires of passes were lit throughout the township. The youth surged into the streets singing, 'Thina Silulutsha (We are the Youth), you will not kill us,' and attacked telegraph poles with their radio reception boxes thought to communicate government propaganda.

On 30 March the government declared a state of emergency throughout the country and followed this with mass arrests. Before the sun cast its first rays there was a hammering on the door of the Mandela home reminiscent of the pre-dawn treason swoop. Armed police surrounded the house and forced entry, pushing family members against the walls as they took up floor space. They searched the house, looked through books on the shelves and took whatever they considered 'dangerous'. When they had all they wanted, they told Nelson to pack his bag and accompany them. Winnie looked on with a mixture of fear and anger. It was her initiation to the police raid, about to become a chronic feature of her life.

Nelson was driven to Newlands police station where he was detained, among others, with Walter, Duma and Robert Resha. There were more detainees at the Fort. About a fortnight later they were all transferred to Pretoria prison.

They followed events outside the prison walls as best they could. They heard that over one and a half thousand people had been detained; then that there was a near revolution in Cape Town. They tensed and waited and heard more: the people were marching to the Houses of Parliament. Whatever his misgivings about the PAC, Nelson thought, the end results were staggering, beyond all expectation. Was Sobukwe's prophecy going to materialize after all?

Then they heard that Philip Kgosana was leading the march. Who is Philip Kgosana? they asked each other. But even before the new leader could register on their minds, they were told that the Government had taken over the march. Kgosana's brief flash into South African history petered out almost the moment it was born. They swore in exasperation. Who had betrayed the exceptional youth? They heard these details. The young man had taken charge of the largest people's march Cape Town had ever seen, or was likely to see for decades to come. The marchers had been heading for the Houses of Parliament, but were persuaded by white liberals to divert to police headquarters in Caledon Square. There, the twenty-three-year-old Kgosana, looking more like a schoolboy in his short trousers than a university student, had fallen into the trap set by the Chief of Police, Colonel I. B. S. Terblanche. 'I was blamed for not using force. I was an outcast even among my colleagues . . . But, if I had used force, it would have been a massacre,' said Brigadier Terblanche, twenty-seven years later, just before his death.

'They wormed themselves into your mind and heart and sold you down the drain.' That, some said, was what Patrick Duncan had done to Kgosana. The young leader the people had chosen and trusted bartered away their power for the promise of a white policeman, because that leader had trusted a liberal. Kgosana spoke to the marchers who, recognizing his voice as their own, responded to him. He told them to go home. He would talk to the Minister of Justice and wring concessions from him. The people turned and as they dispersed so did their power, and young Kgosana's. He was immediately arrested and imprisoned.

Twenty-seven years later, Terblanche would say *he* had betrayed Kgosana who was arrested before he could meet the Minister.*

All Nelson's misgivings about the PAC were confirmed, but it was a heavy-hearted confirmation. It depressed him, as it did his comrades. Had they worked together, perhaps the outcome might have been different and they might have been closer to their day of liberation. An opportunity had come and was now lost. But there was no restraining the Verwoerdian Government which would not have hesitated at another blood bath, albeit on the heels of Sharpeville.

The detained helplessly whiled away their time in prison, but their spirits never dimmed. They were allowed visitors. Winnie came, bringing changes of clothing and tinned foods, since that was all they were allowed. She was pregnant again, and this time glowing.

On 8 April the ANC and PAC were banned.

It can be argued that no government can ban a person, a people, or an organization. A victim of banning, in the final analysis, can only be victimized by himself. Thus neither the ANC nor the PAC, nor for that matter the CP, were destroyed in South Africa. That is the dilemma of the Nationalist Party and the challenge they face today. Thirty years after their attempts to bury these organizations, all three exist, the ANC stronger than ever.

The ANC and the PAC re-emerged within a year in different formations, their presence as ubiquitous as before. Now, since they went underground they took more risks than they had dared in the formal and legal 'above ground', in the vain hope that they might negotiate some gains. But underground there is nothing to negotiate, no prospect for reconciliation. To all intents and purposes, one is non-existent and the existence one projects is on one's own terms, and with whatever power one can muster.

A few days prior to its banning, the ANC declared:

* A. T. Kgosana, *Lest We Forget*, Skotaville Publishers, Johannesburg, 1988.

We do not recognize the validity of this law; and we shall not submit to it. The African National Congress will carry on in its own name to give leadership and organization to our people until freedom has been won and the scourge of racial discrimination has been banished from our country.

An Emergency Committee of the African National Congress has been established which will continue until our elected leaders have been released and our organization restored to legality.

The basis for overseas organizations had been laid before the emergency. The PAC sent Nana Mahomo and Peter Molotsi out of the country on 20 March, on the eve of Sharpeville, to canvass support for their campaign among African leaders.

On 27 March Tambo, anticipating the emergency, crossed the border illegally; Dadoo followed a week later. Frene Ginwala, helped by the Indian Government, organized their flight to Britain.

In the face of their joint bannings, and on the advice of Kwame Nkrumah and Colonel G. Nasser, the representatives of the ANC and PAC formed the short-lived 'United Front' in June 1960.

The emergency ended in August 1960 and Nelson was let out of prison. After a lift to Johannesburg, he and Duma took a bus to Orlando. Nelson caught sight of Winnie's familiar figure on the lawn. She could not believe what she saw and ran barefooted to his embrace.

In December 1960 Nelson went to see his boys in Qamata. Still under banning, still a treason accused, he drove, disguised, drove fast, for he had to make the return trip in a day and a night to avoid being missed by the police. He found Makgatho ill, being nursed by Nobandla, Matanzima's senior wife. He was grateful to her, but believed that his son needed better medical attention than that available in the Transkei. He wrapped the shivering boy in a blanket and left almost immediately for Johannesburg.

Winnie went into labour during his brief absence, weeks ahead of her time, and was urgently moved to hospital. Zindzi's birth was normal, but Winnie ran a high temperature and was placed in an oxygen tent.

Nelson reached home in the early hours of the morning with a sick boy, the news of Zindzi's arrival and a sick wife, and a police raid in full blast on his house.

His first thoughts were for Makgatho. He took him to Dr Abdullah, and then, leaving the boy in the care of Leabie, rushed to hospital. He found Winnie weak but recovering. She was out of the tent, but his tiny new daughter was now running a temperature.

Nelson's anxiety came to an end: Evelyn took over her son and the hospital cared for his wife and baby.

He resumed his roll call at the Treason trial. This trial, too, ended. On 29 March 1961, five years after it had begun, the court dismissed it and Nelson was released from a stranglehold that had cost him his practice and seriously jeopardized his freedom to work for his people. The prosecution had produced 10,000 documents as evidence, eventually cutting these down to 4,000, and had presented 150 witnesses. The court ruled: 'On the evidence before this court, it is impossible for this court to come to the conclusion that the ANC had acquired or adopted a policy to overthrow the State by violence, i.e. in the sense that the masses had to be prepared or conditioned to commit direct acts of violence against the State.'

There were demonstrations of wild joy outside the court. Richard Maphonya, now one of Soweto's most flourishing businessmen, threw a party for Nelson and his friends, just as he had done when the state of emergency was lifted in August the previous year. If Winnie nurtured expectations of a normal family life with a working husband, they were dashed within weeks of Nelson's release as he prepared for the final phase of his life outside prison.

# CHAPTER 17

# The Tribesmen Locked in Violence

While the trial continued its humdrum routine, the country was in turmoil which spread to the reserves. Migrant workers, already exposed to urban resistance and charged by it, returned to discover their land expropriated and their families uprooted and squeezed into rural slums.

For a number of years Nelson had noticed the increase in complaints from rural areas about crops failing, the milk growing thinner. 'The goodness of the old days has gone,' his mother had said. 'We can expect nothing from the land and *amasi* [sour milk] is not as before.'

But Nelson knew that it was not simply a matter of the good old days. He studied reports and census returns and saw to his horror how the ratio of land and livestock to population size had declined, how the people had been deprived of grazing and agricultural land, and how new regulations made it increasingly difficult to move to urban areas to survive. How different, he asked himself, were the reserves from Nazi gas chambers? The people were being deliberately contained to die of starvation.

While the reserves were a pre-Nationalist creation, the Nationalists, under the pretext of establishing Bantu Authorities and independent homelands, were divorcing the people from all the resources of the country. The former government had not been as harsh in its control of movement from the reserves to towns; women were not subjected to passes; thousands of families had been allowed to live as tenant farmers on the vast white farms; and urban workers were not as harassed when they put up their shacks. The Nationalists were completing the process of converting the traditional chiefs from patrons and guardians of the people into lackeys of the oppressor. Influx control was tightened and extended to women; African tenant farmers were expelled from the white farms and pushed into the already overcrowded reserves, after they had been forced to sell whatever livestock they possessed. Their anger descended on those chiefs who had accepted the new and more pernicious system of rural administration under Bantu Authorities and they rose against them. They knew that this was a prelude to the conversion of the reserves into homelands and their legal alienation from their country. The violence in the Cape had demonstrated to Nelson that the African people were so brutalized that they could not wait to be mobilized by politicians, they would hit out blindly, irrationally, against whatever they saw as part of their oppression. That was the rage that had burst out in Zeerust and Sekhukhuniland and in his own Transkei in 1959.

A year later Nelson would be driven to give up non-violence as the means to change, and when arrested he would say:

It could not be denied that our policy to achieve a non-racial state by non-violence had achieved nothing, and that our followers were beginning to lose confidence in this policy and were developing disturbing ideas of terrorism. Small groups had arisen in the urban areas and were systematically making plans for violent forms of political struggle in rural areas. It was increasingly taking the form, not of struggle against the government, though this is what precipitated it, but of civil strife against themselves, conducted in such a way that it could not hope to achieve anything other than loss of life and killing . . . it was precisely because the soil of South Africa is already drenched with the blood of innocent Africans that we felt it our duty to make preparations as a long term to use force in order to defend ourselves against force.

Nelson, intensely rural in his roots, was very conscious that the ANC had neglected the rural areas. Home was never Johannesburg. It could never be, even though by 1960 he had spent half his life there. When it came to roots the rural years mattered more. The ANC had supported the traditional structures and had worked mainly through the chiefs. These structures, however, were only nominal, for the chiefs and headmen were all employees of the Government and the rural councils were all chief-centred. Where the Non-European Unity Movement had penetrated the Transkei and called for non-collaboration, the ANC had supported elections to local council. Nelson was among those who stressed to the ANC that it could no longer support a chief who collaborated with the government to implement the policy of Bantustans. The ANC accordingly issued a new policy statement in its Report to the National Executive in 1958:

The African chiefs on the whole have a tradition of working with the ANC from its inception. To continue on this has become more difficult in recent years, yet many of them are with the people.

There are some, however, who have become loyal agents of the Government. They serve the Government better than the police. It is this group which has become desperate in its efforts to implement the Government's plan and has become very cruel and brutal against the people.

Whether strong or weak, effective or ineffective, the government took no chances with the ANC. In 1958 it was declared an unlawful organization in parts of the rural reserves in the Transvaal and the Cape.

The threat of Bantu Authorities divided communities into those who supported them and those who opposed them. The bitterness of a people without any resources was one without shock absorbers. Its violence was terrible, and the retaliation of the State even more so.

Tribal heads gathered their followers and discussed the situation. The anger of one kraal merged with that of others and so distilled into a storm, into a power of the people. Among the Pondos it was that of *Intaba*, the men who gathered in the 'mountains'. The Thembu rose in similar resistance against Bantu Authorities.

Prime targets were Paramount Chief Botha Sigcau of East

Pondoland and Kaiser Matanzima. But there was consternation among all Pondo and Thembu chiefs, and they organized their own mercenaries to guard the two men and to attack on sight anyone who they thought constituted a political threat to their patrons. Migrant workers, finding such indigenous tyranny intolerable, took their revenge by burning the huts of chiefs and their supporters, and by assaulting the occupants. In Sekhukhuniland several supporters of Bantu Authorities were killed. The State protected its pawns and detained hundreds of people. It eventually convicted twenty to life imprisonment and numerous others to sentences averaging ten years. It was a matter of great personal embarrassment to Nelson that his kinsman Kaiser Matanzima was the pre-eminent chief on whom the anger of the tribesmen was focused. The attacks and counter-attacks divided his beloved country.

Nelson despaired when he heard that Matanzima had sent an impi from his headquarters in Qamata to Rhwantsana, where, protected by the police, it had burnt down a hundred huts. He heard how in Flagstaff the police had surrounded and fired on a meeting of 400 tribesmen who had met at Ngquza Hills to consider action against Botha Sigcau. Eight men shot in the back had died on the spot, many were left injured. The survivors had fled into the forests, remobilized and returned to take effective control of the entire region. It was the power of *intaba* (the mountain revolutionaries), not of Sigcau, that prevailed. The 'liberators' warned the chiefs against working with the government. When these warnings were ignored they sent the chilling message: 'The horsemen are coming!' and then swooped down on their victims. Official administration broke down. The magistrates baulked at the problem and the chiefs fled to refugee camps in Bizana and Umzimkulu.

At Langa in the Cape, Nelson's tribesmen, Thembu migrant workers and members of Poqo (allegedly the violent wing of the PAC), assembled before *inyanga* who incised their skins and rubbed in protective medicines. Thus fortified they set off by train to their home area to kill Kaiser Matanzima. But spies forestalled them and police blocked all entrances to the station. As the train stopped police swooped upon the Poqo tribesmen who gave as good as they got and then fled into the mountains. Police reinforcements gave chase and finally captured them. They were brought to trial; more imprisonments and death sentences followed.

Many things had happened in Winnie's ancestral home by then and her wedding feast and its geniality had become a thing of the past. Her father had thrown in his lot with Matanzima and was serving on his council, which meant he opposed all that she and Nelson stood for. Her brothers had joined *intaba* against her father, even though their filial deference towards him remained unchanged, but there was a brooding and unspoken resentment. Winnie was torn between the justice of the tribal cause and her father's reactionary stance.

She was stricken with grief when she heard that her beloved Makhulu had become the innocent victim of *intaba*. They had asked Kokani for his buses but he had refused. *Intaba* had taken them anyway, holding the drivers hostage. Then at night, while Kokani was in his study and Makhulu was lying in the doorway of the kitchen, as she usually did after a heavy meal, there was a sudden flood of *intaba* men. Kokani leapt through a window and lay prostrate on the ground. Some of the attackers actually stepped over him, but did not see him. He managed to crawl into the garden and to escape. Hilda, Winnie's stepmother, and other members of the household, also escaped, but Makhulu, unable to raise herself in time, was stabbed with *intshula* (spear) and paralysed from the waist down. Kokani's substantial house was set alight. Makhulu refused to be hospitalized, but her pride had gone and she died a short time thereafter.

In 1960 Transkeian tribesmen travelled to 8115 Orlando West to report to Nelson, the ANC and to the Government on the terror they had suffered at the hands of Chief Matanzima and Botha Sigcau. First came a contingent of deported Thembu: Chief Bangilizwe Joyi, Jackson Nkosiyane, Twalimfene Joyi and McGregor Mgolombane, and they were followed by a Pondo deputation. They filled the small front room and sat wherever they could. Winnie busied herself preparing food and wondering how many would have to be put up, for how many nights and what arrangements she should make.

The tribesmen were angry with the chiefs and saw them as selfish and greedy. They questioned Botha Sigcau's legitimacy as the paramount chief of the Pondos and reported their fear that Matanzima would soon control all Transkei and depose the rightful paramount chief of the Thembus, Sabata Dalindyebo.

Nelson stood in the relationship of uncle to both Matanzima and Sabata. While he and Matanzima were about the same age and had both trained as attorneys, Sabata was much younger with little formal education but, unlike Matanzima, was implacably opposed to Bantu Authorities. History was now reversed. Towards the end of the nineteenth century, Sabata's great-grandfather, Paramount Chief Ngangelizwe, had collaborated with the British while his brother Matanzima became a people's hero when he took up arms against them. But his grandson, K. D. Matanzima, collaborated with the Government and eventually deposed his tribal senior, Sabata. They belonged to the Madiba clan and should have stood together at all times but were split from top to bottom.

The tribesmen told Nelson how they had suffered arrest and death. They had scored a significant victory through their consumer boycott and local traders had supported them to ensure goodwill after the boycott. It was news that would not be published, reports that no one would gather. It was as if the illiterate region was not deemed worthy of literate recording. When the tribesmen cried: 'They are killing us!' it was no exaggeration. How else could one describe the situation in this beloved region?

Winnie's pain over the attack on her family and her divided loyalties were compounded that day. The discussion was man's business. The women of the Mandela household heard voices raised in passion and in argument. Winnie recalls:

157

Nelson called in other ANC leaders. A night-long meeting followed. I was kept busy in the kitchen cooking and sending out food. I was simply instructed to prepare dinner for ten people. I didn't know, nor was I told, the business of the meeting. When they had those closed sessions, I didn't dare go into the minute lounge of our home. They served themselves and so it was on this occasion.

I was in the kitchen when the door burst open and one home boy, who had worked for my father as a bus driver and who has now left the country, greeted me cheerfully with a pile of plates. He settled down in the kitchen and, taking a matchstick, started picking his teeth. After exchanging life's pleasantries he said, 'Your father is a lucky bastard, we shall get him yet. We just don't know how he escaped through such a small window. Such a big man. He must thank his lucky stars. He won't be so lucky next time.'

I was transfixed and numb with shock. I was caught in a crossfire in which I dared not show my feelings. I was very angry. That moment, I hated him, but I was helpless. I could say nothing, but when he continued to taunt me in my own kitchen about what he had done to my family all I could say was, 'But you are talking about my father. Can't you see I cannot bear it?' He simply laughed.

My duties done to the meeting I withdrew into my bedroom and cried bitterly. For the first time the horror of my position struck me. I worshipped my father, and here my husband and my people were plotting against him. I did not have the heart to discuss the matter with Madiba nor to reveal to him my feelings for my father. I identified with the Pondos; politically I rejected my father, but this could not and did not wipe out a lifetime of love and mutual respect. Worse was still to come when the rumour was spread that I, his daughter, had harboured his enemies and plotted his murder in my own house.

Deeply troubled, Winnie discussed the brief encounter with her 'home boy' with her husband later that night when they found a few moments to be alone. Nelson assured her that she was not the only one posed with fragmented loyalties. The Government had insinuated itself in such a way into African society that many found themselves in this divisive situation.

The tribesmen returned home with high regard for Moses Kotane and his friends. Walking along Market Street in Johannesburg one day, they met a well-known political figure, John Motshabi. He introduced himself as one of Kotane's comrades and gave them R1,000 to prosecute their struggle.

# CHAPTER 18

# The Black Pimpernel

To sever all ties from Britain, to be completely free of the Empire and its remaining vestiges symbolized in the Union of South Africa, was the Afrikaner dream. The Nationalists had promised themselves a republic; in 1960 they prepared to keep that promise. In practically any other situation, the liberation from a colonial past would have augured independence and freedom from foreign control: in South Africa it meant that the most reactionary, surviving white settler community was shaking off liberal European restraints, however tenuous, and digging in its heels to dominate the indigenous people and all people of colour without restraint.

While white South Africans went to the polls to declare a racist Republic most black South Africans went about their chores uninterestedly. The articulate among them staked their claim to full citizenship rights. Although the ANC and PAC were banned, the personalities associated with them took the lead. Chief Luthuli prepared to call a National Convention of all South Africans to register the will of the people. A Consultative Conference of thirty-six African leaders was set up to pave the way. The problems they encountered were inevitable, given their diverse organizational backgrounds. The PAC wanted the convention to be restricted to Africans and wouldn't even begin talking until the two white representatives of the Liberal Party left the initial meeting. The Consultative Conference nonetheless resolved to call a National Convention of all South Africans regardless of race and set up a thirteen-member Continuation Committee under the presidency of Liberal Party member, Jordan Ngubane, but the committee was riven by dissension. The PAC representatives could not get over their objection to a multiracial conference, and both Africanists and Liberals resented the very strong ANC presence. The dissension was momentarily halted in March 1961 when the Government charged the entire Committee with furthering the aims of the ANC. Not a single member defended himself on the grounds that he was not furthering the aims of the ANC, for none accepted the validity of such a charge. All thirteen were found guilty on 12 October, but all were acquitted on appeal in April 1962.

Dissension within the Committee became more flagrant after the case and the Committee floundered when the PAC, Liberal Party and IDAMF (Interdenominational African Ministers Federation) complained of ANC domination and withdrew. The Convention, called in May 1961, was nonetheless a resounding success, proving the popularity and organizational strength of the ANC despite its banning. *Drum* magazine noted:

The odds were all against success, and yet the outcome was a triumph, an indication of a new spirit of resolve which has emerged among the African people.

1,400 delegates from all over the Union got to Maritzburg and many of them slept out in the veld because there was no other place for them to stay.

They came by train, by car, by foot, by bicycle. They came carrying bundles of food which they shared out as if on a family picnic. Could the Nationalist Party have achieved this in the face of banning orders, with few cars and very little money to spend?

The organizers were well prepared for the police and when they discovered that the conference venue was bugged they immediately abandoned it and walked several kilometres in drizzling rain to the Indian township, where an alternative hall was arranged.

*Drum*, May 1961, reported:

They talked, they listened, they argued and at the end crystallized their feelings into resolutions. They called for a 'non-racial' democratic constitution in South Africa. They demanded the holding of a national convention of elected representatives of all adult men and women on an equal basis, irrespective of race, colour or creed, to be called by the Government not later than 31 May 1961.

The highlight of the Conference was the appearance of Mandela who was greeted with thunderous applause. It was nine years since the public had heard him on account of his banning orders. He cut a heroic figure and his familiar boom filled the hall. The delegates listened raptly to every word. A man sitting close to the *Drum* reporter commented: 'This is like a State of the Nation address by the American president.'

Mr Mandela [the *Drum* report went on] paid tribute . . . to the ANC . . . which for nearly fifty years had been 'the sword and shield of the African people'. Now that it had been suppressed, he said, it had two alternatives, either to accept discrimination and humiliation or stand firm for their rights. They could remain disunited in the face of the Government's arrogance, or they could stand united to ensure that the Government's discriminatory legislation did not work.

Nelson sat down to deafening applause, and was followed by the equally impressive Lilian Ngoyi. *Drum* commented: 'She made a masterful plea for unity. She told delegates that whenever the police decided on a swoop, political opponents would find themselves sleeping in the same cells and facing the same charges. This, she said, showed the futility of wrangling when faced with a common opponent.'

She called for the release of Sobukwe, which the *Drum* reporter correctly noted was a bold thing for her to do, in view of the internecine fighting between the ANC and PAC.

The Conference resolved:

We declare that no constitution or form of government decided without the participation of the African people who form an absolute majority of the population can enjoy moral validity or merit support either within South Africa or beyond its borders.

We demand that a National Convention of elected representatives of all adult men and women on an equal basis, irrespective of race, colour, creed or other limitation, be called by the Union Government not later than 31 May 1961.

The Conference elected a National Action Council and instructed it to organize mass demonstrations, beginning with a national strike if the Government failed to call the Convention. Nelson was placed at the head of the council. The Convention also resolved that the identity of every member of the council, save that of Mandela, would remain secret. Nelson accepted the responsibility unhesitantly. He had reached a point in his life where he was prepared to make any sacrifice to end apartheid. The organization of a strike involving Africans was illegal. There was no way he could hope to pursue the task entrusted to him without risking almost immediate arrest. If he was to succeed at all, he had to disappear 'underground'. This meant he had to leave his family, forget familiar creature comforts and worst of all, sooner or later, face long-term imprisonment.

None of this daunted him. Neither did it occur to him that he should first return to his family and discuss the implications of his new charge with them. He expected his family to give him its full support and that is exactly what they did, despite enormous sacrifices.

Nelson planned a strategy whereby he would keep the government constantly engaged but himself disguised, secret and inaccessible. The black public thrilled at the adventure that Mandela created. For Nelson there was anxiety, loneliness and a change of bed – when there was one – practically every night. There were moments when he wondered why he had chosen the path he had, and the answer was always the same. He had not chosen the path, the path had chosen him. He had been impelled by events over which he had no control. What else could he have done after the banning of the ANC, and especially after Sharpeville? What choice did that leave him? If only blacks could cripple the economy, they could regain what was once theirs.

The Black Pimpernel was everywhere. He cropped up in the dorps and towns throughout the country, at the homes of trusted friends and ANC activists, who could be relied upon to throw in their support behind the directive of the Conference against the white Republic. His disguise, albeit makeshift, worked and confused even those who knew him. He recalls one such incident:

On my way to Durban I stopped at Boom Street, Pietermaritzburg, at about noon. Chota was away in one of his consulting stations. Choti assumed that I was a patient and asked me to return later in the day, but I insisted that I would wait and then spent a couple of hours sitting on the verandah. My corduroy trousers and bush jacket, sandals and unkempt hair provided me with a perfect disguise and I enjoyed the anonymity. It was only when Chota returned that she discovered who I was. Were it not for the fact that she was brought up in the tradition of non-violence, she would certainly have wrung my neck for what I did.

That night we hardly closed our eyes and spent the time chatting with the late Omar, Moses Mabida, Ismail Gangat and Chota.

After his arrest, Nelson told the court:

Early in April 1961, I went underground to organize the May Day general strike. My work entailed travelling throughout the country, living now in African townships, then in country villages and again in cities.

During the second half of the year, I started visiting the home of Mr Arthur Goldreich, where I used to meet my family privately.

In October 1961 Mr Goldreich informed me that he was moving out of town, and offered me a hiding place there. A few days thereafter, he arranged for Mr Michael Harmel, another co-conspirator in this case, to take me to Rivonia. I naturally found Rivonia an ideal place for the man who lived the life of an outlaw. Up to that time I had been compelled to live indoors during the day time and could only venture out under cover of darkness. But at Lilliesleaf I could live differently, and work far more efficiently.

For obvious reasons, I had to disguise myself and I assumed the fictitious name of David. In December, Mr Arthur Goldreich and his family also moved in. I stayed there, my lord, until I went abroad on 11 January 1962. As already indicated, I returned in July 1962 and was arrested in Natal on 5 August.

But there were narrow escapes from the police, and careless communications in an 'underground' which was a very new concept and which had only one member. On one occasion Nelson reached the house of Fatima and Ismail Meer in the early morning. After a short rest, he was up and shaving in the bathroom when the phone rang. 'Has Nelson arrived?' a close friend and official of the NIC asked. Fatima was shocked. 'What Nelson?' she asked. 'No such person has arrived here.' 'We dropped him at your house a few hours ago,' the friend insisted. 'No one has come here,' Fatima reiterated and put down the receiver. She repeated the conversation to Nelson, who swore under his breath. 'Has he never heard of such a thing as tapped telephones?' and wondered whether he should move to another hiding place. But he was tired, wanted some rest and decided to risk staying put. He spent several days with the Meers, taking time off to visit Winnie's sister, who nursed at the FOSA hospital, a few miles from the city, and meeting Alan Paton and Leo Kuper, both of the Liberal Party.

Meanwhile, the Government and the police tried their level best to discredit him. They accused the National Action Committee of planning mass violence. Nelson telephoned the press from a public phone booth and refuted the accusation.

The *Sunday Express* of 21 May 1961 reported:

Mr Rolihlahla Nelson Mandela, leader behind the proposed May demonstrations, told me last night that even though the police were making a nationwide search, he did not think he would be caught before 31 May. He called from a public telephone box and told me: 'So far we have been able to anticipate every move the police have made. I have so much work that I don't even think about arrest. We emphatically deny reports that violence will take place or that the three-day stay-away will be extended. Small organizations which have nothing to do with the demonstrations have made a move to extend the strike, but we have no connection with them.'

The government ignored the demand for the All-in-Conference and forced the National Action Council to announce its three-day stay-away from 29 to 31 May.

The PAC now pre-empted the Government in taking action against the Council. It countered the call and issued a leaflet describing the forthcoming demonstrations as irresponsible and, unforgivably, alleging that the Action

Council was in fact the ANC, thereby exposing the council members to arrest. Nelson had hoped that the ANC and PAC would bridge their differences and work together.

Oliver and Nano Mahomo were working together abroad. Why could they not do so at home as well? Unity was what the ANC needed desperately and it was the one thing that eluded them even in their worst crisis. Whatever the odds, for Nelson there was no turning back. He moved on to visit and inspire the despondent. They told of his appearances and these stories added to treasured folklore. At strategic moments he fed the telephone box its tickeys (threepenny pieces) and spoke to the newspapers.

The last three days of May became the crucial test of strength between the ANC and the racist government. Clearly the key actors were Rolihlahla Nelson Mandela and Dr Hendrik Verwoerd: both had dug in their heels and were determined to stand their ground. The Government had at its command every conceivable power; the banned ANC and Mandela had nothing apart from themselves, their integrity, their faith, and the support of their people.

Monday, 29 May dawned. The white media declared the stay-away a failure and reported feeble responses, varying from 2 to 20 per cent. *Drum*, while declaring the round to the Government, reported considerable countrywide response to the Mandela call. It estimated a 50 per cent stay-away on the first day in Durban and on the Reef (the *Rand Daily Mail* reported 25 per cent), and 20 per cent in Port Elizabeth and Cape Town. Indian shops closed in Durban and on the Reef. Violence and shooting in Port Elizabeth escalated the stay-away to 50 per cent on the following day, but in every other part of the country the stay-away ended when the whites went to the polls.

Whatever the magnitude of the response to the strike call (Nelson himself put it as between 50 and 75 per cent) the black people clearly boycotted the celebrations for the Afrikaner Republic on 31 May. There were practically no takers for the cups and medals.

The July 1961 edition of *Drum*, reported:

In Cape Town it was estimated that only one in ten coloured children had accepted the Republican medal, and school principals said they expected to return about 100,000 medals to the education authorities in Pretoria. They said as far as they knew not one coloured high school pupil in the city had taken the medal and flag. African schools did not receive their stocks. Some were promised them later, but no demand for them was reported. In the Transvaal some Indian children threw away the flags but kept the sticks attached to them. Principals in most Indian schools in Natal were busy packing unwanted flags and medals and sending them back to Pretoria.

Nelson summed up from underground:

In the face of unprecedented intimidation by the Government and employers and of blatant falsehoods by the press, immediately before and during the strike, the freedom-loving people of South Africa gave massive and solid support to the challenging resolution of the Maritzburg Conference.

No organization in the world could have withstood and survived the full-scale and massive bombardment directed against us by the Government during the last month . . . When a government seeks to suppress a peaceful demonstration of an unarmed people by mobilizing the entire reserves of the State, military and police, it concedes powerful mass support for such a demonstration. Who can deny the plain fact that ever since the end of last month, the issue that dominated South African politics was not the Republican celebrations, but our plans for a general strike?

He went on to announce the second phase of the campaign.

We stressed that the strike would be followed by other forms of mass pressure to force the race maniacs who govern our beloved country to make way for a democratic government of the people, by the people, and for the people. A full-scale and countrywide campaign of non-cooperation with the Government will be launched immediately . . . We plan to make government impossible. Those who are voteless cannot be expected to continue paying taxes to a government that is not responsible to them. People who live in poverty and starvation cannot be expected to pay exorbitant house rents to the Government and local authorities. We produce the work of the gold mines, the diamonds and the coal, of the farms and industry, in return for miserable wages. Why should we continue enriching those who steal the products of our sweat and blood, who exploit us and refuse us the right to organize trade unions? Can Africans be expected to be content with serving on Advisory Boards and Bantu Authorities when the demand all over the continent of Africa is for national independence and self government? Is it not an affront to the African people that the Government should now seek to extend Bantu Authorities to the cities, when people in the rural areas have refused to accept the same system and fought against it tooth and nail? Non-collaboration is a dynamic weapon. We must refuse. We must use it to send the Government to the grave. It must be used vigorously and without delay. The entire resources of the black people must be mobilized to withdraw all cooperation with the Nationalist Government. Various forms of industrial and economic action will be employed to undermine the already failing economy of the country. We will call upon the international bodies to expel South Africa and upon nations of the world to sever economic and diplomatic relations with the country.

He pointed to the fact that a warrant for his arrest had been issued and, in an obvious counter to the PAC, which had distributed thousands of leaflets accusing leaders of the Congress Alliance of having run away, he said: 'Any serious politician will realize that under present-day conditions in this society, to seek for cheap martyrdom by handing myself to the police is cheap and criminal. We have an important programme before us.'

The PAC leaflet had stated: 'We, the PAC, have, as you know, broken away from the Congress Alliance because their leaders are such cowards. Where are our leaders? Where is Sobukwe, our Chief? – in gaol with his fellows.'

Nelson emphasized that he had chosen the more difficult course and one which entailed more risk and hardship than being in gaol. In a press statement of 26 June 1961, published in *We Accuse: The Trial of Rolihlahla Mandela, ANC(SA)*, London, he declared:

I have had to separate myself from my dear wife and children, from my mother and sisters, to live as an outlaw in my own land. I have had to close my business, to abandon my profession, and live in poverty and misery, as many of my people are doing. I shall fight the Government side by side with you, inch by inch, and mile by mile, until victory is won. I will not leave South Africa, nor will I surrender. The struggle is my life. I will continue fighting for freedom until the end of my days.

By this time Nelson had become convinced that the battle would not be won through negotiation and passive resistance. Negotiation would occur only when the ANC matched its power against that of the Nationalists. To acquire that power they would have to be prepared to use violence. He told the court in the Rivonia Trial in 1964: 'At the beginning of June 1961, I and some colleagues came to the conclusion that, as violence in this country was inevitable, it would be unrealistic and wrong for African leaders to continue preaching peace and non-violence at a time when the Government met our peaceful demands with force.'

The ANC itself was divided on the use of violence. There were those who thought that the training of recruits was premature. After a full discussion, however, it was decided to go ahead with the plans for military training, because it would take many years to build up a sufficient nucleus of trained soldiers to start a guerrilla campaign and, whatever happened, the training would be of value.

Chief Luthuli never reconciled himself to the violent alternative, though, at the same time, he did not stand against those who had committed themselves to it. Nelson admired Luthuli enormously and considered him to be one of the best President Generals of the ANC, but saw him at the same time to be an individualist. He recalled the time he had been asked to convey to Luthuli the executive decision after the banning of the ANC that Mandela should leave the country and work abroad. Luthuli's response had been that he would discuss the matter with Ismail Meer and Alan Paton, indicating that he placed greater faith in his friends than the organization he headed.

Ironically, Chief Luthuli, the then President General of the

ANC, was awarded the Nobel Peace Prize the same year that *Umkhonto we Sizwe* (Spear of the Nation) announced its first bomb blast. The country awoke to the shock of its first sabotage explosion on 18 October 1961. A small group that would disappear into history, calling itself the National Liberation Committee, later changed to the African Resistance Movement, and not Umkhonto, was responsible for it. The NLC was mainly a radical anti-CP white group with members drawn from the Liberal Party. The first Umkhonto explosions followed on 16 December 1961, simultaneously at three centres: Port Elizabeth, Johannesburg and Durban. The bombs were homemade, the operations clumsy and there was some bungling. One saboteur was killed and another had his arm blown off. A month before this date, units working closely with the ANC had cut telephone wires right across the Witwatersrand from Springs to Randfontein.

Yet a third group, the Yu Che Chen, led by Dr Neville Alexander, with its foundations in the Non-European Unity Movement, planned sabotage. The events of 1960 had convinced a substantial body of South Africans that there was no room for a formal extra-parliamentary opposition in the country, not even as a talk-shop.

The Government on its part appeared unmoved. After eliminating its black opposition, it began carving up the reserves into tribal homelands and accelerated the process of governing these through its black nominees. The anti-apartheid groups – liberals, nationalists, Marxists and Trotskyites – considered their choices in the new situation and became divided between those who counselled a temporary suspension of all activities and those who urged underground military action. To the first group the activists appeared foolhardy, but the militarists themselves saw no other choice. By mid-1961 four underground resistance groups were in operation in the country. The PAC's Poqo responded with a primitive brutality focusing on whites and collaborators.

Nelson found the violence of Poqo reprehensible. His instincts were for talking and negotiating settlements, for restoring friendship and winning confidence. He was essentially a man of peace, but he had been driven to a state of war. He would be as good at war as he was at peace, since his new conviction was that war would lead to peace.

Umkhonto spelled out the position for all four groups when it explained its move to violence in a statement released simultaneously with its first explosion on 16 December:

The time comes in the life of any nation when there remains only two choices – submit or fight. That time has now come to South Africa. We shall not submit and we have no choice but to hit back by all means in our power in defence of our people, our future and our freedom.

We of Umkhonto have always sought to achieve liberation without bloodshed and civil clash. We hope, even at this late hour, that our first actions will awaken everyone to a realization of the disastrous situation to which Nationalist policy is leading. We hope that we will bring the Government and its supporters to their senses before it is too late, so that both government and its policies can be changed before matters reach the desperate stage of civil war.

In despair then, and as a last resort, Umkhonto turned to sabotage as the least violent choice available to it, restricting its violence to property and avoiding violence to the person. Sabotage needed more funding than was made available by the two shillings and sixpence annual ANC membership fee. Umkhonto needed more sophisticated expertise. Nelson was sent out of the country to seek support in Africa and abroad.

Later, when brought to trial, he told the court:

The ANC decided that I should attend the Pan-African Freedom Movement for Central, East and Southern Africa which was to be held early in 1962 in Addis Ababa, and it was also decided that, after this conference, I would undertake a tour of the African states with a view to soliciting support for our cause, and obtaining scholarships for the higher education of matriculated Africans. At the same time the MK [Umkhonto] decided I should investigate whether facilities were available for the training of soldiers which was the first stage in the preparation for guerrilla warfare.

It was on this note that I left South Africa to proceed to Addis Ababa as a delegate of the ANC.

CHAPTER 19

# Mission to Africa

Nelson, dressed in a khaki uniform that replaced his tailor-made suit, slipped across the border into Bechuanaland (later Botswana) without a passport in January 1962.

His brief, among other assignments, was to lead the ANC delegation to the Pan-African Freedom Movement for East and Central Africa (PAFMECA) Conference in Addis Ababa. Before leaving Johannesburg he had waited at an address in Doornfontein for Duma Nokwe and Walter Sisulu to bring the official letter appointing him leader of the ANC delegation. But both Duma and Walter were arrested on the way, so he went on without it.

He felt a sense of ease and belonging in liberated Africa that he had never experienced in his own country. It was a home-coming away from home. Africa, beyond the southern-most corner which was his, invaded his consciousness. He flew through her air-space and bumped over her corrugated roads; the hot dust clogged his nostrils, and the boiling heat of the sandy wastes dried out his skin. He was overawed by the vastness of the continent, the variations in lifestyle and tribal cults, and stimulated by the initiatives towards industrialization.

He found a traditionalism that was far more intense than anything he had known at home and far more extreme poverty. He marvelled at Africa's capacity for religion and was surprised to discover that Christianity was older in Africa than in Europe. He was even more surprised to see how Africa had indigenized Islam: the mosques were convoluted stucco in Mali and Guinea; in Morocco, Tunis and Egypt they were fat domes and tall minarets.

He was moved above all by the vigour with which the continent, once carved and parcelled into European commodities, was returning to itself, discovering its history, realizing its personality; how the cry of *Uhuru* was being transformed into the reality of nation states. The more he saw, the more passionately he yearned for the liberation of South Africa, not only for herself, but for the continent.

Lobatsi, in Bechuanaland, was his first stop, and he waited to travel to Gaberone to see Seretse Khama. He knew Seretse from college as a man of wit and charm, something of a playboy, but astute in student politics. He had told Nelson once that all he wanted of life was to be a magistrate, but that was behind him now, and he was on the eve of leading his country into independence. Umkhonto needed Khama's cooperation to facilitate the movement of recruits through the narrow Kazangula strip across the Zambezi to training bases in liberated Africa.

But he never saw Khama on that trip. The South African police were too active in the region; they had just abducted an ANC colleague, Anderson Ganyile, and Nelson was urged to move northwards, to Tanganyika, where Oliver awaited him. He arrived in Dar-es-Salaam, only to find that Oliver had moved on, leaving instructions with Frene Ginwala to meet him. Nelson knew Frene as a beautiful young Parsee woman who had become a prohibited person in South Africa because of her political profile. She was close to Julius Nyerere, editing his paper. Frene arranged for Nelson to stay with a close friend who was also a Cabinet Minister. There he was joined by Joe Matthews.

Nelson found the land of Kilimanjaro and Lake Nyasa poor in resources, but rich in spirit and ideas. Julius Nyerere had stepped down as Prime Minister and was preparing for elections. They met him informally in his home, a modest bungalow occupied once by a British *bwana*, and he gave them all the attention they required. Nelson compared him with the homeland leaders in South Africa, some of whom earned salaries higher than that of the British Prime Minister and were chauffeur-driven in expensive limousines. He observed Nyerere arrive at a mass rally, driving his own small car, unattended by guards and without any fanfare. It was the people who announced him as they relayed, 'There is Nyerere!' Nyerere was one African leader who understood the poverty of his people and reflected it in his lifestyle.

They spent hours discussing the reconstruction of African society and were thrilled to see how closely their perceptions of African forms matched each others. As far back as 1946, the Youth League had declared that Africans were naturally socialistic – as illustrated in their social practices and customs – and that the achievement of national liberation in South Africa would usher in the era of African socialism. Nyerere identified that socialism as *ujama*. 'Class,' Nyerere asserted, 'is alien to Africa, socialism and democracy, indigenous.' Nelson recognized this in the remnants of the traditional social order that survived in South Africa. He recalled how chiefs and elders spent inordinate hours to reach consensus over small issues. It also explained his own inability to find the class divisions among his people that European academics told him were there.

They discussed the division between the ANC and PAC. Nelson pointed out that moral and pragmatic considerations demanded a multi-racial democracy in South Africa, and there was no justification for excluding a particular group or person from the liberation struggle on account of his or her colour. Nyerere had no difficulty in appreciating this since Tanganyikan society was also multi-cultural, but he emphasized the need to retain the hegemony of the African spirit in Africa. Where else could such a spirit be retained, he argued, as did other African leaders whom Nelson met later. Nyerere urged that the ANC and PAC should unite; that unity was of the utmost importance. He advised the ANC leadership to wait until Sobukwe was released and for the two groups to pool resources, and in unity renew their attack on the white regime.

Nelson briefed Nyerere on the military initiative planned by Umkhonto. Though emotionally opposed to violence, Nyerere conceded that the South African situation, like the

Algerian, left no other option. Tanganyika, he said, would help Umkhonto in every way it could. But, he pointed out, the Tanganyikan force was led by British officers. Not only would these officers be reluctant teachers, but they could be expected also to blow the secrecy. He advised Nelson to raise the issue with Emperor Haile Selassie at the PAFMECA Conference in Addis Ababa and undertook to send a special attaché to brief him so that he would give the South African issue the attention it deserved.

While Tanganyika was calm at this time, the little island of Zanzibar, just off the mainland and destined to unite with her as Tanzania, was riddled with conflict. Only the year before, in 1961, the island had been torn by riots. Babu Mohamed, leader of the Zanzibar National Party, a graduate of the London School of Economics and a confirmed Marxist, filled them in on the details.

Nelson and Joe Matthews flew to Lagos, and there was a joyous reunion with Oliver, Mzwai Piliso and Robert Resha. They attended the Conference of the Monrovian group of African states; Nelson incognito, since it was planned that his presence outside South Africa would only be made public at the PAFMECA Conference. Nelson was impressed with Haile Selassie's ability to stand above political divisions. Where others saw themselves as Casablancans and Monrovians, he firmly declared himself African.

Nelson was struck by Islamism of Nigeria. There were mosques and muezzins everywhere. It seemed to him that praying was the most important single activity. The nation paused and turned to Allah several times a day. It was quite usual to see groups of white-robed, white-hatted men in prayer on little mats on the streets and in odd corners of the hotels, their sandals placed neatly beside them. He learnt that there were more Muslims in Nigeria than in any Arab state in the world.

They were due to be flown to the residence of the Governor General, Dr Azikiwe, who lived outside Lagos, but trouble broke out in the East and practically all members of the Government were rushed out there. Nigeria, smaller in area than South Africa, had twice her population, classified into 250 ethnic groups; problems were inevitable, despite the Islamic bond. The British had added to these problems by breaking up the traditional kingdoms into small emirates.

The ANC and PAC delegates arrived in Addis Ababa for the PAFMECA Conference from 2 to 10 February 1962. The capital put out its red carpet and Ethiopian dignitaries welcomed the delegations.

Nelson was charmed by the people: aquiline-nosed, large-eyed, ebony-skinned. Ethiopia had a deep meaning for South Africa. It was the only African state that had resisted colonialism, and as such reassured Africans of their innate capacity for self-reliance and independence. It had also contributed a distinctly African Ethiopian Christian movement which was very visible in South Africa. Nelson was charged with the history of the country; he recalled the valour of Yohannes Menelik, who had vanquished the Italians in the last century; the perfidity of the League of Nations that had abandoned its members to the fascists in 1936 and forced the Emperor into exile because, as Professor Jabavu put it at the time in his address to the emergency meeting of the AAC, it was only 'black Abyssinian'. The Professor had gone on to refer to the outrage as the 'rape of Italy' which had scratched 'this European veneer and revealed the white savage hidden beneath . . .'

The Italians had poured into the country and set up their own separatist structures. When, at the end of the war, the Emperor had moved to return to his country, the British had tried to block him, fearing that he might wreak revenge on the occupying Italians. The Emperor had defied the British, and to the joyous acclaim of his people had returned to lead his country.

Nelson and his comrades met this defiant and proud man, Emperor Tafari Makonnen, Haile Selassie, a slightly built yet majestic figure, who believed that he was the 225th descendant of the Lion of Judah, of King Solomon and Queen Sheba.

Haile Selassie did not like white South Africans. A South

African battalion had recaptured Addis Ababa after it had been occupied by the Fascists and, like the Fascists, had attempted to impose a colour bar. Ethiopians could see no difference between the foreign occupiers and the foreign 'liberators'. Haile Selassie's sympathies were for the South African liberation struggle and he pledged his whole-hearted support.

Nelson was in his stride at the conference. He thrived on the heady atmosphere of ideas and the cut and thrust of argument.

There was lobbying outside the conference chamber. Foreign ambassadors were very interested in the ANC and, in particular, in Mandela, on account of the wide publicity given to the latest events in South Africa. Nelson met Joe Slovo who set up a meeting with Tass. The Tass correspondent wanted the ANC to align itself with Russia in the Cold War. Nelson adroitly avoided committing his organization to any superpower, pointing out he had no mandate to do so.

Conference assembled and the public gallery was packed. The Reverend Michael Scott was among the observers. Nelson was fond of Scott although he had taken up the PAC cause. It seemed to Nelson that he considered it his duty to support the weaker, minority group. But his PAC protégés shunned him, as if ashamed he was white. This embarrassed and pained Nelson and he took special care of Scott.

The Credentials Committee objected to the presence of a contingent from North Africa, led by A. Dialo, the Secretary General of the All Africa People's Conference. Nelson was shocked to hear a member of the Zanzibar Afro-Shirazi Party say, 'The trouble is that there are some Africans here who are not Africans.' He could not see any legitimacy for the exclusion of the North Africans. To say the least, it contradicted the unity they sought from the Atlantic to the Mediterranean Seas. He spoke up for the admission of North Africa, arguing that while PAFMECA was presently focused on Central- and East-African freedom, it was about to include the Southern African region, so why should the north be excluded – particularly in the face of the fierce war the Algerians were waging against the French. Besides, he emphasized, PAFMECA was an affiliate of the All African Peoples Congress (AAPC) and it was absurd to exclude fellow members of the parent body.

Nelson's arguments found wide support, but an element of resistance persisted. There was a proposal that the North Africans be allowed to attend, but not to speak. A delegate said to all-round laughter: 'Mr Dialo was ill during the last conference and his speech lasted three hours. He is well today, he will speak for three days.' Nelson rejoined that it was unreasonable not to allow them a voice. Oliver, who had been following Nelson's vigorous championing of the North African case with some apprehension, passed him a laconic note 'Shut up!' Nelson complied. But Nelson won the day for the North Africans, and the ANC gained firm friends in Dr Gallal, Vice-President of the United Arabic National Assembly, and Captain Abdul Aziz of the Afro-Asian Solidarity Committee, who was also an officer in the Algerian Army.

The Emperor opened the proceedings. His address was distinguished by his concern for continental unity, and by his deprecation of those European powers that continued to dominate Africa. He outlined the economic problems that faced the continent, warned against the dangers of neo-colonialism, and called for active support for the South African freedom movement.

So much has been said in the past about sanctions and measures to be taken against South Africa, but unfortunately little has been done to force the Union Government to change its policy. It is therefore important that all those who have the interest of the Africans at heart should start thinking on new lines than hitherto undertaken in order to effectively assist our African brothers to deliver them out of bondage under which they find themselves at present in that unhappy country.*

Speeches from others: heads of states and potential heads,

* PAFMECA, 1962, p. 78.

representatives of leading liberation movements, followed. The target of attack was European colonialism. There was an impatience for action, and while the Conference was a conference of words, there was constant urging that the words be translated into deeds.

K. Mpho, Secretary General of the Bechuanaland People's Party, accused: 'The French are murdering our brothers and sisters in Algeria, the Portuguese in Angola, the Belgians in the Congo, the Boers in the Republic of Verwoerd, last but not least, the English in the Rhodesias.'* Sheik Mohamed Farah of Somalia declared, 'Although the Somali Republic is free from colonial rule, I personally will not feel that we have achieved complete independence until every part of Africa is liberated. How can I feel free and my conscience be at peace so long as millions of my brothers are in bondage?'

Nelson was appalled by Portuguese oppression in Mozambique, which struck him as worse than that of the Afrikaners in South Africa. They heard that the *msumbiji* did not even have access to the law courts, that any policeman or agricultural official could sentence people and there was no appeal against such sentences.

Kenneth Kaunda of emergent Zambia explained: 'The question of ideology is not an issue with us now – the issue of Africa today is one of freedom. We shall consider them friend those who behave as such and we shall consider them enemy those who behave like enemies. When we are free, we definitely still want to learn from both the West and the East.'

Peter Molotsi of the PAC waxed poetic. He regretted that 'with the war clouds on the horizon, with the war drums taking on a shriller note every day and every hour ... we cannot pause long enough here in this beautiful city to try and recapture the glory that was Africa'. He hoped that they would have time for this on another occasion when they would excavate the secrets of the African past and find pathways that would take them back into antiquity 'and

* PAFMECA, 1962, p. 76.

throw light on the Azanian civilization which flourished in the territories that are now Tanganyika and Kenya and whose traces extend as far south as Rhodesia, Mozambique and the Transvaal'.

Nelson got up to deliver his address and, for the first time since leaving South Africa, dropped the pseudonym of David Motsamai and publicly announced himself. South Africa immediately knew the whereabouts of the Black Pimpernel. He was speaking on behalf of the ANC and his speech, written in Dar-es-Salaam, had been carefully scrutinized, amended and added to by Tennyson Makiwane, Oliver Tambo, Joe Matthews, Robert Resha and Mzwai Piliso. It was thus, as Nelson saw it, a group effort, in the best tradition of the ANC.

Nelson began by thanking PAFMECA for extending its area of concern to Southern Africa, 'the heart and core of imperialist reaction', and by paying tribute to His Imperial Majesty, a 'rich and unfailing foundation of wisdom' and 'foremost in promoting the cause of unity, independence and progress in Africa'. He thanked those African states that had supported the call for sanctions against South Africa and referred, in particular, to Ethiopia, Somalia, Sudan and Tanganyika.

He also thanked those African states that had 'given asylum and assistance to South Africa refugees of all shades of political opinion and beliefs'. He said, 'the warm affection with which South African freedom-fighters are received by democratic countries all over the world, and the hospitality so frequently showered upon us by governments and political organizations, has made it possible for some of our people to escape persecution by the South African Government, to travel freely from country to country, and from continent to continent to canvass our point of view and to rally support for our cause. We are indeed extremely grateful for this spontaneous demonstration of solidarity and support, and sincerely hope that each and every one of us will prove worthy of the trust and confidence the world has in us.'

He identified the main objective of PAFMECA to be the

liberation of territories still under imperial domination, and emphasized that in South Africa they faced 'formidable difficulties' and the struggle was likely to be 'long, complicated, hard and bitter'. He described South Africa as 'torn from top to bottom by fierce racial strife' and enumerated some of the more brutal incidences of massacre perpetrated by the Government:

Almost every African household in South Africa knows about the massacre of our people at Bulhoek in the Queenstown district when detachments of the army and police, armed with artillery machine-guns and rifles, opened fire on unarmed Africans, killing 163 persons, wounding 129, during which 95 people were arrested simply because they refused to move from a piece of land on which they lived.

Almost every African family remembers a similar massacre of our African brothers in South West Africa when the South African Government assembled aeroplanes, heavy machine-guns, artillery and rifles, killing 100 people and mutilating scores of others, merely because people concerned refused to pay dog tax.

On the 1 May 1950 eighteen Africans were shot dead by the police in Johannesburg whilst striking peacefully for higher wages. Naked force and violence is the weapon openly used by the South African Government to beat down the struggles of the African people and to suppress their aspirations.

According to official statistics, he told Conference, police violence against political demonstrators had resulted in 300 dead and 500 wounded between 1948 and 1960.

He referred to the 1956 Treason Trial as 'unprecedented in the history of the country, both in its magnitude and duration. It dragged on for over four years and drained our resources to the limit.' He pointed to the 'murderous killing' of about seventy Africans in Sharpeville in 1960 and to the state of emergency and detention of close on 20,000 people without trial. The 2,500,000 people of the Transkei, he told Conference, were under martial law. He went on to say:

The Government stubbornly refuses to publish the names and number of persons detained. But it is estimated that close on 1,000

Africans are presently languishing in jail in this area alone. Among these are to be found teachers, lawyers, doctors, clerks, workers from the towns, peasants from the country and other freedom-fighters. In this same area and during the last six months more than thirty Africans have been sentenced to death by white judicial officers, hostile to our aspirations, for offences arising out of political demonstrations.

He told the conference of the revolts against the pass laws, the poll tax and against the government-appointed tribal authorities in Zeerust and Sekhukhuneland. 'Instead of meeting the legitimate political demands of the masses of the people and redressing their grievances,' he said, 'the Government reacted by banning the ANC in all these districts. In April 1960, the Government went further and completely outlawed both the African National Congress and the Pan-Africanist Congress.'

He told Conference of the 'formidable force' the state had assembled when the ANC had called a general strike in May of the year before. Special bills had been rushed through parliament to round up and detain political opponents, meetings had been banned, political workers trailed and hounded by the members of the security branch, and helicopters had hovered over African residential areas and searchlights trained on houses and yards. Despite this, he impressed, thousands of workers had stayed away from work and industry and commerce had been seriously damaged.

The celebrations which had been planned by the Government to mark inauguration of the republic were not only completely boycotted by the Africans, but were held in an atmosphere of tensions and crisis in which the whole country looked like a military camp in a state of unrest and uncertainty. This panic-stricken show of force was a measure of the power of the liberation movement and yet it failed to stem the rising tide of popular discontent.

He stressed that while international pressure was crucial to liberation in South Africa, it was ultimately the efforts of the South African people themselves that would liberate the country.

The centre and cornerstone of the struggle for freedom and democracy in South Africa lies inside South Africa itself. Apart from those required for essential work outside the country, freedom-fighters are in great demand for work inside the country. We owe it as a duty to ourselves and to freedom-loving peoples of the world to build and maintain in South Africa itself a powerful solid movement, capable of surviving any attack by the Government and sufficiently militant to fight back with the determination that comes from the knowledge and conviction that it is first and foremost by our own struggle and sacrifice inside South Africa itself that victory over white domination and apartheid can be won.

Then he turned to the crucial point of his speech, namely that it was no longer possible to achieve liberation in South Africa through non-violence.

During the last ten years the African people in South Africa have fought many freedom battles, involving civil disobedience, strikes, protest marches, boycotts and demonstrations of all kinds. In all these campaigns we repeatedly stressed the importance of discipline, peaceful and non-violent struggle. We did so, firstly, because we felt that there were still opportunities for peaceful struggle and we sincerely worked for peaceful changes. Secondly, we did not want to expose our people to situations where they might become easy targets for the trigger-happy police of South Africa. But the situation has now radically altered.

South Africa is now a land ruled by the gun. The Government is increasing the size of its army, of the navy, of its air force and the police. Pill-boxes and road-blocks are being built up all over the country. Armament factories are being set up in Johannesburg and other cities. Officers of the South African Army have visited Algeria and Angola where they were briefed exclusively on methods of suppressing popular struggles. All opportunities for peaceful agitation and struggle have been closed. Africans no longer have the freedom even to stay peacefully in their houses in protest against the oppressive politics of the Government. During the strike in May last year the police actually went from house to house, beating up Africans and driving them to work.

Hence it is understandable why today many of our people are turning their faces away from the path of peace and non-violence.

They feel that peace in our country must be considered already broken when a minority government maintains its authority over the majority by force and violence.

A crisis is developing in earnest in South Africa. However, no high command ever announces beforehand what its strategy and tactics will be to meet a situation. Certainly, the days of civil disobedience, of strikes and mass demonstrations are not over and we will resort to them over and over again. But a leadership commits a crime against its own people if it hesitates to sharpen its political weapons where they have become less effective.

Regarding the actual situation pertaining today in South Africa, I should mention that I have just come out of South Africa. For the last ten months I lived in my own country as an outlaw, away from family and friends. When I was compelled to lead this sort of life, I made a public statement in which I announced that I would not leave the country but would continue working underground. I meant it and I have honoured that undertaking. But when my organization received the invitation to the Conference it was decided that I should attempt to come out and attend the Conference in order to furnish the various African leaders, leading sons of our continent, with the most up-to-date information about the situation.

During the past ten months I moved up and down my country and spoke to peasants in the countryside, to workers in the cities, to students and professional people. It dawned on me quite clearly that the situation had become explosive. It was not surprising therefore when one morning in October last year, we woke up to read the press reports of widespread sabotage involving the cutting of telephone wires and the blowing up of power pylons. The Government remained unshaken and white South Africa tried to dismiss it as the work of criminals. Then on the night of 16 December last year the whole of South Africa vibrated under the heavy blows of Umkhonto we Sizwe [The Spear of the Nation]. The Government buildings were blasted with explosives in Johannesburg, the industrial heart of South Africa, in Port Elizabeth and in Durban. It was now clear that this was a political demonstration of a formidable kind, and the press announced the beginning of planned acts of sabotage in the country. It was still a small beginning because the Government as strong and as aggressive as that of South Africa can never be induced to part with political power by bomb explosions in one night and in three cities only.

184

But in a country where freedom-fighters frequently pay with their very lives, and at a time when the most elaborate military preparations are being made to crush the people's struggles, planned acts of sabotage against government installations introduce a new phase in the political situation and are a demonstration of the people's unshakeable determination to win their freedom whatever the cost may be. The Government is preparing to strike viciously at political leaders and freedom-fighters; but the people will not take these blows sitting down.

He sat down to sustained applause. It was a seminal speech as it altered the African reluctance to support violence as a strategy for change. In 1958 the All African People's Conference in Accra had conceded support for the Algerian struggle but had reaffirmed its commitment to non-violence. The reason was easy to see. Except in Algeria and in Southern Africa, colonized Africans did not have to contend with stubborn settler communities, but Mandela's 'call to arms' at PAFMECA in 1962 dispelled this reluctance.*

Julius Nyerere reflected the new mood when he stated: 'Our preference, and that of every true Africa patriot, has always been for peaceful methods of struggle. But when the door of peaceful progress is slammed shut and bolted, then the struggle must take other forms; we cannot surrender.†

At the end of that Conference PAFMECA became PAFMESCA, as the Southern African region was incorporated into its zone of concern.

Elated by their impact at PAFMESCA, Oliver, Resha, Matthews and Nelson flew to Cairo where Dr Gallal placed himself at their service. The few days in Cairo, apart from meeting government officials and successfully canvassing military and financial assistance, were spent sight-seeing. Dr Gallal invited them to his home and Nelson was introduced to new tastes. He loved the spicy tea brewed in ginger; took his first and only puff on a communal hookah at a wayside tea stall; stared at the sphinx, marvelled at the size of the

---

* PAFMECA, 1962, p. 39.

† Kenneth W. Grundy, *Guerrilla Struggle in Africa*, A World Order Book, Grossma Publishers, New York, 1971, pp. 30–33.

pyramids and agonized at the thought of the thousands of slaves who had sweated and died to build them. In the Egyptian Museum, he was dazzled by the beauty of an unbandaged, partially restored, mummy of a young woman, thousands of years old, Negro-featured, lovely in death. The mysteries of the continent overawed him. Evidence showed that it was in Africa that man had stood up on his two feet and conceptualized his environment. It was in Egypt that he had first committed those concepts to writing and had created the breathtaking civilization reflected in the ceremonial burial of the Pharoahs: the golden mask of the young King Tutankhamun in his golden chariot, the chips of blue glass and grains of wheat all carefully entombed to recreate a mortal life in eternity. And it was in Egypt that Moses had liberated man from the tyranny of man and inspired a saga of freedom that Nelson identified with.

The delegates walked on the banks of the ancient Nile and saw biblical maidens in blue robes carrying waterpots. One evening they relaxed on an Egyptian barge, relishing spiced foods as Arab musicians fiddled and drummed.

Their business with the Egyptian Government done, their support secured, they flew to the crest of Africa: to Libya, Tunisia and Morocco. They stood on the banks of the Mediterranean and marvelled that they were a stone's throw from Europe. Not so long ago, they had scanned the oceans on the southernmost foot of the continent, at Cape Point in Cape Town, searching for the dividing-line between the Indian and Atlantic.

President Bourguiba clasped Nelson warmly and said how good it felt when African blood from the North embraced that from the South. They settled down to talk, with Nelson outlining the position of the ANC and the formation of Umkhonto. He dwelt on the splintering of the PAC from the ANC, and on Sobukwe's imprisonment. The President leaned forward and, with urgency in his voice, said: 'What are you doing here? When Robert Sobukwe comes out of prison, he will replace you.' Resha gave Nelson an 'I told you so' look. It had been his opinion that they should negate the PAC case when presenting their own. Oliver and Nelson had insisted on explaining it. Nelson assured the President that he would be returning to South Africa as soon as he had completed his mission in independent Africa. The President was impressed by their sincerity and asked, 'How can we help? We are ready to do so.' They told him they needed £5,000 and training facilities for their men. Bourguiba arranged for the money to be deposited in their bank account and told them to meet Dr Mostefai in Rabat who would advise them on military training as the Algerians had a training-base there.

Nelson and Robert Resha parted company with their colleagues in Tunisia and went on to Morocco. They found Rabat to be the meeting place of practically every guerrilla group in Africa: the Algerians, Mozambicans, Angolans, Goans and Cape Verdians were all there. They met Jacques Verges, head of the African division in Algeria, who would later defend the abducted Nazi, Klaus Barbie. A resident of Réunion, and therefore a French national, Verges had been declared a prohibited inhabitant in his own country. Dr L. Khatib, a Marxist intellectual, became particularly friendly with Nelson and Resha and introduced them to Marcellino De Santos of Mozambique and Mario Andrade, the Secretary General of the MPLA. Discussions were intense; there was canvassing of support for each other's causes. The ANC delegates weighed issues carefully and avoided making commitments, particularly when it involved supporting one radical group against another. This brought home to them why the African states had to remain neutral when it came to the ANC and PAC.

Nelson and Resha placed themselves under the tutelage of Dr Mostefai for a week. They learnt about Algerian resistance to French oppression and were encouraged in their own pursuit of guerrilla warfare. The Algerian situation came closest to the South African one. They were both confronted with large, white settler communities, intent on domination. But as Algeria was a colony of France their prospect of independence was less complicated.

Dr Mostefai told them how the Algerians had begun their attacks with a few poorly armed men in 1954, how the guerrilla attacks had breathed new life into the liberation struggle, how the resistance army had grown to 120,000 within three years, and how that army was fighting a French force of 450,000.

Mostefai instructed them in the theory of guerrilla warfare, drawing heavily on the Algerian experience and they made mental notes of the parallels. Dr Mostefai stressed the importance of coordinating the political with the military, of always bearing in mind that the object of the warfare was to take over the Government. In Algeria the FLN (Front de Libération Nationale) coordinated the two sectors. Mostefai warned that the enemy exploited regional and ethnic differences to weaken the freedom struggle and that they had to be on the alert against that tactic.

Everything, he counselled, ultimately depended on establishing bases for training and for retreat. In Algeria the liberation force had retreated into the mountains and had been supported by the Berbers. They had set up training bases in liberated Morocco, and both Morocco and Tunisia had provided refuge for fleeing Algerian civilians when government torture became excessive. Mostefai advised them to read extensively on guerrilla warfare, to understand the tactics used by other liberation forces, but to apply these critically to fit their own objectives and their terrain, the psychology of their people and their enemy.

Guerrilla warfare, he emphasized, rarely resulted in a military victory but it unleashed political and economic forces that brought down the enemy. It attracted international support and bankrupted the oppressor. The Algerian war had cost the French an estimated F200m a day, 24,000 lives and the humiliation of being compared with the Nazis in their torture. He warned that the struggle would be hard and long, but that they should never despair for time was on their side and would exhaust the enemy and give them victory.

Nelson and Resha waited to see the King, Hassan, son of

Mohamed Ibn Yusuf, who had led the rebellion against the French in Morocco. They were told that if the object of the meeting was to present their case that had already been done and the king had instructed that they be given £5,000. The money was handed to them in cash, together with a generous grant for personal expenditure.

Robert Resha left for London with the money; Nelson spent some time visiting the ancient Roman ruins in Nabuel, which inspired in him a life-long interest in archaeology. He then set off for West Africa. He flew across the desert, across vast reaches of rippling sand, arid, dry, with no trace of life. Later when he was imprisoned and seized with intense homesickness, missing the love that had filled his life, he would describe his condition as dry and arid as the Saharan sands.

Mali, landlocked and desert dry, appeared to be living on the pride of independence. Nelson was introduced to several people, all by the name of Keita, and finally to the President, Modibo Keita, and the Minister of Defence, Madiere Keita. He recalled the latter name in Ruth First's *Fighting Talk*; Madiere had contributed several essays to it.

They sat down with the Minister of Defence and Nelson began to elaborate on the ANC programme. He had spoken for less than five minutes when he had the distinct impression that his listener had fallen asleep. Nelson was alarmed and embarrassed but pursued doggedly, determined to penetrate Madiere Keita's mind, through its subconsciousness if necessary. There was a long pause when he finished. Nelson's first thought was that he hadn't heard a word of what he had said. But the Minister's eyes opened. 'Your undertaking is very serious,' he said. 'Your Government will know where you have been. You must exercise the utmost caution. We are very far from you, but if your people come to Dar-es-Salaam, we will train them.' He took Nelson to the President, who told him that they had an agreement with Guinea and Ghana and that they would place the matter on agenda at the next meeting, and put their heads together to see what further assistance they could give the ANC.

Lamine Keita took charge of Nelson's social needs. He was a rare academic who had graduated from Lincoln, Moscow and Cairo universities. Lamine told Nelson that the government would meet all his expenditure in Mali and he instructed the manager of Nelson's hotel accordingly. But the President's secretary apparently had a score to settle with Lamine and decided to settle it at Nelson's expense. She countermanded Lamine's instruction and the nervous hotel manager, thinking that he had a bilking on his hand, almost threatened to throw out Nelson. 'Since when did I come here on your government's strength and when did I say that I was not responsible for my own bills?' Nelson asked angrily. He then marched the manager to his room, where he showed him the bank notes in his suitcase, 'I have enough here to pay you for a year!' The manager apologized. Lamine Keita was outraged when he heard of the incident. It now became a matter of his personal honour that the Government met Nelson's expenses, and it did.

The flight to Guinea had a distinct African flavour. Nelson was relaxed, eyes half closed, when a soft voice asked, 'What will you drink?' The air hostess was not beautiful, but she had great charm. 'Tea,' he answered. She smiled approval for they were flying over Muslim territory and they did not like alcohol. The plane descended between Bamako and Conakry; the new passengers boarded with chickens and groundnuts. The woman who sank into the seat next to Nelson's was so heavily pregnant that she could not fasten her seat-belt. She beckoned to Nelson for help. He obliged but not without some embarrassment at the unexpected familiarity with an expectant mother.

At Conakry Airport the Guinean officials became suspicious of Nelson's passport. Oliver had arranged an Ethiopian passport for David Motsamai. Nelson was asked to step aside for questioning. They eventually released him, but retained his passport. By then, all the transport in the city had stopped. They gave him a lift to the nearest garage from where he got directions to a cheap hotel.

In the morning he set out on foot for the Foreign Office.

He had the distinct feeling of being followed. Turning around he found a group of young boys tracking his footsteps. He stopped, curious about their business, but it was they who questioned him. They asked for his passport and when he told them it was at the airport, they became suspicious and ordered him to go to the police station. He said he was on his way to the Foreign Office. They insisted that he went to the police station. Nelson managed to evade them and reached the Foreign Office. He found the boys there ahead of him. 'Who are they?' he asked, after he had been officially welcomed. 'Volunteer reservists!' he was told.

Guinea was a contrast to Mali as the vegetation was lush and the country appeared to be thriving. Sekou Touré had enormous popularity. He and his party had put the economy back on its feet after the French had practically bankrupted it. Nelson heard how the departing colonialists out of sheer pique had left the state coffers dry and gone off with the maps of crucial public works, causing unnecessary trouble for the new administration.

He didn't meet the President as he was occupied with the American Foreign Secretary. But when Nelson reached Lagos he found a communication asking him to return to see Sekou Touré, which he did with Oliver. Sekou Touré told them that the Democratic Party of Guinea supported their struggle and gave them £5,000 in Guinean currency, worthless outside the country. The Czechoslovakian Embassy obliged and exchanged the money.

From Conakry, Nelson flew to Freetown, the capital of Sierra Leone. The flight was a short fifteen minutes, but it took him over an hour by bus to the city for they had to be ferried across a channel to reach it.

He discovered that parliament was in session and decided that that would be the best place of first call; everyone would be there. He went up to a Cabinet Minister and introduced himself as Chief Luthuli's representative. Luthuli had been awarded the Nobel peace prize and was a well-known and honoured African.

I was given a very prominent seat in the House, right in line with the Speaker, and wondered to what I owed such honour. So too did the Speaker who came up to inquire who I was. I whispered, 'Chief Luthuli's representative.' He bowed and said that not even their most distinguished visitors were conducted to that particular seat, but my case was exceptional. 'I wondered what made it exceptional.

The House adjourned for tea. The Cabinet Minister who had conducted me to the special seat now conducted me to the President, Sir Milton Margai, and bowing deeply, said, 'Sir Milton, I present to you our most distinguished visitor, Chief Albert Luthuli.'

'I am David Motsamai,' I corrected, but he waived my correction aside. 'No! No! You'll do.' He then repeated, 'Chief Albert Luthuli!'

Nelson realized it was useless to protest. They were intent on having the Nobel Prize winner and intent on passing him off as Luthuli. Later they accepted the reality, gave Umkhonto their support and put him up in a government guest-house.

He had been asked by Mzwai Piliso, the ANC representative in Cairo, to look up his sister, who was going through a bad patch following the breakdown of her marriage. Lindi Piliso was a 'home girl' and a medical practitioner who had qualified at Wentworth, Durban, and had married a businessman from Sierra Leone. Nelson had never met her. He introduced himself as David Motsamai from South Africa. The name meant nothing to Lindi, but she was pleased to see him. He accompanied her on her medical rounds and was amused by her mastery of the Pidgin English used by locals. On leaving, he asked if it had not bothered her that though he had given her a Sotho name, he had spoken to her in Xhosa. She said it had. Then he told her who he was. She embraced him, welcomed him anew and begged him to stay with her longer. But he had to go on, to Liberia this time, and so took his leave.

Nelson's first contact in Liberia was a Mr Eastman, who subsequently became head of the Foreign Affairs division. Eastman checked him out in Ronald Segal's *Who's Who of*

*South Africa*, and introduced him to the Foreign Secretary, Mr Grimes, who phoned the President in Las Palmas (a local holiday resort). The Foreign Secretary cut short his holiday there and returned to the capital to meet his distinguished guest.

Nelson waited for the President with a number of ambassadors in the ante-chamber of the stateroom of the Palace. The first name to be announced was that of 'Mr David Motsamai'. It caused a stir and the dignitaries looked around to see who had been given priority over them.

President Tubman welcomed Nelson genially and told him that he did not have to explain anything to him. He was fully behind the struggle against the racist regime in South Africa and ready to help. Nelson was given the £5,000 he requested for the ANC and was asked about his personal expenses. He told the President that he had been given allowances in Morocco and Mali. The President whispered something to his secretary, who left the room and returned with a personal envelope for Nelson. It contained 300 American dollars.

The Liberians didn't like his hotel and suggested he move to the Duke: 'It is more in keeping with your status and we will pay the expenses.' Nelson declined. He thought of the poverty of his people back home and preferred to remain in his third-class hotel which was more appropriate. He was invited to a state banquet that evening but also declined that. He knew it was a formal affair and he neither had nor was prepared to wear a dress-suit at that point in his life.

President Tubman placed a car with telephone and chauffeur at his disposal. He was asked to see the Commander of the Harbour, Colonel Ware. *En route* he discovered a surprising patriotism in the chauffeur. 'What river is this?' Nelson asked. 'The River Po,' the chauffeur replied. He then drew up to the side of the road and pointed to an island. 'You see that island there? That is where our forefathers began this country. God save Liberia! They had been taken as slaves to America. They returned when they had been freed, but they were no longer used to this climate. They found the conditions very rough; only half of them survived and they are our founding fathers. That was in the last century.' Nelson was deeply moved. He showed the chauffeur the letter to Colonel Ware, thinking he would be pleased to see it. To his consternation, the chauffeur snatched the letter from his hand and tore it up. 'They are just showing off,' he said. 'You are the guest of the people of Liberia. The people will show you around. I will take you to Colonel Ware.' And so assuming the role of 'the people', the chauffeur presented him to the Colonel.

In Accra Nelson directed the taxi to the only hotel he knew. It had been recommended by the Ghanaian ambassador in Liberia. He saw himself reflected ten or more times in the mirrors lining the foyer. He decided he would change hotels the next day and telephoned Peter Raboroko. They had worked together during the Youth League days, but now Peter was the PAC representative in Ghana and the assistant editor of *The Voice*, a publication put out by the Ghanaian Bureau of African Affairs. Peter came to see him immediately and invited him over to the PAC office.

The PAC had established itself ahead of the ANC in Ghana. Peter was bent on impressing this on Nelson and gave a demonstration of their tough performance and extensive reach when he visited their office the next day. Peter ostentatiously handed a pile of envelopes to an attendant. 'Post these and be very careful about it. They are going to all the leaders in Africa. Register them and bring back their slips.'

Peter was curious to know exactly why Nelson was in Accra and he was convinced there was a hidden agenda. He discussed this with Mlahleni Njesane, a sociologist who had resigned his post at the University of Natal and joined the PAC. But Njesane was having second thoughts about the PAC. Besides he was Nelson's kinsman, being Winnie's maternal uncle, so he reported the discussion to him, much to Nelson's amusement.

Nelson found Nkrumah's dream of a united federal state of Africa compelling, but the more he travelled in Africa and the more he came to understand the continent, the more he realized that the dream would remain one. There were too

194

many differences and the underdeveloped nature of the continent made access and unity almost impossible. There were
politicians who disputed that the North Africans were African at all, since they were not Negroid in appearance; and
tribal and ethnic consciousness challenged national integration, let alone Pan-Africanism. Ghana had a relatively small
population of seven million but the people spoke seventy-five
different languages and dialects, and there were signs of
tension between the southerners who were relatively western-
ized and had a higher literacy rate than the northerners, who
remained traditional.

But Kwame Nkrumah was a binding force and enormously
popular. Nelson was impressed with the steps he was taking
to rekindle national pride by relating the people to their pre-
colonial civilization through stamps, postcards and easily
readable books, and to lead them to a prosperous, modern
society. High on his list of priorities was the damming of the
waters of the Volta to build the Akosombo Dam that would
irrigate, electrify and industrialize Ghana and the surrounding states.

Oliver joined Nelson in Accra and they flew to Dakar in
Senegal. The city was a cosmopolitan mixture of African and
Arab with a sprinkling of French. Nelson admired the ladies
of high society, richly perfumed, gliding in flowing floral
silks and georgettes, with turbanned heads; their male companions in gold-embroided white robes. He visited the
bustling marketplace dominated by the large, Moorish
mosque, enjoyed the cool sherbets, the Afro-Arab meat and
fish dishes and music. Most of all, he loved watching the
boats as they came in at dawn, silhouetted against the pink
sky, graceful, small, pencil-slim vessels with the fishermen at
the one end rowing upright. Their fish spilled and shimmered
on the beach sand, still alive, and the town's folk flocked to
barter and buy.

Nelson and Oliver had an appointment with President
Senghor and as they approached the presidential building
Oliver was seized by an attack of asthma, brought on by the
heat and humidity in Dakar. He was in such a state of

collapse that Nelson had to carry him on his back up the stairs. The President was alarmed by Oliver's condition and immediately summoned his physician. Medication brought relief and Oliver recovered sufficiently to join in the discussion. But he was bedridden for the next few days. Their cheap hotel proved a liability for it did not serve meals, and bringing in appropriate food for Oliver was a problem. Nelson also had to pursue the rest of their work in Ghana on his own. He sensed that while President Senghor was highly respected his penchant for his former colonizers and their French culture evoked open criticism. Nelson had a taste of it within Senghor's bureaucracy. The President gave him an aide, a beautiful young French woman. They arrived at the office of the Minister of Justice, Mr Dabussiére. His secretary, a young black woman, asked the aide her business with the Minister. 'I have been sent by the President to interpret for Mr Motsamai', she answered. 'So?' demanded the black secretary. 'So, may we go in?' she pressed. 'Minister Dabussiére speaks English fluently. You are not needed here. Go back!' The black secretary was openly hostile. Nelson's French companion protested but the secretary held her own and debarred the former 'colonizer' from seeing her boss.

Nelson and Oliver left the continent of Africa at Dakar for London. As the sun rose the plane descended and revealed the city Nelson knew through colonial literature. He saw the great metropolis through the smog in Lilliputian proportions, serene and harmless, and he thought of how almost three quarters of the world had been invaded and occupied from it.

London was exciting: the Thames, Westminster Abbey, the Houses of Parliament, Big Ben; his responses were mixed. So much of his education was related to British history and symbols that he experienced a sense of identity; but there was a simultaneous recoil against the imperialism of the colonies that had demeaned and brutalized people. He saw a reaffirmation of that imperialism in its inherent racism in the statue of General Smuts prestigiously appointed near Westminster Abbey. But as the Empire dimmed and disappeared, so his rancour slackened and Nelson was ready to forgive and to embrace London as part of his international heritage.

They met leaders of the British Labour and Liberal parties and gave Dr Dadoo a report of their African trip. They emphasized the Africanist ethos that pervaded the continent. They told him that African leaders found it difficult to accommodate an ANC that gave such prominence to other racial groups within its structure and that they saw the PAC as articulating African Nationalism. To them the ANC appeared to represent an amorphous group that could not quite be identified as African. They suggested some reformulation of the ANC image to achieve unquestioned support. Yusuf Dadoo tensed at the suggestion. As Nelson recalls:

He kept asking, 'What about policy?' We tried to reassure him that we were not suggesting any changes in policy: we were concerned about the image we projected. We felt at the time that Dadoo was falling short in appreciating the problem from our perspective. However, when on my return to South Africa, I reported on the Africanist demand of the African states to Chief Luthuli, he retorted, 'What right have they to dictate to us?' I explained that they were not dictating, that I was reporting to him as President General how African leaders saw the ANC. Dr Naicker, on the other hand, readily grasped the dilemma that beset us.

Later, at the Rivonia Trial, Nelson would summarize his African sojourn as follows:

My tour was successful beyond all our hopes. Wherever I went, I met sympathy for our cause and promises of help. All Africa was united against the stand of white South Africa, and even in London I was received with great sympathy by political leaders such as the late Mr Hugh Gaitskell and Mr Grimond. In Africa I was promised support by such men as Julius Nyerere, now President of Tanganyika, Mr Kawawa, then Prime Minister of Tanganyika, Emperor Haile Selassie of Ethiopia, General Aboud, President of the Sudan, Habib Bourguiba, President of Tunisia, Ben Bella, now President of Algeria, Modibo Keita, President of Mali, Leopold Senghor, President of Senegal, Sekou Touré, President of Guinea, President Tubman of Liberia, Milton Obote, Prime Minister of Uganda, and Kenneth Kaunda, now Prime Minister of Northern Rhodesia. It was Ben Bella who invited me to visit Oujda, the headquarters of the Algerian Army of National Liberation, the visit which is described in my diary, one of the exhibits.

I had already started to make a study of the art of war and revolution and whilst abroad underwent a course in military training. If there was to be guerrilla warfare, I wanted to be able to stand and fight with my people and to share the hazards of war with them. Notes of lectures I received in Ethiopia and Algeria are contained in exhibits produced in evidence. Summaries of books on guerrilla warfare and military strategy have also been produced. I have already admitted that these documents are in my writing, and I acknowledge that I made these studies to equip myself for the role which I might have to play if the struggle drifted into guerrilla warfare. I approached this question as every African Nationalist should do. I was completely objective. The Court will see that I attempted to examine all types of authority on the subject, from the East and from the West, going back to the classic works of Clausewitz, and covering such a variety as Mao Tse-tung and Che Guevara on the one hand, and the writings on the Anglo-Boer War on the other. Of course, these notes, my lord, are merely summaries of the books I read and do not contain my personal views.

I also made arrangements for our recruits to undergo military training, but here, my lord, it was impossible to organize any scheme without the cooperation of the ANC offices in Africa. I consequently obtained the permission of the ANC in South Africa to do this to this extent that there was a departure from the original decision of the ANC that it would not take part in violent methods of struggle, but it applied outside South Africa only. The first batch of recruits actually arrived in Tanganyika when I was passing through that country on my way back to South Africa.

I returned to South Africa and reported to my colleages on the results of my trip. On my return I found that there had been little alteration in the political scene, save that the threat of a death penalty for sabotage had now become a fact. The attitude of my colleagues in Umkhonto was much the same as it had been before I left.

CHAPTER 20

# Return of the Black Pimpernel

Nelson returned to South Africa in July 1962, crossing the border, as before, at an unchecked point. Joe Modise, now a commander of Umkhonto, awaited him with a car and they sped to Johannesburg. He meticulously avoided making contact with Winnie. He disappeared into the Johannesburg suburb of Rivonia, where his comrades had established an underground base to pursue the new phase in the liberation struggle: sabotage. He met Moses Kotane, Walter Sisulu, Duma Nokwe, J. B. Marks, Govan Mbeki, Dan Tloome and other friends. He had brought new expertise into the struggle and glowed with a remarkable energy that infected his colleagues.

In June 1962 the newspapers headlined THE RETURN OF THE BLACK PIMPERNEL and the police went on alert. In the Mandela home they became a regular establishment. Winnie told a reporter of the *Sunday Times* on 24 June 1962:

The police have been making visits and searches at my house every night for almost three weeks. Whenever my children and I are about to sleep, security branch police arrive. They ask me where my husband is and sometimes search the house. Some times they joke and at other times they are aggressive which frightens the children. There are rumours that Nelson is back, but I have not seen or heard from him.

On Wednesday, 20 June, the police arrived at 10 p.m. and became vicious when they did not find Winnie at home. Her sister, living with her at the time, barred their way and demanded a warrant. They pushed her aside and ransacked the house. The neighbours gathered outside, angry at the intrusion but helpless against it. Some youths, not sharing their helplessness and tantalized by the parked motorbike, set it alight. The bike exploded just as Winnie arrived. The police rushed outside, revolvers in hand, ready to fire. The crowd melted away. They confronted Winnie and questioned her about the explosion. She scoffed haughtily, 'Don't ask me to do your dirty work.' Nobody was going to identify anyone for the police and the Government was not yet empowered to take the sort of arbitrary actions against citizens that they would in the near future.

Nelson found Lilliesleaf, the sprawling farm in Rivonia, officially occupied by Arthur and Hazel Goldreich, a convenient base. When it seemed safe, elaborate arrangements were made for his family to be brought to see him there.

Makgatho recalls:

We knew Tata was in hiding. I can't say how I felt about it. It made me afraid. I couldn't say then why, but now I know I was afraid because I thought we could lose him. I was excited and happy when I saw him. We saw him at different places. Mum Winnie took us to see him. One time I went to stay with him at Lillies farm. There was a big house which was the main house and there were outbuildings. Tata was staying in one of the outbuildings. The white people were staying in the big house. Mum Winnie stayed one night and left. I stayed for a week, or it may have been two weeks. Tata and I swam in the pool and we went for long walks. He taught me to shoot with a rifle and bought me a pellet gun. He used to cook for me. Thembi was not with us. I didn't know why he was not there. I didn't think about it at the time. I saw a lot of Tata because I was close to Mum Winnie then.

I was very sad to leave Tata but he told me I shouldn't worry that we would go to school in Swaziland and we would have no problems.

In August Nelson said goodbye to Winnie. Her eyes had brimmed with tears, and that is how he remembered them. The next day he left for Durban to consult with Chief Luthuli, Monty Naicker, M. B. Yengwa and others, to check on work and to renew contact with friends. He was disguised as a chauffeur, carried a pass that gave his name as David Motsamai, and drove the Austin of his wealthy white boss, actually the theatre director, Cecil Williams.

On Sunday, 5 August, a number of his friends, among them the Meers, the Singhs, Dr Naicker and M. B. Yengwa, gathered at the home of the *Post* photo-journalist, G. R. Naidoo. Nelson cut a large military figure in khaki, his laugh booming the familiar welcome as he embraced each friend. They drank and ate and discussed politics. They laughed a lot, excited by their intrigue. The police were looking for Nelson and here they were partying with him, virtually under their noses. If Nelson had any apprehensions he did not show them.

The 'chauffeur' and his 'boss' drove out of Durban on the warm Natal Sunday enjoying each other's company and strangely at peace with the world, the 'boss' driving and the 'chauffeur' relaxing beside him. They had been travelling for about an hour and a half and had reached Cedara when they were alerted by a police car, catching up with them. Nelson's mind raced:

I considered the possibilities. There was a steep bank on the side of the road. I could make a dash, scale it and disappear into the countryside. I was well trained in such manoeuvres, but one look in the rear-view mirror warned me that I would take the chance at the risk of my life. There were two more police cars immediately behind us. I thought of my gun and my diary. I could not be caught with these. The diary, though written cryptically, could give the police sensitive information and incriminate those I had met recently. I looked around for a hiding place and found it in the car's upholstery. I stuffed both gun and diary into the parting between the two front seats. I do not know to this day what eventually happened to them. Perhaps Cecil Williams found them. Perhaps they accompanied the car as it changed hands, ultimately to be lost to posterity when the old Austin was finally abandoned and left to rot in the sun.

We were flagged down. The police officer came directly to the passenger's side where I was seated and introduced himself as

Sergeant Foster and asked me my name. I said I was David Motsamai. He said he knew I was Nelson Mandela and he had a warrant for my arrest. He was joined by his superior, a major, who occupied the back seat. We drove in silence, my mind wrestling with the thought of escape. The continuing embankment on the side was tantalizing, but I was not sufficiently familiar with the terrain to take a chance. The debate never ceased in my mind, and stopped only when we reached the police station and the prospect of escape ceased.

They questioned me. I declined to make a statement and requested to see a lawyer. I was told, in good time, and locked up in the police cell for the night. I wondered how they had tracked me down and realized that given the number of people I had been seeing the risk had always been there. I heard later that there was suspicion against G. R. Naidoo, my host at my last party, but I was convinced GR would not do such a thing. Later I wrote and told him so.

Warrant Officer Truter arrived the next morning to identify me. I knew Truter. He greeted me genially, 'Hullo, Mr Mandela,' and added, 'Why do you keep up this farce?' I replied coolly, 'I have given you a name and you must be satisfied with it.' I was returned to my cell.

On the third day Nelson was brought before a magistrate in the Pietermaritzburg court and not allowed to see a lawyer. He refused to make any admissions. The court ordered his transfer to Johannesburg.

Nelson was driven to Johannesburg under close police guard. He resigned himself to rustication for several years, cut off from Umkhonto activity during its most sensitive, formative period. He suffered a bout of recriminations that he should have been more careful. After all, he was the only member of the planning committee with military know how but there was no time for depression. He settled down to polite talk with the police, who were being friendly. They stopped twice on the way, at Ladysmith and at Volkrust; both times at police stations. He declined the food they offered. As they approached Johannesburg, the police tensed and their attitude towards him changed. They became officious, handcuffed him and announced his arrival by radio to their superiors. At Marshall Square he was locked up in a cell.

That night he kept hearing a familiar cough; suddenly he knew whose it was and called out to Walter. It was the first both men knew of each other's arrest.

The newspapers headlined the capture of the Black Pimpernel. Winnie was at work where somebody showed her the paper. She read the headlines: POLICE SWOOP ENDS TWO YEARS ON THE RUN, and under that, NELSON MANDELA IS UNDER ARREST. She swayed but the friend caught hold of her and she steadied herself. She asked for early leave and went home. 'What now?' she wondered. She did not realize that she had effectively lost her husband, that her daughters would grow into women and bear their own children, and Nelson would still remain in prison.

# CHAPTER 21

# On Trial and in Prison

Nelson appeared before the Johannesburg Magistrates Court on 16 August. His sister Leabie recalls: 'Seeing Buti brought in by the police was a shock. We rushed towards him and were stopped. We were hurt as a family. What consoled us was his strength. Buti did not want anyone to cry. Our mother was heartbroken. The family was making a great sacrifice. We knew that the people were badly treated, someone had to take action, and Buti had taken that action.'

Winnie, for all her distraught state, put up a brave front and tried to console her mother-in-law. The lawyers Joe Slovo, Harold Wolpe and James Kantor stood by.

Nelson commented: 'I knew the Senior Magistrate, Mr van Coller. He was a decent chap. I had appeared before him, representing clients. I saw now that he was embarrassed to see me as an accused and avoided meeting my eyes.' The case was remanded to a later date. However, Nelson was allowed to speak to his lawyers and his family in one of the court offices: 'It was very emotional, but we were constrained by the very tight security. The police guard kept poking his head through the door to check that I was still there. Zami was in tears but soon cheered up. She had brought me a dressing-gown and a pair of silk pyjamas. That was the extent of her political innocence at the time but she learnt very fast that one didn't wear silk pyjamas in prison.'

Nelson was removed to the Fort and held in the prison hospital as an awaiting trial prisoner. Many friends and relatives came to see him. Among them were Michael Harmel, Duma and Tiny Nokwe, Albertina Sisulu, Ruth First, Ann-Mary Wolpe, Gordon Bruce, Adelaide Joseph and Fred van

Wyk of the Institute of Race Relations. The Reverend Arthur Blaxall brought him books. A few months later he too would be charged and sentenced.

There were five prisoners in the hospital cell and one of them was Moosa Dinath doing a long term for fraud. Nelson had met Dinath, who had a reputation as a business genius, in happier days. He was the only Indian who had floated a public company and had obtained the franchise for a popular German car. More important, he had been a member of the Transvaal Indian Congress and had given Congress generous support. Financial indiscretion had landed him in prison.

While Dinath had fallen foul of the law for a criminal offence, members of his family distinguished themselves. His wife, Ayesha, was one of the four Nagdi sisters, well ahead of their time in feminist consciousness. Years later his sister-in-law, Amina Desai, would serve a five-year prison sentence for alleged involvement with the ANC and Winnie would spend a few months of that sentence with her.

Nelson came to like Dinath. He was generous, resourceful and handled his imprisonment with remarkable aplomb. He treated the commanding officer as if he was his subordinate and had the warders at his beck and call. Nelson taught Dinath exercises and they jogged together around the prison yard. Nelson shared the special meals that were brought for Dinath with him and the other three prisoners. However, Dinath drew a social distance between them and himself and Nelson. He did not, for instance, like sitting down to dinner with them and very discreetly gave them the choice of eating their share of the food when it was brought to him while still fresh and hot. They readily accepted the offer. The whole matter was organized so diplomatically with Dinath saying, 'Well, I can't be left to eat alone, can I? Nelson you can wait to eat with me later,' that Nelson did not have the heart to rebuke him for discriminating against his fellow prisoners. That object lesson could come later, he thought. For the while there were other urgent issues.

Nelson realized the full extent of Dinath's influence one night. He had already turned in when the cell door was opened unexpectedly and he was surprised to see the Commanding Officer, accompanied by a well-known Pretoria advocate, who was later to become a controversial judge because of his biased sentences. The Colonel warned the sergeant in charge: 'You are going to tell nobody that I instructed you to open the door. Understood!' Dinath walked out of prison with his two 'friends' and returned in the early hours of the morning. This was the first of the several nocturnal visits Nelson witnessed while imprisoned with him.

The friendship between the two prisoners was extended to their wives. Maude Katzenellenbogen, the 'common-law' second wife of Moosa Dinath, introduced herself to Winnie with a welcome cheque for four pounds and an invitation to visit her house. Winnie found Maude exciting. It was probably her first close relationship with a white woman outside the political circle. Close to her in age and, like her, burdened with young children with her man in prison, Winnie found it easy to empathize with her. Maude lived in a dilapidated house not far from the prison, flitted about like a butterfly and talked incessantly. She was warm and resourceful and showered Winnie with groceries and clothing at a time when she was in need of both. She told Winnie not to bother to take food for Nelson. Since she lived so close to the prison it was much more convenient for her to take food for both men. In the weeks that followed, the two women became good friends, their friendship continuing after their husbands parted company. But before that time Dinath apparently planned Nelson's escape. His motive for doing so, Maude's motive for continuing her friendship with Winnie, their motive for giving Winnie a job in their office after Dinath's unexpected and premature release from prison – all remain a mystery.

Winnie accepted the Dinaths' friendship and did not impute ulterior motives. Her first meeting with Moosa Dinath, however, was in very strange circumstances. During one of her visits to Nelson at the Fort, the Commanding Officer called her into his office. His manner was secretive, his eyes moving around furtively to ensure that they were not being watched. For a moment she even suspected that he had designs on her. Her anxiety increased when he closed the door and the window, and lessened only when he asked her to take a seat. He then said that he had a very confidential communication for her, that they were in a very delicate situation and she should not be shocked by what she was about to hear. It was only for her to know that it had Nelson's approval. Winnie was then on the brink of hysteria and could barely stop herself screaming. It was only the entrance of a tall, handsome Arab-looking man, as she recalls, that prevented her doing so. The obvious fact that the man was an Indian did not immediately strike her, nor did it occur to her that he was a prisoner.

The Commandant left the two of them to talk alone. The man introduced himself as Moosa Dinath, Maude's husband and Nelson's friend. He told her that they were arranging for Nelson's escape with the cooperation of the Commanding Officer and that they required a sum of R10,000 to see it through. The matter was urgent since Nelson was shortly to be removed to Pretoria and the escape plan had to be executed before then.

Winnie trusted the Dinaths and so communicated the plan to Nelson's friends. They would have to find the money, if it was to be acted on. His friends were suspicious of the Dinaths and considered the possibility of the whole plan being designed to give the police an opportunity to shoot Nelson dead during the escape bid. However, Moosa Dinath, himself, called off the plan on Winnie's second meeting with him, when he told her that he had serious doubts about the reliability of the Commandant. The man wanted to be paid first and there was no guarantee that he would cooperate thereafter. Dinath told Winnie to decline a further meeting with the Commanding Officer when he would try to arrange for payment of the money.

Twenty years later, Gordon Winter, one of the most successful spies on the ANC, would disclose a plot perpetrated by the Bureau of State Security (BOSS) in 1969 to kill Nelson. A group of British sympathizers, headed by a senior

employee of the British Information Office, Marianne
Borman, would plan to spring Nelson from Robben Island
through the support of the famous British solo-flying ace,
Sheila Scott, who, among other achievements, would have
notched up a non-stop flight from London to Cape Town.
Winter would win the confidence of the ANC and be enlisted
by the Borman group to implement the plan; BOSS would
arrange to take it over. A senior warder on the island would
be taken into the conspiracy and he would drug the coffee of
the two guards to Nelson's cell. This would enable him to
walk out in the warder's uniform, armed with a gun. Unknown to him, the gun would be loaded with blank bullets.
They would board a motor boat, ostensibly belonging to
illegal lobster fishermen, and Nelson would change into a
frogman's diving-suit. On reaching the mainland, he would
be transferred to a waiting car which would whisk him to an
airstrip. He would be shot dead while attempting to board
the plane and the blanks in his gun would be replaced with
real bullets to stamp him as a man of violence.

This plan, however, was aborted because Sheila Scott
turned down the assignment, Marianne Borman became suspicious of Winter and, most crucially, because British Intelligence got wind of it and threatened to blow the whistle since
it involved British nationals.

But in 1962, while Nelson spent dreary hours in prison,
Winnie was invited to open the Indian Youth Congress
Conference, in Johannesburg. The honour would have gone
to Nelson and, in inviting Winnie, the youth saw themselves
as honouring him. Winnie, however, draped in a yellow, silk
sari made the occasion her own. They garlanded her with
yellow carnations. The press, agog with her beauty, reported
little else but Winnie, in her first public appearance, impressed on her audience an independence of mind and a
forthright nature. Attacking the rumour that Nelson had
been betrayed by Communists, she said: 'We shall not waste
time looking for evidence as to who betrayed Mandela. Such
propaganda is calculated to keep us fighting one another
instead of uniting to combat Nationalist oppression.'

The 250 delegates elected Nelson as their Honorary President. Suffused in the fragrance of her garland, Winnie proceeded a few kilometres from the Fordsburg hall with her followers to the Fort to visit Nelson. The flowers festooned about her delighted him. He was anxious to know the contents of her maiden speech and the people's response to it, but the warders warned her to keep conversation to family matters and Nelson had to be content with the leaks that got through, parcelled in family talk.

While Nelson awaited his trial, public opposition to his imprisonment mounted. The Free Mandela Committee organized protest meetings throughout the country. The Government retaliated by banning Mandela, even though imprisoned, so that he could not be quoted or published, and banned all meetings relating to him. This was followed by the house arrest of the secretary of the Free Mandela Committee, Ahmed Kathrada, and six days later of Helen Joseph. By the end of November, twenty-five people were house arrested and the number of banning orders had risen from 64 in 1961 to 105 at the end of 1962.

The trials of Walter Sisulu and Nelson Mandela were set for the same date on identical charges. Joe Slovo argued that they should be tried together as it would greatly facilitate their defence. But not only did the State separate their trials, it also moved Nelson's trial to Pretoria. Before the trial it also moved Nelson to the prison there. This created defence problems since his consultant, Joe, was confined to the magisterial area of Johannesburg. They gave Joe permission to see Nelson in Pretoria but when Nelson announced in court, with Joe sitting next to him, that he would conduct his own defence, they withdrew that permission.

Nelson was transported to Pretoria prison in a closed van in the company of a convicted prisoner, Nkadimeng, who was a member of the notorious Msomi gang. The journey was unusually rough. The floor of the van was splattered with grease and the only available seat was an old tyre. Every time the van lurched, the two prisoners slipped on the floor and banged into each other.

Nkadimeng may have been quite innocent, but my suspicions were aroused when they locked the two of us in a single cell. This was irregular. Prisoners were not, as a rule, locked up in twos to control homosexuality, and awaiting trialists were not locked with convicted prisoners.

I became suspicious that he was a plant and took steps to shake him off. I told the warders that I was defending my own case and I needed a table and chair and a bright light. They declined at first, so I threatened to make a court application. That settled the matter. I was removed to a single cell with the requested facilities. More important, I was rid of Nkadimeng. Denied the assistance of Joe, I turned to Bob Hepple to help me prepare my case.

If the State had hoped that it would divide and deplete public support at each hearing by separating the trials of the two leaders, they were disappointed. Both courts were filled to capacity when their trials opened in Johannesburg and Pretoria.

Walter Sisulu, wearing the traditional Sotho peaked grass hat, and out on bail, was carried shoulder high into the court. The detained Nelson was brought in by the police.

Nelson's Madiba clan filled the public gallery with the sight and sound of his Transkei. Clansmen and women, chiefs and followers in traditional dress, the men bearing sticks, took their positions long before the court assembled and the *imbongi* from White River intoned the ancestral praise song as he traced Nelson's genealogy and focused on the Thembu tradition of resistance against domination. The crowds pressed towards the doors singing 'Nkosi Sikelel' iAfrika' and 'Tshotsholoza, Mandela' (Advance Mandela). The authorities took a grim view of the fanfare. The people were warned that they were violating the order that banned meetings for Mandela: 'I give you five minutes to disperse peacefully or I shall use force.'

There were angry mutterings and someone shouted: 'We have a right to attend the trial.' For a moment it seemed that there would be a disturbance, but ANC orderlies quietened down the crowd and persuaded those who could not get in to stand peacefully outside. Nelson's entry was heralded with enthusiastic applause and cries of 'Amandla!'

His appearance in a leopard kaross was spectacular, but it threatened the police. On his return to prison, Colonel Jacobs ordered him to hand over 'that blanket' as he called it. Nelson refused and told the Colonel that he had no jurisdiction over his court attire, that it was a matter for the court to decide. The court never raised any objection and the kaross remained on the regal Thembu's shoulders throughout that trial. But the prison authorities kept it from the eyes of the general prison population, fearing that it would arouse their latent tribal militancy. So each time Nelson departed for, or arrived from, court any prisoner who might have been around in the course of his duties was carefully locked away.

The court proceedings began with the charges against Mandela. The prosecutor, Mr P. J. Bosch, accused him of organizing protests against South Africa becoming a Republic, of speaking at the Conference in Pietermaritzburg and of printing and distributing leaflets inciting workers to strike. The result, he alleged, was that tens of thousands of people had stayed away from work from 29 to 31 May 1961. Mandela was further accused of leaving the country without proper travel documents and of visiting several states abroad, including Ethiopia, where he had attended a conference at Addis Ababa in February.

Mandela conducted his own case and was brief. He did not call any witnesses. He said: 'Your Worship, I submit that I am guilty of no crime.' The magistrate asked if that was all he had to say. Mandela replied, 'With respect, if I had something else to say, I would have said it.' The case was adjourned to 7 November for sentencing. Walter was granted bail at the end of his first hearing. Nelson was refused bail.

In between the hearings, Nelson met Winnie, accompanied by the Madiba cousins. He teased the girls and told them to look after Nkosikazi (Winnie). 'I am worried about all the young men outside.' They said, 'Those young men think we

211

are the married ones and she the single one. They don't even look at us!' Nelson laughed and said he did not believe it as they were all so beautiful. Winnie was not allowed to bring the children, so he sent Zeni and Zindzi a toy aeroplane each.

Two days before his trial resumed news reached Nelson of Ma Sisulu's death. It was as if he had lost his own mother and he longed to be with Walter. Then he heard that the police had raided the Sisulu home on the evening of her death and charged Walter for violating his house arrest because they found a mourner with him. Nelson was infuriated.

Walter, for all the harrassment, remained optimistic and comforted Winnie that they would be given light sentences. Nelson disagreed; he was sure that they would get the maximum and that there would be no remission. When his friend Gordon Bruce came with a scholarship proposal for Winnie to Kampala University, he urged her to take it. Winnie said she would think about it once he had started serving his sentence. Though the prospect was exciting, the thought of leaving her husband in prison while she pursued her individual ambition was chilling. She declined the scholarship; all too soon too the authorities crowded in on her and it was clear that they would not give her a passport to travel abroad.

The State was on the alert on sentence day. The crowds were even larger than on the day of the first hearing. The Johannesburg *Star* reported: 'When all the seats reserved for Africans were taken, police closed the doors and cleared the street in front of the court. Hundreds of Africans were kept back a block away and traffic was diverted. There was a strong force of police, some of them carrying haversacks containing teargas bombs, all around the premises . . .'

The prosecutor, Mr Bosch, made a Pontius Pilate-like gesture when he stopped Nelson briefly on the way to court, apologized for having to ask for his sentence and then kissed him.

The *Star* report described the scene in the court-room:

212

... inside the court every one of the 150 seats reserved for 'Non-Europeans' was taken up and the European gallery was full. There was a spontaneous, though subdued, acclaim when Nelson appeared under police escort and took his position in the dock. He turned to the crowd and, raising his arm in the traditional clenched fist salute, called 'Amandla!' three times. The crowd rose and responded 'Ngawethu!' [It is ours!] The magistrate read out his judgement. He said Mandela was 'the leader, instigator, main mouthpiece and the brain behind the entire organization', and added 'that to incite people to commit a crime by forcing them to protest a law was the same as committing the crime itself'. He also pointed out that it was an offence for certain classes of Africans to absent themselves from work without cause.

The report also noted that 'during the magistrate's forty-minute summing up, Mandela deliberately avoided looking at him. He glanced around the court, nodding and smiling to friends. Nor were the spectators attentive. The legal terminology was beyond them. But during Mandela's statement they listened closely.'

Nelson's address took seventy minutes. He spoke of his youth, of how his imagination had been fired by tales of tribal heroes who had lived in the good old days before the coming of the white man, and how he had devoted his life to the emancipation of his people. He spoke of the difficulties he and his partner Oliver Tambo experienced in their profession, and how they had been ordered to remove their law office from Johannesburg to an African township and how they had defied that order. He could not live with his conscience, he said, and accept laws which in his opinion were unjust, immoral and intolerable.'

The magistrate ordered a ten-minute adjournment at the end of his address to consider the sentence. That he needed only ten minutes to consider Nelson's seventy-minute address suggested that he had already made up his mind. The court reassembled and listened in tense silence as the magistrate sentenced Nelson to three years' imprisonment for incitement and two years for leaving the country without a passport. Then, as the magistrate's figure retreated from the court, Nelson turned to the gallery and called 'Amandla!' There was the familiar resounding response, followed by the singing of 'Nkosi Sikelel' iAfrika'. It was taken up by the vast body of people cordoned off outside the courthouse by the police. The women danced and ululated, and the people linked arms across the width of the street and walked slowly until they split into smaller groups and made their way home.

Walter was sentenced to six years' imprisonment, but he was allowed bail. He disappeared underground. The police, armed with new power, pounced on his wife, Albertina, and their sixteen-year-old son, Zwelakhe, and imprisoned them under the 90-Day Detention clause. By the end of the year, 544 people had been dumped in prison on the whim of the police. Tales emerged of horrendous torture and, in their wake, followed the deaths in detention.

Nelson began serving his sentence in Pretoria prison. Colonel Jacobs, who had resented Nelson's kaross, now took his revenge. The entire prison staff was assembled to witness his humiliation. 'Mandela, take off all those things,' he ordered, referring to the kaross and beads. 'Here is what you will wear.' He issued him with prison garb: a khaki shirt, a pair of coarse fawn-coloured shorts, a calico jacket and open sandals. Nelson was affronted by the indignity. He refused to wear the clothes and told the Colonel that he could take him to court if he wished. The Colonel's response was that they would give him long trousers but Nelson would be removed from the others. 'We were going to put you with Sobukwe,' he said, 'but now you will be alone.'

Nelson protested again when they brought his 'dinner', a stiff porridge with a teaspoon of sugar. 'This is not food,' he said and refused to eat it. An argument followed. He threatened not to eat at all if they didn't bring him proper food. 'Mandela,' the Colonel said, 'you are impudent and uncooperative. Have it your way. We'll give you food that you will find acceptable, but you are going to pay dearly for it. The others are in the sun the whole day. You will have thirty minutes outside and spend the rest of the time in solitary confinement.'

Nelson soon learnt that solitary confinement was more intolerable than bad food and demeaning clothes.

An hour was like a year. I was locked up in the bare cell, literally with nothing, nothing to read, nothing to write, nothing to do, and no one to talk or turn to. I was guarded by two warders during exercise time; the one was an African. I tried to talk to him. He spurned me, afraid no doubt of his white colleague. I suffered the isolation for two months and finally concluded that nothing was more dehumanizing than isolation from human companionship.

So he accepted the prison garb and food and merged into the nondescript mass of the prison population. He joined the prison gang and willed his body to the labour demanded of it, his mind remaining alert to any information it could grasp about the outside world.

There were seven political prisoners in South Africa in 1962 and Nelson was the only member of the ANC. The others were PAC men and they included Robert Sobukwe. On the whole Nelson got on well with his six PAC colleagues; but there were those who told him 'stories' about his non-African allies, that they were ethnically motivated, that they did not respect Africans and did not believe Africans could rule. Personal friends were pin-pointed and Nelson stood up vigorously for them. The attacks were without foundation and Sobukwe reprimanded his followers and counselled them that nothing could be won through pure emotionalism. In many respects Sobukwe found more in common with Nelson than he did with some of his own colleagues. The prison authorities on their part feared the power of the two men and took steps to ensure that they were separated from each other, but accidents occurred when warders were changed.

Sobukwe saw himself as a seasoned old-timer in relation to Nelson and proceeded to guide him on how to survive in prison. He counselled patience and caution. 'You've got to pull through five years. There is no point in putting their backs up against you. They can be very vicious.' On one occasion they asked the warder on duty to take them to the Colonel to discuss prison conditions. The Colonel was surly and demanded what the prisoners were doing outside his office. The warder said they had asked to be brought to him. 'Take them back,' the Colonel barked. 'They will come when I call them.' Nelson began to protest but Sobukwe restrained him. 'Nel, Nel, don't be rash. You've got to live here.'

If Sobukwe was cautious, and Nelson rash, old man Steven Tefu was foolhardy. He prided himself on his contempt for the warders and boasted that no one had as much guts as he in dealing with them. He made it a point to complain about anything and everything. One day, to Nelson's embarrassment, a warder held him up as a model of good conduct. 'Tefu, why do you complain so much? Here is Mandela, he does not complain like you.' 'Ag!' retorted Tefu, 'Mandela is a small boy. He fears you.'

Nelson overlooked the insult. They were victims of an environment which reduced them to compete with each other for their self-respect. He appreciated Tefu's fighting spirit, but also realized that it was futile to protest for the sake of it. It was not simply a question of one man standing up for himself; the entire prison population had to be taught to demand their rights as prisoners. The warders daily violated these; prisoners had to be liberated as a whole. There were prisoners who grovelled before warders with '*ja baas*'s', convinced that their survival depended on arbitrary mercy. This behaviour sickened him. He and his comrades had gone into military training to combat just that type of subservience. Through confronting the State on its own terms, they could return to their people something of their diminished dignity.

The prison's capacity to degrade the human spirit outstripped anything he had known in the slums and in the famine-stricken reserves. He saw men whom he had known to be respectable and proud, crumble and go to any lengths in their misery – 'eat their own children', as one colleague put it. When prisoners lost their self-respect and fought over food left on the plates of warders, how could they be expected to respect them?

Sobukwe and Mandela talked of these problems. For all Steven Tefu's foolish confrontations with warders, they admired him because he maintained his self-respect and helped them in their task to regain the dignity of the imprisoned.

The date 24 May is indelibly inscribed in Nelson's mind. He was suddenly told that he was being moved and found himself within the hour in a closed van, destination unknown, with three other political prisoners: Steven Tefu, Malete, who had been a *New Age* reporter, and John Gaitsiwe. It was a cold night and they travelled shackled to each other and handcuffed, sitting on the raised platform on the side of the van and using the sanitary bucket when the need arose. They were not allowed out for the whole journey which lasted the night and the best part of the next day. The sun came up in the morning but little light filtered into the van. The stench from the bucket was so overpowering that they could barely eat their food. They talked, they sang and slumbered to take their minds off their chains.

About midday they reached their destination. Unlocked and out of the van, they saw that they were at the Roeland Street jail in Cape Town. That evening they were taken to the small dockyard, with its old warehouses, not far from where Jan van Riebeeck had first landed and laid the foundations of the brand of white tyranny responsible for their condition. They boarded the boat, climbed down the ladder into the hold and set sail for Robben Island, feeling the waves under them.

The boat docked and the prisoners were the last to alight. Prison warders awaited them. 'This is not Pretoria. This is Robben Island,' they announced in tones calculated to terrify. Nelson knew the score, knew that their treatment on the island would depend largely on how they handled this first confrontation. If they submitted to them now, they would probably remain so thereafter.

'Huck!' ordered the warders, expecting them to pull together as cattle. Nelson and Tefu stepped up front and set a dignified, human pace. 'Huck! Huck!' the warders shouted to speed them up, their anger rising. The prisoners' pace remained unchanged. 'You want us to kill you?' The prisoners did not respond. The warders prodded them with their rifles. 'We will kill you!' they threatened. The poking and the threats continued, but the prisoners' pace remained unchanged until they reached the prison gates. Nelson's eyes moved upwards to the guardpost and saw the warders with their guns pointed in readiness. He saw that there were guardposts all around the prison compound and, on the ground, more wardens with sten guns. It was a very grim sight and escape seemed impossible. Inside, the orderlies had prepared for their reception. They had sluiced the floor so that it was almost a shallow pool. 'Trek uit!' (Take off!) thundered a warder and as they removed their clothing it was snatched from their hands and dropped into the water. Their bodies were searched in every crevice and they were left standing completely naked.

Captain Gericke undertook a cursory inspection. 'Why is your hair so long?' he asked Malete. 'Like this boy's,' and he pointed to Nelson. They had managed to resist having their heads shaved in Pretoria prison. The Captain was now impressing upon them that that sort of laxity would not be tolerated on Robben Island. 'Look here,' Nelson began, and Gericke was upon him, wagging his finger in his face, and fuming threateningly. 'I must warn you,' Nelson went on, 'I'll take you to the highest authority and you'll be as poor as a doormouse by the time I finish with you.' The Captain had never heard anything like this from a prisoner before. 'Mandela!' There was an explosion of unprintables, and then, 'You are going to do five years, and you show such cheek!' But Nelson's reply was a cool 'Don't be laughable. I will not allow you to do anything outside the regulations.' Gericke was speechless in astonishment and anger.

When the warders realized the futility of strong-arm tactics, they tried divisive ones. Colonel Steyn told Nelson that he knew he was a decent chap, unlike the others. Turning to Steven Tefu he exclaimed, 'Unlike you. You are rotten! You and I, Mandela, are educated men. *We* have common interests.' Tefu drew his emaciated frame erect and spiritedly declared 'I am Steven Tefu, and I am known all over the world. More people know me than they know your Prime Minister!'

Whereas they had been a small group of seven political prisoners in Pretoria, on Robben Island they were a part of a much larger number. Political convictions increased as Poqo insurgents, rural resisters against Bantu authorities in Sekhukuniland, Thembuland and Zeerust, and urban saboteurs joined them. The Poqo offshoot of the PAC had engaged in chilling acts of murder which horrified Sobukwe as much as it did Nelson. Since 1958 the Government had been imposing a new system of rural control, splitting up regions and chieftainships, and suppressing resistance by deposing and deporting 'troublesome' chiefs and their associates, and by banning the ANC from the Transkei. This turned tribal anger on collaborators and traitors, who were hunted down, assaulted and at times killed. Large-scale imprisonment followed. The new wave of political prisoners came to the Island with the expectation of meeting their leaders in prison, of being protected and guided by them. This deepened Nelson's responsibility.

One of the first tasks assigned to Nelson's unit was to pound stones into gravel. The warders decided on an acceptable measure of work for the day: the allotted measure in the first week was half a bucket; towards the end of the week, it was a full one. Those who did not reach the target suffered additional deprivations. There were many altercations between prisoners and warders about whether or not the allocated measure had been reached.

The most obnoxious warder Nelson confronted in those early days was Kleynhans, one of the four Kleynhans brothers on Robben Island who were overseers of the prison work gangs. One particularly hot day they had been working at a brisk pace for three hours and fatigue had set in. Some of the prisoners sobbed and stretched their bodies. 'Go on!' ordered Kleynhans and called Tefu a 'boy'. Tefu remonstrated with him in high Dutch saying that he was old enough to be his grandfather, then proceeding to lecture him on manners. Kleynhans had probably never heard high Dutch before. The realization dawned on him that although Tefu was black, in education and class he was superior to him. The knowledge confused, frightened and humiliated him. The next day he attempted to re-assert himself. He ordered one of the prisoners to take off his jacket and spread it on the ground for him to sit on. The prisoner refused. Kleynhans could do nothing about it beyond swearing.

Kleynhans number two tried his hand at demeaning prisoners. Nelson was walking past a gang of about 300 prisoners overseen by Kleynhans when Kleynhans number one came along. He stood over a prisoner and ordered him to polish his shoes. The prisoner reluctantly obeyed him while the others stopped their work and looked on angrily. Kleynhans number two fixed his eye on Nelson and ordered, 'Look the other way!' Nelson ignored him; self-respect was at stake. Kleynhans was furious and came up to Nelson. This time he shouted in his face, 'Look the other way!' Even if Nelson had wanted to, he could not have looked away. It was as if he was charged by the 300 prisoners. He saw Kleynhans number two raise his hand to strike him. He looked on doggedly and controlled his anger. He knew that Kleynhans was trying to provoke him, so that he could charge him for assault. Kleynhans number one knew that, if struck, Nelson could charge his brother for assault, so he ran to his brother's rescue, forcing back his arm in mid-air.

Kleynhans two eventually showed signs of softening. One day, when lunch was brought to him, he ordered an extra packet and threw it at Nelson's feet. It was a clumsy effort at reconciliation but Nelson ignored it, for although given in kindness, it had been thrown as if to a dog.

Nelson spent the first few months in near total isolation from the outside world. He could receive neither letters nor visits. Winnie wrote to Mary Benson in London from 8115 Orlando West on 17 December 1962: 'I'm not permitted to write nor see him for the first four months. I suppose I'll see him in April.'

She did not see him in April for in January 1963 she was restricted by a banning order. Nelson heard about it from an old-time prisoner who had earned some privileges and had access to the newspapers. It shocked him for while he kept telling himself that the reprisal was inevitable, it did not console him. He relied on Winnie to handle all the family affairs during his absence. Now she would be seriously hampered. He worried about her and the children, and suffered horrific nightmares. He woke up in cold sweats and the nocturnal warnings pursued him for days, though they they did not affect his routine prison duties. He knew that Winnie could not be contained, that her impulsive and head-strong nature would pit her against the police. Her banning order was a deliberate trap to just that end. As the years unfolded, his deepest forebodings proved to be true.

Winnie's responsibilities were heavy as there were the children to care for. She prepared herself to do the best she could, grateful that she had a job and an income. The vivacious smile never left her face but at night the loneliness at times threatened to drive her crazy. Zeni and Zindzi remained oblivious of the tragic changes that had occurred in the family, but the older children were conscious of them.

Makgatho recalls:

When Tata was arrested, Thembi and I were schooling in Manzini, Swaziland. The teachers told us about his arrest and Thembi talked to me about it. I cannot remember what he said, but I think he understood better than I did what was going on. I began to understand what it meant when Tata no longer came to fetch us from school in the holidays. Mum Winnie came instead and she took us to school to Swaziland. The first time after Tata was imprisoned, she took us in Tata's car. We stayed with Ma Mashwana, Father Hooper's maid, in her small two-roomed house, which was already crowded because there were five people in the family. After a while Zwelakhe Sisulu joined us, and we built our own separate hut.

We came home once a year, and the car would come for us. We had no passports, that's why we couldn't take the train or bus across the border. But when we learnt from our friends how to skip the border, Mum Winnie did not have to send a car for us. We travelled by train or bus close to the border. Then we crossed the border at night by foot. There was an Indian man who had a taxi

221

and he would wait for us on the Piet Retief border and drive us to Johannesburg. Maki started school in Swaziland some years later. She did not follow our route. Mum Winnie had managed to put her on someone's passport and she travelled with them.

But Tata was gone from our lives. Homecoming was not as it was before. We missed Tata terribly. We heard nothing from him. He did not write to us during this time. We did not know how to write to him. He was in prison and it was all very strange and in a way frightening too. I was losing my Tata and I did not know I was losing him. It was all just happening. We lived the whole year in Manzini and the Mashwanas became our family. Our Mama sent us money for the small things but there was no money for the big things, for school fees and for lodging.

Winnie began to be hounded by the police. On 7 May 1963 she wrote to Mary Benson from the Child Welfare office in Fox Street where she was employed: 'The situation seems to be getting grimmer by the day. I am supposed to have violated a certain section of my banning by attending gatherings. The case will be on 30 September. I imagine that these people desperately want to convict me; they can therefore stoop very low so as to build up false evidence.' Winnie's observations were accurate, not only with regard to herself but also in relation to all those who openly challenged the State.

Nelson was granted his first visit, eight months after his imprisonment, on 13 July. On 12 July, the police had made their spectacular arrests at Rivonia. Even if the Mandelas were aware of this, they could not have talked about it.

Robert Sobukwe, whose three-year prison sentence expired in May 1963, was redetained on Robben Island. By mid year the State was boasting that it had smashed the PAC and its offshoot Poqo. It rounded up and imprisoned 3,246 alleged members of the organization. By the end of the year, forty people had been sentenced to death and over a thousand to prison sentences ranging from one to twenty-five years. But Poqo cells re-emerged in the prisons themselves.

Nelson was isolated from the others without explanation. He was told that he had been wrongly transferred to Robben Island and that they were returning him to Pretoria.

(*above*) The thatched hut at Mqekezweni, where Nelson Mandela lived from the late 1920s to 1939 (*author*)

(*below*) His first school at Mqekezweni (*author*)

(*above*) Nelson Mandela in the lawyers' office he shared with Oliver Tambo in Johannesburg (*Jurgen Schadeburg*)

(*left*) Nelson Mandela at nineteen, Umtata, Transkei (*IDAF*)

Yusuf Dadoo and Mandela in the Defiance Campaign, 1952 (*IDAF*)

Nelson and Winnie Mandela on their wedding day, 14 June 1958 (*Eli Weinberg*)

(*above*) Oliver Tambo and Nelson Mandela in Addis Ababa, 1962 (*IDAF*)

(*below*) Soweto students protest against being forced to study in the Afrikaans language, 1976 (*IDAF*)

Unarmed Soweto students defy South African state forces marshalled against them
(*IDAF*)

Zeni Mandela and Oliver Tambo at the unveiling of Nelson Mandela's statue, London 1985 (*Gillian Edelstein*)

CHAPTER 22

# Rivonia

The historic Rivonia arrests were prominently featured in the August issue of *Drum* magazine:

Thursday night, 11 July, 1963. A bakery van and a dry cleaner's van trundle down the long driveway of an elegant house in Rivonia, a smart northern suburb of Johannesburg. From the vans come police. They fan out and surround the house and the out-buildings. With them are two highly trained police dogs. A police officer enters a biggish room in an outbuilding, and 16 people tense in surprise.

One – Mr Walter Sisulu, former ANC secretary-general, whom the police have been hunting for several months – leaps to a window. But on the outside a snarling police dog forces him back. Another man makes a break for it – but a dog brings him down.

Then they realize that it's the end.

Handcuffs are snapped on, and all but one do not resist. The man who declines the proffered handcuffs is Mr Ahmed ('Kathy') Kathrada, popular former Indian Congressman, whom the police have also sought since he skipped his house-arrest order a few months back. The handcuffs are forced onto his wrists.

And, as detectives fan out into the house and spread themselves over the twenty-two-acre grounds, the arrested people are rounded up and taken off to a Ninety-day detention. They include Mr Govan Mbeki of Port Elizabeth, Mr Lionel Bernstein, a twelve-hour arrestee, Dennis Goldberg, former member of the Congress of Democrats, and Mr B. A. Hepple, a Johannesburg advocate.

With them go well-known South African artist, Arthur Goldreich, his wife, Hazel, and Dr Hilliard Festenstein. Mr Goldreich had driven into the grounds of the house soon after the swoop. When he realized something was amiss, he tried to reverse his car back to the road but police clambered onto the bonnet of the vehicle and he was forced to stop at the point of a revolver. Mrs Goldreich was also arrested as she drove into the grounds. Dr Festenstein, a medical researcher, was held in similar circumstances.

After the raid, police announced that they had unearthed many documents, a radio transmitter and other evidence.

And they said they had broken the back of the ANC underground and 'Umkhonto we Sizwe' movement.

All those captured at Rivonia were detained in terms of the 90-Day detention law. Wolpe and Goldreich managed to escape from prison with Mosie Moolla and Abdul Haq Jassat. The police, meanwhile, made other arrests. Nelson, already in Pretoria, was now confronted with new charges and a new trial Titled *The State* versus *the National High Command and others* and also *Nelson Mandela and Nine Others*, opened in the Palace of Justice in Pretoria on 9 October 1963. Nelson was Accused number one. He was eventually allowed to see his lawyers: Bram Fischer, Arthur Chaskalson, Joel Joffe, Vernon Berrange and George Bizos.

The one spin-off in being brought to trial was the pleasure of seeing family and friends in court. But Winnie was not there. She needed special permission to attend court because of her banning and it was refused. To aggravate matters, the police raided the Mandela home and detained a young relative living with Winnie. The families of the other arrested people also suffered. Albertina Sisulu and Caroline Motsoaledi were detained under the 90-Day Detention Act.

The trial began. Winnie still did not have permission to attend and made a personal appeal to the Prime Minister. He relented but with a threat: 'Permission would be withdrawn at any time your presence or action at the court, by the manner in which you dress or in any other respect, leads to an incident or incidents caused by you or others present.' When the trial resumed on 14 April Winnie was there, sedate in European clothes. Her physical presence in court buoyed Nelson's spirits. There was time during recess to touch and to catch up on family news. He told Winnie the results of the law examinations he had been writing.

Winnie wrote to Mary Benson in London on 2 November 1963:

I was thrilled to hear about Nel's results. It was a fantastic achievement against unimaginable odds. Unfortunately I could not congratulate him personally due to the fact that I have to get special permission to communicate with him as he is also banned. My attorney has been fighting to get me permission to speak to Nel about his defence and also permission to travel to Pretoria. I saw him for half an hour under impossible conditions. Besides numerous officers who had to listen, I was not permitted to say a word but to talk about defence. He has lost a lot of weight; he was advised to do so by the doctor. Our local press exaggerated his appearance.

# CHAPTER 23

# Rivonia: The State's Case

The case of *The State* versus *the National High Command and others* opened in the Supreme Court of South Africa (Transvaal Provincial Division) on 9 October 1963.

Nelson Mandela, Walter Sisulu, Dennis Goldberg, Govan Mbeki, Ahmed Mohamed Kathrada, Lionel Bernstein and Raymond Mhlaba were identified as members of the High Command and of Umkhonto we Sizwe. The others, according to the charge sheet, were James Kantor, Elias Motsoaledi, Andrew Mlangeni and Bob Alexander Hepple.

Counsel for the Defence, Bram Fisher, applied for the indictment to be quashed on the grounds of its vagueness. Defence Counsel pointed out that 156 of the 199 alleged acts of violence had occurred during the period when one of the accused, Mr Mandela, had been in prison. The Judge President ruled that the accused were entitled to greater clarity and more information about the case they had to meet and quashed the indictment. The State, however, re-arrested the accused and redetained them under the 90-Day Clause while it prepared a new indictment. Bob Hepple was discharged and he fled the country with his wife.

In the second indictment the trial was referred to as *The State* versus *Mandela and Nine Others*. They were charged with sabotage and with attempting to cause a violent revolution in the Republic through a conspiracy of banned persons and organizations, and assistance to military units of foreign countries. The banned persons included Michael Harmel, Percy Hodgson, Joe Slovo, Harold Strachan, Harold Wolpe, Moses Kotane, Tennyson Makiwane, John Joseph Marks, Johannes Modise, Philemon Duma Nokwe, James Jose

Radebe, Robert Resha and Oliver Tambo. The banned organizations were the Communist Party of South Africa and the African National Congress.

The State Prosecutor, Dr Percy Yutar, in his opening address claimed that:

... the accused deliberately and maliciously plotted and engineered the commission of acts of violence and destruction throughout the country directed against the offices and homes of state and municipal officials, as well as against all lines and manner of communications.

The planned purpose thereof was to bring in the Republic of South Africa chaos, disorder and turmoil, which would be aggravated, according to their plan, by the operation of thousands of trained guerrilla warfare units deployed throughout the country at various areas by local inhabitants, as well as special selected men posted to such areas. Their combined operations were planned to lead to confusion, violent insurrection and rebellion, followed at the appropriate juncture by an armed invasion of the country by military units of foreign powers.

In the midst of the resulting chaos, turmoil and disorder, it was planned by the accused to set up a Provisional Revolutionary Government to take over the administration and control of this country.

The Prosecutor went on to allege that:

By the latter half of 1961, the African National Congress had decided to embark upon a policy of violence and destruction – a policy of sabotage – in order to achieve their political aims and objectives. For this purpose they had formed the Umkonto we Sizwe [The Spear of the Nation], often abbreviated as the MK. This organization was recruited from followers who were prepared, whatever the odds, to die. The MK was placed under the political guidance of the National Liberation Committee and the National Executive of such Committee, representative of all the banned organizations in this country, including in particular, the African National Congress and the South African Communist Party, but for its control and direction the MK placed itself under the so called National High Command.

'These organizations', the State continued, 'went underground and purchased Lilliesleaf in Rivonia and Travelain in Krugersdorp to direct their underground activities.'

According to the State, Lilliesleaf was purchased for R25,000 in August 1961 by one Vivian Ezra (brother-in-law of Communist Party member Michael Harmel) acting as trustee for Navian (Pty), Limited of which he and Harold Wolpe, another named Communist, were directors. All the transactions for the purpose of the property were executed in the office of James Kantor. The property was rented out to Arthur Goldreich at R100 a month, and he moved into it with his wife, Hazel, and their two young children. The Goldreichs employed indoor and outdoor 'Bantu staff' who 'gave the outward appearance that the grounds were being used for legitimate and innocent farming purposes and were required regularly to sell the produce of the land to the neighbours in the vicinity and even to the staff of the local police station.'

The Lilliesleaf outbuildings had been occupied, amongst others, by Nelson Mandela, who went under the assumed name of David, Walter Sisulu, who was referred to as Allah, and Ahmed Mohamed Kathrada, whose code name was Pedro. The other residents included Govan Mbeki, a named Communist and also known as Dlamini, and Raymond Mhlaba. Frequent and regular visitors to the Rivonia house were Dennis Goldberg, who went one step further and had two fictitious names, Williams and Barnard, Lionel Bernstein, a named Communist, Harold Wolpe, Joe Slovo, another named Communist, and Michael Harmel, also a named Communist.

The State said that Rivonia was the focal point of the African National Congress and the Communist Party of South Africa, and the seat of the National High Command. The leaders adopted the so-called M-Plan (the Mandela Plan) which provided for a central authority at Rivonia, and regional, as well as sub-regional, committees throughout the country. The plan incorporated the cell system of the Communist Party and extraordinary steps were taken to ensure the utmost secrecy in every possible way, from the humblest street steward and cell leader to the leaders at Rivonia.

The National High Command, the State alleged, had established a complete radio transmitting set, known as the Freedom Radio, from which Walter Sisulu broadcast a message to his followers and sympathizers after being introduced by Govan Mbeki. A tape recording found at Rivonia and a typed transcript of the tape were produced as exhibits.

The accused, according to the State, had been promised military and financial aid from several African states and by some overseas countries. As evidence of this, it submitted two lengthy documents in the handwriting of Nelson Mandela.

Dr Yutar went on to allege that the MK had taken numerous young 'Bantu males' away from their homes without their parents' or relatives' consent. They sent them across the border in small batches under the leadership of trusted agents and servants of the accused for training in guerrilla warfare as waged in China, Algeria and Cuba. The recruits, he said, were given false names and addresses and prepared in advance with false statements to be given to the South African police should they be stopped en route. He said several escape routes were used and the police had found maps at Rivonia showing some of these. Elias Motsoaledi and Andrew Mlangeni were cited as the prime recruiters. The recruits, once across the border, were airlifted to the training centres at a cost of R30,000 per planeload of twenty or less. The first stop was Tanganyika and from there they were sent to various countries, including Algeria, Egypt and Ethiopia, where they received extensive military training in sabotage and guerrilla warfare.

Dr Yutar told the court, that a special school for the initial training of young 'Bantu' recruits was at Mamre in the district of Darling, Cape, run by, and in the charge of, Dennis Goldberg, who required the recruits to call him Comrade Commandant. Another leading figure at the school was Looksmart Solwandle Ngudle, whom he described as the leader of the Cape Town branch of Umkhonto and responsible for acts of violence in the city. On his arrest he was found in possession of a quantity of explosives and a firearm. (Looksmart subsequently 'died' in prison.)

229

The State produced 250 documents seized at Rivonia which included many standard works on Marxism, histories of European civil war and revolutions, guerrilla warfare, manuals on rock blasting, maps, copies of vouchers, receipts, blueprints and a passport made out to David Motsamai, Nelson's alias in the underground.

The State's case in the final analysis rested on the evidence of two members of Umkhonto who had turned State witnesses, referred to as X and Z, respectively, for their protection. They freely admitted their acts of sabotage, having been promised immunity if they gave satisfactory evidence. They not only exposed their comrades but doctored the facts to assist the police so that the identities of the ANC and Umkhonto were virtually obliterated and more or less converted into the Communist Party.

Mr X described himself as a saboteur, a member of the ANC (joining in 1957) and a member of the SA Communist Party. He had served as secretary of the African Municipal Workers' Union, an affiliate of the South African Congress of Trade Unions (SACTU) in 1962, and was paid odd amounts ranging from R6 to R10 per month. His disaffection, he said, occurred in 1963. Up to then he had seen the Communist Party as an agent of the ANC and had supported Umkhonto as an instrument of the ANC. He had joined the CP, he said, on the understanding that it worked for the ANC. However, in 1963, he discovered that the ANC and Umkhonto were instruments of the Communist Party. He had endangered his life and risked imprisonment for the ANC and had never lost faith in its ideals. 'I will say this, that I thought all the time, that what the ANC was working for was good, and is good, but what made me disillusioned was the action of the leaders.' He excluded Mandela. The other leaders, he alleged, did not represent the ANC. They were Communists. 'The ANC were under the impression that Umkhonto we Sizwe was an organization belonging to them, when in fact, it was an organization belonging to the Communists.' He said that in 1963 the CP directed its members to infiltrate ANC branches and capture the leadership.

This, he said, was discussed in the CP cell and members were instructed gradually to take over the branches and transfer power to the Communists. He said he became disillusioned with Umkhonto because he felt the recruits were not cared for. The leaders had a lot of money and they left the country. He identified the qualitative difference between the ANC and CP as that the first held that wealth belonged to the people and the second that it belonged to the workers. He said that he discovered after he joined the Party that it divided the people into classes.

He was aggressively cross-examined by Vernon Berrange for the Defence, but he stood by his claim. Berrange, however, established that Mr X had a history of petty criminality and had served three terms of imprisonment for theft, totalling four and a half years.

Mr Z testified that he had joined the ANC in 1951 and rose to the position of secretary of the West Bank branch of the ANC. He had lost respect for ANC leaders like Oliver Tambo who had run away. When the ANC had been banned, they had been instructed by Govan Mbeki to organize secret cells, and cripple the Government economically and militarily and watch out for informers. He had been told that two informers had been shot dead. Volunteers recruited to the MK were known as *Amadelakufa* (those who defy death) and were instructed to distribute leaflets and to kill. This was a deliberate falsification of the concept of Amadelakufa, which implied volunteers.

The State case ended after five months on 29 February 1964.

CHAPTER 24

# Rivonia: The Defence Case

The Defence began its case on 20 April 1964. Senior Counsel, Bram Fischer, addressed the court:

May it please your lordship. My lord, your lordship will have realized, from the cross-examination of the State witnesses, that there are certain important parts of the State evidence which will be admitted by some of the accused. Your lordship will also have realized, from the cross-examination, that there are certain equally important parts of that evidence which will be denied and which we shall maintain are false.

He asserted that Accused three, five and six, Goldberg, Bernstein and Mhlaba, were not members of the High Command. Secondly, he pointed out that Umkhonto was not

the military wing of the African National Congress. Here, the Defence will seek to show that the leaders both of Umkhonto and of the African National Congress, for sound valid reasons, which will be explained to your lordship, endeavoured to keep these two organizations entirely distinct. They did not always succeed in this, for reasons which will also be explained, but we will suggest that the object of keeping the two organizations separate was always kept in mind, and every effort was made to achieve that object.

Thirdly, he asserted that the Defence would emphatically deny that the ANC was a tool of the Communist Party:

It will show that the African National Congress is a broad national movement embracing all classes of Africans within its ranks, and having the aim of achieving equal political rights for all South Africans. The evidence will show further that it welcomes not only the support which it received from the Communist Party, but also the support which it receives from many other quarters.

232

Now on this point the evidence will show how Umkhonto we Sizwe was formed, and that it was formed in order to undertake sabotage only when it was considered that no other method remained for the achievement of political rights.

Mr Fischer said that the Defence would deny that 'Umkhonto had adopted a military plan called Operation Mayibuye and intended to embark upon guerrilla warfare'.

In regard particularly to the last issue, the court will be asked to have regard to the motives, the character and political background of the men in charge of Umkhonto we Sizwe and its operations. In other words, to have regard, amongst other things, to the tradition of non-violence of the African National Congress, to have regard to the reasons which led these men to resort to sabotage in an effort to achieve their political objectives and why, in the light of these facts, they are to be believed when they say why Operation Mayibuye had not been adopted, and that they would not have adopted it while there was some chance, however remote, of having their objectives achieved by the combination of mass political struggle and sabotage.

The Defence case will commence with a statement from the dock by Accused number one, who personally took part in the establishment of Umkhonto, and who will be able to inform the court of the beginnings of that organization, and of its history up to August, when he was arrested.

Dr Yutar did not relish the idea of Mandela in the dock. He knew that he would make a strong political plea. He wanted to prevent that, but how? Feebly, he advised 'that a statement from the dock does not carry the same weight as evidence under oath, although I am sure that he knows this already'.

## STATEMENT FROM THE DOCK OF NELSON MANDELA, ACCUSED NUMBER ONE:

### I have done whatever I did ... because of my experience in South Africa and my own proudly felt African background

My lord, I am the first accused. I hold a Bachelor's degree in Arts, and practised as an attorney in Johannesburg for a number of years, in partnership with Mr Oliver Tambo. I am a convicted prisoner, serving five years for leaving the country without a permit, and for inciting people to go on strike at the end of May 1961.

I admit immediately that I was one of the persons who helped to form Umkhonto we Sizwe, and that I played a prominent role in its affairs until I was arrested in August 1962.

At the outset, I want to say that the suggestion made by the State in its opening that the struggle in South Africa is under the influence of foreigners or Communists is wholly incorrect. I have done whatever I did, both as an individual and as a leader of my people, because of my experience in South Africa, and my own proudly felt African background, and not because of what any outsider might have said.

In my youth in the Transkei, I listened to the elders of my tribe telling stories of the old days. Amongst the tales they related to me were those of wars fought by our ancestors in defence of the fatherland. The names of Dingane and Bambata, Hintsa and Makana, Squngatha and Dalasile, Moshoeshoe and Sekukhuni, were praised as the pride and glory of the entire African nation. I hoped then that life might offer me the opportunity to serve my people and make my own humble contribution to their freedon struggle. This is what has motivated me in all that I have done in relation to the charges made against me in this case.

## I did not plan it [sabotage] in a spirit of recklessness, nor because I have any love for violence

Some of the things so far told to the court are true and some are untrue. I do not, however, deny that I planned sabotage. I did not plan it in a spirit of recklessness, nor because I have any love for violence. I planned it as a result of a calm and sober assessment of the political situation that had arisen after many years of tyranny, exploitation and oppression of my people by the whites.

## We believed that as a result of government policy, violence by the African people had become inevitable

I have already mentioned that I was one of the persons who helped to form Umkhonto. I, and the others who started the organization, did so for two reasons. Firstly, we believed that as a result of government policy, violence by the African people had become inevitable, and that unless responsible leadership was given to

234

catalyse and control the feelings of our people, there would be outbreaks of terrorism which would produce an intensity of bitterness and hostility between the various races of this country which is not produced even by war.

Secondly, we felt that without sabotage there would be no way open to the African people to succeed in their struggle against the principle of white supremacy. All lawful modes of expressing opposition to this principle had been closed by legislation and we were placed in a position in which we had either to accept a permanent state of inferiority, or to defy the Government. We chose to defy the Government. We first broke the law in a way which avoided any recourse to violence; when this form was legislated against, and when the Government resorted to a show of force to crush opposition to its policies, only then did we decide to answer violence with violence.

But the violence which we chose to adopt was not terrorism. We who formed Umkhonto were all members of the African National Congress, and had behind us the ANC tradition of non-violence and negotiation as a means of solving political disputes. We believed that South Africa belonged to all the people who lived in it, and not to one group, be it black or white. We did not want an inter-racial war, and tried to avoid it to the last minute. If the court is in doubt about this, it will be seen that the whole history of our organization bears out what I have said, and what I will subsequently say, when I describe the tactics which Umkhonto decided to adopt. I want, therefore, to say something about the African National Congress.

## For thirty-seven years . . . it [the ANC] adhered strictly to a constitutional struggle

The African National Congress was formed in 1912 to defend the rights of the African people which had been seriously curtailed by the South Africa Act, and which was then being threatened by the Native Land Act. For thirty-seven years, that is until 1949, it adhered strictly to a constitutional struggle. It put forward demands and resolutions, it sent delegations to the Government in the belief that African grievances could be settled through peaceful discussion and that Africans could advance gradually to full political rights. But white governments remained unmoved, and the rights of Africans became less instead of becoming greater. In the words of my leader, Chief Luthuli, who became President of the ANC in 1952, and who was later awarded the Nobel Peace Prize, I quote: 'Who will deny that thirty years of my life have been spent knocking in vain, patiently, moderately and modestly at a closed and barred door? What have been the fruits of moderation? The past thirty years have seen the greatest number of laws restricting our rights and progress, until today we have reached a stage where we have almost no rights at all'

Even after 1949 the ANC remained determined to avoid violence. At this time, however, there was a change from the strictly constitutional means of protest which had been employed in the past. The change was embodied in a decision which was taken to protest against apartheid legislation by peaceful, but unlawful, demonstrations against certain laws. Pursuant to this policy the ANC launched the Defiance Campaign, in which I was placed in charge of volunteers. This campaign was based on the principles of passive resistance. More than 8,500 people defied apartheid laws and went to gaol. Yet there was not a single instance of violence in the course of this campaign on the part of any defier. I and nineteen colleagues were convicted for the role which we played in organizing the campaign, and this conviction was under the Suppression of Communism Act although our campaign had nothing to do with Communism; but our sentences were suspended, mainly because the Judge found that discipline and non-violence had been stressed throughout. This was the time when the volunteer section of the ANC was established, and when the word *Amadelakufa* was first used: this was the time when the volunteers were asked to take a pledge to uphold certain principles. Evidence dealing with volunteers and their pledges has been introduced into this case, but completely out of context. The volunteers were not, and are not, the soldiers of a black army pledged to fight a civil war against the whites. They were, and are, the dedicated workers who are prepared to lead campaigns initiated by the ANC, to distribute leaflets, to organize strikes, or to do whatever the particular campaign required. They are called volunteers because they volunteer to face the penalties of imprisonment and whipping which are not prescribed by the legislature for such acts.

## The ANC is not, and never has been, a Communist organization

During the Defiance Campaign, the Public Safety Act and the Criminal Law Amendment Act were passed. These statutes provided harsher penalties for offences committed by way of protests against laws. Despite this, the protests continued and the ANC adhered to its policy of non-violence. In 1956, 156 leading members of the Congress Alliance, including myself, were arrested on a charge of High Treason and charges under the Suppression of Communism Act. The non-violent policy of the ANC was put in issue by the State, but when the court gave judgement some five years later, it found that the ANC did not have a policy of violence. We were acquitted on all counts, which included a count that the ANC sought to set up a communist state in place of the existing regime. The Government has always sought to label all its opponents as Communists. This allegation has been repeated in the present case, but, as I will show, the ANC is not, and never has been, a Communist organization.

In 1960 there was the shooting at Sharpeville, which resulted in the proclamation of a State of Emergency and the declaration of the ANC as an unlawful organization. My colleagues and I, after careful consideration, dedided that we would not obey this decree. The African people were not part of the Government, and did not make the laws by which they were governed. We believed in the words of the Universal Declaration of Human Rights, that 'the will of the people shall be the basis of the authority of the Government', and for us to accept the banning was equivalent to accepting the silencing of the Africans for all time. The ANC refused to dissolve, but instead went underground. We believed it was our duty to preserve this organization which had been built up with almost fifty years of unremitting toil. I have no doubt that no self-respecting white political organization would disband itself if declared illegal by a government in which it had no say.

## The M- [Mandela] Plan . . . was a method of organizing . . . it had nothing whatsoever to do with sabotage or Umkhonto we Sizwe

I now want to deal, my lord, with evidence which misrepresents the true position in this case. In some of the evidence the M-Plan has been completely misrepresented. It was nothing more than a method of organizing planned in 1953, and put into operation with varying degrees of success thereafter. After April 1960, new methods had to be devised, for instance, by relying on smaller committees.

The M-Plan was referred to in evidence at the Treason Trial, but it had nothing whatsoever to do with sabotage or Umkhonto we Sizwe, and was never adopted by Umkhonto. The confusion, particularly by certain witnesses from the Eastern Cape is, I think, due to the use of the words or the phrase 'High Command'. This term was coined in Port Elizabeth during the Emergency, when most of the ANC leaders were gaoled, and a Gaol Committee, set up to deal with complaints, was called the High Command. After the Emergency, this phrase stuck, and was used to describe certain of the ANC committees in that area. Thus we have had witnesses talking about the West Bank High Command, and the Port Elizabeth High Command. These so-called 'High Commands' came into existence before Umkhonto was formed, and were not concerned in any way with sabotage. In fact, as I will subsequently explain, Umkhonto as an organization was, as far as possible, kept separate from the ANC. The use of the phrase 'High Command' caused some dissension in ANC circles in the Eastern Province. I travelled there in 1961, because it was alleged that some of these so-called High Commands were using duress in order to enforce the new Plan. I did not find evidence of this, but nevertheless forbade it, and also insisted that the term 'High Command' should not be used to describe any ANC committee.

## All-In African Conference ... I was the Honorary Secretary ... responsible for organizing the national stay-at-home ... As all strikes by Africans are illegal ... I had to ... go into hiding to avoid arrest

My Lord, I would like now to deal with the immediate causes leading to the formation of Umkhonto. In 1960 the Government held a referendum which led to the establishment of a republic. Africans, who constituted approximately seventy per cent of the population of South Africa, were not entitled to vote, and were not even consulted about the proposed constitutional change. All of us were apprehensive about our future under the proposed white republic, and a resolution was taken to hold an All-In African Conference to call for a National Convention, and to organize mass demonstrations on the eve of the unwanted republic, if the Government failed to call the convention.

The conference was attended by Africans of various political persuasions. I was the Honorary Secretary of the conference, and undertook to be responsible for organizing the national stay-at-home which was subsequently called to coincide with the declaration of the republic. As all strikes by Africans are illegal, the person organizing such a strike must avoid arrest. I was chosen to be this person, and consequently I had to leave my home and my family and my practice and go into hiding to avoid arrest.

## The stay-at-home ... was to be a peaceful demonstration ... the Government's answer was to introduce new and harsher laws

The stay-at-home, in accordance with ANC policy, was to be a peaceful demonstration. Careful instructions were given to organizers and members to avoid any recourse to violence. The Government's answer was to introduce new and harsher laws, to mobilize its armed forces, and to send Saracens, armed vehicles and soldiers into the townships in a massive show of force to intimidate the people. This was an indication that the Government had decided to rule by force alone, and this decision was a milestone on the road to Umkhonto.

Some of this may appear irrelevant to this trial. In fact I believe none of it is irrelevant because it will, I hope, enable the court to appreciate the attitude towards Umkhonto eventually adopted by the various persons and bodies concerned in the National Liberation Movement. When I went to gaol in 1962, the dominant idea was that loss of life should be avoided. I know now that this was still so in 1963.

## What were we, the leaders of our people, to do?

I must return, however, my lord, to June 1961. What were we, the leaders of our people, to do? Were we to give in to the show of force and the implied threat against future action, or were we to fight it out, and if so, how?

We had no doubt that we had to continue to fight. Anything else would have been abject surrender. Our problem, my lord, was not whether to fight, but was how to continue to fight. We of the ANC had always stood for a non-racial democracy, and we shrank from any action which might drive the races further apart than they already were. But the hard facts were that fifty years of non-violence had brought the African people nothing but more and more repressive legislation, and fewer and fewer rights.

It may not be easy for this court to understand, but it is a fact that for a long time the people had been talking of violence, of the day when they would fight the white man, and win back their country, and we, the leaders of the ANC, had nevertheless always prevailed upon them to avoid violence and to pursue peaceful methods. When some of us discussed this in June of 1961, it could not be denied that our policy to achieve a non-racial state by non-violence had achieved nothing, and that our followers were beginning to lose confidence in this policy, and were developing disturbing ideas of terrorism.

**A government which uses force to maintain its rule teaches the oppressed to use force to oppose it . . . Particularly disturbing was [that violence] was . . . increasingly taking the form, not of struggle against the Government . . . but of civil strife**

It must not be forgotten, my lord, that by this time violence had, in fact, become a feature of the South African political scene. There had been violence in 1957 when the women of Zeerust were ordered to carry passes; there was violence in 1958 with the enforcement of Bantu Authorities and cattle culling in Sekhukuniland; there was violence in 1959 when the people of Cato Manor protested against pass raids; there was violence in 1960 when the Government attempted to impose Bantu Authorities in Pondoland. Thirty-nine Africans died in those Pondoland disturbances. In 1961 there had been riots in Warmbaths, and all this time, my lord, the Transkei had been a seething mass of unrest.

Each disturbance pointed clearly to the inevitable growth amongst Africans of the belief that violence was the only way out – it showed that a government which uses force to maintain its rule teaches the oppressed to use force to oppose it. Already small groups had arisen in the urban areas and were spontaneously making plans for violent forms of political struggle. There now arose a danger that these groups would adopt terrorism against Africans, as well as whites, if not properly directed. Particularly disturbing was the type of violence engendered in places such as Zeerust, Sekhukuniland and Pondoland amongst Africans. It was increasingly taking the form, not of struggle against the Government – though this is what prompted it – but of civil strife between pro-government chiefs and those opposed to them, conducted in such a way that it could not hope to achieve anything other than a loss of life, and bitterness.

At the beginning of June 1961, after a long and anxious assessment of the South African situation, I and some colleagues, came to the conclusion that as violence in this country was inevitable, it would be unrealistic and wrong for African leaders to continue preaching peace and non-violence at a time when the Government met our peaceful demands with force.

## The decision was made to embark on violent forms of political struggle ... because the Government had left us with no other choice

This conclusion was not easily arrived at. It was only when all else had failed, when all channels of peaceful protest had been barred to us, that the decision was made to embark on violent forms of political struggle and to form Umkhonto we Sizwe. We did so, not because we desired such a course, but solely because the Government had left us with no other choice. I can only say that I felt morally obliged to do what I did.

We, who had taken this decision, started to consult leaders of various organizations, including the ANC. I will not say whom we spoke to, or what they said.

## Umkhonto was to perform sabotage ... on no account were they [members] to injure or kill people in planning or carrying out operations

The ANC was a mass political organization. Its members had joined on the express policy of non-violence. It could not and would not undertake violence.

On the other hand, in view of this situation I have described, the ANC was prepared to depart from its fifty-year-old policy of non-violence to this extent that it would no longer disapprove of properly controlled sabotage, and hence members who undertook such activity would not be subject to disciplinary action by the ANC.

I say 'properly controlled sabotage' because I made it clear that if I helped to form the organization I would at all times subject it to the political guidance of the ANC and would not undertake any different form of activity from that contemplated without the consent of the ANC.

241

## We felt that the country was drifting towards civil war [sabotage was planned to avoid civil war]

Umkhonto was formed in November 1961. When we took this decision, and subsequently formulated our plans, the ANC heritage of non-violence and racial harmony was very much with us. We felt that the country was drifting towards civil war in which blacks and whites would fight each other. We viewed the situation with alarm. Civil war would mean the destruction of what the ANC stood for; with civil war, racial peace would be more difficult than ever to achieve.

The avoidance of civil war had dominated our thinking for many years, but when we decided to adopt sabotage as part of our policy, we realized that we might one day have to face the prospect of such a war. This had to be taken into account in formulating our plans. We required a plan which was flexible, and which permitted us to act in accordance with the needs of the times; above all, the plan had to be one which recognized civil war as the last resort, and left the decision on this question to the future. We did not want to be committed to civil war, but we wanted to be ready if it became inevitable.

Four forms of violence are possible. There is sabotage, there is guerrilla warfare, there is terrorism and there is open revolution. We chose to adopt the first method and to test it fully before taking any other decision.

In the light of our political background, the choice was a logical one. Sabotage did not involve loss of life and it offered the best hope for future race relations. Bitterness would be kept to a minimum and, if the policy bore fruit, democratic government could become a reality.

## Attacks on the economic life-lines of the country were to be linked with sabotage on government buildings

The initial plan was based on a careful analysis of the political and economic situation of our country. We believed that South Africa depended to a large extent on foreign capital and foreign trade. We felt that planned destruction of power plants and interference with rail and telephone communications would tend to scare away capital from the country, make it more difficult for goods from the industrial areas to reach the seaports on schedule, and would in the long run be a heavy drain on the economic life of the country, thus compelling the voters of the country to reconsider their position.

242

Attacks on the economic life-lines of the country were to be linked with sabotage on government buildings and other symbols of apartheid. These attacks would serve as a source of inspiration to our people.

Umkhonto was to perform sabotage, and strict instructions were given to its members right from the start, that on no account were they to injure or kill people in planning or carrying out operations.

The affairs of Umkhonto were controlled and directed by a National High Command, which had powers of co-option, and which could, and did, appoint Regional Commands. The High Command was the body which determined tactics and targets and was in charge of training and finance. Under the High Command there were Regional Commands which were responsible for the direction of the local sabotage groups. Within the framework of the policy laid down by the National High Command, the Regional Commands had authority to select the targets to be attacked. They had no authority whatsoever to go beyond the prescribed framework, and thus had no authority to embark upon acts which endangered life, or which did not fit in with the overall plan of sabotage. For instance, Umkhonto members were forbidden ever to go armed into operation.

Umkhonto had its first operation on 16 December 1961, when government buildings in Johannesburg, Port Elizabeth and Durban were attacked. The selection of targets is proof of the policy to which I have referred. Had we intended to attack life, we would have selected targets where people congregated and not empty buildings and power stations. The sabotage which was committed before 16 December 1961 was the work of isolated groups and had no connection whatsoever with Umkhonto. In fact, my lord, some of these and a number of later acts were claimed by other organizations.

The Manifesto of Umkhonto was issued on the day the operations commenced. The response to our actions and manifesto among the white population was characteristically violent. The Government threatened to take strong action, and called upon its supporters to stand firm and ignore the demands of the Africans. The whites failed to respond by suggesting change; they responded to our call by retreating behind the laager.

In contrast, the response of the Africans was one of encouragement. Suddenly there was hope again. Things were happening. People in the townships became eager for political news. A great deal of enthusiasm was generated by the initial successes, and people began to speculate on how soon freedom would be obtained.

But we in Umkhonto weighed up the white response with anxiety. The lines were being drawn. The whites and blacks were moving into separate camps, and the prospects of avoiding a civil war were diminishing. The white newspapers carried reports that sabotage would be punished by death. If this was so, how could we continue to keep the Africans away from terrorism?

**All whites undergo compulsory military training, but no such training is given to Africans ... we felt it our duty ... to use force in order to defend ourselves against force**

I now wish to turn, my lord, to the question of guerrilla warfare, and how it came to be considered. By 1961 scores of Africans had died as a result of racial friction. In 1920, when the famous leader Masabalala was held in Port Elizabeth gaol, twenty-four of a group of Africans, who gathered to demand his release, were killed by the police and white civilians. In 1921, more than a hundred Africans died in the Bulhoek affair. In 1924, over two hundred Africans were killed when the Administrator of South West Africa led a force against a group which had rebelled against the imposition of dog tax. On 1 May 1950, eighteen Africans died as a result of police shootings during the strike. On 21 March 1960, sixty-nine unarmed Africans died at Sharpeville.

How many more Sharpevilles would there be in the history of our country? And how many more Sharpevilles could the country stand without violence and terror becoming the order of the day? And what would happen to our people when that stage was reached? In the long run we felt certain we must succeed but at what cost to ourselves and the rest of the country? And if this happened, how could black and white ever live together again in peace and harmony? These were the problems that faced us, and these were our decisions.

Experience convinced us that rebellion would offer the Government limitless opportunities for the indiscriminate slaughter of our people. But it was precisely because the soil of South Africa is already drenched with the blood of innocent Africans that we felt it our duty to make preparations as a long-term undertaking, to use force in order to defend ourselves against force. If war became

244

inevitable, we wanted to be ready when the time came, and for the fight to be conducted on terms most favourable to our people. The fight which held out the best prospects to us and the least risk of life to both parties was guerrilla warfare. We decided, therefore, in our preparations for the future, to make provision for the possibility of guerrilla warfare.

All whites undergo compulsory military training, but no such training is given to Africans. It was in our view essential to build up a nucleus of trained men who would be able to provide the leadership which would be required if guerrilla warfare started. We had to prepare for such a situation before it became too late to make proper preparations. It was also necessary to build up a nucleus of men trained in civil administration and other professions, so that Africans would be equipped to participate in the government of this country as soon as they were allowed to do so.

## The evidence of the witness X

I want to deal now with some of the evidence of the witness X. Much of his account is substantially correct, but much of it is slanted and is distorted and in some important respects untruthful. I want to deal with the evidence as briefly as possible.

I did say that I had left the country early in the year to attend the PAFMECSA Conference, that the Conference was opened by the Emperor Haile Selassie, who attacked the racial policies of the South African Government, and who pledged support to the African people in this country. I also informed them of the unanimous resolution condemning the ill-treatment of the African people here, and promising support. I did tell them that the Emperor sent his warmest felicitations to my leader, Chief Luthuli.

But I never told them of any comparison made between Ghanaians and South African recruits, and could not have done so for very simple reasons. By the time I left Ethiopia, the first South African recruits had not yet reached that country, and Ghanaian soldiers, as far as I am aware, receive training in the United Kingdom. This being the fact and my understanding, I could not possibly have thought of telling the Regional Command that the Emperor of Ethiopia thought our trainees were better than the Ghanaians.

These statements, therefore, are sheer invention unless they were suggested to X by someone wishing to create a false picture.

I did tell them of financial support received in Ethiopia and in

245

other parts of Africa. I certainly did not tell him that certain African states had promised us one per cent of their Budget. This suggestion of donating one per cent never arose during my visit. It arose for the first time, as far as I am aware, at the Conference in May 1963, by which time I had been in gaol for ten months.

Despite X's alleged failure to remember this, I did speak of scholarships promised in Ethiopia, such general education of our people has always, as I have pointed out, been an important aspect of our plan.

My visit to Egypt coincided with that of Marshal Tito, and I was not able to wait until General Nasser was free to interview me. The officials I saw expressed criticism of articles appearing in *New Age* which dealt with General Nasser's attacks on Communism, but I had told them that *New Age* did not necessarily express the policy of our movement, and that I would take up this complaint with *New Age* and try and use my influence to change their line, because it was not our duty to say in what manner any state should achieve its freedom.

I told the Regional Committee that I had not visited Cuba, but that I had met that country's ambassadors in Egypt, Morocco and Ghana. I spoke of the warm affection with which I was received at these embassies, and that we were offered all forms of assistance, including scholarships for our youth. In dealing with the question of white and Asian recruits, I did say that as Cuba was a multi-racial country, it would be logical to send such persons to this country as these recruits would fit in more easily there than with black soldiers in African states.

On my return to Tanganyika, after touring the African continent, I met about thirty South African young men, who were on their way to Ethiopia for training. I addressed them on discipline and good behaviour while abroad.

Of course I referred to Umkhonto we Sizwe, but it cannot be true to say that they heard from me for the first time that this was the name or that it was the 'military wing' of the ANC, a phrase much used by the State in this trial. A proclamation had been issued by Umkhonto on 16 December 1961, announcing the existence of the body and its name had been known for several months before the time of this meeting. And I had certainly never referred to it as a military wing of the ANC. I always regarded it as a separate organization, and endeavoured to keep it as such.

I did tell them that the activities of Umkhonto might go through two phases, namely acts of sabotage and possibly guerrilla warfare, if that became necessary. I dealt with the problems relating to each phase. But I did not say that people were scouting out areas suitable for guerrilla warfare because no such thing was being done at the time. I stressed, just as he said, that the most important thing was to study our own history and our own situation. We must, of course, study the experiences of other countries also, and, in so doing, we must study not only the cases where revolutions were victorious, but also cases where revolutions were defeated.

But I did not discuss the training of people in East Germany, as testified to by X.

## The bombing of private houses of pro-government persons had nothing to do with the policy of Umkhonto

I wish to revert to certain occurrences said by witnesses to have happened in Port Elizabeth and East London. I am referring to the bombing of private houses of pro-government persons during September, October and November 1962. I do not know what justification there was for these acts, nor what provocation had been given, but if what I have said already is accepted, then it is clear that these acts had nothing to do with the carrying out of the policy of Umkhonto.

He went on to explain that there was a difference between a resolution adopted in the atmosphere of a committee room and the concrete difficulties that arise in the field of practical activity. The fact that those who could have guided operations were banned, house arrested or exiled, accounted for the blurring of distinction between Umkhonto and ANC.

Great care was taken to keep the activities of the two organizations in South Africa distinct. The ANC remained a mass political body of Africans only carrying on the type of political work they conducted prior to 1961. Umkhonto remained a small organization, recruiting its members from different races and organizations, and trying to achieve its own particular objective. The fact that members of Umkhonto were recruited from the ANC and the fact that persons served both organizations, like Solomon Mbanjwa, did not, in our view, change the nature of the ANC or give it a policy of violence. This overlapping of officers, however, was more the exception than the rule. This is why, my lord, persons such as X

247

and Z who were on the Regional Command of their respective areas, did not participate in any of the ANC Committees or activities, and why people such as Bennett Mashiyana and Reginald Ndubi did not hear of sabotage at their ANC meetings.

## Rivonia was [not] the headquarters of Umkhonto ... when I was there

Another of the allegations in the indictment is that Rivonia was the headquarters of Umkhonto. This is not true of the time when I was there. I was told, of course, and knew that certain of the activities of the Communist Party were carried on there, but this was no reason, as I shall presently explain, why I should not use the place.

Before I went on my tour of Africa, I lived in the room marked 12 on schedule A. On my return in July 1962, I lived in the thatched cottage.

While staying at Lilliesleaf Farm, I frequently visited Mr Goldreich in the main house and he also paid me visits in my room. We had numerous political discussions.

Up to the time of my arrest, Lilliesleaf Farm was the headquarters of neither the African National Congress nor Umkhonto. With the exception of myself none of the officials or members of these bodies lived there, no meetings of the governing bodies were ever held there, and no activities connected with them were either organized or directed from there. On numerous occasions during my stay at Lilliesleaf Farm I met both the Executive Committee of the ANC, as well as the National High Command, but such meetings were held elsewhere, and not on the farm.

## The objects of the ANC and the Communist Party are [different]. It [the Freedom Charter] is by no means a blueprint for a Socialist state

The allegation that the aims and objects of the ANC and the CP are the same ... is false. This is an old allegation which was disproved at the Treason Trial, and which has again reared its head. The ideological creed of the ANC is, and always has been, the creed of African Nationalism. It is not the concept of African Nationalism expressed in the cry 'Drive the white man into the sea'. The African Nationalism for which the ANC stands is the concept of freedom and fulfilment for the African people in their own land. The most important political document ever adopted by

248

the ANC is the 'Freedom Charter'. It is by no means a blueprint for a socialist state. It calls for redistribution, but not nationalization, of land; it provides for nationalization of mines, banks and monopoly industry, because big monopolies are owned by one race only, and without such nationalization racial domination would be perpetuated despite the spread of political power. It would be a hollow gesture to repeal the Gold Law prohibitions against Africans when all gold mines are owned by European companies. In this respect the ANC's policy corresponds with the old policy of the present Nationalist Party which, for many years, had as part of its programme the nationalization of the Gold Mines which, at that time, were controlled by foreign capital. Under the Freedom Charter, nationalization would take place in an economy based on private enterprise. The realization of the Freedom Charter would open up fresh fields for a prosperous African population of all classes, including the middle class. The ANC has never at any period of its history advocated a revolutionary change in the economic structure of the country, nor has it, to the best of my recollection, ever condemned capitalist society.

**I believe that Communists have always played an active role in the fight by colonial countries for their freedom**

As far as the Communist Party is concerned, and, if I understand its policy correctly, it stands for the establishment of a state based on the principles of Marxism. Although it is prepared to work for the Freedom Charter, as a short-term solution to the problems created by white supremacy, it regards the Freedom Charter as the beginning, and not the end, of its programme.

The ANC, unlike the Communist Party, admitted Africans only as members. Its chief goal was, and is, for the African people to win unity and full political rights. The Communist Party's main aim, on the other hand, was to remove the capitalists and to replace them with a working-class government. The Communist Party sought to emphasize class distinctions, whilst the ANC seeks to harmonize them. This is a vital distinction, my lord.

It is true that there has often been close cooperation between the ANC and the Communist Party. But cooperation is merely proof of a common goal – in this case the removal of white supremacy – and is not proof of a complete community of interests.

My lord, the history of the world is full of similar examples. Perhaps the most striking illustration is to be found in the cooperation between Great Britain, the United States of America and the Soviet Union in the fight against Hitler. Nobody but Hitler would have dared to suggest that such cooperation turned Churchill or Roosevelt into Communists or Communist tools, or that Britain and America were working to bring about a Communist world.

My lord, I give these illustrations because they are relevant to the allegation that our sabotage was a Communist plot or the work of so-called agitators. Because, my lord, another instance of such cooperation is to be found precisely in Umkhonto. Shortly after Umkhonto was constituted I was informed by some of its members that the Communist Party would support Umkhonto, and this then occurred. At a later stage the support was made openly.

I believe that Communists have always played an active role in the fight by colonial countries for their freedom, because the short-term objects of Communism would always correspond with the long-term objects of freedom movements. Thus Communists, my lord, have played an important role in the freedom struggles fought in countries such as Malaya, Algeria and Indonesia, yet none of these states today are Communist countries. Similarly, in the underground resistance movement which sprung up in Europe during the last World War, Communists played an important role. Even General Chiang Kai-shek, today one of the bitterest enemies of Communism, fought together with the Communists against the ruling classes in the struggle which led to his assumption of power in China in the 1930s.

This pattern of cooperation between Communists and non-Communists has been repeated in the National Liberation Movement of South Africa. Prior to the banning of the Communist Party, joint campaigns involving the Communist Party and the Congress Movement were accepted practice. African Communists could, and did, become members of the ANC and some served on the National, Provincial and local committees.

**I am not a Communist, and I have never been a member of the Communist Party ... we count Communists amongst those who support our cause**

There are many Africans who, today, turn to equate freedom with Communism. They are supported in this belief by the legislation which brands all exponents of democratic government and African freedom as Communists, and bans those, who are not Communists, under the Suppression of Communism Act. Although my lord, I am not a Communist, and I have never been a member of the Communist Party, I myself have been named under that pernicious Act because of the role I played in the Defiance Campaign. I have also been banned and convicted under that Act.

It is not only in internal politics that we count Communists as amongst those who support our cause. In the international field, Communist countries have always come to our aid. In the United Nations and other councils of the world, the Communist bloc has supported the Afro-Asian struggle against colonialism and often seems to be more sympathetic to our plight than some of the Western powers. Although there is a universal condemnation of apartheid, the Communist bloc speaks out against it with a louder voice than most of the Western world. In these circumstances it would take a brash young politician, such as I was in 1949, to proclaim that the Communists are our enemies.

I have denied that I am a Communist, and I think in the circumstances I am obliged to state exactly what my political beliefs are in order to explain what my position in Umkhonto was, and what my attitude towards the use of force is.

## I have always regarded myself, in the first place, as an African patriot

I have always regarded myself, in the first place, as an African patriot. After all, I was born in Umtata forty-six years ago. My guardian was my cousin, who was the acting paramount chief of Thembuland. I am related both to the present paramount chief of Thembuland, Sabata Dalindyebo, and to Kaizer Mantanzima, the Chief Minister of the Transkei.

Today I am attracted by the idea of a classless society, an attraction which springs in part from Marxist reading and, in part, from my admiration of the structure and organization of early African societies in this country. The land, then the main means of production, belonged to the tribe. There were no rich or poor, and there was no exploitation.

It is true, as I have already stated, that I have been influenced by Marxist thought, but this is also true of many of the leaders of the new independent states. Such widely different persons as Gandhi, Nehru, Nkrumah and Nasser all acknowledge this fact. We all accept the need for some form of socialism to enable our people to catch up with the advanced countries of the world and to overcome their legacy of extreme poverty. But this does not mean we are Marxists.

## Communists regard the parliamentary system of the West as undemocratic and reactionary ... I am an admirer of such a system ... I regard the British Parliament as the most democratic institution in the world

Indeed, my lord, for my own part I believe that it is open to debate whether the Communist Party has any specific role to play at this particular stage of our political struggle. The basic task at the present moment is the removal of race discrimination and the attainment of democratic rights on the basis of the Freedom Charter and the struggle can best be led by a strong ANC. Insofar as that party furthers this task, I welcome its assistance. I realize that it is one of the main means by which people of all races can be drawn into our struggle.

But from my reading of Marxist literature and from conversation with Marxists, I have gained the impression that Communists regard the parliamentary system of the West as undemocratic and reactionary. But, on the contrary, I am an admirer of such a system.

The Magna Carta, the Petition of Rights and the Bill of Rights, are documents which are held in veneration by democrats throughout the world.

I have great respect for British political institutions, and for the country's system of justice. I regard the British Parliament as the most democratic institution in the world, and the independence and impartiality of its judiciary never fail to arouse my admiration.

The American Congress, that country's doctrine of separation of powers, as well as the independence of its judiciary, arouse in me similar sentiments.

I have been influenced in my thinking by both West and East. All this has led me to feel that in my search for a political formula, I should be absolutely impartial and objective. I should tie myself to no particular system of society, other than that of socialism. I must leave myself free to borrow the best from the West and from the East.

## [Marxist notes in Mandela's handwriting] ... an old friend ...

**was busy writing lectures for use in the Communist Party ... I told him that they seemed far too complicated for the ordinary reader ... I ... set to work [to draft] the lectures in simplified form**

I wish now to deal with some of the exhibits. Many of the exhibits are in my handwriting. It has always been my custom to reduce to writing the material which I have been studying.

Exhibits R.20, 21 and 22 are lectures drafted in my own hand, but they are not my original work. They came to be written in the following circumstances:

For several years an old friend with whom I worked very closely on ANC matters, and who occupied senior positions both in the ANC and the Communist Party, had been trying to get me to join the Communist Party. I had had many debates with him on the role which the Communist Party can play at this stage of our struggle, and I advanced to him the same views in regard to my political beliefs which I have described earlier in my statement.

In order to convince me that I should join the Communist Party he, from time to time, gave me Marxist literature to read, though I did not always find time to do this.

Each of us always stuck to our guns in our argument as to whether I should join the Communist Party. He maintained that on achieving freedom we would be unable to solve our problems of poverty and inequality without establishing a Communist state, and we would require trained Marxists to do this. I maintained my attitude that no ideological differences should be introduced until freedom had been achieved.

I saw him on several occasions at Lilliesleaf Farm, and on one of the last of these occasions he was busy writing with books around him. When I asked him what he was doing, he told me that he was busy writing lectures for use in the Communist Party, and suggested that I should read them. There were several lectures in draft form.

After I had done so, I told him that they seemed far too complicated for the ordinary reader in that the language was obtuse and they were full of the usual Communist clichés and jargon. If the court will look at some of the standard works of Marxism, my point will be demonstrated. He said it was impossible to simplify the language, without losing the effect of what the author was trying to stress. I disagreed with him, and then he asked me to see whether I could redraft the lectures in the simplified form suggested by me.

I agreed to help him, and set to work in an endeavour to do this, but I never finished the task as I later became occupied with other practical work which was more important. I never again saw the unfinished manuscript until it was produced at the trial.

I wish to state that it is not my handwriting which appears on Exhibit R.23, which was obviously drafted by the person who prepared the lectures.

## Our political struggle has always been financed . . . from funds raised by our own people

My lord, there are certain exhibits which suggest that we received financial support from abroad, and I wish now to deal with this question.

Our political struggle has always been financed from internal sources – from funds raised by our own people and by our own supporters. Whenever we had a special campaign, or an important political case – for example, the Treason Trial – we received financial assistance from sympathetic individuals and organizations in the Western countries. We have never felt it necessary to go beyond these sources.

## Umkhonto [sought] funds from the African states

But when in 1961 Umkhonto was formed, and a new phase of struggle was introduced, we realized that these events would make a heavy call on our slender resources, and that the scale of our activities would be hampered by lack of funds. One of my instructions, as I went abroad in January 1962, was to raise funds from the African states.

I must add that, whilst abroad, I had discussions with leaders of political movements in Africa and discovered that almost every single one of them, in areas which had still not attained independence, had received all forms of assistance from the socialist countries, as well as from the West, including that of financial support. I also discovered that some well-known African states, all of them non-Communists, and even anti-Communists, had received similar assistance.

On my return to the Republic, I made a strong recommendation to the ANC that we should not confine ourselves to Africa and the

Western countries, but that we should also send a mission to the socialist countries to raise the funds which we so urgently needed.

I have been told that after I was convicted such a mission was sent.

## Umkhonto was not founded by the Communist Party . . . we do not need Communists . . . to teach us about these things [poverty and lack of human dignity]

As I understand the State case and in particular the evidence of X, Umkhonto was the inspiration of the Communist Party which sought, by playing upon imaginary grievances, to enrol the African people into an army which ostensibly was to fight for African freedom, but in reality was fighting for a Communist state. Nothing could be further from the truth. In fact, the suggestion is preposterous. Umkhonto was formed by Africans to further their struggle for freedom in their own land. Communists and others supported the movement, and we only wish that more sections of the community would join us.

Our fight is against real, and not imaginary hardships, or, to use the language of the State Prosecutor, 'so-called hardships'. Basically, my lord, we fight against two features which are the hallmarks of African life in South Africa, and which are entrenched by legislation which we seek to have repealed. These features are poverty and lack of human dignity, and we do not need Communists, or so-called 'agitators', to teach us about these things.

## The complaint of Africans . . . is not only that they are poor . . . but that the laws . . . are designed to preserve this situation

The whites enjoy what may well be the highest standard of living in the world, whilst Africans live in poverty and misery. Forty per cent of the Africans live in hopelessly over-crowded and, in some cases, drought-stricken reserves, where soil erosion and the over-working of the soil make it impossible for them to live properly off the land. Thirty per cent are labourers, labour tenants, and squatters on white farms and work and live under conditions similar to those of the serfs of the Middle Ages. The other thirty per cent live in towns where they have developed economic and social habits which bring them closer, in many respects, to white standards. Yet forty-six per cent of all African families in Johannesburg do not earn enough to keep them going.

The complaint of Africans, however, is not only that they are poor and whites are rich, but that the laws which are made by the whites are designed to preserve this situation. There are two ways to break out of poverty. The first is by formal education, and the second is by the worker acquiring a greater skill at his work and thus higher wages. As far as Africans are concerned, both these avenues of advancement are deliberately curtailed by legislation.

## The present Government . . . hamper[s] Africans in their search for education

The present government has always sought to hamper Africans in their search for education. There is compulsory education for all white children at virtually no cost to their parents, be they rich or poor. Similar facilities are not provided for African children. In 1960–61, the *per capita* government spending on African students at state-funded schools was estimated at R12.46. In the same year, the *per capita* spending on white children in the Cape Province (which are the only figures available to me) was R144.57. The present Prime Minister said during the debate on the Bantu Education Bill in 1953: 'When I have control of Native education, I will reform it so that Natives will be taught from childhood to realize that equality with Europeans is not for them . . . People who believe in equality are not desirable teachers for Natives. When my Department controls Native education, it will know for what class of higher education a Native is fitted, and whether he will have a chance in life to use his knowledge.'

## Industrial colour bar

The other main obstacle to the economic advancement of the Africans is the industrial colour bar by which all the better jobs of industry are reserved for whites only. Moreover, Africans are not allowed to form trade unions, which have recognition under the Industrial Conciliation Act. The Government often answers its critics by saying that Africans in South Africa are economically better off than the inhabitants of the other countries in Africa. Our complaint is not that we are poor by comparison with people in other countries, but that we are poor by comparison with white people in our own country, and that we are prevented by legislation from altering this imbalance.

## Life in the townships is dangerous

Hundreds and thousands of Africans are thrown into gaol each year under pass laws. Even worse than this is the fact that pass laws keep husband and wife apart and lead to the breakdown of family life.

Poverty and the breakdown of family life have secondary effects. Children wander about the streets of the townships because they have no schools to go to, or no money to enable them to go to school, or no parents at home to see that they go to school because both parents, if there be two, have to work to keep the family alive. This leads to a breakdown in moral standards, to an alarming rise in illegitimacy and to growing violence which erupts, not only politically but everywhere. Life in the townships is dangerous; there is not a day that goes by without somebody being stabbed or assaulted. And violence is carried out of the townships into the white living areas. People are afraid to walk alone in the streets after dark. House-breakings and robberies are increasing despite the fact that the death sentence can now be imposed for such offences. Death sentences cannot cure the festering sore. The only cure is to alter the conditions under which the Africans are forced to live, and to meet their legitimate grievances.

## We want to be part of the general population, and not confined to living in our ghettos

We want to be part of the general population, and not confined to living in our ghettos. African men want to have their wives and children to live with them where they work, and not to be forced into an unnatural existence in men's hostels. Our women want to be left with their men folk, and not to be left permanently widowed in the Reserves. We want to be allowed out after 11 p.m. and not to be confined to our rooms like little children. We want to be allowed to travel in our own country, and seek work where we want to, and not where the Labour Bureau tells us to. We want a just share in the whole of South Africa; we want security and a stake in society.

## I have cherished the ideal of a democratic and free society ... It is an ideal for which I am prepared to die

Above all, my lord, we want equal political rights, because without them our disabilities will be permanent. I know this sounds revolu-

257

tionary to the whites in this country, because the majority of voters will be Africans. This makes the white man fear democracy. But this fear cannot be allowed to stand in the way of the only solution which will guarantee racial harmony and freedom for all. It is not true that the enfranchisement of all will result in racial domination. Political division, based on colour, is entirely artificial, and when it disappears, so will the domination of one colour group by another. The ANC has spent half a century fighting against racialism. When it triumphs, as it certainly must, it will not change that policy.

This then is what the ANC is fighting. Our struggle is a truly national one. It is a struggle of the African people, inspired by our own suffering and our own experience. It is a struggle for the right to live.

During my lifetime I have dedicated my life to this struggle of the African people. I have fought against white domination, and I have fought against black domination. I have cherished the ideal of a democratic and free society in which all persons live together in harmony with equal opportunities. It is an ideal which I hope to live for, and to see realized. But my lord, if needs be, it is an ideal for which I am prepared to die.

It was a long statement, an explanation of the ANC, of Umkhonto, of himself and of his people. Mandela had worked late into the night and slumped in utter exhaustion when he had done the writing. Now that he had finished the speaking, he felt elated. Throughout, he had the feeling that the entire black gallery was hearing his words and approving his thoughts, for he knew they were their own thoughts and words. He had a deep consciousness too of Winnie's penetrating gaze, his mother's silent approval, his sister's pride and his clansmen's loyalty.

His address was followed by the evidence of Walter Sisulu, Ahmed Kathrada, Lionel Bernstein, Dennis Goldberg, Govan Mbeki, Elias Motsoaledi and Raymond Mhlaba. Each impressed the gallery with his eloquence and his integrity; the effect on the bench was mixed. Finally, Alan Paton gave evidence in mitigation. Relief came with the sentencing. They had faced the death penalty. They got life imprisonment.

There are so many ways of looking at things, so many basic attitudes, and in this trial they took on a definition and clarity:

• There was Dr Yutar speaking for the law. It was a long catalogue of crimes that he paraded before the court: sabotage, conspiring to revolution, illegal acts, more illegal acts. There were the accused men admitting most of the acts but denying moral guilt. The attempt by Alan Paton to explain why the men had done what they did; his talk of the two alternatives: 'To bow their heads and submit, or to resist by force'; his assessment of the personal characters of the accused men.

• The appeal by Mr H. J. Hanson, QC, leading evidence in mitigation, for the 'understanding and compassion which has always formed the basis of judicial decisions in this country'. And his theme that 'it was not their aims which had been criminal – only the means to which they had resorted'.

• The Judge President's detailed analysis of Umkhonto organization and the part the ANC played.

• The reason which Mr Justice de Wet gave – with such brevity – for imposing a life sentence and not a death sentence. Even the police, it seems, did not expect such a harsh sentence, as during an adjournment on sentence day a policeman told the press: 'These guys won't really be in for too long – we've learnt a lot from them during the trial, you know.'

Aggery Klaaste recorded the scene outside the court:

I'll never forget . . .
The voices of the crowd raised in song outside the Palace of Justice on Verdict Day (11 June) in the Rivonia Trial at Pretoria . . . the priest who led them in song as they waited for the judgement . . . and the way they burst into 'Nkosi Sikelele' as Winnie Mandela appeared on the steps.

The way Hilda Bernstein rushed up to her husband Rusty when he was found Not Guilty . . . and the expression on her face when, two minutes later, he was re-arrested and the police pulled her away.

The bewildered look on the face of old Mrs Mandela – Nelson Mandela's mother – who had come all the way from Umtata to hear her son found guilty of sabotage and sentenced to life imprisonment.

And the way her daughter-in-law, Winnie, looked after her inside and outside the court.

The expressions on the faces of the accused men when the verdict of Guilty was given – Nelson smiling to his wife; Walter Sisulu waving; Kathy Kathrada shrugging his shoulders. And the way they looked on sentence day – Nelson Mandela in new dark suit taking notes; Sisulu fined down to thinness; Dennis Goldberg, cheerful and almost chubby; Govan Mbeki listening, hand cupped to ear; Raymond Mhlaba staring at the proceedings.

The exchange between Dr Percy Yutar, the prosecutor, and Mr Alan Paton, who gave evidence in mitigation.

The biting sarcasm when Dr Yutar, questioning Mr Paton on his forecast of sabotage, asked: 'So you are a prophet?' And the quiet dignity with which Paton replied: 'Yes, a prophet.'

The quiet voice of Mr Justice de Wet saying: 'The sentence is life imprisonment on all counts for the accused.'

The hush in the court that followed – an almost deathlike, motionless silence. Then the eight men in the dock – who had stood erect showing no sign of emotion – turning to the packed courts and smiling.

The moment when their wives and relatives and friends caught their last glimpse of them as they descended from the court.

The car back-firing like a pistol shot. We all stepping briskly back. A police dog barking back. And somebody nervously whispering 'Sharpeville!' But a police captain near me, his row of buttons gleaming, standing impassive and aloof.

The women – in their black and green uniform – standing quietly, almost bored as the time crept to noon. Then 12.15 and the inevitable policeman and his dog walking up and down the pavement again.

The first spectator walking out of the Palace. We all looking anxiously at her, she saying, 'Amandla!' The crowd saying 'Amandla!' if doubtfully.

The ripple that went through the dense crowd as She walked out. Winnie Mandela. A whisper of 'life' passing from mouth to mouth as in a movie.

Those who stood next to Winnie say there were tears in her eyes. Yet there was no weeping.

Then the women began singing and afterwards the unfurling of banners, the spontaneous outburst of freedom songs.

The women marching, chanting, up Church Square, Pretoria will never forget this either. About fifty of them, some youngsters trying to trip them, somebody kicking at them.

But the women continued marching, right round the Palace of Justice.

A bucket of water flew from a window. Right on to the singing women. They marched on regardless.

Only a fool would forget the back of the Palace where the prisoners were to be driven out.

People were peeping from windows. Some stood on balconies. Others stood on shop roofs.

A further crowd waited patiently at the back of the Palace of Justice, their eyes fixed expectantly on the ornamental wrought-iron gates for the van that would transport the prisoners. In equal expectation, police on motorbikes revved their engines. Then the black gates opened and a deafening screech rent the air and was taken up almost instantly by the burst of sirens from the accompanying police vehicles. The crowd was momentarily stunned by the might of the State manifested in the terrifying noise of the roaring engines that sped past them. The prisoners' van came into view and prisoners and supporters strained in vain to catch a last glimpse of each other through the meshed steel that covered the windows. Then a great cry of 'Amandla!' went up and the two were bonded in the historic instant.

The conviction did not allay the fears of the State: on 10 June the Minister of Justice, Mr Vorster, said: 'We are prepared for anything that might be planned by the Communists after the Rivonia Trial,' and, again on 12 June, 'We are prepared for anything.' On 13 June Brigadier C. J. Joubert of the Security Branch said: 'Things are very quiet, but we are prepared. There may be trouble – but we don't expect anything.' What he wasn't expecting happened the next day, 14 June, when saboteurs blew out the front of the Vrededorp Post Office in Johannesburg.

# CHAPTER 25

# The Prisoners

Nelson and his comrades were taken to Pretoria Central prison, where all except Nelson, who was already a prisoner, went through the usual admission procedure; the stripping, the searching of naked bodies, and the changing into prison uniforms of coarse shirts and shorts. They spent until about midnight in single cells, then Colonel Aucamp told Nelson that they were being transported to Robben Island. At the crack of dawn they were loaded into closed trucks and driven to the military airport. Manacled together in pairs, they fell against each other as they struggled to get on to the aircraft. After several hours, the familiar landmark of the Cape mountains came into view. They landed on the military strip, were driven to the docks and ferried across to Robben Island.

The first man to be imprisoned on Robben Island was one of the Khoi-Khoi, men of men, Autshumao, who had swum out to Jan van Riebeeck's ship in 1652 as the contingent of three vessels had dropped anchor in the Cape Bay. Autshumao, whom Van Riebeeck, called Herrie (Harry), had offered his services as interpreter and guide to the first Dutch East India commander at the Cape, but he and his people soon realized that the white people sought to dispossess them of their cattle and their land, and to bridle their labour. So he fought a relentless guerrilla war with the Dutch. Van Riebeeck had imprisoned him on Robben Island, but he had managed to escape in a little boat left carelessly by an official.

Over three hundred years later, the Island prison had a reputation of being so heavily fortified that few prisons in the world could match its security.

Neither Nelson nor his colleagues believed that they were in prison for their lives – perhaps the Prime Minister's life, but certainly not theirs. They had been spared death and their lives were their own, for all the controls imposed on them. In time the Government would realize this, and find their incarceration an embarrassment and a problem.

The Rivonia Trial, was not the only Umkhonto trial that had engaged the States attention in 1963. In Pietermaritzburg Ebrahim Ismail, Girja Singh, Natvarlal Bebebenia, Billy Nair, Kisten Moonsamy, George Naicker, Kisten Doorsamy, Riot Mkhwanazi, Alfred Duma, Msizeni Shadrack Maphumulo, Mfanyana Bernard Nkosi, Zakela Mdhlalose, Matthews Meyiwa, Joshua Thembinkosi Zulu, Mdingeni David Mkhize, David Ndwande and Siva Pillay were also on trial for sabotage.

Neither was MK the only sabotage group on trial. The National Liberation Committee was also on trial in Cape Town, and the accused were Neville Alexander, Don Davis, Marcus Solomons, the three van den Heydons (Elizabeth, Doris and Leslie), Fikile Bam, Lionel Davis, Dorothy Alexander, Dulcie September and Gordon Hendricks.

Nelson knew some of them personally, but most were strangers to him. On the island they became a fraternity against apartheid. He was particularly attracted to Fikile Bam and Neville Alexander whose intellects he admired. They talked during work and held discussions whenever they could, always surreptitiously and at risk.

The original prison at Robben Island was an old stone building with eleven cells. As political prisoners came flooding in, a corrugated iron block, the zinc jail, was added, and during 1963–4, the main blocks accommodating political prisoners: blocks A, B, C and D were built.

The daily routine during Nelson's first decade of imprisonment was rigorous. The morning bell rang at 5.30. The prisoners rushed through their ablutions, folded their bedding, lined it against the wall and queued up in double file at the centre of the cell. The loud jangling of keys heralded the opening of doors and the entry of wardens. From that point onwards, they were not allowed to talk to each other except during the lunch-break. The wardens went up and down the line counting the prisoners and then marched them out of the cells down the passage to the kitchen where they queued for their breakfast. They ate in silence, seated in twos in double rows on the ground in the open space next to the kitchen. The sick parade followed breakfast. Prisoners reporting illness were sent off to the hospital. The rest were marched in double file, closely guarded by armed warders, past the guardpost to the stands where they were again counted and then marched off to work in groups of fifty or so. They worked until the lunch-break when they were allowed to talk to each other.

Lunch over, the prisoners were again stood in double file and counted. Work stopped at 4.30 when the prisoners were marched back to the compound, stripped naked, searched, marched to the kitchen to collect their supper and then led back to their cells, re-counted and locked up for the night. The cell lights remained on throughout the night. It was during this period that the prisoners entered into discussions and planned strategies.

Nelson and the other political prisoners settled into their prison routine. While imprisonment is inhuman, dreadful beyond words, its dread and horror are not experienced as one continuous, unremitting ordeal. The prison is, after all, a social institution and, as such, constitutes its own society even if its inmates are coerced into membership. Most important of all, human nature is malleable and inventive and so it adjusts to whatever situation it finds itself. The redeeming features about the Robben Island prison was its political prisoners. There was a concentration of courage, intellect and integrity, probably not found easily in any other part of South Africa. The men of Robben Island, the saboteurs of 1964, came from diverse ideological foundations. Yet they had all come to the same conclusion: sabotage as the revolutionary strategy, they had faced the same judges and suffered similar sentences.

These crucial common experiences were, in themselves, a

strong binding force. They made the ideological differences, which had been seemingly irreconcilable outside prison, quite reconcilable inside it. The prison became a university. The political prisoners talked out their differences, learnt from them and learnt to cope with them. They talked as they laboured relentlessly in the lime pit, as they waded collecting seaweed, and as they sat and ate their fugal meals, at first uneatable but later becoming more palatable. Nonetheless there were the frustrations: the moments, the hours, when they could not tolerate each other and felt trapped in each other's company.

They discussed their approach to the prison authorities, rules and regulations. There were disagreements and arguments, but they built a fraternity in that completely closed, strongly guarded, highly restricted society. Their relatives met each other at the Cape Town docks, in the hold of the ferry that brought them to the Island and they, too, developed a sense of fraternity.

In his cell each Robben Islander notched up the years. All except the Rivonia group, Wilton Mkwayi, Jeff Masemola and a few other PAC members, knew when they would be released. The destiny of the Rivonia group depended on the changing political climate.

'A child, and children's voices, that is what I missed most,' said Neville Alexander. Ahmed Kathrada described gobbling up the contents of letters from home, wanting more, like Oliver Twist; he yearned for personal communication, and hungered for little titbits about births and marriages, schooling, games, picnics, film shows, theatre, books, flowers, travels, rain, new inventions, social problems, changing attitudes. In the shrunken prison world these seemingly little things become immensely important.

Ahmed Kathrada wrote on 9 September 1982:

I think it was in 1971 or thereabouts that you, Shamin and Rashid came to Cape Town with your mummy. She wrote and told me how you all went up to Table Mountain and looked at Robben Island through the telescope. And how 'their little hearts went out to you', she said. At that time we were not allowed to get any news, and the letter must have had something that was considered 'undesirable', so I only got a portion of the letter. And we spent a lot of time speculating what important information could have been cut out.

Let me tell you of a book I read many years ago. I think it was called *Mistress of Kafka*. Somewhere the author describes her prison experience, and says that in jail it is the minutes and the hours that are the most difficult to get through. The years go by with relative ease. How true!

The hard labour continued. The most difficult job of all was quarrying the lime. As Nelson recalls: 'You begin the task briskly, full of zest, song and swing, but soon the hard rock takes it all away. The lime is soft, but it is embedded in almost impregnable layers of very hard rock. You strike and it remains implacable. Then the singing changes to swearing and there are altercations with the warders.'

Verwoerd's assassination in 1966 reflected on the political prisoners. The assassin, Tsafendas, was a white parliamentary messenger, later declared insane. The movement had no hand in his death but the burden of anger of the white prison staff fell on the prisoners.

In January 1967 Nelson, Eddie Daniels, Dr Neville Alexander and Laloo Chiba became involved in an altercation with the warders in the quarry. The prisoners were charged with being 'idle, careless and negligent'. This incident brought them closer and they bonded together in defence, engaging lawyers to represent them. The charge was dropped.

The attitude of the prison staff never remained constant. New staff came; a new round of abuse took its course. But, inevitably, the political prisoners succeeded in breaking in the warders or somewhat humanizing them. The authorities took precautions against familiarization between prisoners and warders by continuously changing warders.

Nelson remembers Warrant Officer Van Rensburg as one of the more vicious warders. He was brought to the Island from Brandvlei, which had the reputation of being a veritable Hades among prisons. He was animal-like in his crudeness:

266

He would lean against our food table and think nothing of urinating right there if the urge took him. He could stand alongside his puddle and be totally unaffected by its stench and pollution. Each day he would choose his victim for persecution. One day Fikile Bam and I became the targets. 'I want to see you,' he announced at the end of the day and took us to the lieutenant and charged us for lazing on the job. *Te lui om te werk* was the official classification in Afrikaans. We defended ourselves and invited the lieutenant to come and examine the pile of stone that testified our work. 'They are small piles,' Van Rensburg countered. The lieutenant said he would see for himself, and we had an inspection *in loco*. Van Rensburg was shocked to see our large piles of broken rock. 'That's a whole week's work,' he protested, but his lie was obvious, and the disgusted lieutenant did what a superior prison officer rarely does, chastised his subordinate in the presence of prisoners. 'You are telling lies,' he said. It was a vindication that heartened all of us.

There were other instances of fair play:

In 1972 we were plagued by Colonel Badenhorst who had been brought out of retirement. He was rude beyond words, and lazy. It was his duty as commanding officer to carry out a daily inspection. He came once a month. If you complained, his stock reaction was to abuse you with the most scurrilous Afrikaans swear words. 'Jou ma se moer!' was a favourite. When three judges, Steyn, Corbett and Theron, visited us, I complained on behalf of the prisoners. Badenhorst threatened me in their presence. 'You are going to get into trouble,' he said. I pointed out to the judges that that was a typical example of what was going on, on Robben Island. Badenhorst was transferred.

Our strategy of not arguing with the prison warders when accused of misdemeanours, but waiting for them to initiate charges against us worked. We defended ourselves before the higher ups and won practically every time and this toned down the warders aggression against us.

The warders also learnt that surliness on their part resulted in a 'go slow' on ours, that if they wanted our cooperation they had to approach us in a civil manner. Sergeant Opperman wanted more lime from the quarry. 'Gentlemen,' he addressed us, 'the heavy rain yesterday washed away the markings on the roads. There is an urgent need for lime. Can you help?' We did.

Food was always a problem, bad in itself and bad in quality and discriminatory by race (Indians and Coloureds got better food than Africans), it disappeared almost altogether at times; warders stole and sold it. Coffee was crushed mealies in the early period of imprisonment; at one point we were deprived of our daily allotment of a teaspoon of sugar per day, the servings of porridge grew smaller on our plates, and we began to fear that one morning we would wake up to find nothing at all. We didn't relish the porridge but we lived on it. When General Steyn took over it was as if a great burden was lifted from our shoulders. He was outraged when he heard our complaints. The food returned, sadistic warders were replaced, regulations were strictly adhered to, letters that had been suppressed from arbitrary vindictiveness, materialized. I had complained to Zami during a visit: 'Why aren't you writing to me?' She had protested, 'I have been writing to you every month.' I took up the matter with the commanding officer. The following day I received six of my letters.

Nelson wrote an autobiography in the late 1970s. He smuggled out one copy for publication, and concealed the other in an empty pipe under concrete. One day work began there; the concrete and pipe were smashed, and the original copy of the manuscript lost in the debris.

The prison is above all punitive, it operates to break the human spirit, to exploit human weakness, undermine human strength, destroy initiative, individuality, negate intelligence and process an amorphous, robot-like mass. The great challenge is how to resist, how not to adjust, to keep intact the knowledge of the society outside and to live by its rules, for that is the only way to maintain the human and the social within you. Our survival as ourselves depended on us understanding this and sharing it with each other. We were not all alike, our responses to the hardships differed. We were all living under stress, but some of us were more capable of handling that stress than others. The worst part of imprisonment is being locked up by yourself. You came face to face with time and there is nothing more terrifying than to be alone with sheer time. Then the ghosts come crowding in. They can be very sinister, very mischievous, raising a thousand doubts in your mind about the people outside, their loyalty. Was your sacrifice worth the trouble? What would your life have been like if you hadn't got involved?

Ultimately, it is only you who can save yourself and a latent talent brought to the fore helps. Everyone has some talent. Often the prisoner does not even know that he has that talent; there is so much to do in the life outside that it may remain buried. In prison, that talent can become your life-line. It can be a wonderful therapy that redeems you and helps to redeem your comrades. There were men on Robben Island who were good with their hands and men good with their minds, and men who excelled at both. Jeff Masemola, a PAC man, taught me maths and he made a master key that could open any prison door. They took him away from the general section. He was too ingenious and therefore too dangerous. Mac Maharaj, Laloo Chiba and Henry Fozzie made their own tools with pieces of zinc and whatever they found. They brought back what appeared to be débris from the work place, wood and stone, and during lock-up time fashioned these into exquisite pieces of sculpture or furniture.

There were among us men who were prepared to make every sacrifice for their fellows and no political grouping held a monopoly over this, and there were men who degraded humanity. The latter became our problems. In the course of time, we established our committees; disciplinary, educational, political, recreational, literary, and these helped to ensure that we shared the meagre facilities available to us equitably. The authorities came to recognize, unofficially of course, that, in the final analysis, order in the prison was preserved, not by the warders, but by ourselves.

We had to build our own social life and we modelled it in terms of the life we had lived and would live outside the prison walls. We encouraged, above all, study. We helped each other with the knowledge of our own disciplines and expertise. In that constricted, deprived environment, we placed the highest value on sharing, sharing everything, every resource, material and intellectual, and on the whole we succeeded.

Kathy was the youngest of the Rivonia group, in his early thirties, but from the outset, he pursued two causes in prison, unity and discipline. He was mainly responsible for developing channels of communication between the Rivonia group and other political prisoners and the system he developed survived. Walter was the beloved father. Prisoners found him compassionate and always helpful.

They were separated from the non-political prisoners but there was always contact. Nelson recalls one particular incident.

I was going about my usual business in our section. The sun was high and I had on my broad-brimmed cardboard hat, ingeniously crafted by Jeff Masemola. A group of prisoners were working on a higher level and so could see me in my yard. 'Amigos!' they called. I ignored them, knowing that the warder overseeing me would get into trouble. The prisoners were angry. 'Mdala!' (old man) they retorted in contempt. Later they came to know my identity and when they saw me again, they renewed their attempts to engage me, this time resorting to a strategy bound to succeed. 'We are also your children,' they said. 'Why do you only talk to the Xhosas? Why do you discriminate against us? (Most prisoners in the Western Cape are Coloured and most Africans Xhosa.) The accusation stung. 'How can you say that?' I asked. 'You have not seen me talk to Xhosas. You can't accuse me of discrimination. No! No! No! We are one. But can't you see there will be trouble if I talk to you?' They were satisfied I had talked to them.

They were like our fathers: Govan Mbeki, Walter Sisulu, Nelson Mandela [said one comrade]. Mandela helps everyone. He does not discriminate against a man because he is PAC or BC. You have a problem you go and talk to him, personal, any kind of problem. Family problems, above all, can depress you. If someone dies, and, worse, if your wife or girl friend goes off with another man. It can be killing.

On one occasion, there was a deadlock between ourselves and the wardens. Nelson persuaded the authorities to hold a discussion about the problems. Each cell was asked to send representatives. We were conducted to the small office. There weren't enough chairs, so some of us were standing, others sitting two to a chair. The officials were seated comfortably. Nelson was about the last to join us. He cast one look and said, 'We can't hold a discussion under these conditions. We must be properly seated.' They brought in more chairs and the discussions were conducted in a more appropriate environment.

Strini Moodley was one of the nine members of the South African Student Organization (SASO), convicted in 1976 for terrorism by thought. They had not exploded a single bomb, but the court found their poetry, drama and political speeches, terroristic. They were young men under thirty and

they brought fresh revolutionary energy to that grim Island.
  Strini recounts:

We arrived on Robben Island on 22 December 1976. We looked
forward to meeting our leaders who were our legendary heroes.
That was the one bonus of our long-term sentences. But we didn't
see them, not immediately. We were put into 'C' Section and
locked up in single cells. Our only view of the Rivonia men was the
dim figures we made out as we looked from our high cell windows,
across the passage, and through the high cell windows of the
opposite cells, into their yard in 'B' Section. We could not distin-
guish anyone.

Our section had not been used for a while and was referred to as
the observation or punishment section. It was so damp that the
paintwork kept peeling off and if one kept one's foot on the
cement floor for ten or fifteen minutes, and lifted it, one found a
puddle of water beneath. There was a passage down the centre of
the block; the cells were on either side. The warden's office was at
the one end of the passage and beyond that was a narrow walled-in
yard with six showers and a couple of toilet pans. There was no hot
water, only cold sea water.

Our cells were small, about three paces each way. There were
two high windows and from one, the third glass pane was removed
so that the wardens could look in. The windows were barred from
the inside. All I could see from my back window was the concrete
walls of other cell blocks. We were locked up with a sanitary
bucket, a bottle, a towel, a face cloth, three sleeping mats (one
grass and two felt), and four blankets. That meagre space and
those few belongings constituted our world for six weeks. We were
let out of it for an hour each day: in the morning to shower and
use the toilets, and in the afternoon to breathe fresh air and stretch
our limbs.

Once in the yard, we deliberately defied the warders. We shouted
*Amandla!* as loud as we could so that the other prisoners could
hear us. Failing to restrain us, they built a high wall so that the
others could not see us.

On the day before Christmas, Kathy (Ahmed Kathrada) and
Frank Anthony of the Non-European Unity Movement visited us.
They brought us sweets and tobacco from their committee, Ulundi.
We were very excited to see Kathy. He asked for me by name; he
told me that he knew my father. He was quite emotional and

271

wouldn't leave me and asked me endless questions about people in Durban we both knew.

We discussed how we could maintain communication with them. We discovered that there was a gap in the iron gate between our yards and we could leave messages there. We told Kathy we wanted to see Nelson and suggested that he should stand in their yard at a certain spot at a certain time when we were outside in our yard, so we could identify him. At the time of his arrest, most of us had been toddlers and some not yet born, but he was part of our psyche and our political culture and we were most anxious to see him. He did as we requested and we saw him standing, tall, slim, very regal. We did not speak, and we made no signs, we looked in wonder at the man and, later, we talked about him with excitement.

We were later moved to Section 'D', which was a communal block, and which, like all the communal blocks, had a number of advantages. The toilets and showers were built inside the block so that we had continuous access to them and, more important, we had each other's company. At night we discussed, planned activities or attended to our reading and our studies when these were allowed to us.

Non-political prisoners were housed about two to three kilometres away from us. We saw them when they came to clean the ground near our compound or worked near us in gangs. They worked on the runway and generally kept the island clean.

There were two forms of hard labour that were particularly grim on Robben Island, collecting bird droppings and lime quarrying. The bird droppings made us dirty and stinky that we could hardly accept our own bodies at the end of the day.

At the quarries, the sun shone on the white lime and blinded our eyes. We could barely see, and we feared that we would strike into each other in error. We were expected to pick, shovel and load without a break and we feared that we would pick into each other. We asked that there should be breaks between the tasks, but the warders refused. We had an argument. We struck work. There were about 150 in our gang. A reinforcement of warders arrived. We were ordered to return to work. We refused. We were conducted to our cells. That evening, just as we began to eat our supper, we were told we had to stop. We protested. We had only just begun. They set the dogs on us. Canine teeth sunk into our flesh. Made wild by the dogs, we picked up our picks and spades and lashed out at them. There was a reinforcement of warders. They baton-charged and overpowered us and we were locked up in Section 'C', seventy-seven of us.

There was outrage among the prisoners. Nelson and his colleagues slipped us notes of encouragement and support. We went on a hunger strike; they joined in. Eventually the Red Cross intervened and the hunger strike was called off.

Our case went on trial. A magistrate was brought in from the mainland because we had insisted on the recusal of the Officer in Command, Richardson, who was a real fascist. Eight of us went on trial and the charge against us was withdrawn. We received constant support and advice from the Rivonia men and especially from Nelson.

Later, Saths, Aubrey and I were moved into the 'B' Section and I got to know Nelson at close range. He came up to all my expectations. He stood head and shoulders above the others. Everyone looked up to him and respected him. When he spoke, we listened. He was patient, tolerant and I never saw him lose his temper.

Nelson was very eager to understand our political approach and arranged for us to present papers, so that they could catch up with the post-Sharpeville political activity and understand the Black Consciousness movement first hand.

I felt that he had no problems identifying with our position, but was, at the same time, constructively critical. He said we were somewhat rash. I suggested that what he really meant was that we were just a little more radical. I told him my father used to say I was rash, but finally conceded that I was more radical than he was. Nelson did not argue against that.

His tolerance of the range of attitudes that prevailed among us was remarkable. I found him more tolerant of differing points of view than most of the others. I remember a film that was shown to us, deliberately chosen, I suspect, to impress on us the righteousness of authority. It showed two groups of men: a group of bikers, Hell's Angels, and an army contingent. The army went about its war business and there were shots of action in Vietnam, quite brutal, but all according to rules; the Hell's Angels broke the law outrageously and eventually horrifically molested and raped some girls. The army caught up with them, and the film ended with the Hell's Angels being marched off by the army. There was unanimous agreement at the end of the film that the Hell's Angels had richly deserved their punishment. I disagreed and said that we should look at the symbolism of the movie; the Hell's Angels really symbolized the revolutionary youth of the seventies, Cohn-Bendit and his generation; and that the film condoned institutionalized violence, but condemned anti-system violence. There was a furor against me. I was accused of supporting a bunch of rapists and of downright unmitigated evil. My talk of symbolism, I was told, was just so much hogwash. Nelson alone remained aloof from the attack and brought calm when he said. 'No, Strini may well have a point. Let's try and understand it. We have missed out on these trends.' He suggested I should be asked to prepare a paper on the subject. I prepared the paper and there was great interest and unemotional intellectual discussion, in which Nelson played a key part.

I also found Nelson to be a great social companion. He loved playing chess and dominoes. He was never patronizing to us because we were of a younger generation. When we sat together and joked, as men joke, the jokes getting a bit risque at times, he didn't withdraw. He remained with us.

One particular incident stands out in my mind: We had grouped ourselves into sports teams in our section to introduce some healthy competition. We would choose a commentator from among us to round up the day's happenings. On this particular occasion, I was the commentator and I had to report on a volleyball match in which one team had made a blue and everyone had laughed. Nelson had retained a subdued decorum during the match. Now I related the incident, exaggerating the event to make it humorous. Nelson threw back his head and slapped his thighs and guffawed in abandoned enjoyment. My cell was opposite his so I could see him through the grille.

George Sithole gives an account of life on Robben Island in the eighties. By then physical conditions had improved considerably. He reports:

The Robben Island prison is a walled-in compound, about the size of four football fields. There are ten, large, sprawling buildings on it, seven of which are cells and the rest, the administration block, the recreation-hall-cum-library and the hospital.

When I got to the Island, Mandela, Sisulu and Kathrada had already been removed to Pollsmoor. Motsoaledi, Mhlaba and

Mbeki were still there. But it was as if the other Rivonia men had never left.

We constantly heard stories about them, about Mandela and Sisulu and Kathy. John Ganya, a PAC man, said that one of the first things Mandela did when he arrived on Robben Island was to help a group of PAC men. Nelson was convinced they were wrongly sentenced and he prepared their appeals and succeeded. Ganya had declined to be represented, holding the view that he did not want favours from a white court, but he regretted his attitude when the others were released.

The Rivonia men exerted great influence and it is as a result of the rules they laid down that political prisoners concentrate on studying, and writing and passing exams.

The prison authorities respected the Rivonia men because they feared them. They also respected the authority of other leaders, but not the way they did that of the ANC leaders. The ANC leaders could disrupt the prison if they wanted to, and they knew this. The ANC authority worked because it was democratic, and it was in the main the Rivonia men who had laid the foundation of that democracy.

But, says Sithole, they also feared the leadership and therefore separated it from the rest of the prisoners in Block 'B':

The administration buildings overlook Block 'B' and it is under constant surveillance. You step down to a lower level to reach the cells. They are cold and dismal and they get the sun for only a few hours a day. The Rivonia men spent most of their prison lives there. It has its own library and tennis court, so that the leaders and men of influence remain among themselves.

The prison today has a capacity for approximately 700 prisoners. When I was there during 1983–8, about 600 were ANC comrades, 50 AZAPO, 30 PAC and about 20 Namibians.

We got on well with each other and to some extent learnt to be more tolerant of our ideological differences. The ANC people were at times accused of arrogance and they tried to bring us down a peg or two by insinuating that if there were so many of us in prison, it was because we had made so many slips. We, of course, pointed out that we were so many in prison because we were so many many outside prison.

Each political organization had its own approach to the prison authorities. The Namibians saw themselves as in a foreign country, the PAC and BC adopted a policy of non cooperation when they could; the ANC approach was to observe regulations, utilize the amenities and concentrate on strengthening our unity. This was the policy laid down by the Rivonia trialists and particularly by Mandela. I found it to be a very positive approach. It strengthened our commitment to the ANC. It also resulted in winning us recruits from the PAC and BC.

Life inside the prison is highly organized and the organization is on three levels. Firstly, there is the official bureaucracy, then there are the general committees set up by the prisoners to utilize the sports and library facilities, and then there are the cell committees of the political organizations to maintain organization discipline, to share the monies that came from outside and to decide how these should be spent. Prison discipline depends on the last committee, and the prison authorities know this.

I learnt more in prison than in all my years outside. If we had problems among each other that we could not resolve, we took them to the 'B' Section, a commission went into the dispute, its findings were discussed in each cell, and that way we tried to reach a consensus.

Conditions have improved considerably on Robben Island, specially since the mid 1980s. Prisoners get up to piped music today, have running water and showers in the cells, have access to radio and TV, and may subscribe to newspapers and periodicals. Prisoners are also taught a trade. None of these amenities were available in the 1960s and 1970s. It was only in 1984 that beds were provided in common cells and a year or so earlier in the single cells. Television was allowed in 1986 and the radio about five years earlier.

When the Rivonia trialists were imprisoned, conditions were very primitive. They slept on jute mats on the floor, their uniforms were indecent and they were not given pyjamas. They were locked into their cells with sanitary buckets and a bottle of water. They had no access to reading material, or the radio, or to any media. They could not study. They fought for improved conditions and succeeded.

When I was on Robben Island, prisoners who had completed a year were given the option to learn a trade: tailoring, upholstery and brick-laying. Hard labour involves going out to the 'span' (work place). Prisoners, of course, are graded from A to D. Newcomers have practically no privileges. It could take a prisoner more than a decade to be promoted to the A grade, which allows you to buy sugar, tea and sweets, and technically to have forty visits a year. In fact, the prison bureaucracy cannot handle that many visits per person, and prisoners' families cannot afford the visits because of the long distances they have to travel and the cost. The International Red Cross gives each family twelve tickets a year.

But as Nelson says today: 'It was a hard and bitter struggle to humanize the prison and improve conditions so that political prisoners could live with some resemblance of dignity.' Penal reform is today high on the list of priorities that Nelson would like to get down to, if given the opportunity.

In June 1967 Nelson had his third visit from Winnie. They met for half an hour. She brought him news of Thembi, whom she had just seen, and Nelson was delighted to hear that there had been a pleasant reunion. Nelson was allowed four visits a year at the time, restricted to next of kin. It was not always easy for the 'next of kin' to take those visits because of the long distances and the expense of travel.

Nelson concentrated on his studies and tried to put meaning into the hard labour allocated to him. He saw it as an opportunity to breathe fresh air, see the sea and bird life. They worked in the lime quarry, digging and then loading trucks. He became interested in rock formations and in archaeology. He read whatever he could find on the subject in the sparse prison library. The privilege to study, to enrol on a correspondence college, to order and receive books, write assignments and receive them marked, to knotch up grades, courses, degrees, to share each other's academic achievements – these became the sustainers.

In 1978 Nelson wrote to Zindzi:

On some days the weather on the island is quite beautiful, in fact, beyond words, as Aunt Fatima would put it. Early one morning, I looked out through the window and the eye could see eastwards as far as the distant horizon. The power of imagination created the illusion that my vision went much further than the naked eye could actually see. I could survey vast regions behind the long mountain ranges where I have never been. Later, I walked out into the courtyard and the few living things there, the seagulls, wagtails, the plants, small trees and even grass blades were gay and full of smiles. Everything was caught up in the beauty of the day. I looked into the vast dome of blue emptiness that stretched out above me in all directions and the illusions was still there, the size and speed, and what information they were sending to mother earth.

5 March 1978

CHAPTER 26

# Loss of Comrade and Kin

Three months after their imprisonment, in September 1964,
they heard of the death in detention of Babla Saloojee.
Nelson had known the Fordsburg youth – elusive, childlike
in innocence and completely committed to the movement.
Whatever the official explanation, he knew the boy had not
killed himself.

The year 1965 brought news of the arrest of Bram Fischer.
It cast a gloom on Robben Island and the comrades
wondered how much damage had been done. Bram had been
captured in Johannesburg in disguise. The white press gave
pictures of the 'before' and 'after', and distorted Fischer's
sacrifice. Nelson knew immediately that Bram, too, would
spend his life in prison and his heart went out to him.

Nelson loved and admired the man. He regarded him as the
foremost legal brain in the country. He had everything going for
him: the son of a revered Judge President, marriage to Molly
Krige, who was closely related to General Smuts. He could have
had immediate power, but he opposed the power of the racist
state and made common cause with the powerless. Soon after
the Rivonia Trial, and at the height of his legal eminence, he had
abandoned his chambers, his gracious living and congenial
company, and gone underground. Nelson rated Fischer's
sacrifice greater than his own, for he had abandoned his 'tribe'
in order to do so, something that he had never had to do. Bram
Fischer humbled him in a way no man did. Quiet and controlled,
and above all gentle, he was not the stuff of the underground. He
was the man of brilliance to be heard in every court, every
assembly. He deserved to be not just a Judge President, but the
President of the new South Africa they dreamed of.

Nelson recalled Bram's quiet sorrow when his wife died. He had come to visit them on Robben Island with other lawyers, soon after their conviction following the Rivonia Trial. Nelson had inquired after Molly and the children. Bram had behaved strangely; he had muttered something and suddenly turned and walked away from him. After his departure, a prison official, who had monitored the visit, told Nelson that Molly had died in a motor car accident. 'I was shocked. I had known and admired Molly, and knew how close she and Bram had been. My heart went out to him and that evening I wrote him a letter which I hope comforted him in his grief, so deep that he could not even talk about it.'

Bram was also sentenced to life imprisonment, but he spent it at Pretoria maximum security prison. He died there in May 1977, and was mourned by family and friends.

The year that followed the arrest of Bram Fischer brought the sad news of the demise of Chief Albert Luthuli. Banned and ageing and forced to put aside his political duties, his passion for righteousness remained as strong as ever. He spent his days in enforced retirement in the small mission station of Groutville. Delegations and friends came to see him and usually he met them at the home of his friend in Stanger, E. V. Mohamed, his self-appointed Honorary Secretary. When Bobby Kennedy came to South Africa, he had spiralled down into the Groutville sands in a helicopter to the excitement and wonder of the clanspeople. The doomed senator and the wise revolutionary had spent an hour talking.

The Chief and his gracious wife, Nokukhanya, were happy in their children: Albertina, a doctor, Hilda, a nurse, Jane, a social worker, their son, a lawyer. Hilda and Albertina were overseas but the others visited their parents regularly, and grandchildren came to stay. The Chief farmed a little, read a lot and regularly took a walk across a small railway bridge. He knew this walk so well, his son-in-law said later, that he could have walked it blindfolded. Yet, one morning in July 1967, he was found dead, knocked down by a train on that very familiar route. The mystery of his death remains unsolved.

The worst burden Nelson bore in those first four years was

the death of his mother. He remembered her gentleness when he was a growing boy, her Christian counsel that remained in his consciousness despite the ideological strains that entered it. He thought of her with Evelyn, with Winnie, with his children. Above all he was haunted by the memory of her lean, silent image on the day of his sentencing. He was her only son; she had been widowed young. As one of his father's junior wives, she had suffered neglect, but through it all she had preserved her stoic dignity. He allowed his grief to take possession of him and felt somewhat comforted. He was in total control when his comrades came to sympathize with him. Alone again, he thought of the time he could have spent with her but had not because politics had claimed him.

He wrote on 1 March 1981: 'Even to my mother, I was not so attentive as I should have been. I rarely wrote to her except to try to persuade her to come to live with me in Johannesburg.'

Nosekeni Mandela's funeral in October 1968 was in high contrast to her humble life. Two states made their presence felt: the Transkeian in honour of a kinswoman and the mother of a kinsman they honoured despite political differences; and the South African as a grim reminded of the power that kept her son imprisoned. A quiet and very private person, Nosekeni's funeral became a police rendezvous. There had never been as many police at any other Transkeian funeral. They had never visited her at Qunu, though she had felt their invasions regularly at her son's home in Orlando.

Winnie was given permission to travel to the Transkei for the funeral. She broke down and wept bitterly at the graveside; her grief merging with that of her sisters-in-law, Evelyn and the other Madiba women who were close kin.

Three months after Nelson's mother's funeral, Winnie visited him with first-hand news of his mother's illness and burial. Neither realized that it would be two years before they would see each other again, that Winnie would be arrested within months and placed in solitary confinement for almost a year and a half – that as a family they were about to face their worst ordeal yet.

# CHAPTER 27

# Attempts to Destroy
# the Mandelas

In 1964 the first thing that wives and relatives of the Robben Island prisoners did after their conviction was to apply for permission to visit their husbands, sons and brothers. Winnie and Albertina Sisulu were banned and therefore depended on the Minister of Justice's 'grace' to be allowed the normal 'privileges' due to wives of prisoners. Permission was granted, but the two women had to travel separately since, as banned persons, they were not allowed to communicate with each other.

Winnie travelled by train to Cape Town. Friends took her to the docks and she stepped down into the claustrophobic hold of the small motor boat. She felt the engine under her feet and, beneath it, the waves but saw nothing of the sea. When they reached the Island and she had clambered to the top deck: she saw that a festive crowd accompanied her on the boat, young girls visiting the police and warders for a good time, she assumed. As she walked towards the prison building, she saw the watch tower and the sinister guns. They sent a chill down her spine and she realized how impossible it was to escape from that island prison.

She walked on the gravel path into the visitors' waiting-room and waited her turn. When called she went down the narrow passage, past window panes pressed with faces of prisoners. For a split second she was numb with shock at the sight of the 'dismembered' faces but then she recovered and responded to their smiles. A comrade called: 'Nelson is down at the end,' and then she saw him, beaming his welcome. She

282

smiled back and a precious half an hour followed. For Nelson, it was sufficient just to have her there, to talk about the children, to get the news at first-hand.

Winnie returned to Johannesburg, despondent. A few weeks later she was served with her second banning order which confined her to Orlando. More serious, the Child Welfare office terminated her services. Her job had been under threat for some time as the Government refused to subsidize her salary. Winnie's immediate superior a Mrs Uys, had taken a stand and told her that they would find a private source to make up the subsidy. State pressure, however, proved too much. The police pursued Winnie to the office, and armed with warrants went through her files.

Winnie commented:

They were convinced that Nelson was communicating with me and believed that they would find some evidence in my papers. Or perhaps they were just being vindictive, but their presence had an intimidatory effect. Our office was multi-racial. I got on well with everyone, except Mrs Tiny Kruger. We had had clashes before, but now they increased and became more personally pointed. She complained about me to Mrs Uys and demanded an apology. Mrs Uys said, 'I can't sacrifice a white worker for you. You realize the situation in the country.' My instincts revolted against an apology. I knew Mrs Kruger was very wrong and unjust. But I needed the job so I said I would think about it. The banning order spared both of us from making decisions against our consciences. The order automatically deprived me of my job.

Winnie took both her banning order and dismissal from work in her stride. There had been a time when she had thought herself indispensable to the agency. She and Janet Makiwane had the heaviest case load. But then they also had numerous clashes with the Commissioner of Child Welfare over the placement of children. He took a tribalistic view, they a humanist one. She had got into deep trouble over Lydia Mudzawane, abandoned with seven children by her husband and thrown out of the house rented to her husband. Winnie had placed the family in the only available refuge home, and was then ordered to remove them from it because the Mudzawanas were Venda and the home was for Xhosa people. That the children were sick with asthma made no difference.

Speaking about her profession, Winnie says:

I loved my work as a social worker. I really believed I was making an important contribution there, despite all the human pain I had to suffer. My work also entailed the placing of babies for adoption. Orlando had the only sorting-out depot for all non-white babies awaiting adoption. I had a call one day from Aziz who told me of a family that wanted to give away a baby in adoption. He wanted the family's identity to be kept secret, and wanted the adoption to be arranged in such a way that the family would not become involved in the adoptive process at any stage. I collected the baby and placed the child with an adoptive family. I did not question the race of the baby or of the real parents, but I soon learnt from this experience that one has to match babies and parents, that not only was this required by law, but also by the people conditioned by the law.

The adoptive mother loved her baby but the neighbours would not let her be. They kept pointing at the straight hair of the baby so that she began keeping the baby's hair completely covered. How long could that continue? I discussed this with my colleague, Zora Dangore, and we came to the conclusion that our society was not ripe for cross-cultural adoption. The baby was eventually placed in a Coloured home, for that was what had been made of it, in that spontaneous moment of love which had blinded the lovers to their racial identity.

The State wanted to rid itself of the Mandelas, so it followed Nelson's imprisonment with the banning of Winnie. Thereby it gave the world a second Mandela. Winnie was kept under close observation and arrested for trivial infringements of her banning order and, on occasions, imprisoned. The nightmare of police raids was compounded by those of vandals and nocturnal attackers who, judging by their behaviour, appeared to be an extension of the system, or its close sympathizers.

Nelson anguished over Winnie's persecution. It deprived Zeni and Zindzi of the effective presence of both parents. He worried about the effect that it was having on his daughters. He worried about Winnie's isolation and loneliness, about her loss of a job, and deprivation of friends and relatives. He was tortured that he was not there to protect her from the police and thugs who violated her life. And, always, he was deeply grateful to those who helped her.

Winnie was charged for contravening her banning order almost as many times as the number of years she was banned. On two occasions she served prison sentences for technical violations.

For Winnie, survival without Nelson became possible only by surviving like him and she threw herself into political activity. She sought out victims of political persecution and set about finding assistance for them. Excluded from practising her profession, she practised it anyway, without remuneration, focusing on specialized clients. She attracted a body of workers and liaised with other political activists. Emissaries would arrive at the dead of night with leaflets that had to be distributed. Messengers were never questioned, their *bona fides* taken for granted. On one occasion at 4 a.m., while distributing leaflets, she was surprised by a man who greeted her, 'Sakubona, Mama.' She had believed that no one would recognize her in a large overcoat and a headcloth concealing most of her face.

Even if Winnie had chosen to stay clear of politics, the State would not have left her alone. As a banned person, she was constantly under police surveillance as the wife of a man they feared. Winnie clashed constantly with the police, and each time she made an issue of it. Where others would have left it and got on with their lives, she made her life one of confrontation with the police and the system.

In October 1964, four months after Nelson's departure to Robben Island, Winnie was at the Johannesburg police station, taking food for 90-Day detainee, Paul Joseph. The Josephs were special friends and firm compatriots in the struggle for liberation. They had stood firmly with her during Nelson's trial. Paul's interrogation was particularly vicious and he had applied to the courts for relief. 90-Day detainees were only allowed pre-packed foods and Winnie adhered strictly to the requirements but the police refused to take her food. An argument followed and Winnie lashed out at the police. The police, unable to take this, lunged forward and assaulted her. She then laid a charge of assault against them. Perhaps this was what brought about their second-level attack on her, more sinister than the invasions into her privacy and direct arrests for contravening her banning order. They now hatched a sinister plan to destroy the Mandelas by destroying Winnie's reputation.

A woman is vulnerable. A beautiful young woman, deprived of her husband, is a hundred-fold more vulnerable. Beauty itself becomes a target of envy. Tongues wag without cause and how much greater the wagging if some is offered.

Brian Somana was a family friend. Nelson, anxious about Winnie's welfare after his imprisonment, had asked his friends to look after Winnie. Among them was Brian, a 90-Day detainee whom Nelson trusted implicitly. Brian took Nelson's request seriously. But he was a plant, the instrument used by the police in their attempt to destroy Winnie's reputation, morally and politically. Mrs Somana started divorce proceedings and cited Winnie as co-respondent. But once this reached the press, the divorce proceedings were dropped.

The movement was infiltrated by police informers, as the Rivonia trial had so shockingly revealed, and these 'informers', accepted as committed members of the ANC, began their whispering campaign with confusion and malice resulting. Winnie became conscious of friends who began to isolate her but one comforted her. The police tried to pin an allegation of adultery against her. Winnie remained unscathed, her reputation intact.

In July 1966 the Mandelas had their second prison visit. Winnie was told that she would be allowed to see her husband only if she carried a pass. This was another attempt to humiliate them. Nelson had burnt his pass in defiance. Winnie had gone to prison rather than carry the pass imposed on African women in the mid-1950s. But their need to see each other was so desperate that it would have been a self-defeating gesture not to get that piece of paper. They had not seen each other for two years and so much had happened to them.

For Nelson the years and events fell away as he gazed on her. He wondered how he had pulled through without seeing her. She sat there, so young, so vulnerable; his heart went out to her across the glass pane. He wanted to reach out, to touch and to hold her. Vain dreams. They talked embarrassedly in the presence of the warders, feeling like young lovers. Nelson was helpless, hemmed in by police and guards, bars and high walls, and a sea he could not cross.

The police pursued Winnie to Cape Town airport on her departure for Johannesburg and demanded her name and address. Irritated, she retorted that they already knew. How else could they have identified her? They charged her with refusing to identify herself to the police and failing to report her arrival in Cape Town. She was sentenced to one month's imprisonment on the first charge and a full year on the second. The magistrate probably felt that the haughty black woman needed to be taught a lesson. However, all but four days of the sentence were suspended. Her lawyer pleaded that the magistrate should suspend all but one day. The magistrate disagreed saying: 'It is rather unfair that this court has been asked to give judgement in this matter. She is a woman and she may have been upset after seeing her husband but whether this gave her licence to refuse to give her name and address is a moot point. I assess her intellect very highly and I think she knew what she was doing.' The Defence was given leave to appeal and she was released on bail of R20.

Meanwhile, Winnie found a job as a clerk at a correspondence college but the State forced her employer to dismiss her, holding that her banning order did not allow her to be at an educational institution.

With one case still pending, the police brought another. Lieutenant Fourie barged into Winnie's bedroom one day as she was undressing, having just returned from work. Angrily she braced herself against the door frame, lunged at him and forced him out. He laid a charge of assault against her. In court Mrs Mandela scarcely cut the image of an Amazon and the case was dismissed.

That was one occasion for jubilation. Nelson took pride in her guts. He enjoyed the admiration the episode earned her from his comrades on Robben Island. But she lost her appeal in the Cape Town case and the State demanded four days' imprisonment. She served these and came out all smiles. Among those waiting to welcome her was her friend, Maude. A policeman apologized to Maude in deference to her whiteness, 'I'm sorry, I didn't know you were waiting to take her home.'

In 1974 Winnie and Peter Magubane were employed by a debt-collecting company. The director, Francois Squibble, prided himself on the high wages he paid them, but he also recorded his great regard for their competence. Yet while they worked for the same company, they were not allowed to communicate with each other being banned persons. The police kept a close watch in the hope of catching them talking to each other. During the holidays, when Zeni and Zindzi returned from school, Peter would fetch them in his Combi. He would park the van, stand aside, and she would lunch with the girls in it. On one such occasion the police arrested them, alleging that they had been communicating. They served six months in prison for that offence. Winnie spent her sentence with Dorothy Nyembe and Amina Desai, two political prisoners from Kroonstad.

In 1981, while banished in Brandfort, Winnie was charged with receiving a visitor, Mathew Malefane. But Mathew, as it turned out, was a lodger not a visitor, and so the charge failed.

Between 1966 and 1969, Winnie was charged three times and detained for 491 days. Between 1970 and 1978, she was charged on three more occasions and imprisoned for six months. In 1977 she was banished to Brandfort.

Her banning order forced her to live alone. In 1972 two men broke into the house and tried to strangle her in bed. Her screams brought the neighbours and her attackers fled.

A few months later, her garage door was broken and the windows of her car smashed. In 1976 vandals cut her telephone wires, smashed the windows of her house, broke down the door and dumped anti-government leaflets in her yard.

Nelson lived through all this and more, much more, because he blamed himself for her victimization. He loved her and he suffered for her on account of that love. He had a sense of patriarchal obligation and his inability to protect her was unbearable. In his mind her persecution took on a limitless proportion and gruesome forms.

CHAPTER 28

# Winnie's Ordeal

It was 12 May 1969 and Winnie had not yet celebrated her thirty-fifth birthday. Nelson had already served seven years in prison, two under the first conviction for incitement and leaving the country without a permit and five of life imprisonment. Their two little girls, Zeni and Zindzi, were at boarding school in Swaziland; Winnie's sister Nonyaniso was living with her.

At about 3 a.m. the occupants of house No. 8115 were asleep. There was suddenly a loud knock on the door and Winnie was instantly awake. She knew it was the police and alerted her sister. By then the whole house was shuddering with the knocking at both doors and windows. Winnie was putting on her dressing-gown when there was a shattering sound and the front door almost fell in on Nonyaniso. Winnie was furious but Major Johannes Jacobus Viktor ignored her and instructed his men to search the house. They became particularly excited when they found a copy of *Black Power and Liberation: A Communist View* and a book of poems on South Africa. Then they told Winnie to pack her bags: 'You won't be back for a long time, Mrs Mandela.'

Winnie was driven to Pretoria prison and put into solitary confinement. The cell was dark and small: in it were a blanket, a sanitary bucket, a mug and herself. She unrolled the blanket and bugs crawled out, biting her fingers. She then rolled the blanket and hurled it into a corner. But it was cold and she realized that she would need it. She unrolled it again and set about killing the bugs. An hour or so later, there was a heap of dead bugs and the blanket was reasonably clean, but her hands felt unbearably dirty and she was nauseated by the smell of bug blood.

She improvised a calendar and knotched up the days that passed. She had no idea for how long they would keep her, who else had been arrested with her and why. The warders did not speak to her. They simply pushed plates of foul-looking food into her cell and removed them, untouched. She was allowed to leave her cell to empty her bucket and to wash.

She was relieved when the police came to fetch her. Winnie recalls: 'It was company, but my relief evaporated when I saw the chief of the team, the dour-faced, strong-bodied Major Theunis Jacobus Swanepoel. Swanepoel had the reputation of a killer and Babla Saloojee's death at the then Grey's building was connected with him.'

She learnt for the first time of the others who had been detained with her. Her sister and Peter Magubane were among them. She panicked about the children. Who would care for them? The police told her they had eighty witnesses. They named those known to be her close and trusted friends, who, they claimed, had told them just about all they needed to know. They simply required her confirmation. A police-man was sitting at a typewriter, hands poised, to type her con-fession.

Her interrogation alternated between gentle persuasion and outright aggression. Their tactic was to make her believe that they knew everything anyhow; her colleagues, her sister and Peter Magubane had told all.

*Q:* When did you start the ANC?
*A:* The ANC is banned.
*Q:* Don't give us that. Rita has told us all about it. So what's the use? We know all the details about your meetings – in Ndou's storeroom, in Diepkloof, in Alexandra – we know about the oaths you administered, come on, don't be a fool now,. You will stand alone in the court, and they will all be state witnesses against you. You want a cigarette?
*A:* I don't smoke.
*Q:* Some coffee then?

He did not wait for her answer. In Afrikaans he ordered

one of the policemen to get a cup of coffee and then, changing to English and smiling down at her, said, 'Get some toasted chicken sandwiches too, while you are about it. Mrs Mandela will enjoy them. Let us go on.'

'Go on about what? There is nothing to go on. What we did we did openly. We were helping our people.'

The exchange went on for about half an hour. Then Swanepoel got up and complained that she was being tedious. 'Just boring and useless and you have too much to tell. Don't think that you won't tell. You'll tell all before we're through with you. Gert, take her on.'

Gert was a big man with a very red face. His manner was rough and his attitude threatening, and he came at her as if at any moment he would assault her physically. He did not talk to her, he shouted. The others were cooperative. What was she being so special about? Who did she think she was protecting? They had it all there, taped: her meetings with her husband, his secret instructions to her; the telephone calls, her conversations with Oliver Tambo. All recorded. They were going to put her away, so what was the point?

The time dragged. How long had she been sitting on that chair? A day, a night, two days, two nights? Just what did they want? She learnt to measure time in that room where the electric light shone through the shifts of interrogators. Each one, it seemed, spent four hours with her. The first bombarded her with questions; the second shouted, insulted and threatened; the third was all compassion and commiseration, offering to help her if only she would cooperate and satisfy them with some answers. Food came during the 'kindness shift'. She told her interrogator that she was dizzy and had terrible palpitations. He promised to get the doctor and advised, 'Why go through all this? You are young and beautiful and you have two young children. You owe it to them and you owe it to yourself to live a happy normal life.' He then offered her a job with the police. She had class, he said, she should become one of them.

'Think of it, all your problems over.' Think, think, think, the word hammered in her brain. She visualized Nelson saying to her: 'Zami, next month we will go to Durban and have a holiday away from it all.' A holiday on the beach, the foam curling around her toes, the sun on the water, Zeni and Zindzi making sandcastles . . .

'Winnie, don't go off to sleep. We have to talk so that you can get out of here.' She was pulled out of her reverie.

Get out of here, get out of here, get out, get out. Her mind wandered to Bizana. She was with her father and they were picking mealies. 'They are very good this year,' he was saying. 'And so many. We will get a good price. We will put it away for next year when you go to boarding school.'

'Winnie?' Another tone, another man. She was dragged out of her semi-coma. The kindness man had gone and the torture man was looming over her. Her hands and feet were blue and swollen. She thought she would die. Swanepoel was shouting at her: 'For God's sake, leave us some inheritance when you decide to pop it. You can't go with all that information.' The pain was overpowering, her heartbeat thundering, her head in a dizzy whirl, her eyes closed, her head slumped. They banged on the table and clapped their hands. 'Not yet!' they shouted 'You haven't told us all!'

The night passed; it was morning again, the third in her chair. Her head was in a perpetual spin. The new man was all kindness. Would she like to take a shower? he asked and then, without waiting for an answer, led her out of the room down the corridor into the shower cubicle. She saw that her whole body was blue. She applied soap limply; she felt fresher and somewhat relaxed afterwards.

She returned to her chair. The 'kindness man' told her that everyone was very concerned about her and they respected her a great deal. 'That is why we don't make you stand. We know you have a heart condition. Now that meeting with Mr Platt-Mills . . .'

Platt-Mills? she thought. Who could have told them about that?

He continued to give her details about other meetings. They knew a lot. The others had obviously broken but she must keep firm.

It was Major Swanepoel's time again. She feared him most, but not sufficiently to accept the case he was inventing against her. He was shouting:

I will tell you what you are, Winnie Mandela! You are just a bitch! You did it all for money. You got it because you pretended to be such a saviour of your people. But you took it for yourself, most of it, to buy all those fine clothes you wear. Who for, Winnie Mandela? Your husband is in prison. For who do you dress up like a tart? Don't think we don't know. That innocent act won't work with us. We are the police. You'll tell us, if you don't want us to tell them. That will end it all, won't it? Your desire to be a great leader? All you are good for is a kick on your backside. Come on, get smart. You know all the secret plans. They write to you in code and invisible ink. We'll decipher it all, but you have a chance to do it yourself.

He was strutting up and down the room and it seemed to her at any moment he would pick her up and fling her down. She wished he would. Then she could lose consciousness, maybe die. Then it would be all over. What happens after death, she wondered. Like they said in the Bible? Her mother knew, she could go to her. She would ask her, there in the cattle kraal where she prayed. Swanepoel's voice came piercing through her consciousness. 'Why do I waste my time with you? What did you bring all these scum into politics for?'

He was giving up, she thought. The dizzy spells in her head worsened and she began to have blackouts. A policeman allowed her to place her head on her knees. Major Coetzee, the kind one, said his wife was concerned about her. Winnie hardly heard him. She was seized by an acute pain under her left breast and her body was shaking uncontrollably. Suddenly her mind was alerted. Her ears trained to understand the fearful sounds that came from the next room, screams of pain. Her interrogator paused in his work so that she could hear better, and then jeered: 'That will fix him. You want to know who that is? One of your men. Not so brave now, is he? By the time they have finished with him he'll be of use to no one. Not even himself. But he'll talk. He's reached the end. Now what is it going to be with you? Broken bones or the statement we want?'

'I am guilty. I am the one. I did it all. I confess to everything. Just leave the others.'

Swanepoel was beside himself with excitement: 'We got her. It works every time, no matter who it is.'

More policemen came; the room filled with interrogators as if to relish this last assault on the Mandelas. The police walked up and down, reading to her from piles of paper and files, stopping every now and again to ask for explanations and confirmations. She kept on saying: 'Yes, yes. It is true, I was there, I did it. I called the meetings, I wrote those letters, I posted them.' Anything, she thought, anything other than her comrades be tortured.

Major Coetzee had the letters in a large book. It seemed to her that he had every name of those to whom she had written in the last year or so. She had to explain cryptic messages that appeared unintelligible or decipher handwriting they could not read. They drew their own inferences and asked her whether these were correct. She said 'Yes, yes!' to everything as if mesmerized. The interrogation continued through the afternoon into the night and the team changed, she did not. Then, at last, at dawn Swanepoel told his team: 'That's it. We have as much as we need for now.'

They returned her to her cell, a shadow of the woman who had left it five days ago. The wardress peeped through the slit in the door and heard her talking to herself. She was delirious and could not sleep after five days of staying awake. They brought her food and she said it was poisoned and vomited. Then she had an attack of diarrhoea. There were nights when the other prisoners were startled by her screams; the days passed and with them some healing of body and spirit.

On 18 July, as reflected on Winnie's hand-made calendar, the wardress announced that she was wanted in the super-intendent's office and instructed her to come immediately. Major Swanepoel wanted to know who Thembi was. 'My eldest son,' she replied. He told her that he had died in a car accident. Her mind flashed to Nelson in prison. Her body convulsed and she sobbed unashamedly. They led her back to her cell. She lay on her mat and thought of the boy Nelson had presented to her, the son the father had so loved. She saw Nelson's anxious face through the glass pane on Robben Island, asking for news of Thembi. She wailed uncontrollably.

The news of Thembi's death was conveyed to Nelson by the commanding officer on Robben Island. He received it, his every muscle taut, struggling to contain his feelings in the presence of his jailers. He wanted only to get into his cell, to lock himself up and give vent to the emotions that almost choked him.

When his terrible agony subsided, he wrote a letter to Evelyn, the only one after their parting. He consoled her for he knew her pain was as great as his. Then he wrote to Thembi's widow and told her that he hoped she would come to see him and tell him about his two granddaughters.

Nelson expressed his feelings about deaths in the family in a letter of 26 October 1976, after a cousin died: 'I don't have words to express the suffering I endure when family members pass away and I cannot attend their funerals. The news of Thembi's death was shattering.'

Makgatho recalled: 'I did not see the effect of Thembi's death on Tata. I saw it on Mama. She was heartbroken. I felt more lonely than ever.'

The police now plotted to replace Winnie's attorney, Joel Carlson, with a more pliable lawyer. They knew of the conflicts between them and they exploited these to achieve their ends. They knew that if they alienated Winnie from Carlson, it would cause a split among the accused. That, in itself, would weaken the Defence. They told her that Joel Carlson was not available to represent the accused, that he would never be allowed to see them and that if she wanted the case to be brought speedily to court, she had better settle for Mendel Levine. They offered to arrange for her to see the other accused so that they could come to an agreement in the matter.

Later, in court, Laurence Ndzanga said that he was summoned to Major Swanepoel's office one day where Mrs Mandela was also present. 'He gave me a paper and said Mrs Mandela will explain everything and left us to talk together ... I refused to sign the paper, stating that I wanted to be represented by Mr Carlson.' Elliot Shabangu testified that Major Swanepoel had told him there was a possibility that Mr Carlson would not appear in court. Major Swanepoel had asked him to sign the paper agreeing to Mr Levine representing him. Rita Ndzanga recalled how one day she had met Winnie while they were being taken to Compol (headquarters of Security Police in Pretoria). She had asked why they were being told that Mr Levine would work for them. Winnie had answered that the police were saying that Mr Carlson was prohibited from entering prisons.

When the twenty-two accused were brought to court on 29 October 1969, both Joel Carlson and Mendel Levine claimed they represented Mrs Mandela. After an adjournment, all twenty-two agreed to be represented by Carlson. The accused told the court that the police had tried to persuade them to engage Levine as their attorney.

When the case began in the Pretoria Supreme Court in the Old Synagogue on 1 December 1969, most of the accused had served seven months in detention. They were charged with reviving the ANC by establishing groups and committees, recruiting members, holding meetings, arranging funerals of ANC members, distributing ANC propaganda, canvassing funds, organizing support for families of political prisoners, planning to assist guerrilla fighters, acquiring explosives and propagating Communist doctrines.

The State Prosecutor, Mr Liebenberg, alleged that they had revived the ANC during 1967, had established contact with old ANC members in Soweto, Diepkloof, Alexandra, Durban, Port Elizabeth and Umtata, that they had been briefed by the ANC members imprisoned at Robben Island and Nylstroom prisons and exiled in London and Lusaka, and that they held secret ANC meetings in private houses, in cars and in the veld.

As the case unfolded (and the police produced their witnesses, many of whom had been tortured and promised indemnity if their evidence was satisfactory), it became clear that all that the State could substantiate was that Winnie's group had organized relief for the families of political prisoners and for the prisoners themselves on their release. It also became evident that the police relied on the witness of detained 'co-conspirators' promised indemnity if their evidence was satisfactory. Two witnesses, Shanthi Naidoo and Nondwe Vricine Mankahla, refused to testify for the State and were sentenced to two months' imprisonment. Five 'comrades' who gave evidence for the State admitted under cross-examination that they had been tortured before they had made their statements. Even then, their evidence did not establish the State's case.

Philip Golding, a UK national, had been assaulted during interrogation and promised his freedom if he gave evidence in accordance with the statement made to the police. He said he had become friendly with one of the accused, Samuel Pholotho, whom he had tutored in Economics and that he had taken messages to ANC contacts in the UK on behalf of the group. Mr Herbert Nhlapo said that he had attended meetings where the need for an organization to take up African grievances had been discussed. Mohale Mohamyele said he had discussed funeral arrangements for Mr Lekoto and that he had allowed Mrs Mandela the use of a duplicator at the United States Information Centre where he worked to print leaflets opposing the Urban Bantu Council elections and to publicize the funeral of Mr Lekoto.

Winnie's sister, Nonyaniso Madikizela, admitted that she had been so threatened and brainwashed by the police that she could no longer tell the difference between her knowledge and what the police had suggested to her.

Eselina Klaas of Port Elizabeth, who had already served two and a half years' imprisonment for furthering the aims of the ANC in 1964 when Winnie's group had contacted her, and was now serving the second iternment, was too fearful to admit that she had been tortured by the police. She had distributed forms to be filled in by the families of political prisoners and had come up to Johannesburg to be briefed by Winnie and Rita Ndzanga.

*Mr Bizos:* How many times were you requested to make a statement?
*Eselina:* Seven times.
*Mr Bizos:* Was your lip not cut? Was your face not bruised?
*Eselina:* They just spoke to me from Monday to Thursday, all night and all day. I stood all the time. I slept when I could not stand.
*Mr Bizos:* Did you ask why you were standing?
*Eselina:* I was standing to make a statement.

She finally admitted that she had discussed welfare work and never the ANC with some of the accused.

The evidence of the police, too, did not add up to much. Major Viktor's evidence was restricted to the two books from hundreds he had found in the Mandela home. Johannes Jacobus found a pamphlet titled 'We are at War' on Accused number seventeen. W. O. Jordaan found press-cuttings on the lack of school facilities for African children in Ndzanga's house, and W. O. Smith found a copy of the M-Plan, a copy of the ANC oath and English translations of articles published in the Afrikaans magazines, *Dagbreek* and *Landstem* in Accused number four's locker.

In February 1970 the State withdrew the charge against all twenty-two accused but they were immediately re-arrested and re-charged under the Terrorism Act. That charge failed too and they were acquitted. The State, however, banned them.

She had been held in solitary confinement for seventeen months and Nelson had not been allowed to communicate with her during that time. He had written her several letters and a senior prison official had assured him that they had been delivered. They never were. He had agonized over Winnie, and over Zeni and Zindzi. Mercifully the girls were at Waterford boarding school in Swaziland, and there were friends they could turn to. But he knew that nothing could make up for the absence of their parents.

Winnie's first thought on release was to visit Nelson. The prison authorities gave her a visiting date for 3 October, but on 30 September she was banned again for five years. To boot, she was put under house arrest between 6 p.m. and 6 a.m. on weekdays and from 2 p.m. to 6 a.m. on weekends and public holidays. The local magistrate refused to allow her to leave Johannesburg and travel to Cape Town. The police raided the Mandela home yet again in October. They found Peter Magubane (who had also been banned) Winnie's sister and brother-in-law at home. They laid a fresh charge against her for breaching her banning order and, for good measure, arrested her sister Nonyaniso for being in Johannesburg 'illegally'. They gave her seventy-two hours to leave the city for the Transkei. Winnie's younger brother was charged for not having a pass.

Winnie was distracted from her concern about visiting Nelson to arranging defence for herself and her relatives. In the midst of that turmoil, her second application to leave Johannesburg for Cape Town succeeded and she set off to visit Nelson.

After two years, they had thirty minutes to discuss the vast number of domestic problems that had accumulated and to commiserate with each other on the unbearable loss of Thembi. Nelson came well prepared for the visit, all the issues that had to be discussed neatly itemized on paper. He knew that if he did not do that, he would be so distracted by the sheer emotionalism of the reunion that the urgent matters would remain unattended and that he would later suffer a flood of recriminations.

Winnie had been allowed leave of absence from Johannesburg for only one day and so had to rush to the airport immediately after the visit. The excitement and tension of the visit proved too much for her and that night, in Johannesburg, she suffered a mild heart-attack.

Nelson expressed his feelings about his wife's arrest in the following words:

However trivial the actual charge, every one of your cases are more than ordinary court trials in which luck hardly played a part in your discharge. Only the loyalty and skill of professional friends brought you out. I am confident that whatever the final verdict might be they will do their best. Although I always put on a brave face I never get used to you being in the cooler. Few things disorganize my whole life as much as this particular type of hardship which seems destined to stalk us for quite some time still. I will never forget the actual distressing experience we had from May 1969 to September 1970, the six months you spent in Kroonstad. To ask someone to live with you (if you did) was a necessary precaution on your part and was by no means intended to be an act of defiance against anyone.

It was a perfectly reasonable action which ought to raise no alarm. I expect you to inform me of the date of the hearing and the final outcome. Meanwhile, I will be thinking of you especially as you are ordered to the dock and as you listen to the expected and unexpected turns in the state evidence. I am solidly behind you and know too well that you suffer because of your love and loyalty to the children and me, as well as to our large families. It is an ever-growing love and loyalty which strike me more forcefully every day you come.

When you were detained I wrote to the daughters, telling them not to worry about your absence from home. But I am worried about you and your health. I have sleepless nights thinking about the children alone at home. I do not know anything about family affairs, who pays the rent, the telephone account, who cares for the children. You have lost your job, your relatives are passing away, you cannot write exams after paying so much money to do so, and we do not know when we will meet.

The daughters have visited me and they assure me you are well.

7 March 1981

The lives of the Mandelas settled into a routine of letters, visits, police harassment, arrests and court appearances. By the end of the 1960s, and after five years in prison, Nelson had had five visits – one of these from Makgatho who had turned sixteen. Winnie, in that period, had been served with two banning orders, had been detained for almost two years, and had been arrested and brought to trial more often than

301

she had been allowed to visit her husband. Police raids on the Mandela house increased in frequency. In 1976 Winnie was detained again, without trial, for six months, and this was followed by her banishment to Brandfort.

In the beginning she was the victim of the State's vendetta against Nelson, but as she turned each attack to her advantage, she began to be hounded in her own right, and, in the course of time, to be honoured herself.

For Winnie, the banning order was a state strategy for constant harassment. The police kept her under closer observation than other banned persons and became personally vindictive. They wanted her behind bars and became acrimonious when the law courts gave her suspended sentences. The Appellate Court came in for their special rancour. 'This time you are going to prison for a long time. This time your friends in Bloemfontein [Appellate Court] won't help you,' gloated Sergeant van Niekerk, arresting her on the corner of Jeppe and Troye Street for allegedly communicating with another banned person, Peter Magubane, and violating her banning order in May 1972.

# CHAPTER 29

# The Children's Revolt

As the 1970s dawned, the ANC almost disappeared from the articulated consciousness of the country; a new generation of blacks grew into the Black Consciousness and confronted white tyranny with a surly anger. Winnie was drawn towards this movement as the youth surreptitiously visited and consulted her. In 1975–6 she had a brief respite and her banning order was not renewed. She became a founder member of the Federation of Black Women and of the Black Parents Association.

Addressing a meeting in Durban in April 1976, she commented on the discriminatory media reactions to black and white bannings: 'Eight NUSAS [National Union of South African Students] leaders were banned recently and the voice of white protest shook the rafters. It was hardly a week later when eight SASO [South African Students Organization] leaders were banned. There was a muffled outcry which lasted a few days. Such is the white man's hypocrisy.'

Towards the end of that year the country moved into violence from which it has not yet recovered. The Government introduced Afrikaans as the medium of instruction in African secondary schools. African teachers could barely teach the language; African pupils barely understand it. There was genuine fear that they would fail their examinations. The African matriculation pass rate was already abysmally low and they were way behind other population groups in academic and technological skills. The anxiety of pupils, parents and teachers was excruciating. They pleaded to be spared the infliction of Afrikaans which would further block African advancement but their pleas fell on deaf ears.

Mthetheleli Zephania Mncube, presently on death row awaiting the results of an appeal against his sentence (1989), was
fifteen years old at the time. He describes his ordeal.

Mistress Tabele began to teach us in Afrikaans – all the subjects,
social study, history. She was apologetic. She couldn't teach, we
couldn't learn. Previously we were instructed in English or Zulu.
Mistress Tabele was a little bit better than other teachers, but she
was not good. We were getting worried about our exams. The
teachers mixed English with Afrikaans. We wrote tests and failed.
The language was too heavy for us. This went on for five months.
We felt that we had to do something, but we didn't know what.
Then in June during lunch two students called us to assembly and
we decided we would boycott school until Afrikaans was removed.

The pupils called a rally on 16 June 1976; the Black
Parents Association supported them. The State lost its nerve
and police fired on the children. The world was shocked the
next morning to see the picture of a young boy carrying the
dead child, Hector Pieterson.

Youth consciousness was aroused throughout the country.
Overnight the children became the defenders of their people
against the Government. Where previously they had gathered
in the streets for play and mischief and petty-crime, they now
mobilized to take on the police and the State. They coordinated the student councils of the numerous high schools into
the Soweto Students Representative Council. The official administration of Soweto fell into disarray, and the SSRC
took effective control. The police retaliated and focused on
the youth, thousands of whom fled the country to join
Umkhonto.

The political vacuum created by the banning of the ANC
and the PAC was filled in the 1970s by Black Consciousness.
The ideology developed among black students and was a
direct result of Bantu Education and the isolation of blacks
on ethnic campuses. The Soweto rebellion was a manifestation of that consciousness. Strongly influenced by the protago-
nists of black power in the United States, and by the writings
of Frantz Fanon and Albert Memmi in Africa, South African

Black Consciousness focused on the psychological liberation of the disenfranchised, self-realization, self-worth, self-dependence and self-power. Their objective was to forge a united black force that would overpower white domination. To the extent that it focused on black (African, Coloured and Indian) unity, it was critical of the ANC which had worked closely with white radicals. It was also critical of the PAC for excluding bodies of the disenfranchised on racial grounds and for their behind-the-scenes dependence on white organizational and monetary support. While Black Consciousness saw race as the foundation of conflict in South Africa, it later modified this view and admitted the concurrence of race and class.

The mid 1970s saw a number of Black Consciousness formations: students, pupils, workers, teachers, women's and professional. Black theology revolutionized the Christian approach to liberation. The church, formerly reluctant to support Christian justice and stand by men like Michael Scott, Bishop Reeves and Beyers Naude, began taking radicalized positions in the seventies, and by the mid-eighties became a strong bastion against apartheid. Many former members of the Black Consciousness movement joined the ANC. South African Police intelligence estimated 4,000 in military training outside South Africa in 1978; other observers put the figure as high as 8,000, of whom 75 per cent were reported to be with the ANC.

The year 1976 clearly paved the way for a sharpening of the military confrontation between apartheid and its 'opposition'. Reported incidents of terrorism rose from 55 after 1974 to 210 between 1976 and 1983. Simultaneously, there was an escalation of political trials conducted in the country. Targets showed less regard for the official ANC ruling to avoid injury to civilians. The ANC also extended and intensified its political missions internationally. The campaign for sanctions was as important, if not more so, than the military campaign and it was joined by anti-apartheid organizations in the country and throughout the world.

Nelson came face to face with the Black Consciousness

leadership when the SASO trialists joined the Robben Islanders in 1976. Nelson found it ironical that Bantu Education intended to make the youth servile, had produced the angriest blacks in the history of the liberation struggle. Their pride in being black was reminiscent of his own pride in Africa in early Youth League days. They turned the prison upside down; they refused to conform to discipline; they pitched their fury at the wardens. But they turned to the Rivonia men with respect. These shared the benefits of their experiences, and gave them wise counsel on the strategies of survival in prison. They reached a consensus with them. Nelson grew fond of Ben Koape, Strini Moodley, Saths Cooper and Muntu Myeza.

Winnie was rebanned and then detained with almost the entire executive of the Black Women's Federation during the Soweto uprisings of 1976. This was followed by a swoop on practically all Black Consciousness organizations which were subsequently banned. The Black Women's Federation was one of the casualties.

The Government, however, was not content with simply banning Winnie. They also banished her from Soweto where her sphere of influence had been growing. Surveys conducted in 1977, 1978 and 1979 identified her as the second most important black political activist after Buthelezi. In 1980, when she had been banished for three years, her popularity in Soweto and the East Rand dropped to third position and Bishop Tutu emerged as the most popular black activist. Buthelezi had by then dropped to fourth position.

On the morning of 16 May 1977, Winnie was surprised by four carloads of police who invaded her home. They were instructed by the Minister of Justice, Mr Jimmy Kruger, to remove all her belongings and transport her to Brandfort. It was the self-same man who had wagged his finger at her at the airport and warned her about her behaviour. He obviously liked her even less in 1977 than he had in 1976. Now dead, Kruger is remembered for his statement in response to the murder of Steve Biko in prison 'Dit laat my koud' (It leaves me cold). Winnie had not heard of Brandfort and had no idea where it was. Zindzi insisted on accompanying her mother and was allowed to do so.

Even now, the police announced that they were investigating a charge against Mrs Mandela for contravening her banning order.

All the household furniture was loaded onto a truck and they set off for Brandfort, fifty kilometres from Bloemfontein. Winnie was being banished to the racist Orange Free State province. They reached the village after four hours, tense and in need of a wash. They were taken to the laundry of the local hotel, a dilapidated annexe, as Zindzi described it. It was their first taste of discrimination. The hotel was out of bounds to 'non-whites'. Later Zindzi would say: 'They don't even serve blacks on the counter; there are special serving hatches for them where they queue.'

They arrived at their new home in the African township of Phathakahle. House number 802 stood bleakly, semi-detached with the neighbour a policeman for good measure. They unlocked the door and the sight that met them shocked even the police. It was worse than anything Winnie had experienced in a prison cell. There was no flooring; a great mound of hardened soil stood in the centre. The only door to the house was too narrow to allow most of the furniture to be moved in. Mother and daughter sat outside on some boxes, too exhausted and resentful to take any initiative. The police got labourers to dig out the earth, moved in what furniture they could and took away the rest, including Winnie's stove, for storage at the police station. Winnie was then taken to the local magistrate, who informed her that she would receive R100 a month for maintenance and rental on the house. She had been deprived of her well-paid job at Frank and Hirsch, and the temerity of this pittance galled her.

The first night was spent in despair but mother and daughter roused themselves in the morning, determined to face the challenge. They went to purchase provisions and did not queue at a hatch but walked right in to the shop. News had got around about the identity of the new residents and newspaper men suddenly came flooding in and police gathered. The attendants had the feeling that some celebrities, albeit 'native', had entered their dorp, and did not think it suitable to apply their whites-only rule; they served Mrs and Miss Mandela politely.

The mayor said he had not been given prior notice of the new resident, but she was welcome. The deputy mayor observed that Mrs Mandela had put their one-street town on the international map. The ex-state President who had retired to his farm a few kilometres from the town grumbled at Jimmy Kruger. He could have chosen a place further afield for Mrs Mandela. He winced at the thought that he might knock into her at the local post office when he went to collect his post.

Winnie settled into Brandfort. For all her initial resistance and despite the fact that police observation was even more suffocating than it had been in Soweto, she came to love it. The security had no other 'client' and devoted all their attention to her. At times they even performed small errands. Zindzi's friend, Oupa Seakamela, moved in with them and was clever with his hands, improving and adding to the house. But there was no running water, or bathroom. They washed in the bedroom, moving in a tin bath of water, and used a bucket toilet in the small garden. Gradually, a paraffin fridge, a battery TV and a coal cooker provided some 'luxury'.

While the white community had not been forewarned to keep its distance from Mrs Mandela – the authorities assumed that it did not need to be – the black community was cautioned against associating with her. Albertina Dyasi learnt the hard way. It was a neighbourly, across-the-fence, over-the-doorway encounter. Winnie was passing by and stopped to ask Albertina where she could buy coal nuts. As she began directing her, Boeta came by and stopped to show off the chicken he had bought cheaply. He inquired about the photograph that the newspaper people had taken of Winnie. He was in it and he wanted to know when it would appear in the papers. Sergeant Prinsloo was watching them talking: three was a gathering and Mrs Mandela was violating her banning order. He questioned Mrs Dyasi as to what they had been talking about. She was petrified and confused. Was it wrong to speak to Mrs Mandela? If the police said so, she had better listen to them.

But gradually Winnie's neighbours turned to her, police or no police, because they discovered that she was a good woman who cared for them. They were a very impoverished, exploited and demoralized community. Winnie put some self-respect into their lives and gathered together resources. She was soon running a mini-welfare agency and clinic from her home, and providing temporary shelter for the homeless in the garage she built. She took in an abandoned child and an old man she found lying outside her door.

The initial period was hard for Winnie but more so for Nelson who could only contemplate the injustice of this latest assault on his family. He could no longer visualize their movements and had to re-orientate himself to their new physical space. He had been able to picture Winnie in every part of their Orlando home. Gradually he structured her new surroundings: the house comprised a kitchen and two small rooms. There were 725 similar houses in the township, which had a total population of 5,000. The fact that the people spoke Sotho and Afrikaans, both foreign languages as far as his family was concerned, disturbed him, but Winnie informed him that she was making friends, not only with the local blacks but also with the Afrikaaners. The De Waals and Hattinghs became firm friends. Piet de Waal was also her lawyer and Dr Hattingh offered her a job. It seemed that his friendship with her might have cost him his life for on the very day she was due to start employment, he was mysteriously killed in a car accident.

Nelson relaxed somewhat when Winnie and Zindzi wrote to say that they were adjusting and even beginning to enjoy Brandfort. He marvelled at Winnie's capacity to inject meaning into practically everything she did. Winnie, Zindzi and Oupa got down to their studies. There was expectation that Zindzi and Oupa would marry and they had a daughter.

Zeni's children also came to live with Winnie, and the cottage bubbled with their laughter.

The police charged Winnie for contravening her banning order when Zindzi's friends visited her. The magistrate found her guilty and gave a six-month suspended sentence, saying, 'The accused should not be allowed to get around the order by saying every time a magistrate refuses permission, the visitors were Zindzi's.' This was contrary to a previous judgement when the magistrate had said that if there was a second person in the house it could not be assumed that the accused had received visitors.

Friends travelled great distances to visit Winnie; among the earliest were Helen Suzman and Helen Joseph from Johannesburg. But such visits were charged with risk. Helen Joseph, Jackie Bosman, Ilona Kleinschmidt and Barbara Waite all served prison sentences for refusing to testify against Winnie when she was charged for having visitors.

Zindzi, however, found Brandfort unbearable after a while. Her relations with Oupa cooled, she became depressed and returned to Johannesburg. Her parents worried about her living alone in Orlando. Finally, some local white MP's began agitating for Winnie's removal from Brandfort, and towards the end of 1983, life was becoming difficult there.

Matters came to a head on 5 August 1985, when the unrest in other provinces erupted in the Orange Free State as well. Brandfort's white community, accustomed to respect from its black folk, was shocked when the school pupils of Phatha-kahle demonstrated on the roads. The police baton-charged. On 6 August, Winnie left for Johannesburg for a medical check-up. Her sister and Zindzi's son, Gaddafi, remained at home. There was another demonstration by the school children. The police were fiercer than on the day before, and children ran into the Mandela house. In the ensuing mêlée, Gaddafi disappeared.

I was in Ayob's [Ismail Ayob, Nelson's lawyer] office when he told me of the news from home. I went cold. He drove me immediately to Brandfort. The sight that met our eyes was unbelievable. The house I had left in good order only hours before, stood in ruins. There was no door and the wind was blowing through the house with its debris of blasting and broken furniture. They had bombed the house but had used strange explosives that had melted away the sink in the clinic. There was blood on the wall and ominously the gift of a Kennedy bust, presented by American admirers, was draped in a blood-sodden cloth.

Mercifully, my neighbour, the policeman's wife, brought me Gaddafi safe and sound. He had run into her house when the police had started their beatings and she had kept him safely.

I had nowhere to sleep in Brandfort. I was by law prevented from being in my house in Orlando. I moved into a hotel in Johannesburg while the authorities wrangled over whether it was legal for me to be there or not. After three months of living in the hotel, I decided I would just go home to Orlando. That is how I am staying here now in my own house.

The police tried to get me to return. They said they had repaired my Brandfort house, but I decided not to return to Brandfort.

The townships were then in a state of open revolution. In the midst of this black fury, Winnie moved back to Soweto against legal advice. She felt that with the international focus on her, the Government could not afford to aggravate the situation further. Winnie began addressing public meetings after years of silence, forces grew around her; the security police resumed their watch but at a distance. Winnie set up the Mandela Family Office as an advice bureau, and troubled youth, fleeing police persecution and in need of refuge or funding for schooling, flocked to her. She set up a temporary home for some of them in her small backyard.

Police presence intensified in the townships. Black town-boards became the immediate targets of black anger. They engaged professional guards, vigilantes who unleashed their violence on families, invading their privacy and abducting youth. The military and police gave their tacit approval and at times abetted them. In Langa in the Eastern Cape and in Mamelodi, near Pretoria, the police opened fire and scores lay dead. Winnie addressed the mass funeral of forty killed at Mamelodi, and came face to face with infuriated youths who now resorted to their own bizarre violence, 'necklacing' suspected collaborators in burning tyres.

Many factors were responsible for that violence; at base was the deteriorating economic condition of the black people. International banking concerns were calling in their loans; the Government put the squeeze on millions of black tenants and raised rentals to cope with public expenditure. This widened the resistance base. While black masses remained ignorant of the full extent to which they were exploited to keep the Bothas and van der Merwes in power, with the army and police active against them, they understood what went on in their own townships and their anger focused on the black agents, the township councillors, responsible for collecting rentals and other service dues. Apartheid strategy had regionalized and localized black administration, placing immediate responsibility on the black agents. Violence, supported by the United Democratic Front, was internalized in the townships and concentrated on government-sponsored community and regional councils, homeland authorities and residents.

Nelson had warned the court during his trial in 1964 that the country was drifting towards civil war. In the mid 1980s that was realized. The townships flared up as the price of basic commodities rose and wages remained comparatively low. The cost of every service provided by the Government escalated as it struggled to uphold apartheid and keep itself solvent at the expense of the disenfranchised.

# CHAPTER 30

# The World Honours
# Mandela

As the intensity and magnitude of state repression increased, so the pressure against apartheid grew. The one name that resounded above all others was that of Mandela. He was not the only political prisoner serving a life sentence, nor could it be said that his sacrifice towered over all others. Steve Biko had been tortured to death. Mortally ill, he was left naked and in chains in his cell; the doctor called in to attend to him colluded with the police that he was shamming. He was then moved from Port Elizabeth to Pretoria, over a thousand miles, and the ordeal killed him. Neil Aggett, according to the evidence of fellow prisoners, was interrogated continuously for six days. He was seen hours before his death bloodied and staggering by a fellow prisoner. There were scores like them but Mandela came to represent them and to be celebrated internationally as the human symbol of freedom and human resistance against tyranny.

India led the way in 1979 and honoured him with the country's highest civic award, the Nehru prize. Students of the University of London nominated him for the Chancellorship against Princess Anne in 1980. In 1981 a United States Congressional delegation, led by Harold Wolpe, requested to see Mandela, but were refused. In France envoys from six organizations, including the Mitterrand Socialist Party, delivered a petition bearing 17,000 signatures to the South African embassy, calling for his release. By 1983 awards and honours poured in from universities and colleges, peace and human rights foundations in Europe and the

United States. Glasgow made him a freeman of the city; the Students Union of London University made him a life member. Parks and streets began to be renamed after him: First Avenue in north-east London became Nelson Mandela Avenue; Selous Street in Camden became Mandela Street; a park in the port of Hull became Mandela Park, and the committee room of the Amalgamated Union of Engineering Workers (AUEW) became the Mandela Room.

And Winnie did not just share the honours with Nelson. She began to be honoured in her own right. The people of Grenada invited her to their first independence anniversary celebrations; Rome invited her to a conference, Haverford University awarded her an honorary doctorate; the AUEW sent her £1,000 to pay airfares to visit Nelson.

International pressure for reform and for the release of Mandela coincided and sharpened towards the mid-1980s. The world now clamored for the return of Mandela to his people. But it became clear that it was no longer a matter of releasing a prisoner to his family and to private life, it was the return of a national leader to lead the country to a new society. The Nationalist Government was under severe pressure to change and negotiate a new society. The Commonwealth Conference, despite Mrs Thatcher's predilection for the Nationalists, put together an impressive team, the Eminent Persons Group (EPG) to help effect a peaceful transition to a new South African society. They flew into South Africa, consulted with radical groups and gave fair hearing to everyone with whom they talked. When they met Nelson in prison they had the feeling that he raised their stature and came away inspired and refreshed.

The EPG raised black hopes and it seemed that the Government was ready to release Mandela and talk out a new constitution. Preparations began to be made for his reception but on the very morning of the most crucial meeting with the South African Government, Pretoria chose to launch attacks on three neighbouring Commonwealth capitals: Harare, Lusaka and Gaborone. The message was clear. Pretoria had no wish to respond formally to the EPG's proposal and was closing the operation down. On 16 June, even as the EPG were announcing their conclusions to the world press, Pretoria re-imposed a state of emergency.

In January 1985 the Rivonia men were offered their release by the Nationalist State President, P. W. Botha. It was a typical, awkwardly worded statement. They discussed it and rejected it. Then Nelson got down to responding to it. It was heavy going. He put away the document and returned to it again. At last it was done, but the problem of communicating it to the people took more time. This was not just a letter for Mr Botha. It was a letter for the people. He was determined that it would be made public and Zindzi read it out with aplomb at the Jabulani Stadium in Soweto on 10 February 1985, where over 10,000 had gathered for a UDF rally.

She read:

I am a member of the African National Congress. I have always been a member of the African National Congress and I will remain a member of the African National Congress until the day I die. Oliver Tambo is much more than a brother to me. He is my greatest friend and comrade for nearly fifty years. If there is any one amongst you who cherishes my freedom, Oliver Tambo cherishes it more and I know that he would give his life to see me free. There is no difference between his views and mine.

I am surprised at the conditions that the Government wants to impose on me. I am not a violent man. My colleagues and I wrote in 1952 to Malan asking for a round-table conference to find a solution to the problems of our country but that was ignored.

When Strijdom was in power, we made the same offer. Again it was ignored. When Verwoerd was in power we asked for a national convention for all the people in South Africa to decide on their future. This, too, was in vain.

It was only then when all other forms of resistance were no longer open to us that we turned to armed struggle.

Let Botha show that he is different to Malan, Strijdom and Verwoerd.

Let him renounce violence.

Let him say that he will dismantle apartheid.

Let him unban the people's organization, the African National Congress.

Let him free all who have been imprisoned, banished or exiled for their opposition to apartheid.

Let him guarantee free political activity so that the people may decide who will govern them.

I cherish my own freedom dearly but I care even more for your freedom. Too many have died since I went to prison. Too many have suffered for the love of freedom. I owe it to their widows, to their orphans, to their mothers and to their fathers who have grieved and wept for them. Not only I have suffered during these long, lonely, wasted years.

I am not less life-loving than you are. But I cannot sell my birthright, nor am I prepared to sell the birthright of the people to be free. I am in prison as the representative of the people and of your organization, the African National Congress, which was banned. What freedom am I being offered while the organization of the people remains banned? What freedom am I being offered when I may be arrested on a pass offence? What freedom am I being offered to live my life as a family with my dear wife who remains in banishment in Brandfort? What freedom am I being offered when I must ask for permission to live in an urban area? What freedom am I being offered when I need a stamp in my pass to seek work? What freedom am I being offered when my very South African citizenship is not respected? Only free men can negotiate. Prisoners cannot enter into contracts. Herman Toivo Ja Toivo, when freed, never gave any undertaking, nor was he called upon to do so.

I cannot and will not give any undertaking at a time when I and you, the people, are not free. Your freedom and mine cannot be separated. I will return.

Mandela had spoken to his people and made his promise. Three years later, with violence escalating and practically no indication that the Government had any serious intention of abandoning domination, Nelson celebrated his seventieth birthday and the world celebrated with him, making it an occasion where all those supporting human dignity, justice and peace stood up to be counted.

Pope John Paul expressed his admiration for Mandela and the West German Chancellor, Helmut Kohl, challenged the South African Government: 'Show your readiness to speak to Nelson Mandela and the other previously outlawed political forces in your country. Only then can the national dialogue you have repeatedly called for become a reality.' The Polish Communist leader, Wojcieh Jaruzelski, commended Mandela's heroic struggle; the French president, Francois Mitterand, praised Mandela for devoting his life to the ideals of justice, dignity and liberty; the Scandinavian countries hoped that soon he would be able to celebrate his birthdays 'in freedom in a South Africa liberated from all the bonds of apartheid'; the European Community's foreign ministers called for the unconditional and immediate release of Mandela and other political prisoners. The World Council of Churches warned that Mandela's continued imprisonment was proof 'of the policy of repression of the South African Government and its intransigence in dealing with the just demands of the black people'. Mike Tyson, the world heavyweight boxing champion, sent Mandela his world-title-winning boxing gloves. *New Nation*, 27 July 1988, reported that from Holland came 170,000 letters and birthday cards. London held a big birthday concert and paved the way for concerts all over the world. A young enthusiast, thrilled by the incredible concentration of the world's most famous musicians, asked, 'And when will Mandela sing . . .?'

Indeed when?

# CHAPTER 31

# Murmurs of Change

Soon after the celebration of his seventieth birthday, Nelson fell ill. The years of imprisonment took its toll on his body. One late August evening Winnie was disturbed in her Orlando house by a phone call from Pollsmoor prison. The Officer Commanding told her not to be too worried but that they had removed her husband two hours earlier to the Tygerberg Hospital. It was then 11 p.m. The Officer told Winnie that her husband had stopped eating after her last visit, when she had told him about the burning down of their house and the total loss of all family records. According to the Officer, he had noticed that Nelson's speech had become slurred a few days earlier, but on the morning of his removal to hospital the prison doctor had given him a clean bill of health. He told Winnie that she could visit him the next day. The following morning she and Zindzi, accompanied by Ismail Ayob, flew into Cape Town.

They found Nelson in good medical care, but his appearance was shocking:

He was unable to recognize us at first. They had removed two litres of fluid from his left lung and he was heavily sedated. He mumbled and was in obvious pain. I regret to this day that I took Zindzi with me, for even now she shudders and breaks into tears, when she recalls her father's condition at that time. He had been reduced to a shadow of his former physical self. His weight had dropped to 68 kilograms; his face had suddenly wrinkled and looked old. Yet even in that state, when he became aware of our presence, he told us not to worry, that he would be well and up and about soon.

Professor De Kock, his doctor, reported that he had all

the symptoms of an acute attack of tuberculosis, but that they had arrested it in the early stages. There was no lesions or spots on the lung and it was not infectious.

Winnie later commented: 'On our second visit, a week later, we were relieved to see the improvement in his condition. Tygerberg is one of the best medical centres in the country and it was clear that he was receiving the best of attention.'

By October Nelson was considerably improved. He told Winnie that he had regained his lost weight, resumed his morning press ups and felt as strong as an ox. Winnie found that his face had filled and the wrinkles disappeared. His expression was lively and his complexion normal.

Weeks and months went by; the Government announced that Mandela would not be returned to Pollsmoor. There were predictions that he would be freed and the press focused on Winnie's views in the matter. She said that she had no idea as to what was going on in the mind of the Government; 'The South African Government has serious problems. It has to create the correct climate for Mandela's release and that climate does not exist. There would be no point in releasing Mandela to the South Africa of today. He would simply be returned to prison the next day, if he was not shot dead before that.'

His release, she said in an interview published in *South*, 17 November 1988, was equated with liberation. 'He has to return to a situation where he can negotiate the transfer of power from the minority to the majority. To millions of oppressed blacks in this country and to the millions of oppressed people of all colours Mandela's name is equated with the freedom we sacrificed our lives for, for the liberation of our country.'

At the end of the year expectations for Mandela's release reached an all-time high. The country was abuzz with the news that Mandela and all the Rivonia prisoners had in fact been released, or were about to be released. In Port Elizabeth, Govan Mbeki was inundated with calls as if, despite his banning and separation from his colleagues, some sort of telepathy kept him minutely informed of their position. In practically every centre, community organizations summoned urgent meetings to prepare for the great reception, important personalities and media personnel flew into Cape Town and crowds began to gather outside Pollsmoor prison. When, after much waiting, nothing happened, thousands congregated on the campus of the University of the Western Cape where they heard that the Government was not about to release Mandela or any of the life-time prisoners.

In December the State announced that Mr Mandela had been removed to a house at the Victor Verster prison about fifty kilometres from Cape Town, and that his family would be allowed to live with him there. The media published photographs of the police cottage and focused, in particular, on its swimming pool.

Nelson, as could be expected, declined the 'privilege' of sharing his imprisonment with his family. For in every respect, save in the quality of his confinement, the conditions of his incarceration remained unaltered and, in fact, had worsened for he was now totally isolated from his comrades. Above all, he declined any 'privilege', apart from that forced upon him, denied his comrades in prison.

His family visited him in his new prison. His sister and grandchildren followed. His granddaughter Nandi describes the prison as set in idyllic surroundings but says that little of it is within her grandfather's eyesight.

Once checked through security, a prison kombi takes you to Tatomkhulu's quarters, an isolated three-bedroomed house, about two kilometres from the main prison building. He has never been more alone in his life. On Robben Island and Pollsmoor there was the companionship of other prisoners, now there are only the warders and guards, some of whom live in an adjunct to his prison cottage. He is not allowed to step out of the gate of his compound, and every parcel or document he is allowed to receive is closely censored. The house is comfortable but his loneliness is terrible. Tatomkhulu doesn't complain, but we can feel it.

In February 1989 this loneliness was compounded by the

intense pain he suffered as Winnie's name was implicated in a scandal of abduction and murder. The insinuations were not spearheaded by the State but by the English language press and supported by a statement from the ranks of two highly respected anti-system organizations, COSATU and UDF. This strengthened the hand of the State and the Mandela family was once again the target of police raids and harassment. Nelson did not only read reports, he saw on his television the police invade the house, filmed by state-owned television. He saw the police ransack the annexe to the main house and heard the commentator referring to bloodstains as the police went through old clothes and pointed to a wall. He saw his wife, taken unawares in her nightgown, smiling even in adversity; his daughter huddled in the kitchen with her children, shocked and bemused. When Winnie and Zindzi came to see him, they discussed the matter and considered the events.

Ever since her return to Soweto in 1985, Winnie had been involved with youth fleeing township violence and seeking refuge. She had taken responsibility for sixteen boys, housing them in an annexe, providing them with board and lodging, and seeing to their schooling. They were eventually organized into the Mandela Football Club and as such began accompanying her to meetings, where they served as a guard of honour and choral group, leading in the singing and 'toyi-toying' (dancing in the semi-military fashion characteristic of African youth at rallies).

Winnie explains that the police saw the soccer team as an Umkhonto cell and began attacking it, so that within a year the original team was disbanded, the last of the boys breaking out of jail in December 1987 and fleeing to Angola. But Winnie had gained a reputation for helping youth and new groups replaced the original one, living with her and accompanying her on public occasions in the soccer team track-suits.

Winnie accepted the boys at face value. It is highly likely that they were infiltrated by elements over which she had no control, that among them were informers and police spies.

321

Some became involved in altercations with other youths; there were attacks and counter-attacks. Winnie's boys began to be seen by some as one more 'gang' in an environment infested with them.

Matters came to a head when the Orlando house was burnt down in mid-1988, allegedly following a feud between the said boys and another gang. The Mandelas declined to lay charges against the arsonists, but Nelson impressed on Winnie the inadvisability of continuing to maintain the boys and she began to find placements for them elsewhere. Towards the end of 1988 she had eight boys living with her.

In November, Winnie found herself at the centre of a new crisis. A woman political activist, Xoliswa Falati, who had become involved with the local Methodist Boys' Home, brought her a young teenager whom she had alleged had been sexually asaulted by the official in charge of the Home. Winnie took the boy to be examined by Dr Abubaker Asvat, a prominent AZAPO member, who confirmed the assault and advised psychiatric treatment. Xoliswa also took the boy to the police and laid a charge against the official. She then, with the help of Winnie's former football coach, a man in his forties, removed four other boys from the Home, who she claimed had become abusers themselves. These boys were accommodated in an out-house several metres away from Winnie's house where they were questioned and reprimanded. There are allegations that they were also assaulted. Four of the boys ran away, one of whom, Stompie Moeketsi Sepei, was never seen again. A body was found and identified as his, though many close to Stompie doubted it was his body. This was followed by a number of arrests of boys who at some stage or other had lived with Winnie and of Xoliswe, her daughter and Jerry Richardson, the football coach.

Nelson considered the facts, consulted his lawyers and, weighing up the forces aligned against Winnie, advised her to be patient and to give no interviews to the press. Those who visited him at this time saw his distress, his capacity to assess the situation objectively and his unswerving love for his wife.

To a friend he wrote on 28 February 1989:

Errors of judgement repeatedly committed by those who are in the centre of controversy are in themselves enough to fuel dangerous levels of anger. I will not at all be surprised if, right now, you are suffocating from frustration and despair. But your sister [Winnie] is a wonderful girl; like you. I would accordingly urge patience and that you be as supportive as you have always been.

Opposition to Winnie had by no means been as widespread or as uncontroversial as the media made it out to be. Some top-ranking personalities of the organizations that had distanced themselves from her expressed their personal support and Winnie lists among these the Reverend Alan Boesak, the founder of the UDF; Cyril Ramaphosa and Sydney Mufamadi, Secretary and Assistant Secretary respectively of COSATU, and Frank Chikane of the South African Council of Churches. There was also considerable rank and file support and this was expressed, in part, in letters in the black press. AZAPO issued a thirteen-page analysis of the situation and condemned the UDF statement, as did Chief Buthelezi.

By the end of February 1989 the media focus on Winnie began to wane. By March the prospects of an early Mandela release were once again making headlines following Prime Minister Margaret Thatcher's talks with the South African Foreign Minister, Pik Botha, her visit to several African states and developments in Namibia.

Kathrada wrote to a friend:

I got the message that you and Joel were among the folks who waited till late outside Pollsmoor to welcome us. I believe you had gone to the trouble of cooking a special meal for the occasion. The loyalty, devotion and friendship which you and others like you have shown towards us has been truly astounding. It is painful to think of the inconvenience, the enormous preparation, the expectation – and the invariable discomfort which you people have been experiencing; while we, who are the cause of the excitement, continue with twenty-five years routine in splendid relaxation – by and large unaffected by all the rumours and speculation. It would be interesting to trace the source of these stories, which have been cropping up with monotonous regularity. One cannot easily discuss reports that they originate in official quarters, but the role of sensation-hungry journalists is quite apparent. And one must also not forget the not inconsiderable contribution of some well-meaning member of your profession!

I personally don't expect any dramatic developments in the near future. But if the powers-that-be have anything in mind, you can rest assured that, in keeping with their style of doing things, they'll simply pounce on us and give us the shortest possible time to pack. And within hours, we'll find ourselves far away from Pollsmoor. You know when Uncle Nelson and them were transferred to Pollsmoor in 1982, they were suddenly confronted and told to get ready in half an hour! The next thing they were in the boat, having said goodbye to Robben Island, their home for eighteen years.

## EPILOGUE

In July a government communique suddenly informed the world that Mr Mandela had made 'a courtesy call' on State President Botha at the Tuynhuis and that the 'two leaders' had talked for forty-five minutes. The country was agog with expectation. Change was in the air. The impossible suddenly appeared possible. Gone was the fear that the Government might one day just release Mr Mandela from prison, ban him to Soweto and get on with its racism. The Government had openly referred to him as a 'leader'. What appeared to have happened at Tuynhuis was a *toenadering* (rapprochement) of African and Afrikaner nationalism, of two 'super powers' in the South African context. It was the most significant sign yet that the stronghold of Afrikaner domination was crumbling, that the time had come for the African to moderate the Afrikaner.

Those who had been monitoring the country's economic and political climate, and particularly those who in recent times had met Mandela and then the ANC in Lusaka, were not too surprised by the announcement. Apartheid was in serious trouble; in the final analysis it was the country's deteriorating emotional situation that had sent the State President to Mandela as his only hope. The rand had plummeted to a fraction of its value. South African money could barely pay for overseas expertise and technology, let alone overseas holidays, and the Government had become increasingly dependent on its citizens to keep it in some state of solvency. Sixty per cent of the country's inland revenue was derived from personal and other taxes,* These monies were raised largely from blacks and the share of blacks to the inland revenue could only increase.† How long could the disenfranchised be expected to finance the police and army that daily harassed them?

Influx control had failed to stem the tide of African urbanization; the demographic projection was that there would be 40 million urban South Africans by 2000, 34 million of whom would be Africans.‡ Bantu Education, the Afrikaner dream to contain black advancement, had failed in that the volume of black matriculants had grown a thousandfold since 1971.§ The isolation of the black student was largely responsible for the youth revolution of the 1970s which remained unabated.

Most significantly, black workers had become powerfully organized and were exerting pressure on both the economy and polity. African wages, following concessions to African trade unions, were rising at a higher rate than any other.

Associated with the social and economic dynamics of black life was the changed dynamics of the Afrikaner. Afrikanerdom was no longer the impregnable monolith it had appeared to be in the fifties and sixties. It had become factionalized, stratified and grown its own capitalist class, ramified into the international corporations and vulnerable to their vested interests. At the beginning of the century white workers had brought down the Government of Smuts because it had pursued the interests of capital and opened 'white' jobs to

* *South African Barometer*, Volume 3, No. 5, 24 March 1989. Figures abstracted from the Budget of the Minister of Finance for 1989/1990.
† Jill Natrass, *Indicator*, February 1983. In 1983 40 per cent of total personal income was earned by blacks; in 1973 the figure was 26 per cent.
‡ John Brewer, *After Soweto*, Clarendon Press, 1986, p. 12.
§ John Brewer, op. cit., p. 18. The Unit for Future Research, Stellenbosch University, estimates that by 2000, 80 per cent of the country's matriculants can be expected to be black (Africans contributing 68.2 per cent).

blacks at black pay rates; the new pact government of labour and Afrikaner Nationalists had emphasized, above all, the rights of white labour. Now those who had rebelled against General Smuts and his relations with international foreign capitalists, and subdued the forces of the market to their racist *volk's wil*, had become partners in foreign capitalism themselves.

White labour, which up to the sixties had exerted a determining influence on policy, was practically disappearing from the South African economy. Constituting 8 per cent of the labour force in 1982, it was expected to decline to 7 per cent by 2000. The Afrikaner capitalist and not the Afrikaner worker, is now calling the Nationalist tune. Dependent on black labour, they have removed uneconomic colour bars protecting white labour and have given black labour the right to organize through registered trade unions. Black labour today has political clout. Gone are the days when homeland leaders attracted overseas capital for South Africa by offering potential investors docile, trouble-free labour – the prime South African commodity (black gold they called it). Black labour now knows its power and is using it.

South Africa had never been so isolated. The strategies of the disenfranchised, internal resistance, sanctions and military combat were having effect. It has taken four decades since the accession of Nationalist rule for social, economic and political forces to reach the present potent compound. The Nationalist State President, F. W. de Klerk, dare not pull back from negotiation. If he does it is at the peril of Afrikanerdom for it has reached its nemesis and survival in any form depends on this negotiation. Mandela might be the supreme prisoner of the Nationalists but he holds the lien on Afrikanerdom itself. It is in recognition of this that Mandela's position has been so considerably relaxed.

There are strong indications that members of the Government have been talking to Mandela for several years. The talking proceeds slowly. Towards the end of the year all but one of the Rivonia Trialists were released and the Government conceded the right of the disenfranchised to protest.

There were rallies and marches of dimensions never known in the country before, and talk of dialogue became the vogue. The new Nationalist State President met Mandela and further increased expectations. All concerned parties began stating their positions on the issue – the two Nationalist groupings, African and Afrikaner favouring it, but with understandably different ends in mind; and the extremists to the left of the ANC and the right of the Nationalist Party opposing it. Mandela has made it quite clear that he will not enter into any unilateral negotiations, that he stands with his people, the ANC, the Mass Democratic Movement, and his fellow prisoners. He also emphasizes that his own release is inconsequential. What is crucial is that the Government addresses itself seriously to creating a political climate in which meaningful negotiation can begin.

In the meanwhile he has had statements of support from the disenfranchised of all political shades from radicals to homeland leaders. His own approach is one of reconciliation; he will not stand aloof for the sake of it from any political grouping. He favours the broadest front against apartheid, and concedes the right of all South Africans to participate in that struggle, and to formulate a new race-free society. He is, above all, concerned about strife in his country and wants to help the situation.

And that man, in slacks, a loose jersey and a sun hat made of corrugated cardboard, sits and waits in the Cape sun at Victor Verster. Cabinet Ministers, members too of the Mass Democratic Movement, come and go. Outside the crowds grow restless; they wait for him and though they know that time is on their side, their patience is wearing thin. That is the ominous message with which Afrikanerdom must contend.

On 18 July 1989 Nelson celebrated his seventy-first birthday, and for the first time since his imprisonment he was allowed to see his whole family. His children, grandchildren and great-grandchildren (through Evelyn) came from Cofimvaba in the Transkei; Winnie and Zindzi and her children came from Soweto. Zeni and her family came a month later from the States to see him. His eldest daughter, Maki, who had flown in with her family from Massachusetts, gives the following account of the 'party'.

We were met at the airport in Cape Town by Dulla and Farida Omar, a barrage of reporters and a discreet contingent of police. It was the same as far as the press and media was concerned at breakfast the following morning.

Dulla Omar had arranged three cars to transport us to the prison. The scene at the prison gates was quite chaotic. To the press and police were now added toyi-toying supporters, many of whom pressed greeting cards into our hands for Dada.

We were taken by prison transport from the gate to Dada's house. It took us about five minutes. I was amazed by the house I hadn't expected it to be that good. We entered through the kitchen and were led through the dining room, into the living room. Standing there was this handsome young man, slim, and in good shape. I couldn't believe it. I had to look again: Is this him? I had last seen Dada in Pollsmoor. He had looked old and grey and his skin had grown dark. I had thought then: Dada is ageing! Now he was almost as I had known him as a child. His face was full then; it was lean now, but he was handsome again.

He had on a pair of brown slacks, a blue shirt, a brown jersey and brown hunters. He greeted each one of us in turn, starting with the children, and then going up to the grown-ups, embracing and kissing us. The children were at ease with him, though I think the older ones held him in a little awe. My children had heard of their grandfather's greatness at school in Massachusetts; I had told them that their grandfather had carved out his own image and they should carve out theirs and not expect to live on their grandfather's name.

Dada told Nandi* she was getting fat. Ma Winnie chided him and said that he shouldn't say that to a young lady. He told Makgatho's wife, Zondie, whom he was meeting for the first time, 'My child, you are beautiful. I didn't know you were such a lovely young woman,' and Ma Winnie laughed and said to Makgatho, 'Didn't I tell you that's what he would say?' and we all laughed.

The house was cosy; there was a crackling fire in the TV room; the dining table was full of food: lots of meats and salads and fruits

---

* Second daughter of Nelson's deceased son, Thembi, who is a second-year student at University of Cape Town.

and desserts. Gaddafi and KweKwe* wanted to get right into the desserts. Zindzi and I restrained them. Dada was all for indulging his grandchildren but we were very firm and insisted on the rule 'dessert after the main meal'.

Dada started us with appetizers, tuna and prawns, and he urged the children to eat it because it would make them clever. After dinner Dada and Mamma settled the children in the television room and Dada put on a video, *The Aliens*. The children settled; the grown-ups retired into the living room, where we caught up on family news, exchanged notes about what we had been doing, and talked and joked.

Dada kept dropping in on the children and making happy comments as they watched the video. KweKwe wanted to know if there was a toy-shop nearby; then he demanded hot chocolate. Mamma Winnie said, 'This American child wants hot chocolate. Where are we going to get that from?' But Dada said, 'You will be surprised,' and went to the kitchen and made KweKwe a hot chocolate.

All too soon the happy time ended and at about 5 p.m. we began our 'goodbyes', kissing and embracing Dada. We had never felt as close to him as on that day.

As we returned home, I thought how lovely it would be to have Dada at home, for us to have more family reunions like the one we had, but then, I thought, he would be taken over completely by the public and we would have little private time, and then I thought again, but Dada, being Dada, would always find time for his family.

* Five-year-old grandsons.

PART V

# LETTERS FROM PRISON

———

# Letters

The Robben Island prisoners settled down to the mindless timetable of imprisonment, filling hours with manual labour which mercifully distracted them from dwelling on their plight and aching for the social contact they had lost. At night their bodies slumped in sleep through sheer exhaustion. The work routine repeated itself in the endless rising and setting of the sun, in the waxing and waning of the moon.

The letters and visits, twice a year, and then gradually more (by 1981 two letters and two visits a month) became their lifeline. There was economy in the number of words that could be exchanged, in writing and in speaking. Every word transmitted through the glass panes and written on ruled foolscap was carefully censored. To help the censor each word had to be distinctly written, and spoken by the prisoners. They learnt to write closely and neatly, and they, and the recipients of their communications, learnt the art of double meaning.

Letters did not always reach their destination; visits could not always be taken because of travelling distance and financial problems. In Winnie's case visits were hindered by her banning, her movements controlled by the state, or because she too was imprisoned.

The waiting for letters and visits, the joy of expectations fulfilled, the despondency following disappointment, the letter-counting, letter- and visit-treasuring, are expressed in the following extracts from Nelson's letters to the family.

TO WINNIE:

I have been fairly successful in putting on a mask behind which I have pined for the family, alone, never rushing for the post when it comes until somebody calls out my name. I also never linger after visits although sometimes the urge to do so becomes quite terrible. I am struggling to suppress my emotions as I write this letter.

I have received only one letter since you were detained, that one dated 22 August. I do not know anything about family affairs, such as payment of rent, telephone bills, care of children and their expenses, whether you will get a job when released. As long as I don't hear from you, I will remain worried and dry like a desert.

I recall the Karoo I crossed on several occasions. I saw the desert again in Botswana on my way to and from Africa – endless pits of sand and not a drop of water. I have not had a letter from you. I feel dry like a desert.

Letters from you and the family are like the arrival of summer rains and spring that liven my life and make it enjoyable.

Whenever I write you, I feel that inside physical warmth, that makes me forget all my problems. I become full of love.

26 October 1976

I feel sad that I write letters to you and you never receive them.

26 May 1978

You witch! You've numerous ways of keeping me hitched to you. But this is a new one. I've not heard from you for more than a month now. Your last letter to me being that of 17/8 which came on 30/8. Maybe that you've written as you've done in the past but that we're having the usual bottlenecks which occur in our correspondence the moment you're hardpressed.

1 October 1975

You left me in high hopes when you visited me in January and promised that Zeni would visit me and it would be your turn in March. But then I knew you could not afford the visit since you had just been released from prison. Yet my heart longs for you.

27 March 1977

Last year I collected a harvest of fifteen visits and forty-three letters. Of these, fifteen came from you. There were seven birthday cards and the card from Helen Joseph was in the form of a letter. I had five more visits than in '77 but although the letters were more than in the previous year I have not reached the record number of fifty that I got in '75. These wonderful visits and lovely letters make the atmosphere around me relatively pleasant and the outlook bright.

21 January 1979

During this year you were here six times and I got nine letters from you, each one bringing more love and good wishes. Apart from the several telegrams you sent, I also received from you, birthday and Xmas cards. All these help to iron out the wrinkles of advancing age, make old limbs flexible and the blood to flow smoothly.

27 January 1980

Last year I got fifteen visits which I enjoyed very much. This year I did not think I would have as much as ten since on request from the SAP [South African Police] you did not turn up in February and March and since Zindzi could not come on 5/4 due to illness. With you and Zindzi coming down this month I expect to have a total of fourteen, which is as much as that of last year. I have received no letter for December except four Xmas cards. December is always my worst month in this regard. In 1977 I got only two and in 1978, three, quite a poor harvest in comparison to what I normally get. Nevertheless for the year I received no less than sixty-seven, sixteen from you, all of which have been most enjoyable. I am quite happy and always try to hide my joy. Not all of us are as fortunate. But I'd like you to know that you have spoilt me very much and a spoilt baby is always difficult to control.

3 February 1980

TO ZINDZI:

Your disappointment with my brief letters is quite reasonable because it coincides with my own feelings when I get a stingy note, or nothing at all, from those I much love.

4 September 1977

TO MAKI:

By the way, do you know how many letters I got from you this year? Believe it or not, a whole twelve, as against only thirteen I

335

received during the period 1967–78. That is a fine harvest for 1979 already. I hope you will keep it up.

2 September 1979

I should like to mention that I am surprised that you attach no significance whatsoever to such important things as birthdays and Christmas cards. Not only have you never sent me one, you have never even had the simple courtesy of thanking me for the numerous birthday and Christmas messages I have sent you during the past eight to ten years. Every year I get beautiful greetings from many well-wishers, messages which I value. But I always feel that there is something missing, a message from you and Makgatho. Nevertheless, your letter has made up for all that. It has brought springtime into my heart and I feel really proud of you. Looking forward to seeing you in January. Tons and tons of love and a million kisses. Affectionately, Tata.

31 December 1978

I think of Mum and all the children, of the pride and joy you all give me. Among us is Nobutho, the beautiful Mantu, whose love and loyalty, visits, letters, birthday and Xmas cards are essential parts of the efforts of the family to help me endure many of the challenges of the last two decades.

1 March 1981

# Photographs

To someone cut off from friends and relatives, restricted to seeing only a selected few people and even these not as frequently as in normal social relations, photographs become very important. Nelson requests photographs and comments on them. He marvels at the growth of grandchildren.

They come with their mothers as infants in arms, and as toddlers, and then for fourteen years he cannot see them. He keeps in touch through photographs.

I am also keen to see Zazi [Zeni's daughter] before 16/6 when she turns two. I won't be able to see her after that until she turns sixteen unless she comes to fetch me before then.

15 April 1976

TO ZENI:

I got the three pictures you sent via Mum even though I become terribly homesick when I see you look well and it pleases me very much to see you full of smiles, to know you are with close family friends. Zazi's picture at once reminded me of you shortly after your Mum returned from Baragwanath maternity ward in 1959. You'd be fast asleep even as she bathed, dried, smeared you with olive oil, turned your skin white with Johnson's baby powder and stuffed your little belly with shark oil. It's family photos, letters and family visits that keep on reminding me of the happy days when we were together, that makes life sweet and that fills the heart with hope and expectation. Thanks a million, darling. Zindzi tells me that Zazi visited Waterford without your permission. The students must have had real fun.

30 October 1977

TO WINNIE:

The collection of photos you left behind gave me, as usual, the false but flattering feeling that I was free and surrounded by you, the members of the family and lifelong friends. I have since spent a lot of time admiring the photos and each time I feel really tremendous, like one who is beginning and not completing a term of more than two decades of hard labour. The sight of Zeni and Muzi and of Zinhle [Zeni's son] and sisters particularly delights me. They look like a happy couple and the kids seem to be growing up well. Zeni and Muzi are striking even when they try to do the impossible, that is to look at them, not as parents but purely as impartial observers. I had never imagined that our daughter would become such a fine, quiet, dignified lady as she appears to be. All her pictures and the way she conducts herself during visits confirm this impression. Her and Muzi's attachment to you is a source of comfort and joy and I sincerely hope that their relationship with Lashongiwe [a kinswoman] is just the same. Is it Nomsa [Nelson's niece] who is standing next to you at 8115? I suspect that the young lady in front of you is Zindzi, except that she appears slightly taller than I would expect. I was also able to recognize Mary Benson. She still looks almost as she was when I last saw her in London.

31 March 1983

Had it not been for your visits, wonderful letters and your love, I would have fallen apart many years ago. I pause here and drink some coffee, after which I dust the photos on my bookcase. I start with that of Zeni, which is on the outer side, then Zindzi's and lastly yours, my darling Mum. Doing so always eases the longing for you.

6 May 1979

TO MAKI:

I have not seen you for a long time and I miss you a great deal. I also long to see Nobuhle [Zindzi] and Dumani [Makaziwe's son]. Ndindi [Thembi's daughter] sent me a group photo but without Nobuhle. Where was she when the picture was taken? Both Mandla [Makgatho's son] and Dumani looked handsome, even though Mandla was a bit serious. The ladies Ndindi and Nandi [Thembi's daughter] were stars of course. It was surprising to see just how fast they have grown. Tons and tons of love and a million kisses.

26 November 1978

TO WINNIE:

You look perfectly holy and saved next to Mantu [pet name for Zindzi]. Vainly did I try to make out the book and chapter of the open Bible you were reading. But the expression in your respective faces seems to suggest that you see on the pages not just a collection of sacred words, but God himself.

31 March 1983

Your beautiful photo still stands about two feet above my left shoulder as I write this note. I dust it carefully every morning, for to do so gives me the pleasant feeling that I'm caressing you as in the old days. I even touch your nose with mine to recapture the electric current that used to flush through my blood whenever I did so. Nolitha stands on the table directly opposite me. How can my spirits ever be down when I enjoy the fond attentions of such wonderful ladies?

15 April 1976

Who was this other lady in his life? He teased Winnie but confided in Zindzi.

By the way, has Mum ever told you about Nolitha, the other lady in my cell from the Andaman Islands. She keeps you, Zeni, Ndindi and Nandi, Mandla, Maki and Mum company. It's one matter over which Mum's comments are surprisingly economic. She regards the pigmy beauty as some sort of rival and hardly suspects that I took her picture out of the *National Geographic*. I heartily laugh when I read Mum's letters, and suppress my laughter when I talk to her face to face and notice her own struggle to hide her anger. I may have to send the picture to Zeni on my return, because I know quite well that our old tannie will be waiting at the gate with chopper and block.

20 October 1976

# Problems

The people sent a hero to prison, but generally ignored the fact that he had responsibilities and dependants. Nelson, in the loneliness of his cell, worried about the survival of his family. He had left behind a mother, a wife and five children. But his sense of responsibility did not stop with them; it extended to his sisters and to their children and to the children of kinsmen who had supported him.

There was no doubt that the State, through its police, sought to ruin the Mandelas as a family by destroying the Mandela financial base, however humble. Winnie had lost her job as a social worker and then her clerical job at a tutorial college because it was held that in terms of her banning order she could not be on the premises of an educational institution. Winnie's salary was important to the family as it was their only livelihood. She took on jobs as salesgirl and clerk, earning half the amount she would have as social worker. Then, when she found a good job as a credit controller, she was imprisoned. In the circumstances the goodwill of others became crucial, but it was in short supply in the 1960s and 1970s. It was only in the 1980s that the Mandela name became an international legend and began to carry a 'goodwill' in itself.

Mandela's imprisonment in 1962 made the local headlines, but not the international. As the 1960s closed so the memory of Mandela dimmed, leaving Winnie very much to her own resources. Without the help of close friends, and admirers from home and abroad, the family's plight would have been worse. It is only in recent years, with international awards, film rights and book royalties that the Mandelas have become solvent. Both in good years and lean, Nelson ultimately turned to Winnie to find the necessary funding and she has proved remarkably resourceful at all times.

The R200 Mum sent me in April is finished. Things are expensive and I also went on a spree buying essential literature which ate deeply into my funds. Neither you nor Mum work. If you think it is wise please ask Benjie [Benjamin Pogrund, political journalist of the *Rand Daily Mail*] to send me at least R250.

9 September 1979

These expensive air trips must have sucked the family dry. I had hoped things would improve a bit from the end of this month when Mum gets her first pay packet after living on the dole for so long.

15 April 1976

This is a special letter Ngutyana [Winnie's clan name], which I would like you to treat as a matter of urgency. Can you telegram me by return post R300 for my personal requirements. Not only are my funds exhausted, but I have also overdrawn the account. As it is I have not even got the cash to make my Christmas orders. Will you be able to raise it? I was also anxious to register for law as early as possible and I hope you are experiencing no difficulties in the matter.

1 December 1980

I note that you recently had an interview with Sigma Motors. I do not possess sufficient facts to be able to give you good advice on the question. I am still as uncertain of your financial position as I was on 15/5/77 when you were deported to that isolated country village. But I consider it dangerous and unwise to move to any new place these hectic days, other than back to Johannesburg.

1 June 1980

Nelson's main worry in prison has always appeared to be the education of his children and the children of those he accepts as having a claim on him. At times the claimants' demands irritate him, but at all times he feels responsible; his irritation flowing out of helplessness rather than the fact of the demands. He complained to Winnie:

The children do not appreciate that in my current position I am

341

powerless to help them. Xoliswa [a niece] has written again to say that she left the University of the Transkei because of the inferior tutelage there. She now works in the Department of Justice, and her ambition is to be a professor in Political Science. She would like me to arrange for her to study abroad. Chrissie [a niece] wrote to make a similar request. She is now twenty-five and she would like to settle down with her man, George, in Europe or America. She sent me two photos. Next week I will write to Mr Fletcher [Leabie's contact] to find out how Leabie [a sister] is doing. She would like me to arrange for the education of Phathiswa, the daughter of Leabie. For this purpose I should like to write to Alan Paton to arrange for a scholarship for her, but am no longer certain of his address. In view of the assistance he gave to Rennie [Makgatho's first wife, now divorced] it would be better to entrust him with this additional task as well, so as to avoid the impression that many people and agencies unknown to one another are being used.

27 May 1979

Yesterday I also received a letter from Nandi [grandaughter] writing from Inyanga High School, Engcobo. She explains that her application for admission to St Philomena was refused. According to her she will go to the Inanda Seminary next year and she expects me to pay her school fees. She reminds me of my promise to pay but adds, 'But you aren't paying none. I am paying my school fees with my fixed deposit.' Her birthday card which I sent to St Johns was returned. By the way she adds, 'At the present moment I am stranded about pocket money. Please ask Grandmother living at Brandfort to send me pocket money.' The load I keep piling on your shoulders is colossal and I am amazed you have not developed a hunchback. It is to me quite understandable if my darling now and again betrays a flashy temper like a Penelope whose chastity has been questioned.

15 April 1977

But if he apologized to Winnie for such impositions he also sounded a note of reprimand if she questioned the requests:

You don't need anybody's consent, no matter how close or helpful, to arrange for Xoliswa's overseas bursary. She is as much our child as any other. Her father's kindness to us is a debt we are bound to repay.

25 May 1979

342

I would also like you to give attention to the position of Dan [a nephew]. He has unusual literary potential, especially in poetry and his skill would even be more developed with a university background. Bear in mind that those boys love you and it is your duty to give them all the assistance they need. You could confer with Mpilo [Bishop Desmond Tutu] with regard to the funds for both Ntonto and Dan. There is a sense of desperation in me about Ntonto [a niece] and I know you will not falter on Dan, if he still wants to carry out the promise he gave me.

Perhaps Christina [a niece] will do much better in Germany. I wish to know her address so that I could continue to be of some help to her. I never stop thinking that some of the children are unable to fulfil their life dreams simply because I am not there to help them solve their numerous problems. I will ask Aunt Judie [Nelson's cousin] to send me her address if she has it.

9 September 1979

# Winnie

Winnie, above all, is Nelson's constant companion in his cell and his contact with the outer world. Throughout these long years of separation, the separated have grown closer. There is no dimming in the relationship which has withstood malicious gossip and every kind of State persecution. He addresses her filially, as is customary among Thembu and Pondo, as Mum (the mother of his children), as Dadewethu (sister), Nomabandla (the name his Mandela clan gave her) as sister, as Zanyiwe and Ngutyana (reference to her tribe). The love-making has continued at a distance, and always in the presence of strangers; the love talk contains its privacy in signs and gestures.

Throughout the years, Winnie has made every visit an event for him to remember and relish, presenting herself with meticulous care, in toiletry, jewellery, and in the dress or kaftan chosen for the occasion.

And each visit is celebrated in the letter that follows:

You looked really wonderful on 17/11, very much like the woman I married. There was colour in your face. Gone was the choleric appearance and glazed look in your eyes when you are under pressure of over-dieting. As usual I kept addressing you as Mum but my body kept telling me that a woman is sitting across this platform. I felt like singing, even if just to say Hallelujah!

22 November 1979

You looked really sparklingly attractive in your outfit during your last visit, especially on Sunday. There was hardly any evidence that Zeni and Zindzi sucked away your youth and part of your physical beauty.

31 March 1983

WINNIE

Your visit last month was quite unexpected and that may be one reason why I enjoyed it so much. At my age I would have expected all the urges of youth to have faded away. But it does not appear to be so. The mere sight of you, even the thought about you, kindles a thousand fires in me.

Though cheerful on 19/2, you nonetheless looked a bit ill and the tiny pools of water in your eyes drowned the love and tenderness they always radiate. But the knowledge of what I have enjoyed in the last twenty years made me feel that love even though physically denied by illness.

On 29/10 you were even more queenly and desirable in your deep green dress and I thought you were lucky that I could neither reach nor confide to you how I felt. Sometimes I feel like one who is on the sidelines, who has missed life itself.

Travelling with you to work in the morning, phoning you during the day, touching your hand or hugging you as you moved up and down the house, enjoying your delicious dishes, the unforgettable hours in the bedroom, made life taste like honey. These are things I cannot forget.

21 January 1979

You may not know that one of my best moments in the old days was to listen to youngsters' compliments of Dadewethu, youngsters who were also caught in the web of intrigue Mother tried to spin around her.

2 September 1979

I love you all the time, in the miserable and cold winter days and when all the beauty, sunshine and warmth of summer returns. My joy when you're bursting with laughter is beyond measure. This is how I always think of you – our Mum with plenty to keep her occupied; with a smiling face whatever the circumstances.

10 February 1980

On 30/8 I was hardly out of the visiting rooms and I thought of you as I walked back to the cell. I said to myself, there goes Msuthu like a bird in hand returning to the bush, to the wild jungle and the wide world. I miss you, Mhlophe, and love you! Devotedly, Dalibunga.

1 October 1975

345

These days I spend some time thinking of you both as Dadewethu, Mum, pal and mentor. What you perhaps don't know is how often I think and actually picture in my mind all that makes you up physically and spiritually – the shape of your forehead, shoulders, limbs, the loving remarks which come daily and the blind eye you've always turned against those numerous shortcomings that would have frustrated another woman.

Sometimes it is a wonderful experience to sit alone and think back about previous moments spent with you, darling. I even remember a day when you were bulging with Zindzi, struggling to cut your nails. I now recall this with a sense of shame. I could have done it for you. Whether or not I was conscious of it, my attitude was: I've done my duty, a second brat is on the way, the difficulties that you're now facing as a result of your physical conditions are now all yours.

15 April 1976

Your love and devotion has created a debt which I will never attempt to pay back. So enormous is it that even if I had to pay regular instalments for another century I would not settle it. All I can say Mum is *Nangamso!*

21 July 1979

The tenderness and intimacy which exists between a man and his Mum, Dad, and the special friend that you are. This particular relationship carries with it something that cannot be separated from self.

21 January 1979

Your affectionate letters, Xmas, birthday and wedding anniversary messages always arrive at the right moment, leaving me with the hope of getting an equally stimulating letter the following month. Hearing from the same person every week for fourteen years should have created that familiarity which takes away the freshness and joy of novelty. But I light up immediately your letter comes and I feel like flying where eagles cannot reach. Although I know your ability to put things simply and clearly I was at once attracted by the beautiful way in which you summed up our eighteen years together – eighteen years of the greatest horror in your life. That message, as usual, shocked and thrilled me all at once.

19 July 1976

346

In times like these I miss you more than ever before. I have told you many times before about the simple things in life that I have missed most these last sixteen years: with you in Jeppe, Chancellor, boxing tournaments, music festivals, film shows, at Nqonqi's in the open veld, the unforgettable days at 8115 and the greatest of all moments – closing the bedroom door.

19 November 1979

Your letters are more than a tonic and I feel different every time I hear from you even when you don the mantle of Nogqwashu and sting me from every direction. Such stings have come to be part of our life, our mutual love and our happiness. They give me some idea of the ravages and damage caused on us by the life of hardship that we must live. On such occasions I always concentrate on the salutation or on the very last words in the concluding paragraph.

31 March 1983

## TO ZINDZE, RECALLING WINNIE'S JEALOUSY

One Saturday after 1 p.m., and about a month before Mum and I got married, she came with friends to fetch me from the office and found me waiting for the secretary of a foreign statesman with whom I'd an appointment. Like Mum, she was shatteringly beautiful and about the same age, and although they had not met, Mum was at once surprisingly hostile. Then I was in top physical condition and going to the gym regularly. In spite of all that, and in the presence of onlookers, she caught me by the scruff of the neck and dragged me out. I never saw that lady again.

On another occasion when Zeni was still suckling, we were having supper when a comrade came and asked me to drive one of Mum's lady friends to what was then Sophiatown. The Ngutyana at once retired to the bedroom, literally shaking with anger. I kissed and rubbed her gently between the shoulders and she cooled down. I'm quite ashamed to say it, darling, but I must tell you that, in spite of the raw deal she gave me those days, Mum soon settled down. Today we've a high-souled and tolerant shepherdess who has made a man of me.

4 September 1977

# Anniversaries

The Mandelas commemorate birthdays whenever possible, and wedding anniversaries almost without exception, in prison during official visits. The occasions are, in addition, observed with cards and letters. Nelson recalls his and Winnie's wedding day in the following extract:

I remember 14 June nostalgically. In spite of the difficult times, we went to the altar. The treason trial, confined to Johannesburg, the debts that were piling up, the inability to honour obligations, on occasions remaining in the background when she had every right to share the limelight: all these things shock me as nothing else has ever done before. That was our cross which I hope we carried reasonably well. I spent a lot of time on this day thinking of you. Every time I do, I literally glow and long to embrace you and feel the electric shocks that your flesh rubs onto me, your navel and heartbeat. Three years from now we celebrate our Silver Jubilee – where and how? Till we meet again.

29 June 1980

His mind rests on times past; of relations who have died, of things he ought to have done and did not.

Dear Sister, Today we have been together for nineteen years. Many things have happened in that time. C. K. Nozipho, Phyllis, Tshawuza Ntwasa and Makhulu who were at our wedding are all gone. So is Ma who welcomed you as a bride to our new home and Thembi, whom you loved as your own child. May they all rest in peace.

I remembered you with a real feast on 26 September [Winnie's birthday]. I put four teaspoons of Nespray powdered milk in a mug, 3 teaspoons of Milo, 2 teaspoons of brown sugar and buried the whole mixture in hot water. It was a magnificent brew fit for a monarch.

1 October 1975

I wish I could drive you on a long, long journey just as I did on 12/6/58, with the one difference that this time I'd prefer us to be alone. I've been away from you for so long that the very first thing I would like to do on my return would be to take you away from that suffocating atmosphere, drive you along carefully, so that you could have the opportunity of breathing fresh and clean air, seeing the beauty spots of South Africa, its green grass and trees, colourful wild flowers, sparkling streams, animals grazing in the open veld and be able to talk to the simple people we meet along the road. Our first stop would be to the place where Ma Rhadebe and CK [Winnie's parents] sleep. I hope they lie next to each other. Then I would be able to pay my respect to those who have made it possible for me to be as happy and free as I am now. Perhaps the stories I've so much wanted to tell you all these years would begin there. The atmosphere should probably sharpen your ears and restrain me to concentrate on those aspects which are tasty, edifying and constructive. Thereafter, we would adjourn and resume next to Mphakanyiswa and Nosekeni [Nelson's parents] where the environment would be similar. I believe we would then be fresh and solid as we drive back to 8115.

29 June 1976

# Regrets, Nostalgia, Dreams

Nelson's letters reflect the volumes that remain unsaid because of the censorship rules that prescribe and proscribe the thoughts of a prisoner. The one thing that he could have expressed freely was remorse and regret. There is not a glimmer of this in any of his letters with regard to the position he has adopted about his country and its freedom and that of his people.

The regrets he does express are about the time he could have spent with his family. There is an underlying consciousness of the price his children have had to pay for the father who withdrew from his family and gave himself to the people, of the husband who left his young wife to serve his country, a consciousness of their pain when he was not there, when they needed him as an intimate, personal presence.


TO WINNIE:

I lead a life where I hardly have enough time even to think.

15 April 1976

Our daughters raised in hardship are grown women today. The first born has her own house and is raising her family.

We couldn't fulfil our wishes, as we had planned, to have a baby boy. I had hoped to build you a refuge, no matter how small, so that we would have a place for rest and sustenance before the arrival of the sad, dry days. I fell down and couldn't do these things. I am as one building castles in the air.

26 June 1977

My arrest for treason on 5/12/56 and the lengthy proceedings that followed worsened the position. The world around me literally crumbled, income disappeared and many obligations could not be honoured. Only the coming of Ngutyana [Winnie] into the picture helped to bring about a bit of order to my personal affairs. But the chaos had gone too far even for her to bring back the stability and easy life I had just begun to lack when misfortune struck.

It is all these things which keep turning up as the mind strays over days in the Golden City. But this soul-searching melts away altogether when I think of Mum and all the children, of the pride and joy you all give me. Among us is Nobutho [Zindzi], the beautiful Mantu whose love and loyalty, visits, letters, birthday and Xmas cards are essential parts in the efforts of the family to help me endure many of the challenges of the last two decades.

1 March 1981

The regrets and anxieties prod him in his dreams which are vivid, often harrowing, nightmares; at times pleasant sublimations.

I've plans, wishes and hopes. I dream and build castles. But one has to be realistic. We're mere individuals in a society run by powerful institutions with its conventions, norms, morals, ideals and attitudes.

1 September 1975

I don't know how to interpret these dreams. But they at least indicate that there is far less steel in me than I had thought, that distance and two decades of separation have not strengthened the steel in me and deepened by anxiety over the family.

28 June 1980

I had a long dream as if it went on the whole night. It started in the mountains, across the Orange River. We were walking on green grass beside a clean stream, holding hands like we did before Zeni and Zindzi were born. We were in Brandfort and we travelled to Kroonstad where we met a lot of friends. All Ngutyanas and Dhlomos and our relations were there.

23 April 1978

Last month's dreams put you and me at the bottom of Selborne Road. We got a lift to First Avenue and then walked to King's bioscope. But we never reached it because you blocked my way

351

and pestered me with affectionate kisses. These are mere dreams but dreams I like to have.

27 May 1979

The world is truly round and seems to start and end with those we love. In this regard the 23/6 was one of those unforgettable nights when the subconscious opened up a romantic world, with all the wonderful thrills I have missed. A lady sat on the floor with her legs stretched out as our mothers used to relax in the old days. Though I can't remember the actual words, she sang with a golden voice, the face radiating all the affection and fire a woman can give a man. She turned and twisted her arms. That lady was none other than our darling Mum. These moments are increasing and make life worthwhile in spite of everything. I love you.

1 July 1979

Perpetual dreams about those we love! On the night of 21/9 you and I were driving the Olds at corner of Eloff and Market when you rushed out and spewed out porridge. It was hard and old with a crust on top. Your whole body quivered as each lump came out and you complained of a sharp pain on your right shoulder. I held you tight against my body, unmindful of the curious crowd and the traffic jam. I was still quite upset when I got up but was immediately happy when I realized that it was all but a dream.

26 June 1979

I dreamt I was with the young men of my kraal. They gave me herbs to strengthen me against you. They were saying that I should fight with you so that you would run away. And you were shouting at me to throw away those leaves, they were bad medicine. A whole audience was listening to this conversation. I threw the leaves away.

16 July 1978

On 20/6 I woke up to see Ngutyana and her man travelling from Brandfort to Johannesburg. They came across two opposing regiments of boys facing one another across a wide stream and spoiling for a fight. For security reasons we separated but I kept you under observation all long the line. The scenery was breathtaking as I watched down the fall towards the river below. Suddenly I was horrified when I noticed that you had disappeared and I rushed across the valley to check. There you were bathing unconcerned in the river with two girls. But when I reached the spot I discovered that all three were strange boys and you were nowhere to be found. Panic again welled up and as I set out to search the area. I saw you lying flat on the Transvaal side of the river shaking from high fever. A Bloemfontein official had walked past you and refused your request for a doctor. It was with an agitated mind I woke up.

I had a similar dream on the night of the 26/6. I was playing dominoes with three friends when I again saw you lying in a spot with giant pine trees and thick undergrowth. This time a hospital atendant brought hot water, sterilizing instruments and swabs for your treatment. Only then did I realize how ill you were. I rushed and embraced you. Later we reached a town where I had lived away from you for years. It was so flattering for me to show you around the place.

29 June 1980

My dreams tell the same story and keep on reminding me that I can't break away from the spell in which I was caught twenty-two years ago. The other night both Zeni and Zindzi dragged me to a second-hand shop in Eloff Street between Commissioner and Main Street to get some household furniture that we badly needed.

When I woke on the morning of 25/2 I was missing you and the children a great deal as always.

14 April 1976

I had one of my perpetual dreams. Returning home late, in fact, towards dawn, I raced through the house and met you as you staggered through the back door looking sickly and depressed. I embraced you for some time, feeling guilty and unable to look at you straight in the face. In the dream, Zindzi was still a baby of about eighteen months and I was stunned when I discovered that she had swallowed a razor blade. It was such a relief when she spewed it out. I dreamt about you and the girls on the following day. This time Zindzi asked me to kiss her. When I did she complained that my kiss lacked warmth. Zeni also insisted on a kiss and appeared to be satisfied.

1 June 1980

# Education

Nelson has a commitment to education. Both Mandelas have continued to study and to write exams throughout their imprisonment. When there was nothing to do, there were studies. In prison Nelson reads everything he can lay his hands on. Political prisoners were initially denied all news, but snatched bits surreptitiously, through newspapers left carelessly by warders. After years of protest they graduated to a restricted number of papers and to the radio, and eventually to TV.

Nelson has developed an interest in archaeology, mythology, philosophy and religion, and has a deep interest in social and cultural forms. He has studied law and economics through UNISA and London Law Correspondence College. In the following letters he discusses his and Winnie's studies.

My college work keeps me busy. I'm required to score 200 marks to be able to write the Business Economics exam at the end of the year. I've got up to date 142 marks through five assignments. Now I am struggling for 58 marks.

I feel guilty that I pursue my studies with ease while you carry a heavy load on your shoulders.

Dear Girl! At last you're back at UNISA. What are your subjects and do you remember you were at the same varsity when we met eighteen years ago? I hope you'll enjoy the course. But remember that I expect you to live up to the high standard I know you're capable of. But it really shook me to learn that in the evenings you drive to the public library. How can you take such a risk? Have you forgotten that you live in Soweto, not in the centre of town where you'd be safe at night. For the last decade you have been the subject of cowardly attempts on your life in which they

354

tried to drag you out of the house. Your life and that of the children is more important than any educational certificate!

15 April 1976

It will be a terrible setback if the registrar's ruling in regard to your degree in social science while in the Free State prevails. You have a strong case for exemption since you hold a diploma in social science which is recognized by provincial municipalities and many welfare organizations and industry. You could refer him to the various kinds of social work you have done since you qualified in 1955 at Baragwanath and the Child Welfare Society.

1 July 1979

About your study problems, I must tell you that I feel disappointed and even disgusted, for I know that social work is second nature to you. To get your degree would be such a compensation for the rough and raw deals that you have experienced during the last twenty-two years.

1 June 1980

The prisons department has announced that studies are being restored, including post-graduate studies. Prisoners may begin their respective courses individually. But at present I have no information as to whether Legal Studies with London University will be allowed ... If I am allowed to proceed with the final, I will tackle Jurisprudence, International Law, African Law and Mercantile Law or Family Law. My only fear is that the books will be prohibitively expensive. I will probably enrol for lectures with Wolseley or Cambridge and subscribe to the *Law Quarterly Review* and the *Modern Law Review*. To get all this I will require no less than R350. If refused, I will continue B. Com. with UNISA.

1 June 1980

# Health

Apart from a prostate operation in 1985 and equally successful treatment for TB in 1988, Nelson's health has been good.
At a time when the Press reported that he had cancer, he
wrote to Winnie:

Mhlophe, I feel tremendous both in flesh and spirit. I am active
during the day, relish both my physical and mental work, trot
around in the early morning as I used to do with Jerry Moloi in the
1950s. My appetite is good and I sleep well. Above all, strength
and supreme optimism runs through my blood because I know you
love me and that I enjoy the good wishes of countless family
members. I wish neither to be sick nor sickening. Only twice in my
life have I ever been to hospital, for only two days; in 1937 due to a
minor stomach complaint, and for the removal of tonsils in 1945.
I've never been to Groote Schuur Hospital at all and last saw that
place from the road in 1961. An occasional indisposition is but
natural and in this regard I've had my share of ailments of a minor
nature but I can't remember suffering from a major illness during
the last fifteen years. Several times during this period the country
as a whole has been hit by epidemics, but not once did I go down.
This is not a boast Kgaitsedi [Winnie's clan name], but a statement
of fact to one who is conscious about sensational but completely
unfounded press reports on the breakdown of my health. The day I
catch that mischievous reporter I'll harpoon him to the ring and
hammer him out in his own corner. I can't predict what will
happen tomorrow but at the moment I am right on!

24 May 1976

Do you still remember 20 December many years ago when you
found me with a deep cut on the left eye and my head in bandages.
I've hardly seen you so upset as you were on that occasion. To this
day that painful look across your face still haunts me. I gave you

all the facts but one day our nephew Zwangendaba will give you a little detail I omitted to tell you then . . . My eyes are quite alright, Ngutyana, and health good.

18 July 1976

On 16/8 I saw an orthopaedic surgeon and he examined my right heel which worries me now and again. I will discuss the matter further with Dr Edelstein on his next round to the Island.

27 February 1979

I have already sent you a medical report in my last letter. I must again assure you that I feel well and alert.

1 July 1979

We took off the plaster of paris on 19/11. The cut looks fine and according to the report of the orthopaedic surgeon the recovery will be uncomplicated. I have started using the foot.

25 November 1979

On 9/5 I saw an eye specialist in Cape Town. A virulent virus had been eating up my eye since 28/3 but the poor creature had no idea of just how strong in me is the will to live. I have eaten it up and the infection has cleared.

The specialist who also attended to me for the same complaint on 7/4/76 says my eyesight is excellent although the test revealed some slight changes in the eye since the last time. I changed reading glasses in 1972. He felt that the change was so small that he would not recommend that I get new glasses unless I wanted a fancy frame, but he nevertheless gave me a prescription just in case. I was somewhat relieved when you and Zindzi did not turn up on 3/3. I injured my left eye with a tennis racket on 28/2 and by 1/3 it had swollen up with a black ring around it. I must also tell you that the left heel has been troubling me for some time. It pains when I run and has thus considerably reduced my mobility. To the naked eye it would seem that there is something wrong with the bone formation. Last month the local X-ray pictures revealed that your hubby has an extra toe in each heel. On the painful spot there is a scar, perhaps an injury long forgotten. On 17/5 I had a cortisone injection and we hope that it will at least subdue the pain.

27 May 1979

The heel is healing well and I walk around in slippers without a walking stick. Maybe that sometime in February I will resume light exercises. I am not used to seeing parts of my body loose and sagging as if I am sixty-two. You know well that I am only forty-five and hardly anyone will have the courage to challenge that statement when I resume my exercises.

December 1979

On 23/5 I saw a radiologist in Cape Town who X-rayed my right heel. Though I have not yet seen the plates, he remarked there was hardly any difference between the right and left heels. The same morning I also had a cardiogram test. I had last seen the heart surgeon on 3/5/77 on the occasion the blood pressure was a bit up. It remained stable until the early hours of 30/4 when there were symptoms that it was high. Late on 1/5 an official from the prison hospital tested the pressure. He pumped the instrument and listened carefully as he released the pressure. Suddenly he exclaimed, 'What?' and quickly pumped again, his face distorted by concern and his eyes shining. The needle shot up and again he listened to the heartbeat. This time he abandoned the instrument still wrapped around my arm and phoned the doctor. The doctor and sister were quite unruffled and relaxed and their apparent calm made me feel better. They confirmed that the pressure was disturbingly high. An Aldomat a day brought it down significantly on the next morning and in the afternoon of 3/5 it was back to normal and I stopped the Aldomat treatment. I don't know what raised it in the first instance. The specialist thought it might have been due to family worries which I naturally pooh-pooh. As if to stress this speculation the night I came back from Cape Town I had one of my perpetual dreams.

1 June 1980

But he worried about the family's health:

I had no idea whatsoever, darling, that you and Zeni are allergic to certain foods and that several doctors have been trying to find the cause. I hope that both of you will accept Dr Variawa's offer and be admitted to Coronation for medical tests. To find the cause of your allergy is normally a difficult matter and the sooner they begin the better. What form does the allergy take? Please give me all the details in the next letter. But the important thing is not to worry about the disorder at all. Remember that regular sports, especially those that involve running around, go a long way in controlling physical and psychological disorders.

5 March 1978

358

I'll be happy to know that your injury has healed, and your health improved. You've hardly paid attention to my pleas in regard to your physical appearance. I just never get used to you; every time we meet I get a shock. You don't look well at all to me even though you claim to be, I don't know exactly how to put it, Msutu, but you look spent, run down. It is not good. I know you will say you're not on show and that you would prefer that people should accept you as you are. But you have always been fresh and full of blood.

What a sense of pride and joy it would have been to me to know that my concern over your appearance during the last thirteen years would have jolted you to do something about it. My anxiety would have gone. I've a conscience and every time I see you carrying visible signs of suffering, I am tortured by a sense of guilt and shame. Nevertheless, you look wonderful to me even when you appear like one whose lungs have been eaten away by a pack of *impundulu* [witchcraft birds]. You should know that if you wish me to be at ease, you'll write one day and tell me that you are back to your old form and that you have put on at least five kilograms.

1 October 1979

# Sons

---

## THEMBI

Thembi, alone of all Nelson's children, was old enough at the time of his imprisonment to visit him. He never did, and while members of his family have placed different interpretations on this, Winnie's explanation is as follows:

When Nelson went underground, he relied heavily on Thembi. The other children were too young to understand. Thembi almost lived underground with his father. Being of an arrestable age, his father instructed him to keep an extremely low profile and not to disclose, even to his mother, his visits to Lilliesleaf. I took him out there personally to spend weekends with Nelson, and he joined me in many dangerous missions. His very closeness to his father and his involvement with him forced him to maintain a façade of distance and aloofness, a façade he maintained even in the presence of his brother and his sister and his mother. I was amazed that as young as he was, he was able to keep that façade so completely. He worshipped his father and was fully committed to his role in Umkhonto. I, in turn, worshipped Thembi.

When he was killed in a motor accident, Nelson wrote to me where I was in the condemned cell for eighteen months in solitary confinement. He reminded me of how Thembi had visited him at Lilliesleaf wearing Nelson's oversize suit jacket. He had said to Nelson, 'Tata, now I am in your place and I will try to be you and look after the family.'

Thembi was the most hurt by his parents' divorce. He was old enough at the time to understand the meaning of divorce and it left him traumatized. He suffered too on account of the extreme positions his parents took, his father committed to politics, his mother to religion.

360

Thembi fell in love with Thoko at school in Swaziland. She fell pregnant and returned home, forced to end her schooling. He followed her to Retreat in Cape Town, where her mother had a retail business. Thoko helped in the store and Thembi had a good clerical job. Their eldest daughter, Ndileka, was born, followed by their second daughter, Nandi. Ndileka was three and Nandi only six months old when Thembi was killed. Thoko survived the accident and continued to live with her mother.

Later the granddaughters joined Evelyn in the Transkei and went to high school there. The granddaughters are grown women now and between them have given Nelson two great-grandchildren. Nelson arranged a scholarship for the younger granddaughter, Nandi, and she is presently studying in Cape Town and sees 'Tatomkhulu', her grandfather, as regularly as she is given visits. Ndileka is a nurse.

Nelson's mind often turns to Thembi; when Zindzi informs him she is learning to drive, he writes:

It pleases me that you're taking driving lessons and hope you will be as careful a driver as Mum is. Thembi could drive the colossal Oldsmobile at ten. But if you get your licence, you'll have done better than Mum and I. We were twenty-six and thirty-three respectively when we got ours. Good luck darling!

4 September 1977


## MAKGATHO

Makgatho says:

I made my first visit to Robben Island when I was sixteen years and nine months old. It was in June 1967 and I was schooling in Orlando. I had not seen Tata since his first arrest in 1962. We did not attend the Rivonia Trial. We were schooling in Swaziland at the time. I only left Swaziland in 1964.

The only news I had of Tata during this time was what I read in newspapers. I could not write to Tata. Tata could not write to me. When I returned to Orlando I visited Mum Winnie and she gave me news of Tata. I liked going to Mum Winnie's. I would play records and relax for the day I was there.

Mum Winnie arranged for me to see Tata. She arranged my fare to Johannesburg and left me at the station. Thembi met me in Cape Town. Thembi had left to live in Cape Town in 1965. He was already married then and seemed to be doing well. I knew he loved Tata. Maybe he went to live in Cape Town because Tata was there. I took the boat and went into the hole. There were four of us travelling together. We were all visiting relatives on the Island.

I had a good visit with Tata but the time was too short. Tata told me to stand back so he could look at me. He said I had grown tall and was good looking. He asked about my schooling and said I must apply to go to Fort Hare. He told me about his days at Fort Hare. We talked a lot. He smiled a lot. The thirty minutes were too short.

After that I used to visit Tata twice a year. The SACC [South African Council of Churches] paid our fares. I had two visits in 1968, two in 1969, two in 1970. Then I had one visit a year, right up to 1978. I last saw him in 1983.

Makgatho's visits became irregular after 1983 and then stopped. 'I just got lazy,' he explains. He resumed his visits to his father only in 1987. The reason perhaps went deeper than laziness. It was basically that he could not cope with his father's persistent exhortations to return to school. Speaking about his education, Kgatho says:

I wrote my standard nine at St Christopher's and passed, but I did not return to write my matric. The fact is that I was expelled. We had organized a strike. I stayed with Mr M. B. Yengwa in Manzizni for three years, and then started schooling in Orlando. Mama paid. She got help from the Institute of Race Relations.

I wrote my matric and got a school-leaving certificate. I had applied to Fort Hare but I did not have a university exemption. I wrote the supplementary but failed again.

Nelson had faith in his son's intellectual capacity and felt he should return to school. He wrote to a friend in November 1974:

My son Kgatho, twenty-four, owes two subjects for his matric. He did very well up to JC [Junior Certificate] passing with honours, though he wrote the exams several months after being expelled from the boarding school for organizing [so it was alleged] a

362

student strike. He has since lost all his sharpness and has through private tuition twice attempted matric without success. The real trouble is that at his age and in my absence he finds it a bit hard to resist the attractions of city life. I have been trying to get him back to boarding school – Clarkebury or St Johns, both in the Transkei – where he would be able to study full-time, far from the influences that make it difficult for him to concentrate on his work. He has a powerful argument to fall back on: a comfortable job which he may lose if he accepts my suggestion and he is also engaged. However, I feel he could take time to study for a year to complete at least matric. Thereafter, I told him, I would discuss further plans. Perhaps if he could be invited to Durban, taken around places like Ngoye, Westville, M. L. Sultan College, to see at first hand what young people are doing elsewhere, such an opportunity might arouse his ambitions and induce him to improve his perform-ance.

1 November 1974

But instead of returning to school, Makgatho married and fathered a son. Nelson was sceptical about the marriage but grew fond of his daughter-in-law, Rennie. She kept closer contact with him than his son. She brought him the first grandchild, Mandla, to visit him. He gazed on the baby he could not touch and saw in the broad healthy face the renewal of the Mandela line, and felt reassured.

Then Rennie did what Kgatho wouldn't do. She expressed a desire to return to school. Nelson discussed the matter with Alan Paton and Paton arranged for Rennie to be enrolled at Inanda Seminary and he, Peter Brown and Ismail Meer paid her fees. Nelson's ambition for his son continued unabated. He wrote to his eldest daughter Maki:

The fact that Rennie is at school and her own decision will make Makgatho realize that he will be the only black sheep in the family. Keep writing and urge him to think of his future and to go back to college.

31 December 1978

In 1979 it seemed that his entreaties to Kgatho to return to school were at last having an effect. He wrote cautiously:

I'll not comment on Makgatho's promise to go back to school. It is what he has been saying these last nine years. When he does actually enter a school I will do everything in my power to help him, but definitely not before that.

But Makgatho did not have a matric exemption and therefore could not be admitted to college. He was deeply frustrated and full of pain because he could not please his father. Nelson heard that his son was not bearing up to his responsibilities and was drinking a little too much. Maki felt that he would be better off living with his mother in the Transkei and blamed her father for discouraging him from doing so. Nelson replied:

In a previous letter you referred to Makgatho's behaviour and blamed me for having influenced him not to come to the Transkei. But the truth is that on the question of education he has given me as much trouble as you have done. There is nothing I have not tried in the last eight years to get him back to school. But all my efforts have been in vain. Even the fact that Rennie went to the Morris Isaacson School in 1975 and she is now at Inanda is all due to the efforts of Mum Winnie who is keen to do everything in her power to help all the children attain their ambitions. We are all trying even now and keeping our hopes up, but both Mum Winnie and myself are far from him and it is not easy at all to persuade him by telephone calls and letters only.

However, there was more to the problem than a waywardness and a refusal to return to school. Makgatho's marriage was hitting the rocks. The family blamed Rennie; Nelson remained neutral. He wrote to Zindzi:

I have taken no sides in this dispute, firstly because I have not heard Kgatho's version. Even when the impossible occurs and Kgatho writes, I will lean towards an amicable settlement. I will think of both parties as well as Mandla who will certainly suffer far more than any other person when his parents break. Imagine, darling, just what our reaction would be if someone urged Mum to pack her belongings and find a new home because of my faults. You are the product of the love and affection of your parents, and throughout your life you have drawn strength and hope from that love and security. Destroying that love and home, for whatever reason, would be like a beautiful rose whose tender roots are exposed to the frost.

Was Nelson thinking of Thembi? Of the frost that had settled on his heart when his father had parted from his mother? Kgatho and Rennie divorced, and Kgatho married again and had another son. It was K. D. Matanzima who brought him and his second wife and son to Cofimvaba to join Evelyn. Proudly, KD claimed, 'I sent a Jack to catch a Jack.'

In Umtata, he presented the prodigal Madiba to the Thembus, flew him to Port St Johns to meet his senior wife, who had looked after both Kgatho and Thembi when they had lived with her for a year while schooling in the Transkei. Kgatho joined his mother in her business and they are today running the Mandela Trading Store in Cofimvaba quite successfully.

# Daughters

_____

## MAKAZIWE

Maki, as she is affectionately called by the family, Evelyn's youngest child, is the oldest of Nelson's three daughters. She was eight years old when her father was first sentenced. She has vivid recollections of visiting him at Lilliesleaf in Rivonia, of being taken there by Mum Winnie, of going for long walks in the country with Tata. It was at school in Swaziland that she heard of her father's arrest. She was overcome with tears and confusion. She did not quite understand what it all meant. She did not see her father again until 1970, when she had grown into a young woman, and father and daughter rediscovered each other.

Nelson found her frank and open, not mincing her words, nor pulling punches. She had an independent approach to black political groupings, but this he grasped only indirectly and read between the lines. Like Kgatho she had taken to Winnie as a child, but then as she grew older she became affected by the separation of the two families and by her mother's bitterness. She absorbed the last unconsciously, for it was her mother she criticized for being bitter.

Maki was the first of Nelson's children to matriculate and that delighted him. Then to his deep disappointment she announced that she was getting married. He tried to dissuade her, and to persuade her to go to university, to put aside all thoughts of marriage until she graduated. Maki, however, would not be influenced. She married and had two children in quick succession. As Nelson had feared, the marriage floundered and the couple separated. Nelson consoled Maki and exhorted her to get on with life.

My Darling, Mum Winnie told me about her visit to you in Port St Johns last November, but as she does not want to upset me (she hardly gives me family news that might worry me), she told me that you would write to me on an important domestic matter. I suspected that your marriage was not going smoothly. I must confess that ever since you told me about your problems with Camagu I feared that this is how it would finally end up. But you must be realistic and act at once. If you are convinced that your marriage is on the rocks and that there is no hope of saving it, you must sue for divorce without delay and forget all about Camagu. Under no circumstances must you neglect this and keep a marriage that has failed. You are still young with a bright future, if from now on you plan carefully and are really determined to go forward. This is not the time to worry yourself about your failure to take our advice on continuing your education by going to varsity. Many children have made that mistake before. What is important is what you can do from now on.

8 June 1978

About the marriage you seem undecided. That is quite natural to a truly virtuous and proud young lady who was devoted to her married life. To be cautious on a question of this kind is something I admire, but you ought to know your mind and act decisively. If you think you can still save it, say so and try again. But if you are convinced the marriage is on the rocks, then you must dissolve it without delay. Your aim should be to lead a free and dignified life. All that you should do is to instruct an attorney, most preferably Mr Fikile Bam, who is practising at Umtata and Engcobo. Failing him, you can consult Mr Mkentane, also at Engcobo. Even more difficult to understand is the fact that you allow Camagu to neglect his duty of supporting the children. If you see an attorney you should easily get a maintenance order against him as well as an order forcing him to pay part of your litigation expenses.

I was also happy to know that you work as an invoice clerk. Although I don't know what your income is, at least you have something to keep you going. I was even more happy to hear you say that you have now learnt that life without a profession is futile. I also note that you are determined to do nursing on the simple ground that, in that way, you can both study and earn a bit of cash. In the circumstances your decision is quite reasonable. In the end you will have achieved something and the children won't be stranded.

You should remember the dilemma in which you may be at present. It would be quite natural for you to save the marriage in the hope that Camagu may change and be the same darling who once so loved and respected you in the early days. But you may be nursing a false hope which will lead to further disappointment at a time when you will be too old to make a fresh start. The children will naturally be shocked by the divorce and tortured by the stigma of growing up without the security of a home where both parents live together. What you decide to do now will be important for their future. But by furthering your education and having an independent profession, say a doctor, lawyer or social worker, you will really inspire them to aim higher than you. Please write back to me as soon as possible and let me know what you have decided.

26 November 1978

I would like to tell you again that I am very sorry to learn of the breakdown of your marriage and the rough experiences you have had. Such a turn is always disastrous to a woman. I must remind you, darling, that members of the family and close friends had a high opinion of you as a girl. They were full of hopes for your conduct inside and outside school, for your serious-mindedness and your natural intelligence. I once hoped that the profession of your choice would match you in these qualities and I urge you to develop them. Divorce may destroy a woman but strong characters have not only survived but have gone further and distinguished themselves in life. I want to think that you are such a strong person, that far from discouraging you, this experience will make you richer. This is the challenge, darling, please take it. We love and trust you and are confident that a wonderful future awaits you.

The thought that his daughter was not aiming high enough grew stronger and he urged her to be more ambitious.

I must ask you to think very carefully about your future and to aim a little higher than you are doing now. This is a second chance you have, Maki, and there may be no third.

I was disappointed to note that you have no higher ambition than to be a nurse. I suggest that you abandon your intention to take nursing and immediately apply for admission to Fort Hare. Mum Winnie will try and arrange for payment of your fees and your clothing and perhaps even for a small allowance whilst you are studying, and your mum can help you with regard to the payments for the divorce case. As you know Mum Winnie lost her job in Johannesburg when she was sent to the Orange Free State. She is herself struggling. But she loves you and I am sure she will try her best. It is not at all easy, darling, to discuss such confidential problems through letters and I hope you can see me soon.

8 June 1978

I have told you before, I repeat it now, that we are able to arrange for you to go to university and to get an allowance while working. These days a university education is essential even if your ambition is to become a mere nurse. More ambitious girls first take a degree and then nursing with the result that they rise to positions of responsibility and influence quicker. Those without real ambition and drive are left to work hard in inferior positions for the rest of their lives. I am really surprised to note that in spite of your cruel experiences you are not able to think of anything more than to be an ordinary nurse. At least your mum was able to reach that position thirty-four years ago, quite an achievement in those days. Later she did a midwifery course. Do you mean to tell me that all that you think you are worth is to be no more than your Mum was more than three decades ago? In doing so you are throwing away a golden opportunity which other people less able than you will never miss. All you need to do is tell me or Mum that you have now decided to go to varsity in January. We will attend to the rest. Think, Maki, think, you are only twenty-four and the whole world is at your feet. Think clearly, and at once. Do not miss this chance of entering university next year.

6 November 1978

Maki decided to go to college. The fact that her mother had given up nursing and settled down as a storekeeper in Cofimvaba had helped to improve financial problems considerably. K. D. Matanzima had been instrumental in bringing about this change in Evelyn's status.

Matanzima was family. Politically he and Rohlihlahla stood in opposite camps but the tie of blood was strong. Whatever Evelyn's own feelings about the Transkei, Matanzima had persuaded her to give up nursing and take up shopkeeping. He advised her of the properties that had become available on the market. The Government, anxious for the first independent homeland to work, was reselling the properties for which whites had been handsomely compensated to the Africans at whatever price they could afford. Matanzima had driven her along the main road in Cofimvaba and pointed out all the properties that had become available. She remembered the place from childhood when they had come to buy from the European storekeepers. Everything had been reserved for whites: white travelling salesmen had sat drinking beer on the verandah of the one and only hotel; blacks had been allowed to enter the tearooms only through side entrances. Now the whole town had become black. She had taken the shop Matanzima advised and by 1978 was doing sufficiently well to take over the care of Maki's children, so that she could pursue her studies.

Nelson was overjoyed when Maki enrolled at Fort Hare and wrote:

My darling Maki, thank you for your letter of 15/2 and for your telegram which I got on 2/3. It read as follows: Registered at Fort Hare with borrowed money. Fees not yet paid. Lectures start March 1. Doing BA. A week later I recieved a letter from Messrs Mkentane telling me that you were going back to school. I am really happy to know that you are at varsity at last and I wish you the best of luck in your studies. You have been out of school for seven years and you may probably be rusty, but I am confident that you will soon recapture your old form and do well. If you work hard from the beginning and according to a definite timetable from which you should not depart, you can pass with distinctions.

11 March 1978

TO WINNIE

Maki says she is the happiest soul and cannot believe that it is herself who has been admitted to Fort Hare. 'I came to Fort Hare through Mum Winnie's manoeuvres' to put it in her own words, but I was shocked to learn that the fees are R707. I have requested Granny [Helen Joseph] in Johannesburg to ask Amina and husband

[Yusuf Cachalia] to attend to the payment of fees. In view of the large amount involved, the allowance she requires and the length of the course, I am compelled to ask her to consult Benjie too.

19 November 1978

There was tension between the two houses he had founded. It was always a matter of deep pain that those whom he loved did not love each other, or did not love each other as much as they should. Maki complained of insufficient support; her complaints reflected on Winnie and Nelson defended her.

Your letter raised other important family matters that cannot properly be discussed through correspondence. I will therefore not comment at this stage. Perhaps we can talk a bit if and when you visit me. All that I wish to remind you at the moment is that Mum Nobandla [Winnie] loves you and Kgatho as much as she loves Zeni and Zindzi. She tried to keep you, Kgatho and the late Thembi at a boarding school. I would like to assure you that Mum Winnie will do everything in her power to cover your tuition and boarding fees. If you want to pick up quickly in your studies you should be a full-time student and stay at varsity. Mum Winnie was here on Boxing Day and we discussed the matter at length. Please get in touch with her at once and give her the full details; that is, the varsity to which you have applied for admission, the course you have chosen, the tuition and boarding fees, the train or bus, if any, to and from varsity, the cost of the varsity uniform.

He told her that he would like her to do medicine, but was realistic in his expectations.

That career has become even more important today, and your ambition was really worthwhile. But we must be realistic; you are now twenty-four and have lost a number of valuable school years. Your immediate aim should be to have some definite academic qualifications and a definite occupation which will make you secure and independent. It would certainly be a good idea to take a BSc with a view to becoming a doctor. The difficulty is that you may perhaps feel that you are now too rusty in maths and physics. In that case it would be better to try another course.

There are certain precautions you should take to prepare yourself for a fruitful study career. You must brush up your knowledge

371

through systematic reading of literature and newspapers. Try to read a novel, even if just for an hour a day and, say, the *Daily Dispatch*, if they are available at Fort Hare or the Transkei University College. You may also subscribe to the *Sunday Times* if it is not available at varsity. Make it a point, no matter how busy you may be, to at least read the editorial carefully and understand it thoroughly. If you do so diligently you will be surprised just how fast your general understanding of facts will become.

You should also do regular physical exercises, especially track running. It has the advantage of exercising all parts of your body and giving you a feeling of well-being. Such activities sharpen interest in your studies and also raise the level of your performance in the classroom. Please consider my suggestions objectively.

31 December 1978

You should also learn to play a few fast-moving games like tennis and basketball to take your mind off books. You will find that extremely helpful. Exercise will give you a feeling of well-being and sharpen your mind. You should also read carefully at least two newspapers a day, especially editorials and feature articles. A varsity career is not just a question of studying books and passing exams. One should have more than a general knowledge of current affairs and the world. You can supplement by having a well-informed friend with whom you can discuss the news.

You should also not discuss your domestic problems and religious views with others even if they are your intimate friends. Keep these matters strictly to yourself. In this way you will come to enjoy your varsity days and later look back at them with fond memories.

11 March 1979

I agree with you when you say that one benefits a great deal by meeting people from different walks of life and that conversations with people from such differing environments tend to widen one's general knowledge. I hope that you will take full advantage of such contacts, and if you do so imaginatively, your entire outlook will be considerably enriched.

With regard to the building of a library, I would suggest that you ask the following agencies for book catalogues from which you can choose your favourite titles: the Ravan Press, No 409–16 Dunwell House, 35 Jorissen Street, Braamfontein, Johannesburg,

2001, and the South African Institute of Race Relations, PO Box 97, Johannesburg, 2000.

Ravan Press concentrates on publishing fiction and non-fiction literature by progressive black and other writers, which are not normally available in the country's other book firms. The SAIRR publishes an annual survey which is one of the country's best sources of information and I would advise you to order a copy of it every year. It is a valuable mine of information. Carefully selected books from the Ravan Press will give you the good feeling that you are reading about your country, your people and yourself. I don't know whether you ever consulted Aunts Helen and Amina as I suggested. Their knowledge and experience on these things are wide and they would be very valuable to you in this regard.

Speaking about Cowley House, you may be aware that the House was bought by the South African Council of Churches to provide accommodation for visitors to political prisoners on Robben Island. The members of its staff are all employees of the SACC. The International Red Cross, PO Box 29001, Sunnyside, 0132 (telephone: 211597) Pretoria, helps in paying the travelling expenses to and from Cape Town. I do look forward to seeing you and Abazukulu [grandchildren] soon and I hope you will this time co-ordinate your visits with those of the family from Brandfort. Nobody can ever question your right to visit Pollsmoor, but you must appreciate the inconvenience that may flow from not informing the family at Brandfort about your proposed visit.

31 January 1983

I was pleased to learn that you are back at college and that you are now busy writing the remaining subjects. I am, however, sorry to hear that you dropped statistical methods because you find the subject somewhat difficult. Perhaps you will manage it better next year.

2 September 1979

Your letter reached me on 20/2, luckily on the day the family paid me a visit. I immediately sent out a message about your registration fee and I sincerely hope that this year you will be saved from the problems you experienced last year. It is a pity that you did not confirm that you were in Johannesburg during the holidays as I would have arranged with friends there to meet and discuss problems directly with you. But let's hope for the best. I look forward to seeing you again. But I would suggest that you apply in time, especially if you intend coming down in June; there are now more visitors to the Island and you can never be sure to get a particular date unless you apply several months in advance. You could apply to see me on two successive days – Saturdays and Sundays. I must also remind you that on 20/2 Ndindi [Thembi's daughter] turned sixteen and is now entitled to visit me. I would suggest that you stay with our cousin Mrs Grace Matsha, No 5, Sandile Street, Langa, a township which is much nearer the town. Cape Town has now become very rough and it will be necessary for somebody to accompany you to and from the docks. By the way I am told that during the disturbances at Fort Hare last year you were seriously injured, so much so that you were hospitalized. Can you give me particulars if this information is true? I sent the children's Xmas and birthday cards to Cofimvaba and I hope they all got them. Makgatho and Aunt Judy visited me in August last year; he later sent me an Xmas card. I have been unable to send him a birthday card. Please tell me where he is. I miss you very badly and look forward to seeing you, possibly next June. Meantime, I send you tons and tons of love and a million kisses. Affectionately, Tata.

20 February 1979

There is a bit of research I should like you to do for me, but only if you have the time, preferably when you are saturated with studying. Though I graduated there in 1942, I left the college at the end of 1940. That year I took part in the inter-varsity sports which were held at Lovedale. For the mile race Mr Mokgokong and I represented the college. It was then the practice for the athletic team to take a photo which was then hung up in the main dining hall. I am not so sure whether that year's team was ever photographed. In November 1940, I was also elected vice-president of the Athletic Union for 1941 but I did not return to complete the course there. Can you check on these matters and let me know?

2 September 1979

He was pleased when he learnt that his daughter was showing interest in the opposite sex again. He took a lively interest in all his daughters' boyfriends and adopted a very liberal attitude in the matter.

It came to me as a big surprise to know that you have a boyfriend who takes you out. I am also glad to know that you have not hidden the true facts from him. I have full confidence in your

374

honesty and know that you will always try to act according to the best of your ability. It was correct and dignified for you to tell him the truth. But you must give me the particulars, e.g., his name and surname, and what his parents do, the course he is taking and his age.

2 September 1979

I was very happy to receive your letter containing the exam results. Two B's out of four subjects is an achievement, and your performance up to now promises even better results this November. Meantime, I send you heartiest congratulations. I note that this year you will be doing Sociology 3, Social Work 3, and Philosophy 1. Will this be your final year, or are there still some courses outstanding? I also note that you spent your December holidays doing practical work at the Child Welfare Society in Johannesburg and that you visited Van Ryn's Home in Benoni, as well as some homes in Soweto. I was not at all aware that Van Ryn's was still there. I visited it several times in the 1950s to consult juvenile clients, and the mere mention of it in your letter aroused pleasant memories.

1 March 1981

In another letter he wrote:

My ambition is that on completing your studies at Fort Hare you should do a senior degree abroad. Although it is still too early to discuss the project, you should consciously have that in mind as you start your varsity career. At present I have some good friends both in England and the USA who have powerful contacts.

Maki graduated from Fort Hare and took on a job as a social worker. Her father wasn't content:

I must point out how disappointed I am to hear that you will not be studying this year. I have discussed this whole question with you as carefully as I could and I am sorry to discover that despite all my efforts and in spite of all your promises you have chosen to condemn yourself to the status of an exploited and miserable social worker of moderate academic qualifications who sadly lacks the ambition and drive that motivate the more serious-minded youth of today. Many of your mates of the fifties are now doing senior degrees – MA's and even doctorates at overseas universities while you remain shut up in a backveld and unable to give meaningful assistance to the people you would so very much like to help.

Again you have not told me whether you ever contacted Aunt Fatima as I requested you or thanked Aunts Helen or Amina for all the help they gave you. Please let me know.

31 January 1983

Her father's cajoling did not fall on deaf ears. Maki contacted 'Aunt Fatima', went to live with her and Uncle Ismail in Durban, and enrolled at the University of Natal. She completed her Honours in Sociology and won a Fulbright Scholarship to the United States. Remarried, she is now living with her husband and three children in Massachusetts and completing her doctoral programme.

## ZENI AND ZINDZI

Zeni and Zindzi were born during the most difficult years of the Mandelas, at the height of Nelson's political activities during 1959–60. Zeni was born prematurely; her mother had to be urgently moved into hospital at 1.30 a.m. on 4 February. Nelson was not present when she was born, though he arrived some hours afterwards. When Zindzi was born a year later, Nelson was away from Johannesburg and only saw her two days later, in the midst of a full-blast police raid on his house. Zindzi was to say in later life, 'I felt I was more or less raised by the police.' Winnie was in full-time employment as a social worker with the Child Welfare Society and had to return to work soon after Zindzi's birth. By the time the infants were toddling, both parents had been banned and their father imprisoned. Neither of the girls had any recollection of their father and virtually met him for the first time when they turned sixteen. The experience was at once awesome yet charming.

When they were still at a pre-school age, and Winnie's life was in jeopardy, Ama Naidoo (whose father-in-law had worked closely with Gandhi and whose son, Indres, would serve a long prison sentence on Robben Island, and whose daughter, Shanthi, would go to prison rather than testify for the State against Winnie) took them over and enrolled them at the Coloured school in Rockie Street. The girls were

376

happy there and doing well, 'But,' says Winnie, 'the terrorizer of the Indian community, Van Tonder, bent on ensuring the racial purity of the Group Areas cast out any African children from the Indian area. Van Tonder's terror eventually unnerved even himself. I hear that he eventually tried to redeem himself by marrying an Indian woman and converting to Islam.' The girls were forced to leave school just before the end of their school year there. Winnie then enrolled them at Our Lady of Sorrows convent school in Swaziland. Later Sir Robert and Lady Birley took over their school education and they went to the Waterford, also in Swaziland.

When Zeni was nine and Zindzi seven, their mother was imprisoned for a year and a half. They grew close to Peter Magubane and their Aunt Nonyaniso, then they too were imprisoned. No one remained in their home and the girls were obliged to live with friends during their school holidays. They were rarely happy with the arrangements and often complained or became the targets of their benefactors' complaints. So they grew into adolescence.

In 1974, when Zindzi was thirteen and Zeni fifteen, Winnie was sentenced to six months' imprisonment. Zeni, coaxed into speaking by the media, was reported as saying: 'We wept, but we tried not to show any grief. Mummy has been through hard times. To us she has been a wonderful mother. Now we are old enough to share her sorrow and grief with her. We have many friends.'

When their mother was not in prison, she was subjected to repeated arrest. The house was continually invaded by police and exposed to attack from reactionary fanatics. The home atmosphere was so bad in January 1973 that Zindzi appealed to the Special Committee on Apartheid to urge the South African Government to provide them with security: 'The family and mummy's friends fear that an atmosphere is being built for something terrible to happen to Mum. As you know, my mother has been a victim of several attacks and we believe that these attacks are politically motivated.'

Zindzi still lives with her mother and has shared some of her most harrowing moments. The bond between mother and daughter is particularly strong. Zindzi's two young children and her boy, named Gaddafi, also live with Winnie.

In 1974, following the parcel-bomb death of Kgopotse Tiro of the South African Students Organization, there were suspicions that the Mandela girls, then at school at Waterford, would be next on the list. The girls lived in fear after their Orlando home had been attacked.

With both parents in prison, they suffered extreme insecurity. They had to rely on friends and on their guardian, Dr Nthato Motlana, to take them to school in Swaziland. Conscious of their double deprivation, and that he had not been at home for almost the whole of their lives, made Nelson even more concerned about his younger daughters than he was about his older children, who at least had their mother. He was aware too, particularly due to their exposure at Waterford to wealthy children, that their expectations were beyond his means. He wrote to a friend in 1974: 'Judging from the girls' letters, travelling to Europe and America has become quite a craze at their school. Now and again, in discussing matters of this nature, I am tempted to remind them that they are my children, a fact that may place insurmountable difficulties in their path. But hard reality does not often coincide with the people's wishes, especially when these people are children.'

## ZENI

Zeni is an open-natured, graceful young woman who has integrated well into the Swazi Royal Family since her marriage in 1977 to Prince Thumbumuzi, a son of King Sobhuza. Their marriage interrupted her studies at high school. Neither Nelson nor Winnie was at first in favour of the marriage; they believed that Zeni was much too young. They wanted her, above all, to complete high school and gain at least a first degree before settling down to marriage. The disappointment was expressed in a letter to Zindzi, dated 4 September 1977: 'You should have seen just how pitiful your mother looked when Zeni came to tell me about Muzi. I would not like to see that frightful sight again. You are the last straw to which she now clings and her happiness now is very much in your hands. Priority Number 1, I repeat priority number 1, is your studies.'

Zeni had three children in quick succession. Nelson's letters to her express his fears that she might so settle into complacent domesticity as to spurn all opportunities to develop her own individual attributes. He continues to urge her to complete her matric and to go to university. He counsels her on her figure and on spacing her children judiciously. He is generally proud of her and happy that her marriage has worked out so well. His letters express his delight with his grandchildren, chastisement for not being more regular in her letters to him, and constant urging that she resumes her studies. He arranged scholarships for both Zeni and her husband, and the couple are now studying in the United States.

Mavelengekacingi is a beautiful well-thought out name. Mum and I would love to see it on the birth certificate. Failure to include it would deeply hurt your in-laws and you and Muzi should avoid that at all costs. Please, darling, consider the matter carefully and let us know what you decided. We will not feel happy until you assure us that you have accepted the name and the birth certificate accordingly amended by adding it to that of Zaziwe.

30 October 1977

I was also worried about the arrangement for Zeni's confinement, and I was relieved when you told me about the arrival of Zuzeka Zanele. I have written to Zeni congratulating her and welcoming the new Mzukulu.

1 July 1979

I want you to know the old hope we have been discussing since 1977 – education. I hope you will leave for the USA as soon as Zazi is old enough to feed on a bottle. I am getting really disturbed by all these delays. This is the third year in which you have been out of school and Mum and I will be terribly disappointed if for any reason you do not leave for the USA before next June. I have already asked her to contact some of our friends there to make arrangements should it be necessary for you to leave without Muzi. It would be tragic if Mum has neglected that request.

TO WINNIE

I am surprised at Zeni's lack of ambition and finesse. She is gambling away her entire future. Without proper academic qualifications they cannot be quite secure in any position they now hold. The Swazis like all other people of Africa have discovered the value of education. They are trying to give their children the best opportunities within their means. Though she may appear secure and happy today, time will soon leave its marks on her, and the affections that now seem so strong may gradually wear out and even loosen. Zeni will be lacking in imagination and foresight if she allows herself to be reduced into the position of an outsider who is deficient in so crucial an aspect. I hesitate to suggest that they should at least study privately. I do not think they would have the real drive to do so. They may just seize the opportunity and use our advice as a sort of defence to any further pressure you may still use. You know the other fears I have about the reluctance to go abroad. These may occur sooner than we expect. I hope Zindzi will carry out my request and have a confidential chat with her sister on the whole question.

26 September 1979

I hope the telegram in which I congratulated you on the arrival of Zuzeka Zanele reached you in time. Every sentence and every word in this letter has been inspired by the pride and joy of being two times a grandpa. I am looking forward to seeing Zuzi as soon as it will be safe for her to fly down and sail across the waters of the Atlantic. I hope Zazi will love the baby as a sister and future playmate who will complement her life in many ways.

Mum's telegram came when I was just on the point of writing to suggest that this time the honour of naming the baby should be reserved for the Swazis. They may be easily offended if we ignore them in such matters. The only redeeming feature is that the baby is a girl. If it were a boy they would probably have insisted on exercising their prerogative. Maybe the next time you will be luckier than Mum and that your third child will be a boy. I can well imagine the security and excitement the birth of a son will bring. I sometimes expect that the expression of concern and uncertainty on the part of Mum may be partly due to my absence from home and partly to the events that overtook us before we had a son. The thought of you and Zindzi married and away, leaving her alone without anybody to look after her in her old age is eating deep into her soul. But I hope that the eagerness to get a son will not obsess you. Relax completely in regard to things beyond your control and do not allow them to interfere with your happiness. You must plan the birth of your next one a little better, during the holidays. Have the Swazis seen the baby?

26 March 1979

Nomadabi [Zeni] seems to be maturing well and I enjoyed the conversation with her a fortnight ago. I wished I could talk to her confidentially on a number of topics. In her last letter she tells me that she and Muzi are planning to write a history of the Dlamini House and to present a balanced picture of the Royal House. Such a desire on their part is of course understandable. The Swazi Royal House is one of the most famous families in Southern Africa and the popularity of the father-in-law highlights the fame. But if they must tackle such a project they must prepare themselves thoroughly academically and otherwise. Although I did not discuss the matter with her, the matter is, in the light of modern trends of thought, a particularly sensitive one, requiring careful handling. I would certainly prefer Nomadabi to enter the book market with a less controversial subject.

29 July 1979

TO WINNIE

It disturbed me very much to learn of Zeni's operation. I do not know, Mhlope, how to persuade Zeni to get used to the pen. What you have told me about the operation are details that I ought to have got directly from herself and I find her silence to be equally disturbing. I do not even know whether or not that silence is due to her illness. I am trying hard to get used to her rather casual approach towards correspondence. Her indifference contrasts so strongly with your promptness and with that of Zindzi and it will take me a lifetime to accept the fact that I must accept less from one darling child in this respect.

1 June 1980

Did you send Fatima and Ayesha [Dr Ayesha Arnold, with whom the family stayed for many years when visiting Cape Town] some Swazi national dresses as I once suggested? You have not acknowledged receipt of your birthday letter-card. Few children find it easy to write to parents and failure to do so on their part is not anything so serious. But the habit of attending to small things and of appreciating small courtesies is one of the important marks of a good person.

1 August 1978

TO WINNIE

I was taken aback when you told me that Zeni and Muzi had not left after all. She has now wasted three years which may, in the long run, bring further complications. I hope you are discussing the matter with her and that she will leave soon after she has confined.

27 February 1979

Although Mum tells me you have been writing regularly I have received no letters at all from you since April and nothing whatsoever, absolutely nothing, can make up for the emptiness within me caused by my longing for you and your letters. I am confident I will see you soon, but the months that have passed since we last met seem like a lifetime. The only thing that comforts me are Mum's reports that she is in touch with you, even if by telephone only. I wonder just how you spend your free time, what you are reading, and whether you find time for physical exercises. Whatever you do darling, please do not neglect your health. Both Mum and Dad are natural heavyweighters, a characteristic which has both its advantages and disadvantages. A tall person can be quite impressive if he/she has an athletic figure and be repulsive if burdened by too much weight. The best way to keep yourself fit is to have regular physical exercises and by playing for a definite club, say hockey, basketball, tennis, provided your in-laws have no objection.

30 October 1977

I sent Zeni the two volumes of *War and Peace* by Tolstoy plus a box of chocolates. These were preceded by a 21st birthday card with a beautiful picture of a horse's head on the outside cover. Today I wrote her another letter wishing her well after her last operation and stressing to her the importance of physical exercise, especially regular running, that will certainly improve her breathing mechanism. It is such exercises that contributed to the clearing of my own sinus ... She must refrain from using nose drops.

10 February 1980

## ZINDZI

While Zeni settled down to a happy married life and also
fulfilled her father's desire that she study, Zindzi has
remained with her mother and is very close to her. When
Nelson saw her for the first time since he had left her as a
toddler, he wrote to a friend on 1 January 1976: 'I had a
lovely time on 27 December with Zeni and Zindzi. I was
seeing Zeni for the third time and the youngest for the first
time since 1962. She has a lot of fire in her and I hope she
will exploit it fully.'

Zindzi is by far the most articulate and well known of
Nelson's four surviving children. She has unusual talents and
published an anthology of poems at the age of fifteen. But
this is the only occasion when she shared her hidden spark
with the world. She has since been overwhelmed by too
many problems, both hers and her mother's with whom she
identifies deeply. There is little doubt that she has been the
most affected by the ordeals of her parents, and the continuing traumas inflicted on the family have left their scars. She
has ceased to write and says, 'It has dried up.' With the two
elder daughters studying in the United States, she is the one,
apart from Winnie, who keeps in closest touch with her
father. She invariably accompanies her mother on her visits,
apart from making her own. During the year she spent at the
University of Cape Town she saw him quite often.

Nelson's relations with his two elder daughters tend to be
patriarchal but with Zindzi he tends to be more of a confi-
dante and friend.

My Darling, 23 December! How do you celebrate your 17th birthday so far away from home and from where you have spent 16
years of your life, from relatives and friends, from those who love
you and would have brought you beautiful presents and even
invited you into their homes or taken you out. How does poor
Mum show her love to our last-born in a strange place where she
has no income, where she faces numerous problems? For the first
time in your life, 23 December will find you without your beloved
sister Zeni, and far away from your brother Makgatho, from

Rennie and Mandla. In such circumstances is it at all correct to talk of a birthday?

30 October 1977

I still remember when I saw you on 21/10/79. You were really striking in your pantaloons and every fabric in your garments seemed to be crying out for attention, urging all round to take note that this young lady across the partition is Mantu. The impact of your visit on 23/12 is still fresh in my mind. It is a significant gesture for a young lady to spend her nineteenth birthday crossing and recrossing the polluted waters of the Atlantic. Your visits calm the nostalgic feeling that inevitably wells up when I think of how you and I used to play at home and in the other dens in which I used to live. As usual you left me in a tremendous mood. I will always treasure the memory of that visit.

## Zindzi's Literary Talents

Zindzi's writing abilities pleased Nelson.

I'm also pleased to learn that you're a *True Love* columnist and that you have already received your first cheque. That's no small achievement at your age and it is very nice of J.B. to give you such a challenging opportunity. Writing is a prestigious profession which puts one right into the centre of the world and to remain on top, one has to work really hard, the aim being a good and original theme, simplicity in expression and the use of the irreplaceable word. In this regard, you have many able friends who could help you. Benjie is one of them. From your poem which is full of much promise, you have the makings of a professional in this field.

4 September 1977

He proved correct, for two years later, when she was fifteen, she published her first anthology of poems in the United States. He longed to see them but was not allowed to do so for some time. Meanwhile he read reviews of the anthology.

TO WINNIE

Zindzi's anthology has not been received but I was allowed to read, but not make notes of, Dr Paton's article in *Fair Lady* (31/1/79). It

384

is a powerful review written by one whose main purpose was not to introduce Zindzi to the readers of that magazine but to inspire her 'to make joy great and sorrow small'. For that he certainly deserves our thanks.

I am still struggling to get your anthology. I have already told you that I was allowed to read, but not to take notes, from Dr Alan Paton's review of your poetry. I thought your themes were well chosen and your language simple and crisp, so much so that I can still see the black bird insulting the wall, giving you its back and flying off gracefully at an awkward angle; the black beauty 'who reminds me of who I am' I can still see the two hands, the impossibility of having them in one pocket for 'that would be too uncomfortable'. Hope and expectation well up as you call 'come tomorrow, I eagerly await you ...' Nevertheless, Darling, Dr Paton makes a good point when he advises you to go over your poems carefully. Raw feelings will be refined and the rough edges will be polished, putting down words on paper will become an art. As Ernst Fischer says in *The Necessity of Art* the artist is not mauled by the beast, he tames it. But Mantu, neither Dr Paton's remarks nor mine should be taken as a criticism. They are merely a tip to a girl we both love and respect.

*Black as I am* turned out to be something quite different from what I had expected. You will no doubt realize the permanent impact good literature can make. Remember that Homer wrote about 1200 BC and yet his works still appeal to this day. But this is an aspect which need not at all worry you. All things considered you have done more than I expected. What Kenneth Roscroft has said about your poetry sums up my own view remarkably well. Your pen is as talkative as our darling Mantu. But the ideas reveal a depth that should be reserved for older hands.

27 January 1980

I don't know to what extent you and Mum were in actual control of the joint project. The arrangement of the outside cover, the precedence of the biographical notes and the contents of each note gave the impression that you were both on the sidelines. I was also not aware that the same firm that published *Black as I am* was given the right to bring out *Black and Fourteen*. I wish you had consulted me first and fully about the matter, because I would have discussed the matter with you and Mum and advised differently.

Good use of photography can give even poverty with all its rags, filth and vermin a measure of divineness rarely noticeable in real life. The old man on page twenty-nine looks really strong and majestic. I find it difficult to forget his calm and confident bearing. The weeping lady on page forty-eight looks like our neighbour, Mrs Mtimkulu. The only difference is that she looks younger than our neighbour should be now.

TO WINNIE:

I laughed and laughed when I heard about Zindzi and FH [Fort Hare]. I realize that more than ever before just how deep-seated the environment in which they were schooled – Rockie Street, Kliptown and then Waterford. It is a real pity that she is losing another year, but I fully understand the reasons, emotional and otherwise, behind her protest and return from FH. Zindzi is a poet and capable of grasping deep meanings with ease. All the same Zindzi's work would serve wider issues and its main aim should not be commercial or desire for publicity.

6 August 1979

Anticipating Zeni's Swazi wedding and knowing the Swazi custom of young women dancing bare breasted, Nelson wrote to his Zindzi:

Talking about the wedding, I feel confident that you'll do nothing that might embarrass your sister and Muzi. The beauty of a woman lies as much in her face as in her body. Your breasts should be as hard as apples and as dangerous as cannons. You can proudly and honourably display them when occasion demands. In our days it was a common sight to see unmarried women move around with nothing else on their bodies except a 'mini mbaco'. I think it was the famous ballerina, Duncan, who first introduced the modern ballet scanty outfit. She astonished her audience by tearing her clumsy and conservative costume during a performance. With part of her body exposed she yelled, at the same time pointing to that part, 'This is the beauty of a woman!'

I badly miss you and hope to see you this month. I've become so selfish, that I find it quite difficult to suppress the temptation of arranging for you to do your first degree in Cape Town when I'd see you monthly. Life would have been ideal, in spite of everything, if I could put you, Zazi, Zeni and Mum into my shirt pocket so that you could press against my heart. Perhaps the longing that has been eating me up for years would lessen considerably and I might even feel younger. Also I could peep into that pocket when hard times knocked at my door. The hope that I will see you soon, that I will get a nice letter from you, that perhaps I will be with you for days, weeks and months on end fills my life with expectation and optimism. Meantime, lots and lots of love and a million kisses to you, Mum, Zeni and Zazi. Affectionately, Tata.

5 March 1978

## Zindzi's Education

It was real pleasure for me to get some details as to what you're now doing in connection with your 'talents'. Your subjects should be quite interesting. I have forgotten all the history I ever knew and my memory of the Stuart and Tudor periods is very hazy. All that now stands out in my mind is the film *Mary, Queen of Scots* in which Vanessa Redgrave played the role of Queen Elizabeth. That period is not only important for England but for the entire world, since it marks the end of feudalism and the beginning of the contemporary era of capitalism.

I don't know what text book you are using on the Cold War and I should certainly like to be told. But the Cold War is the product of two conflicting systems of society – socialism and capitalism – which are competing today in practically every field. But with more contact between the two systems throughout the world and in which they are forced to handle common problems jointly, to co-operate in the space field and the love of peace by the people of the world, the Cold War is now melting away. Finally, darling, I must tell you that I miss you badly for I always enjoy your letters and, of course, I love you very much and get worried whenever you remain quiet for a long time. With lots and lots of love and a million kisses. Affectionately, Tata.

10 July 1978

TO WINNIE

I have written to Zindzi and also sent her a telegram of good wishes. If nothing disturbs her, she should pull through and we should see her in Cambridge or Wits next year.

27 May 1979

I hope Zindzi, whatever else she may be doing, will not neglect her studies. By all means she must pass the June exams and go to varsity next year. I do not know how children reason at times!

19 November 1979

I am waiting to hear from you whether you have finalized the question of Zindzi's studies. I am aware that you are as worried as I am over the question and you may even be annoyed by the pestering.

29 June 1983

I was also sorry to hear that Zindzi was not admitted at Wits. Whatever she is now doing, that can never be as good as advancing her academic education. That means that she will also lose three years, something we cannot afford.

27 February 1979

In regard to your interview with Professor Dugard, you should not at all regret that he has recommended that you first complete your A levels before you enter varsity. This will prepare you more thoroughly for Cambridge and give you more confidence in your academic work. Very happy indeed to note that you are back at the school desk. Try and get your A levels out of the way as soon as possible and thereafter start with your varsity course. Meantime let me know the subjects you are doing. I hope Oupa will also take his studies seriously. From all that you have told me he seems to be a gifted child and with suitable academic qualifications, he should be quite precious. Have you given up your music lessons? Please don't, if your otherwise heavy programme allows you.

5 March 1978

Oupa Seakamena became a strong family support and both Mandelas came to love him as a son. Zindzi and he became lovers but the relationship cooled and the couple parted. The following extracts express Nelson's welcome to the young man and then his disappointment at the parting.

Our dear Oupa, Zindzi, Zeni and their Mum are full of warm praise for you and have told me how you are helping at home in various ways and that now the shack looks somewhat tolerable with nice fittings which you made and a garden with trees. They have lived under frightful strains during my absence and it is much safer to have someone like you around most of the time. I am happy to be told that your dad and mum have approved of the

388

arrangement. I am also pleased to know that you have now resumed your studies even if by correspondence.

23 April 1978

Though I last saw you only fifty-seven days ago, I miss you very much and my mind frequently wanders between the OFS and Transvaal, between Brandfort and Norwood. I see you yapping with Mum and Oupa and Granny, gossiping about this and that, asking this and that question, listening to the radio, looking at TV in the evening and suddenly grabbing pen and paper as some new idea strikes you, as some inspiration feeds your thoughts and feelings. I say yapping, not yelping, because my old girl and granny are too peaceful to make you cry.

9 September 1979

TO WINNIE

Oupa, 'the dream of an otherwise wonderful boy', who has considerably endeared himself to us and who we once hoped would be a permanent member of the family. I am just as sorry about the whole affair as you are, but we must also respect Zindzi's feelings and views and avoid everything which may suggest that we are forcing her into a relationship she no longer wants. Let us accept the situation and forget altogether about this particular dream.

29 June 1983

By the end of 1979, Brandfort, close police observation and the fact that her mother was persecuted even on account of the friends who came to visit her proved too much for Zindzi and she returned to their Orlando home. Nelson wrote to Winnie:

I am also disturbed by the fact that Zindzi now lives alone at home. As you know I have complete confidence in her and I fully appreciate her desire to be back where she spent but two years of her life. But she is just too young to live alone or with just Nomfundo [Nelson's niece]. Let Niki [Nelson's sister-in-law] and Marsh [Nelson's brother-in-law] try to get some elderly Aunt to live with her if possible.

10 February 1980

I am equally unhappy about the position of Zindzi, even though I know you are doing your utmost best to solve the problem. We cannot stop the child from insisting on staying at her home, the place where she, her sister and her Mum spent some of the happiest days of their lives, pleasures which were sweet, despite all the harsh experiences that you went through. Home, ever ours, is a home-sweet-home and Zindzi's determination to live there is something natural, to be admired and encouraged. Yet common sense and experience demands that she should never live alone or with just some old couple living in the back yard. She needs a mother who can be at her side twenty-four hours a day who will try and make her life full and happy. Any couple that Niki or Nthato [Dr Motlano] may get will not last long because of calculated harass-ment as the young Makgatho and many others found out.

1 June 1980

Zindzi, who up until recently has been such a good correspondent seems to have burnt herself up. If waiting to see her results is such a torture to me, I wonder how she feels.

1 June 1980

Sensitive to the fact that Zindzi was undergoing spells of depression, he wrote to encourage her and to rekindle her self-esteem.

My darling, Moodiness is but a common condition that affects many people. In your case it is quite understandable. For you, Zeni and Mum it has been an uphill struggle for more than a decade and a half. After so many years it does not seem that real relief is in sight.

3 February 1979

I have reminded you before now, and I do so again, that you are one of the luckiest girls in the country. You have the whole world at your feet if you make proper use of your opportunities. You have ripened before your time and already you have made achieve-ments which are a source of real pride and happiness not only to the family and relatives, but to friends and members of the public who have never met you. You have a lovely personality and people take easily to you. Your picture on my book case between that of Mum and Zeni reflects your personality very well. You look alert, full of go and relaxed; at peace with yourself and the world. If you consciously remember this, moments of depression will be at a mini-mum.

What you have every reason to do is to be angry with the fates for the setbacks you may have suffered from time to time, to vow that you will turn those misfortunes into victory. There are few misfortunes in this world that you cannot turn into a personal triumph if you have the iron will and the necessary skill. You have both darling, and if you give them a chance to develop, you will score even more successes. 'Count your blessings one by one' and your system will be immune against all forms of depression.

When I say to you, in confidence, and as a father advising a beloved daughter facing unusual problems, that your inquisitive mind, relaxed disposition, lovely sense of humour, ability to make friends, extra-mural activities, all put you in a position to conquer new worlds and to fulfil even your wildest dreams. That is our Zindzi! That's the reason why the family, relatives and our friends have so much confidence in you. We love you very deeply, darling, and Dr Farb's [a local physician] solemn views are a real tonic to me.

Your stimulating poem, your letters to me, even the revenge cards, above all the numerous friends you now have and which make even Brandfort a nice place, after all, go to confirm much of Dr Farb's sober views. I never had the slightest doubts about your sound health. You make a wonderful impression to me whenever I see you and in all your letters to me. Love and kisses to you and mum and my very best regards to all your friends. Affectionately, Tata.

25 March 1979

# Friends

Nelson, above all, is concerned about the education of his children and grandchildren. When he reached out to friends for help, it was nearly always with regard to their education. He felt that he owed each child and grandchild a good education and that his imprisonment had deprived them of that right. So he asked those who expressed their love and admiration and sympathy, and whom he knew he could count on. Among them were Helen Joseph, the Cachalias, the Meers, Benjamin Pogrund, Alan Paton and Peter Brown. From overseas Sir Robert Birley undertook the education of Zindzi and Zeni. David Astor and Mary Benson have always been helpful.

He was and continues to be grateful to them and expresses thanks in his letters.

Wahali Fatimabehn. Even if you had not sent that marvellous telegram of 14/10, I would have been quite sure that you and Ismail would take care of the girls, that they would not be orphans as long as you were alive, that in Zanyiwe's absence there would be someone to whom they could turn when problems arise, someone conversant with our background, outlook, aspirations and dreams, one should add even our shortcomings.

1 November 1974


**Friends in Exile**

Zeni is doing a good job when she goes abroad. Her contact with Adie, Paul and Zoya arouses fond memories which form an important part of our life. I cannot help imagining just how different life would be if it was possible to write an unlimited number of letters to family and friends and to reach all those whose friendship and love give us so much strength and hope.

## TO ZINDZI

Tell Dr Abdulla that I have not forgotten him and that a few years back the publication *Alpha* even contained pictures of his new mansion. I was only sorry that his own picture and that of his family were not included. I was friendly with his children and used to shadow-box with them as I waited our turn to be examined.

5 March 1978

## TO WINNIE RE HATTINGH

With regard to Susan [Chris Hattingh's sister] I will send her a message of good wishes for her exams. That will be my contribution to your efforts to help her out of the shock of her brother's unfortunate death. But please do not mention the matter to her. I want the card to come as a surprise. I hope you immediately contacted David Astor and Gwen to arrange an overseas scholarship for a senior degree for her.

26 September 1979

Matlala and friends have sent you some cash for a car and I sincerely hope that our Johannesburg dealer will provide you with a reliable new wagon. My love and respect for our friends inside and outside the country has deepened considerably. I always shudder to think just what would have happened if we were all alone. We would have survived but the task would have been far more difficult. I have already informed the Head of Prison about Matlala's forthcoming letters. But I repeated my earlier promise not to write to her again.

1 March 1981

I think a lot about our friends, especially those who try to be of some help to you and the children. They are countless and I am grateful to all of them. I was heartened by the warm manner in which they responded after 15/5/1977. That response helped us to get through it all. What I had never expected was the fact that you could win friends from both sides of the colour line in that Province. Thinking about it now, I should have known that there would be people like Drs Moroka and Stofile, Molefe Litheko and the youth who soon streamed to the shack. But I must confess that

393

I never imagined that you could be helped by people like De Waals, Van Aswegens and the late Chris Hattingh. The very fact that Chris offered you a job and waited so long while you negotiated for the relaxation of your restriction order was significant.

19 November 1979

You will probably like to tell Ismail or Zamila about an article on leukemia in the *Huisgenoot* of 28/6 entitled 'Hope for Children'. It describes the work of St Jude's Hospital for Children in Memphis, USA. According to the article, since 1962, hundreds of children with leukemia from various parts of the world have already been treated free of charge. Hotel accommodation for parents is also free. I don't know whether they are aware of this institution, but no harm can be done by mentioning the matter to them. Please give them and the children our best regards. I sincerely hope that the child's heath will improve.

29 July 1979

TO ZINDZI

I will certainly not comment here on the very special memories the Johannesburg Amina arouses in me, except to say what you already know, that is, she always reminds me of an unforgettable chapter in our lives. I am writing to thank her for spending so many precious moments with you at the clinic. The Cape Town Amina appears to be an equally wonderful person and I suspect that a lot of talent and humanism lie buried behind her hubby's bushy face. Perhaps next time you visit Cape Town you will take a photo together with Peggy Delport and the Prof and his wife, so that I can at least have the pleasure of seeing them. It was a fine gesture for Mum to visit you and to drive you here on your recent visit. I will also like to see her paintings of the family when she completes the work.

29 June 1983

# Kinsfolk

The politics of the Transkei, the intrigues within the Madiba clan that destroyed unity, weakened those whom Nelson supported and strengthened those who collaborated, were matters of deep concern and even from his prison Nelson exercised whatever influence he could to the tribesmen who came for advice.

Paramount Chief Sabata, the nephew of his benefactor Jongintaba, the great-grandson of Ngangelizwe, who had collaborated with the British, had bravely and honourably rejected the conversion of the Transkei into a homeland. K. D. Matanzima, whose great-grandfather had refused to sell out to the British, and thus became a famous man in Thembuland, collaborated with the Government, deposed a people's hero, Sabata, and forced him into exile where he died.

In a letter written just when the conflict between Sabata and Matanzima came to a head, when Sabata, faced with the invasion of the Thembu palace by fifty police, and fearing for his life, fled the country, Nelson wrote:

I wish you could immediately phone and warn Jongilanga [Sabata] and family. He has an unfortunate manner of being slow and negligent in matters where he should act quickly. He should long have been here so that we could talk matters over. If he had given me that opportunity I would have advised him on how to be effective without exposing himself. His position would probably have been stronger and safer, and few people would have dared to touch him. I cannot discuss such confidential matters through letters. But I have previously warned him against the danger of staying away when many people with whom he has difficulties are able to put their own side of the story to me. Naturally I will do everything possible to protect him, even when I thought he could have handled a particular problem differently and nobody will ever use it again. Even with his current problem I am fully behind him and at Port St Johns I will work hard to turn the tables against those who dragged him into the dock. But are you aware that up to now I don't even know precisely what remarks he is alleged to have made in Butterworth of the law that is quite unsatisfactory? Nxeko [late Thembu Regent] was here on 15/9 and I asked him to see Jongilanga at once.

With regard to other urgent family matters, I was happy to hear that you visited Jongilanga. I was sorry to learn about his illness. The visit must have cheered him. If we succeed in bringing together the parties, i.e., rival factions, you would also have to be present so that you would tie up the loose ends in my absence. By the way I found it quite strange that you saw Mafungwashe [Matanzima's senior wife] at Qawukeni because I was also thinking about the matter only a few weeks back. It pleased me to note that you were well received.

Our dear Sisi [a cousin]
Our families are far larger than those of whites and it's always pure pleasure to be fully accepted throughout a village, district or even several districts occupied by your clan as a beloved household member, where you can call at any time, completely relax, sleep at ease and freely take part in the discussion of all problems, where you can even be given livestock and land to build free of charge.

As you know I was barely ten when our father died, having lost all his wealth. Mother could neither read nor write and had no means to send me to school. Yet a member of our clan educated me from elementary school right up to Fort Hare and never expected any refund. According to our custom I was his child and his responsibility. I have a lot of praise for this institution, not only because it's part of me, but also due to its usefulness. It caters for all those who are descended from one ancestor and holds them together as one family.

It's an institution that arose and developed in the countryside and functions only in that area. The flocking of people to the cities, mines and farms makes it difficult for the institution to function as in the old days. You and Winnie are up there whilst Leabie, Maki and the grandchildren live across the Kei. Can you imagine how I must have felt at Xmas and New Year when I could not send you, of all people, the compliments of the season? You, who is not only our sister, but a loyal friend whom Winnie and I love and admire, even though the two of you are always locked up in all sorts of nonsensical rows that you both blow up. I certainly will not again waste my time by trying to make peace between two big women who should know better than they seem to be at present. I had expected that both of you would spare me the countless headaches you had brought on me.

But the real aim of this letter is to let you know that you are still as dear to me and Winnie as the unforgettable day when you accompanied us across the courtyard at Bizana almost twenty years ago now. I have said it before, I repeat it here, that I miss the rice with seedless raisins you served to Winnie and me when we dined together shortly after our return from Pondoland. We think of you and pray that you may be blessed with sound health and that you may live even longer than the Old Lady did. It is against this background that, with all my heart, I wish you, the children, grand and great-grandchildren a Merry Xmas and a bright and happy New Year.

One of my fondest wishes these last fourteen years has been to be with you again, listen to your humorous stories, hear you make your many vows and then break them repeatedly. Do you still remember telling us that you'll never eat potatoes again? Also I have attended many services when I knew you would be asked to pray. When divine words come from you, they are realistic, simple and inspiring. But there have been times when you reminded me of Nongqawuse. When you prophesied that Sekwati would soon rise as Christ did. I still remember when you were at Twist Street and the Pretoria Temple when Libhebheke [Prosecutor Liebenberg] and Vanikeke [Prosecutor van Niekerk] reminded you of those un-fulfilled promises.

Perhaps that had its advantage as it may have sobered you up and made the daily experiences of believer and non-believer the subject of your prayers even more than ever before. I was, of course, baptized in the Wesleyan Church and went to its missionary schools. Outside and here I remain a staunch member, but one's Church outlook tends to broaden to such an extent as to welcome efforts towards denominational unity. I have listened to sermons by priests of several denominations here – Anglicans, Dutch Re-formed, Hindus, Methodists, Moravians, Presbyterians, Moslems and Roman Catholics. Most of them are eloquent and experienced men and some of their sermons have been memorable. I'm strongly in favour of a move towards the merger of all South African churches, so long as the doctrine of the new church is progressive and moves away from the rigid and backward dogmas of olden times.

Finally, all people throughout the world have, at one time or another, had clans and some clans were certainly mightier and better known in history than ours. But to you, Winnie and me, ours is the whole world, our umbrella, the source of all our strength and efforts; the navel that links us together as a family, that binds you and me, Sisi. I have not seen you for a long time, but this letter is a reunion and calls to mind all the lovely moments we spent together in the past. Winnie shares all these sentiments. I believe you have become rheumatic and that it is difficult for you to write. Dictate the reply to the children. Once again, a Merry Xmas and Happy New Year!

Very sincerely, Your Buti

# House and Land

━━━━━━━

Nelson's attachment to property is sentimental rather than material and this is reflected in his attitude to his Orlando home and to land at his birthplace Qunu.


## HOUSE

With regard to the so-called ownership scheme our main difficulty is that we are not in occupation and consequently do not qualify. When your man is 1,000 miles away, and if the expectation was that you would not have the constitution nor the guts to stick it out so long at Brandfort, then we cannot expect to share in such schemes. If we could, I would certainly have suggested that we take the ninety-nine year lease and a bond to put up a better house.

The house itself was originally a municipal one, and like all other municipal houses, the plan was drawn up by their own draughtsmen. The outbuilding was built, if I remember correctly, by Mr Molefe, Ma Dlomo's late husband. The garage, as you know, by my gym mate, Peter, who is probably now back at his home in Bloemfontein and our friend, Japan, from O. East. In both cases the plan was drawn by the builders and approved by the superintendent, Mr Griffiths.

1 July 1979


## LAND

Have you negotiated with Jongilanga or Nomoscow [a kinsman] about the site at the upper end of Xami's residence? That place may already be occupied, but it was my desire to spend my last days there.

27 March 1977

I wrote two letters to the Magistrate of Umtata, asking for the transfer of the residential and garden lots at Qunu. I also sent the required affidavit to Sabata who was handling the matter. I also paid all the rates up to and including the year 1977. But up to now I have received no acknowledgement or reply from that official. Perhaps you may discuss the matter with Sabata with the suggestion that somebody else, like Mlahleni, should now handle it if Sabata has no objection.

10 February 1980

# Brandfort

Nelson's response to the Brandfort sojourn are recorded in extracts from the letters that follow:

I have thought of you since I heard of the heavy snowfall in various parts of the country. A few days before the cold spell reached the Island, I saw at last the picture of the spectacle in which you and the children were dumped. I fear that no fire can ever warm that ramshackle shack. With such an infirm structure and poor workmanship the cold must be seeping through the crevices and rickety walls with ease, keeping temperatures quite low inside. Not only do you need to protect yourself with warm clothing during the day and warm blankets at night but there must also be a bit of fat in your food to keep the body from freezing. These are things you cannot afford without an income. I hope the faith and miracles that kept you going all these years will keep you on your feet and well until we meet again. The cold weather, coming so soon after your illness, has made me anxious.

29 July 1979

I have no idea as to where Phathakahle is, in what district, and least of all the situation of 802. But my mind carries a vivid picture, imaginary, but nevertheless vivid, of that shack. Uppermost in that picture is the position of the bedroom. I think of you always and love you.

19 November 1979

Zindzi likes reading and it is a shame that you have a paraffin lamp. Do you remember the lamp we had before we had electricity? It is expensive but try to buy two of them for the house.

7 October 1977

It pleased me to know that people as far afield as Pietermaritzburg have visited you. Apparently Dr Biggs is a well known orthopaedic surgeon in that city and his wife and Mrs Corigall all familiar names in that province and beyond. Give them a big hug on my behalf when you meet them again.

2 September 1979

## TO ZINDZI

I really hope it will be possible for me to see you on the eve of your departure. I know how you will miss that miserable outpost which has been so hard on you. I have the hope and confidence, that, at least, it has given you the opportunity to sit down and take stock of your life during the fifteen years preceding your arrival there.

6 August 1979

Keeping in touch by telephone must be an extremely difficult task for you since you must inevitably rely on the public telephone. But who else can I burden with these requests. I can easily invoke the assistance of the old families, confident that they would eagerly respond. But you would probably have fits or suffocate with anger if I did so.

31 March 1983

Brandfort becoming a nice place! I can't believe it. Mum lost almost everything. She'll never get any job there except perhaps as a domestic or a farm-hand or washerwoman, and will spend all her days in poverty. She's described the sort of structure in which you must now live and the type of toilet and water facilities that you have to use. I fear to ask her the fortune she'll have to pay to make that place really fit to live in. You will never eat and dress as well as you did in J-B, nor will you be able to afford a TV set, see a decent film or go to a theatre or have a telephone.

Nevertheless, darling, I'm glad to note that you are adjusting yourself and trying to be happy all the same. I feel tenderness when I read the line 'A nice place after all'. As long as you have an iron will, darling, you can turn misfortune into advantage, as you yourself say. Were it not so, Mum would have been a complete wreck by now.

4 September 1977

## TO WINNIE

I would also like to know your estimate of the amount you spent to make the Brandfort shack habitable.

About the improvements at 802, including the expensive trees you planted, I am waiting for the information requested in my last letter before I can give you proper advice.

Meanwhile I should like you to give me some information about your employer, the names of his other employees if any, the nature of the work and the average number of people you have to attend to daily. Please think carefully about Cape Town.

27 February 1979

It is not easy to advise you on the question of the job at Welkom. It is the work you love most and in regard to which you have a lot of training and experience. It will keep you busy for the day and give you the pleasure of helping people in their numerous problems; something for which you have the natural ability. Of no less importance is the fact that the job will give you a regular income and guarantee you some measure of financial independence, all of which are of enormous importance.

I fully approve of your stand in regard to the suggestion or veiled hint that you should shift to Welkom. You were deported to that place and there you should remain. Even though Brandfort is no more than a farming village, you have found your feet there and paid heavily for doing so. I do not want you to start all over again, turning a cave into a habitation. Your arrival in Brandfort was followed by harrowing experiences.

27 January 1979

I have the feeling that contrary to what we had hoped – your removal from Brandfort would be done only after proper consultation with us – you may be deported again without further reference to us. In this regard I still support your original stand of refusing to go to any other place voluntarily other than Johannesburg. This is so even though I would have liked us to examine the question of us coming to live in Cape Town, as well as the problems relating to your departure from that world. Meantime I should like you to come down immediately so that we could at least consider the most urgent household matters.

6 May 1979

Speaking from the point of view of the family moving, Cape Town would be better if we can get a good job. Do you realize that I could see you twice a month and that you could forget completely about the old families? It would probably also be wonderful therapy for Zindzi and Oupa. You could all probably study at UCT. But I

403

do not think we could ever discuss that proposition under the conditions in which we have to see each other.

I should also endeavour to contact Helen in Cape Town to find out whether she can get you suitable work so that we could fruitfully consider the possibility – I stress the word possibility – of the family moving to the mother city.

19 November 1979

I am in full agreement with your refusal to shift to Welkom or any other place except Johannesburg. I have other reasons which worry me even more, about the mere fact of your being connected with that place, to say nothing of your living there. I do not think I can ever sanction that. It also worries me that you should be on the road for no less than 2.20 hours a day. From the mileage it would seem that you can make that time only if you step on the gas. Moreover, petrol and oil have become very expensive and taking into account the wear and tear as well, they will swallow up your small income.

27 February 1979

The sudden death of Chris shook me so badly as if he was a life-long friend. I should be pleased if you would kindly give his parents my deepest sympathy.

His tragic death on the very day you started work under him was a shattering blow to you, the children and me. Even before I got your letter of 20/2 I knew how keenly you looked forward to the 1/3. In spite of my great concern about your travelling such a long distance daily all alone, working for twelve hours a day and my opposition to your ever moving to Welkom, I felt that you should nevertheless try out for the three months stipulated. His death has destroyed all your hopes for a new and challenging experience in your stay in that world. I note that with Chris you would start work at 8h00 to 20h00. Even if you lived in Welkom, working twelve hours a day would have been a considerable strain. Add to that, travelling daily between Brandfort and Welkom for about 2–3 hours; that would tax the capacity of the toughest constitution and would make it difficult for you to continue your studies.

19 November 1979

I have been thinking about your study problems. The possibility that you may have to move to Klerksdorp disturbs me immensely and I advise against it. To rove around at this stage in your life is undesirable in spite of all the advantages it might have in regard to your study course. We have had so many nightmares in Johannesburg and Brandfort and I should like to avoid them at all costs. We were able to overcome them in the former place and we are only beginning to settle down in the latter. To move again to what are practically platteland areas where the police, superintendents, magistrates, have no experience at all in dealing with people like you and me will revive all the ugly problems we have experienced in the past seventeen years. Such a step may even prove more disastrous to Zindzi, who is adjusting to Brandfort despite the atmosphere of dislocation and isolation that surrounds it. It will expose Oupa to fresh onslaughts from which he should be spared. While I have no alternative to offer, I would suggest that we try to get an agency in Bloemfontein to which you could be attached . . . The head of the sociology department in University of the Orange Free State may have similar contacts and it may be useful to discuss the matter with him. The advantage of being allocated to a special agency in that city is that you can travel daily between it and Brandfort. That would save you all the problems entailed in moving to a new place. In the meantime I wish you all the luck, darling Mum.

25 November 1979

TO ZINDZI

I am happy, darling, that you're around to look after Mum. It was a real relief to see her emerge clean, erect and strong from all the problems she has had since last May. That was due mainly to your earnest love and inspiration. At forty-three, Mum is no longer young. At that age the average woman usually feels depressed when she sees her hair turning white and ugly wrinkles distorting her once pretty face. Children grow and become independent of her and it is easy for her to think that she's neglected by those who were once deeply attached to her. I'm very grateful to you for all that you're doing for her.

Are you studying now? I hope your trip has made you rich in experience and given you material for your second anthology. A million kisses and tons and tons of love. Affectionately, Tata.

# The World Celebrates
# the Mandelas

Winnie's banning order expired in September 1975 and thir-teen years of silence was broken. She was in a sense pulled back from the dead. Durban welcomed her on Sunday, 12 October, at a tumultuous rally which began at the airport where some 600 people waited, led by Dr Naicker, Bishop Manas Buthelezi, Fatima Meer, George Sithole, David Gasa and M. J. Naidoo. The authorities baulked and disrupted the arrangements by changing the passengers' entrance. The care-fully structured reception fell into disarray, the rank and file ran ahead of the 'leadership', someone swooped up Winnie and paraded her willy-nilly shoulder-high to the parking lot. Eventually she was brought to Dr Naicker and Bishop Manas Buthelezi and some fifty Zulu dancers joined in the formal welcome.

Her motorcade took a roundabout route through Umlazi and residents rushed out of their houses to see this Mandela. At last Winnie, dressed in the tribal robes of Xhosas, arrived at the packed hall of the YMCA, where over a thousand people had waited patiently to hear her speak.

Returning home on Monday following the meeting, a reporter, Farook Khan, drew Fatima Meer's attention to the Minister of Justice and Prisons, Jimmy Kruger, whose car had just pulled up outside the airport. Fatima eased Winnie towards the indicated car 'to have some fun and games'. The Minister, a short man in wide-rimmed spectacles, was at that point half buried in the boot of the car, withdrawing a suitcase. 'Mr Kruger, I don't think we have met. I am

Fatima Meer and this is Mrs Mandela.' The little man beamed at the two women and said he was pleased to meet them. Winnie asked, 'When are you releasing my husband?' 'That's up to you,' he said, wagging a finger. 'Listen to him,' Winnie guffawed. 'He says it's up to me. What have I got to do with my husband's release?' 'If you behave yourself,' the Minister said. 'Behave myself?' The two women laughed derisively and left the Minister to join their friends.

Winnie described her exciting time to Nelson and he wrote back:

I was even more happy to hear of your visit to Durban, about the presence of Ma Nokukhanya [Mrs Albert Luthuli], Monty [Dr G. M. Naicker] and others and hope that the experience made you forget about the host of problems that worry you. Moments of complete relaxation and happiness when you are in the hands of warm and devoted friends who are ready to offer you their love and give you that feeling of security and confidence, born of the knowledge that you are beyond the reach of the wicked and surrounded by countless men and women who think fondly of you, who could pull you out from the claws of the hyenas and jackals that have been prowling around the house for so many years, is always a memorable occasion and a tremendous inspiration not only to you but also to the children, the family and myself.'

One day you'll relate everything to me and my chief interest will be whether the details will fill in the gaps between the lines as the picture took form in my mind with your account and that of Fatima. Your closeness to Fatima made me assume that you had seen Ismail as often as Fatima. He's always been nice and humorous.

1 December 1975

To Fatima, who had couched the whole event in Hindu mythology and thereby escaped the intelligence of the censors, Nelson replied:

A good head and a good heart are always a formidable combination. But when you add to that a literate tongue or pen, then you've something very special and a simple story one has heard repeatedly suddenly evokes significant moral lessons. Interest me in mythology? I'd try even magic if only you recommended it. As for mythology, my interest in that particular field has a long history, my mother having fed me on it from the earliest days of my childhood. I'd plenty of it at college, but outside the lecture room mythology can be even more challenging and absorbing and that is why I've found your theme so particularly exhilarating.

An element of hindsight can't be completely eliminated in statements made after the happening of a relevant event. But I'd like you to know that since October 1974 I've missed a great deal and the idea of the goddess Zamona [reference to Winnie] descending into the third heaven repeatedly preoccupied me. This was then nothing more than a mere whim which came and passed like the winds and I attached no significance whatsoever to it. Only when I got your marvellous letter and that of Zami [Winnie] did the thought occur whether the whim was a premonition or not. Perhaps we ought not to pursue this point much further less we end up in the supernatural world.

Suffice it to say that this particular narrative, rendered with characteristic skill, has dispelled all the pessimism that might flow out of the belief that all sparks have been drained off the Vhoras, Kolas, Hadas and Biharas [references to the black peoples of South Africa – Indian, African, 'Coloured'] and that the evil spirits are invincible. The simple lesson of religions of all philosophies and of life itself is that, although evil may be on the rampage temporarily, the good must win the laurels in the end. Your story expresses this truth very well. I've always regarded the multiplicity of gods in Greek mythology as yet another manifestation of the widespread belief that the destiny of all natural and human affairs is in the hands of the divinities whose superhuman excellence is a source of inspiration and hope to all creation, an excellence which will ultimately rule the world.

We, who were brought up in religious homes, and who studied in missionary schools, experienced the acute spiritual conflict that occurred in us when we saw the way of life we considered sacred being challenged by new philosophies and when we realized that amongst those who dismissed our beliefs as opium were clear thinkers whose integrity and love of their fellow men was beyond doubt. But at least there was one thing in which both the adherents of the scriptures as well as atheists were agreed: belief in the existence of beings with superhuman powers indicates what man would like to be and how throughout the centuries he has fought against all kinds of evil and strived for a virtuous life.

You say that myths are not to be taken at their face value and that underlying are the great moral lessons. I accept that completely and whatever shifts may have occurred in my own outlook, I realize more than ever before the dynamic role of mythology in the exposition of human problems and in the moulding of human characteristics.

A few years ago I was browsing hurriedly through a review of the works of Euripides, Sophocles and other Greek scholars when I came across the statement that one of the basic tenets we have inherited from classical Greek philosophy was that a real man was one who could stand firmly on his feet and never bend his knees even when dealing with the divine.

Passage of time tends to blur even immortal teachings such as these and your story has revived all my interest in symbolic abstraction. If I had access to the Vedas and Upanishads I'd plough through them with all zest.

1 January 1976

In March 1979 Fatima wrote to Mrs Gandhi, temporarily out of office as Prime Minister of India, to consider Mandela for the Nehru Award. She replied on 6 July 1979 from her home in 12 Willingdon Crescent, New Delhi:

I share your hopes for South Africa and Nelson Mandela. The Indian Government's attitude is such that any recommendations made by me is sure to be turned down. But I have tried to suggest Mandela's name indirectly. I shall certainly send a card to him, but my mail, incoming and outgoing, is very irregular.

Give my warmest greetings to all friends and comrades in your gallant struggle.

Mrs Gandhi's suggestion worked. Mandela was awarded the Nehru prize for 1979. His obvious pleasure at the Award was expressed to Winnie:

With regards to the development of the last three months, 1979 has been a lucky year for the family, and I could literally picture you beaming with joy and pride for the first time after so many years of hard struggle, unemployment and loneliness. It is such a contrast to your experiences during the same months a decade ago. I am tremendously pleased to share the honours with you and I have serious doubts if that would have been possible without Ngutyana [Winnie] around.

409

I hope that when next you come you will give me more information about the Nehru Award.

3 February 1980

1979 was a good year. The pressure that Mum has endured for so long continued to ease. At the worst of times she has been able to give me a seductive smile. But the smile has flickered through a lifeless skin stretched out over bone and cartilage. This time there was blood in her cheeks, fire in her eyes and she became an inch taller after getting the UNISA results. Seeing her in that healthy and gay mood makes me feel really good.

21 January 1980

He was keen for Winnie to go to India and almost believed for a while that she would get a passport.

Fatima suggests that you and the girls and family take a trip to India and Britain. That's a fine idea and if you're able to get the passport the suggestion enjoys my full support. But taking the whole family across the Indian Ocean would be too costly and I'd suggest that you leave the girls behind so that there'd be somebody to arrange my visits in your absence. Besides, India once had wealthy princes with magnificent palaces and in case their glitter and attraction make Dadewethu change her nationality I'll not lose everything if the girls remain behind. Perhaps we're too optimistic in even thinking that the proposition is discussable but there's no harm in trying. I'll keep my fingers crossed.

I hope you are attending to the matter and that you will on no account allow it to go by default. You may already have contacted Matlala [Adelaide Tambo] to let her know of your plans and to ascertain the exact date of the formal ceremony. I also hope that you are keeping Zeni and Muzi informed about your plans in case she has to step into your shoes.

10 February 1980

With regard to the Nehru Award it is time that you tell me something about Zeni and Muzi's trip to India. If you find it difficult to go over this matter with them, I would suggest that you put more pressure through Reggie. Incidentally, I was shocked to hear about the sudden death of Indira's son. Such a tragedy is a disaster not only for Indira personally, but for the whole of India. From all reports he appeared to have been a reasonable young

410

man and Indira may find it quite difficult to close the gap he has left.

29 June 1980

There was some confusion about the album of the proceedings at New Delhi. On 21/2 I understood you to mean that you had left it at Ayesha's place and I only discovered the misunderstanding when I got *Eternal India* on 23/2. Let Zindzi bring the album along when she visits me this month.

1 March 1981

Other awards and honours came in 1981 and through into 1983.

I hope you have already thanked Senator Tsongas. It is no small gesture for members of the American Congress to respond so magnificently and a personal letter under your signature would be a most appropriate way of responding. A personal letter to the Greeks will also be necessary. They are a new force with a bright future and an invitation to you to attend the Bundelog must be seen in this light.

31 March 1981

The Simon Bolivar Award which we share with Spain coincides with our twenty-fifth anniversary. These honours which have come from many parts of the world are a measure of support for our close friends, those with whom we grew up, schooled together, worked and lived in the same ghettoes, and with whom we shared unique experiences difficult to explain in our present circumstances, men and women who have denied themselves the pleasures, comforts and honours which they so richly deserve, so that you and I can enjoy some sort of security and happiness wherever we may be. They and they alone are primarily responsible for whatever delightful news may warm our hearts.

29 June 1983

This letter was written after Nelson Mandela had been nominated for the Chancellorship of London University.

The support of 7,199 against such prominent candidates must have inspired the children and all our friends inside and outside the country. To you, in particular, it must have been even more flattering making that miserable shack into a castle, making its narrow rooms as spacious as those of Windsor. I would like all our

411

supporters to know that I did not expect to poll even 100, to say nothing of 7,199 against a British Princess and against so distinguished an English reformer as Mr Jack Jones. That figure has a significance far more than can be expressed in a note written under my current circumstances.

1 March 1981

PART VI

# MEMORABILIA

---

# Mandela Milestones

**1918,** *18 July*: Rolihlahla Nelson Dalibhunga Mandela is born to Hendry Gadla Mphakanyiswa and Nosekeni Fanny Mandela at Mbhashe in the Umtata district. He grew up at Qunu in the same district. His father, a chief, had four wives, his mother being of the Right-hand House. She had three daughters, all of them younger than Nelson. He was baptized in the Methodist Church.

**1927:** Hendry Mandela dies entrusting his son to his close relative, Acting Paramount Chief of the Thembus, Jongintaba David Dalindyebo. Nelson takes up residence at the Great Place, Mqekezweni, and goes to the local school there, and then on to Qokolweni in the Mqanduli district. He matriculates at Healdtown in the Ciskei in 1938.

**1939:** Enrols at Fort Hare where he meets his nephews K. D. Matanzima and Sonto Mgudlwa. Wonga Mbekeni and George Matanzima were then at nearby Lovedale. Oliver Tambo, Congress Mbata (both later foundation members of the ANC Youth League), Knowledge Guzana, Gamaliel Vabaza, Lincoln Mkentane – all future attorneys were fellow students.

**1940:** He is expelled from Fort Hare. His guardian presses him to return to university. He and his cousin, Justice, set out for Johannesburg without telling Jongintaba.

**1941:** Nelson and Justice arrive in Johannesburg and Justice is employed at Crown Mines as a learner *mabhalane* (clerk) and Nelson as a mine policeman. Jongintaba demands their immediate return home, and when they refuse to do so, they are expelled from the mine. Shortly after he is introduced to Walter Sisulu, then an enterprising estate agent in the centre of Johannesburg. Walter, in turn, introduces him to the firm of Messrs Witkin, Sidelsky and Eidelman where he becomes articled. He finds lodgings in Alexander township.

**1942:** Nelson obtains his BA degree and enrols at the Witwatersrand University in the Faculty of Law. He moves in with Walter who lives with his mother in Orlando West.

**1943:** Nelson meets students of all races and is exposed to radical, liberal and Africanist thought.

**1944:** Nelson joins the ANC and marries Evelyn, Walter's cousin, a nurse and a 'home girl'. They live with Evelyn's brother, Sam Mase, at Orlando East and later with Evelyn's sister, Mrs Kate Mgudlwa. Nelson Mandela, Anton Lembede, A. P. Mda, Oliver Tambo, William Nkomo, Victor Mbobo, Lionel Majombozi, Congress Mbata, David Bopape, Jordan Ngubane, Msikinya and Walter Sisulu found the ANC Youth League.

**1945:** Evelyn gives birth to their first child, Madiba Thembekile (Thembi). They are allocated a house, first in Orlando East and later No. 8115, Orlando West. Nelson's mother and his young sister, Nomabandla Leabie, come to live with them.

**1947:** Nelson is elected Secretary of ANC Youth League and A. P. Mda succeeds Lembede as President after the latter's death. Oliver Tambo is elected Vice President.

**1948:** A daughter is born to Nelson and Evelyn Mandela, but the infant dies at nine months.

**1949:** Walter Sisulu is elected Secretary General and Oliver Tambo is among those elected to the executive of the ANC. Nelson Mandela, who was unable to attend the Conference, is later co-opted on to the executive of the ANC. The Bloemfontein Conference adopts their programme of action which calls for a militant, African campaign.

**1950:** The Youth League opposes the one-day stay-away

called by the Communist Party and the Indian Congress, and supported by Dr Moroka, in protest against the banning of Dr Dadoo, Moses Kotane and J. B. Marks. The stay-away is a great success. The Communist Party is banned. Nelson's second son, Makgatho, is born.

**1951:** The Youth League throws in its lot with the Indian Congress and joins it in organizing a national work stoppage on 26 June. Walter Sisulu and Yusuf Cachalia are appointed joint secretaries of the Planning Council. The response is significant in Durban and the Eastern Cape. Mandela is elected President of the Youth League.

**1952:** ANC and Indian Congress organize Defiance of Unjust Laws Campaign. Mandela is appointed volunteer-in-chief, with Moulvi Cachalia as his deputy. He and Yusuf Cachalia, and about twenty others under the leadership of Flag Bosielo, are arrested at midnight on 26 June and kept in custody for a few days. Dr Lowen defends them and they're discharged.

● Evelyn Mandela leaves for Durban to study midwifery.

● Nelson is elected President of the Transvaal ANC to replace the banned J. B. Marks.

● Nelson, James Moroka, Sisulu, Dadoo, J. B. Marks and sixteen others are charged under the Suppression of Communism Act. Moroka appoints his own separate defence and falls out of favour.

● Chief Albert Luthuli is elected President General of the ANC.

● Riots break out in New Brighton (Eastern Cape), eleven are killed, including four whites. Riots spread to Port Elizabeth and Kimberley and twenty-five Africans are killed. In East London enraged blacks kill two whites, including a nun.

● The Government bans fifty-two persons, including Nelson Mandela and the newly elected President General of the ANC, Chief Luthuli.

● The Defiance Campaign comes to a halt after 8,577 volunteers, mostly from the Eastern Cape, had courted imprisonment.

**1953:** Mandela's first banning order expires. He throws himself into the campaign against removals from Sophiatown, and the Western Areas, and is banned for a second time.
● He sets up his legal practice in partnership with Oliver Tambo.
● The Congress of Democrats is established following a meeting addressed by Tambo and Yusuf Cachalia.

**1954:** The Transvaal Law Society petitions the Supreme Court to strike Mandela off the role because of his involvement in the Defiance Campaign. Walter Pollak, QC, head of the Johannesburg Bar Council, successfully defends him *pro amico*.
● Mandela revises ANC organizational structure and introduces the M (for Mandela) Plan based on small, street cells.
● Makaziwe, Nelson's eldest surviving daughter, is born.
● The Congress Alliance of ANC, South African Indian Congress, Congress of Democrats (white), Congress of Trade Unions and Coloured Peoples' Organization is established, and the Congress of the People planned.

**1955:** The Congress of the People is convened in Kliptown. 3,000 delegates, including 320 Indian, 230 Coloured and 112 White, adopt the Freedom Charter.
● The Government intensifies its bannings. By the end of 1955, forty-eight ANC leaders are banned.

**1956:** Nelson separates from Evelyn.
● Mandela is brought to trial for treason with 155 others.
● Passes are extended to African women. The Federation of South African Women is founded and women take centre stage in the resistance movement.
● The Treason Trial Defence Fund is set up in South Africa and Britain.

**1957:** Nelson meets Winnie Madikizela.

**1958:** The Congress Alliance calls for a national stay-away. Tension erupts within the ANC in Orlando and the Africanist wing challenges Luthuli's leadership, accusing it of deviating from the 1949 ANC plan of action, handing over initiative to non-Africans and participating in the Advisory Board elections. The Orlando branch is accused of corruption.

● Potlako Leballo, Peter Molotsi, Zeph Mothopeng, Peter Raboroko and Josias Madzunya spearhead the formation of the Pan-Africanist Congress under Robert Sobukwe.

● Nelson marries Winnie Madikizela at Bizana.

**1959:** ANC and PAC organize separate anti-pass campaigns.

● Zeni is born.

**1960,** *21 March*: police shoot dead sixty-nine and injure 180 at Sharpeville, following the PAC call to hand in passes at police stations. The pass protest develops into a two-week-long stoppage in the Western Cape when police open fire and kill two Africans. Ninety-five per cent of the workforce go on strike. PAC youth take control of the townships of Langa and Nyanga, setting up roadblocks and distributing food. Strike continues for six days. The Cape resistance culminates in the march of 30,000 on Caledon Square; the march is checked when the leader, Philip Kgosana, is persuaded to turn the marchers back; the State calls in the military and marines, the townships are cordoned off and the situation brought under Nationalist control. A state of emergency is declared, thousands are arrested throughout the country, the ANC and PAC are declared banned organizations. Mandela is among those imprisoned.

● Zindzi is born on 23 December.

● Defence and Aid is set up in South Africa to help with the legal defence of political trialists, and the support of their families. Funding comes mostly from overseas: USA, New Zealand, Australia, Belgium, Switzerland.

**1961:** The ANC and PAC establish front organizations with religious and welfare tags.

● Mandela and a group of ANC members set up Umkhonto we Sizwe, independently of the ANC, to pressurize change through acts of sabotage. There is a strict undertaking that life will not be endangered, only installations will be attacked. A central High Command and regional commands are set up under the direction of Mandela. The first explosion occurs on 16 December in Durban, followed by explosions in Johannesburg and Cape Town. The President General of the ANC, Chief Luthuli, is awarded the Nobel Peace Prize a week before the first explosion. Although the ANC still remains committed to non-violence, Luthuli refuses to condemn violence.

**1962:** Meets Emperor Haile Selassie and Colonel Boumedienne, Commander-in-Chief of the Algerian army of National Liberation, and undergoes military training in Ethiopia and Algeria. Meets, among others, Julius Nyerere, who had already been Prime Minister, and Kaunda, who later leads his state, and Oginga Odinga, opposition leader in Kenya. Meets the first batch of about twenty recruits in Tanganyika on their way to Ethiopia. He visited Britain where he met Hugh Gaitskell and Jo Grimond, Labour and Liberal leaders.

● He returns to South Africa, is met at the border and driven to Johannesburg. The COD is banned; SA Communist Party collaborates with ANC but remains separate from Umkhonto. Mandela visits Luthuli on his return to Johannesburg, disguised as a chauffeur. He is arrested on 5 August, seventeen months after going underground, near Howick, by the police who had been tipped off by informers.

● *12 October*: Mandela is banned while in prison to prevent him being quoted or published. Free Mandela Committee set up.

● *13 October*: All meetings relating to Mandela are banned. Helen Joseph is the first person to be served with a house arrest order.

● *15 October*: Mandela's trial is moved to Pretoria, thereby depriving him of the services of his Counsel, Joe Slovo. He defends himself. Walter Sisulu is tried on the same charge in Johannesburg.

● *20 October*: Ahmed Kathrada, Secretary of the Free

Mandela Committee, and Walter Sisulu are house arrested together with twenty-three others.

• *7 November*: He is sentenced to five years' imprisonment for incitement to strike and leaving the country without a passport. He is held on Robben Island.

• There are Poqo uprisings in the Cape resulting in vicious killings, particularly of whites. Mass arrests quell the riots.

**1963,** *March*: Walter Sisulu is sentenced to six years' imprisonment but is allowed out on R6,000 bail.

• *20 April*: Walter Sisulu goes underground and is heard on the ANC's pirate broadcasting service, Radio Freedom. Police detain his wife, Albertina, their sixteen-year-old son, Zwelakhe, and Caroline Motsoaledi under the 90-day Clause. Winnie Mandela is banned.

• *May*: Robert Sobukwe is redetained on Robben Island after the expiry of his three-year sentence.

• *9 October*: Mandela is brought to trial again with Walter Sisulu, Govan Mbeki, Ahmed Kathrada, Rusty Bernstein, Dennis Goldberg, James Kantor, Andrew Mhlangeni, Elias Motsoaledi and Raymond Mhlaba, and charged with sabotage and attempting to overthrow the State. The trial comes to be known as the Rivonia Trial. The State simultaneously conducts two other political trials: Neville Alexander, Don Davis, Marcus Solomons, Elizabeth van den Heyden, Fikile Bam, Ian Leslie van den Heyden, Lionel Davis, Dorothy Alexander, Dulcie September, Doris van den Heyden and Gordon Hendricks are brought to trial in Cape Town; Ebrahim Ismail, Girja Singh, Natvarlal Bebenia, Billy Nair, Kisten Moonsamy, George Naicker, Kisten Doorsamy, Curnick Ndhlovu, Ragoowan Kistensamy, Riot Mkhwanazi, Alfred Duma, Msingeni Shadrack Mapumulo, Masinyane Bernard Nkosi, Zakela Mdhalose, Matteys Msiwa, Joshua Tembinkosi Zulu, Mdingeni David Mkize, David Ndwonde and Siva Pillay are tried in Durban.

**1964,** *April*: Winnie is given permission to attend Rivonia Trial on condition she does not dress or behave in a manner to cause 'incidents'.

- *June*: Nelson Mandela and all other accused, except Rusty Bernstein and James Kantor, who are discharged, are found guilty of sabotage and sentenced to life imprisonment. They are flown to Robben Island. Dennis Goldberg is held in Pretoria.
- *August*: Winnie and Albertina given permission to visit Robben Island, but are forbidden to travel together since they are banned.
- *9 September*: Babla Saloojee 'mysteriously' falls from the seventh floor of police headquarters and dies in detention.
- *October*: Winnie lays charge of assault against police. The incident occurred while she was at the police station, bringing food for 90-day detainee, Paul Joseph. Chief Luthuli calls on Britain and United States to apply sanctions against Pretoria.

**1964:** Professor Z. K. Matthews reports on refugee camps in Francistown and Dar-es-Salaam, financed by Amnesty International, the Sudan Joint Committee for High Commission Territories, the African-American Institute and the Government of Tanzania. London sets up its own Defence and Aid under Canon John Collins, funded by private organizations, the churches and by Sweden, Denmark, the Soviet Union, India and Pakistan.

**1965:** Bram Fischer goes underground.

**1966:** Bram Fisher is sentenced to life imprisonment for sabotage. Andimba Ja Toivo of SWAPO joins Mandela on Robben Island.
- Winnie makes second visit to Island.
- Defence and Aid Fund placed under the Suppression of Communism Act.

**1967,** *April*: Mandela, Neville Alexander, Eddie Davis and Chiba are charged under section 99(1) of the Prisons Regulations for being 'idle, careless and negligent' at work, later dropped.
- *July:* Death of Chief Albert Luthuli under suspicious

circumstances. He is knocked down by a train while taking his walk on a familiar route at Groutville.

• *September*: Makgatho visits Nelson, their first meeting in four years. He is allowed visits at three-monthly periods. Winnie loses her second job.

**1968,** *September*: Nelson's mother, Nosekeni Fanny Mandela, dies of heart attack. Winnie and Paramount Chief Dalindyebo of Thembuland apply for permission for Nelson to attend the funeral. Permission is refused.

• *20 December*: Winnie gets permission to visit Nelson.

**1969,** *May*: Winnie is arrested with twenty-one others and detained for five months. She is interrogated and tortured. A group of British activists plan to rescue Mandela from Robben Island. BOSS uncovers the plan which is then aborted.

• *July*: Nelson is informed in prison of the death of his son Thembi.

• *September*: Winnie and her co-accused are acquitted after 491 days in solitary confinement.

• *October*: Winnie is served with a five-year banning order and placed under house arrest.

**1970,** *November*: Mandela is allowed his first visit from Winnie in two years.

**1971:** A gunman is found prowling in the yard of the Mandela home.

**1972:** Two men try to strangle Winnie in her bed. They flee when her screams attract neighbours.

• The Mandela house is attacked: windows are smashed.

• Winnie and Peter Magubane are arrested for communicating with each other. They are prohibited from doing so in terms of their banning order.

**1973:** The State offers to release Mandela to the Transkei. He refuses. Security police raid the Mandela home. This is followed by an attack by vandals who cut off the telephone wires, smash windows and doors, and dump anti-government leaflets in the yard.

**1974:** Winnie and Peter Magubane lose their appeal and begin their six-month jail sentence for communicating with each other. Winnie is cited Woman of the Year by British women.

**1975:** Winnie's banning order expires. She is not rebanned. She attends a welcome meeting in Durban and is elected to the executive of the Federation of Black Women.

**1976:** Soweto burns. Winnie is elected to the Black Parents Committee. Mass detentions follow. Winnie is one of six executive members of the Federation of Black Women to be detained. She is banned again.

**1977:** Steve Biko is killed.
● Winnie is charged on seven counts of breaking her banning order, four for having visitors and three for attending gatherings.
● Dr Aaron Matlhare accuses Winnie and Dr Nthato Motlana of attempting to kill him. He later apologizes publicly and pays both for defamation.
● Black organizations, including the Federation of Black Women and the Black Parents Association, are banned.

**1978:** Winnie is sentenced to six months' imprisonment suspended for four years.

**1979:** India awards Mandela the Nehru Award.

**1980:** Police charge Winnie for receiving a visitor.
● Mandela is nominated for Chancellorship of London University. While he loses to Princess Anne, he receives substantial support.
● Dalindyebo Sabata, Paramount Chief of Transkei, is deposed and flees to Swaziland. Thembu chiefs visit Mandela to discuss the issue.

● Grenada invites Winnie to its first freedom anniversary celebrations.
● Release Mandela Campaign begins.

**1981:** Winnie's banning and banishment orders are renewed for another five years. Winnie is cleared of the charge of receiving a visitor, Mathew Malefane, on grounds that he was a lodger not a visitor.
● United States Congressional delegation, headed by Harold Wolpe, request to meet Mandela.
● Envoys from six French organizations, including the ruling Socialist Party of France, deliver a petition with 17,000 signatures calling for the release of Mandela to the South African Embassy in Paris.

**1982:** Zindzi Mandela is raided in her father's house. Books are confiscated.
● Students of the Witwatersrand nominate Mandela for Chancellorship.
● Haverford College confers honorary doctorate on Winnie.
● A Dorset woman sends Winnie her air fare to Cape Town to visit Nelson. The AUEW of Britain follow this up with a grant of £1000 for the same purpose.
● Nelson, with Walter Sisulu, Ahmed Kathrada, Raymond Mhlaba and Andrew Mhlangeni, is moved to Pollsmoor.
● President Kaunda of Zambia urges South African Prime Minister, Botha, to release Mandela.
● Winnie is invited to attend a conference in Rome.

**1983:** Local authorities in Britain name streets and parks after Nelson. The AUEW name executive committee room after him.
● City College of New York confers honorary degree.
● Greek village of Ancient Olympia confers honorary citizenship.
● Glasgow awards him freedom of city.
● University of London makes him a life member.

- The British Labour Party invites him to its party conference.
- Bruno Krensky Foundation awards him the Austrian Human Rights Award.
- Twenty-six US Congressman replace a quilt vandalized by thugs with a Pennsylvanian bedspread.

**1984:** The Nationalist Government announces a new constitution. Release Mandela Committees are established. The world demands his and other political prisoners' release.

**1985:** Botha offers Mandela and other Rivonia trialists a conditional release. They refuse.

**1988:** The world commemorates Mandela's seventieth birthday.
- Youths burn down Mandela house, No. 8115, Orlando West.
- A Mandela Crisis Committee is formed, consisting of Reverend Frank Chikane (Chairman), Dr Beyers Naude, Cyril Ramaphosa, Sydney Mafumadi, Aubrey Mokoena and Sister Bernard Ncube who appeal for calm in response to Mandela's request that no criminal action be taken against the youths. The community rallies to help rebuild Mandela's house.
- Mozambique Government grants its highest award to Nelson Mandela. Mandela is admitted to the Tygerberg Hospital in Cape Town and Winnie visits him. He is diagnosed as suffering from tuberculosis. Later, he sends a message to a friend, saying that he has regained his normal weight, is regularly doing his press-ups and is as strong as a bull. Overseas calls for his release are echoed.
- *31 August*: Mandela removed to the Constantiaberg Medic-Clinic for recuperation.
- *7 December*: Mandela is removed to an isolated cottage at Victor Verster prison, fifty kilometres from Cape Town, and enters into the loneliest phase of his life sentence.

**1989,** *4 July*: Mandela meets the State President, P. W.

Botha, and there are expectations of change through negotiation.

● *15 October*: All the Rivonia trialists except Mandela are released.

● *13 December*: Mandela meets State President, F. W. de Klerk.

Mandela Family Tree

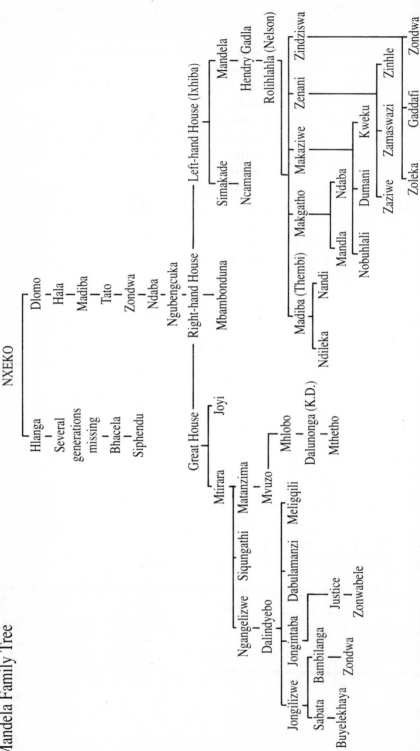

As the Thembu genealogy opposite shows, Hlanga and Dlomo were the sons of Nxeko. Hlanga was the elder and the heir of Nxeko, He was a man of moderate habits who respected custom and tradition. For this reason he was much liked by his father and was popular with the tribal elders. Dlomo, on the other hand, was an enterprising man who distinguished himself fighting and who was very popular with the youth. When Nxeko died Dlomo claimed the chieftancy, and in a battle at Msana near the Mbhashe river Hlanga was defeated and fled to Pondoland. Years later when Dlomo was firmly established in his position, he fetched his brother from Pondoland and gave him land where his descendants still rule. (Family tree and notes compiled by Nelson Mandela.)